THE PANDIT

Traditional Scholarship In India

SOUTH ASIA INSTITUTE, NEW DELHI BRANCH
HEIDELBERG UNIVERSITY
SOUTH ASIAN STUDIES NO. XXXVIII

Festschrif Parameswara Aithal

THE PANDIT

Traditional Scholarship in India

Edited by
AXEL MICHAELS

MANOHAR
2026

First published 2001
Reprinted 2026

ISBN 978-81-7304-435-9

Published by
Ajay Kumar Jain *for*
Manohar Publishers & Distributors
4753/23 Ansari Road, Daryaganj
New Delhi 110 002

Printed at
Replika Press Pvt. Ltd.

Contents

IV. Transmission and Scholarship

Foreword

by

HERMANN BERGER

Dr. K. Parameswara Aithal was born into a family of village priests and Sanskrit scholars in Kota, an idyllic hamlet of Canarese brahmins, on 18 January 1934. He received his early education in the traditional method at home and was initiated according to family tradition at the age of eight. After studying Śrauta-, Gṛhya-, Dharmaśāstra- as well as related literature, and the knowledge specifically pertaining to priesthood with traditional pandits, he participated and officiated in Śrauta rituals and Gṛhya ceremonies and other rites of the family procession for a period of ten years. After studying Sanskrit at home and in the Vani Vilasini Sanskrit School at Saligrama (two miles from his home) for five years, he appeared for the Sanskrit Entrance Examination of Madras University in 1951, joined the Maharaja's Sanskrit College at Mysore in 1952, studied *śāstras* for five years, taking the *advaitavedānta* of Śaṅkara as a special subject, and passed both the Inter (1955) and the Final (1957) "Vidvān" Examinations with highest honours. In 1959, he joined the A.P. College of Arts and Commerce in Bangalore and was awarded the Bachelor of Arts in 1961. In 1965, he was awarded the Master of Arts by Karnatak University of Dharwar as an external student. For his dissertation "Non-Rigvedic citations in the Aśvalāyana Śrautasūtra" he was awarded the doctorate of philosophy (Ph.D) by the Karnataka University at Dharwar in 1970.

He joined the Adyar Library and Research Centre, Madras, in 1962 as a pandit and was the Curator of the Sanskrit Mss. Section of the Library until 1970. During this period he worked on Sanskrit Mss. and published several volumes of descriptive catalogues and edited rare Sanskrit texts. After many years of research, a sudden change took place in Pandit Aithal's life. Professor J. Duncan M. Derrett of the University of London, who had worked with him previously on Dharmaśāstra, recommended him for appointment as a teacher at the South Asia Institute of the University of Heidelberg. The late professor Günther Sontheimer (1933 - 1992) and I got the opportunity of meeting Pandit Aithal at the library of the Theosophical Society at Adyar, Madras, during the International Congress of Tamil at Madras in 1968. We felt that Professor Derrett had been right in his assessment and were happy to learn that Pandit Aithal was willing to come to Heidelberg as a staff member.

It must have been an unexpected and exciting change for him to leave India and the idyllic atmosphere of his home in Karnataka, the Ashram where he spoke Sanskrit as the language of everyday life, and his training as a Śrauta priest. However, in a remarkably short period of time he and his family became true Heidelbergers and he was able to teach his students in excellent German. He fully accepted the Western approach to philology, at the same time remaining faithful to panditship and Indian thinking.

The South Asia Institute of the University of Heidelberg stands in considerable debt to Pandit Aithal for his untiring efforts over the course of nearly thirty years. He was an infallible authority on Sanskrit grammar and literature both for students and staff members who sought his advice in difficult matters. With his help we completed our syllabus of Indology. Together with him we had lectures and seminars on Pāṇini, Alaṃkāraśāstra, the Dhvanyāloka, and the text highly admired and feared by Western scholars for its difficulty, the Vākyapadīya of Bhartṛhari. Unforgettable for those who took part was a seminar of two semesters on Paśubandha, the description of Vedic animal sacrifice. The terse text of the *śāstra* was illuminated by a man who had performed the sacrifice himself and was, therefore, able to explain details which would otherwise have remained obscure to a Western reader.

In addition to his teaching duties, Pandit Aithal made invaluable contributions to research on *vedalakṣaṇa* or Vedic ancillary literature, a field little known in Western philology. As a brahmin and Śrauta priest he had easy access to orthodox circles, and was thus able to rescue valuable materials that otherwise would have fallen into oblivion.

Pandit Aithal possesses all the qualities that have been expected of a true pandit since time immemorial in India. His modesty is only equalled by his learning; he selflessly grants his help to anyone who asks for it. His balanced, cheerful character makes him a most pleasant companion. He has now left our institute, but, we are happy to say that it will not be forever. What is left for me to do is to thank him for all his efforts and help, and wish him good health and happiness for many years to come.

Preface

The present volume is a result of an international colloquium "The Pandit: The Future of Traditional Sanskrit Scholarship" organized at the Internationales Wissenschaftsforum Heidelberg, July 12-14, 1999, in honour of Pandit Parameshwara Aithal, who served at the South Asia Institute, Ruprecht-Karls-University of Heidelberg, for about thirty years.

My intention in organizing this conference was twofold: Firstly and above all, I wished to thank Pt. Dr. Aithal for his long selfless service at our institute. Secondly, I held the occasion of Dr. Aithal's retirement an apt possibility to combine it with a discussion on the future of the institution of the pandit in the educational system not only of India, but also of the West. For both these reasons pandits and scholars from India, who worked in Western indological institutes for many years, were invited: A. Aklujkar, M. Deshpande, S. Sharma Peri and G. C. Tripathi, although, G. C. Tripathi could unfortunately not participate in the conference due to administrative reasons. However, he kindly faxed his paper to the conference hall where it was summarized by A. Aklujkar.

To our deep regret, Sarweswara Sharma Peri, who displayed enjoyable examples of his recitation skills at the conference, passed away on March 17, 2000, during the preparation of the present publication. S. Sharma Peri was born on May 15, 1926, in the village Pedanandipalli Agraharam, Viskha District, Andhra Pradesh. From 1964 until his retirement in 1991 he was a "Lektor" in the Department of Indology, University of Marburg, teaching Hindi, Telugu and Sanskrit. He has come to be a renowned specialist in Sanskrit grammar, particularly Bhartṛhari, and Indian astrology. In 1972 he published in New Delhi his thesis entitled "The Kālasamuddeśa of Bhartṛhari's Vākyapadīya, together with Helārāja's commentary translated from the Sanskrit for the first time". In everything he did, the traditional Sanskrit training combined with philological methodology in the tradition of his teacher Wilhelm Rau (1922-1999) was evident. Many students used his collection of one hundred *subhāṣitas* called "Śataślokena Paṇḍita" ("By learning hundred verses one becomes wise"), which he published 1982 in a mimeographed form and which was praised by Wilhelm Rau in his preface with the following words: "All who peruse these Sanskrit subhāṣitas will certainly get a whiff of the indiscribably enchanting atmosphere to be met with only in an Indian pāṭhaśālā!" Since S. Sharma Peri's early years in India are typical of a traditional pandit, I shall also refer to his training and education in India in my paper in the Introduction, based upon the manuscript of the paper he presented during the conference.[1]

---

1 See also his autobiographical poem *Madvṛttānta katham atha ca me Jarmanīdeśavāsa*

I am extremely grateful to many friends, colleagues and institutions for their help during the conference and the editing process: Hermann Berger, my predecessor at Heidelberg University, for his long support of Pt. Aithal, Ashok Aklujkar for his kind offer of a second introductory paper to this volume, and Albrecht Wezler, my indological "guru", for his guidance and encouraging comments throughout the years. I am deeply thankful to Thomas Lehmann, a student of H. Berger and P. Aithal, who helped not only in proof-reading but also carefully prepared the camera-ready copy of this book with the LaTeX programme. My colleagues at the South Asia Institute, Jörg Gengnagel, Srilata Müller, Thomas Lehmann, Birgit Mayer-König, kindly supported me in the editorial process. Elfrun Linke helped me to organize the conference. Last not least, many thanks are due to Audrey Chapot, Michaela Dimmers, Katja Ehrhardt, and Carmen Hoffmann for the organizational help during the conference and/or re-typing manuscripts. It goes without mentioning that I alone am responsible for any editorial mistakes or shortcomings.

We received generous financial support from the Deutsche Forschungsgemeinschaft, Stiftung Universität Heidelberg, and Gesellschaft der Freunde des Südasien-Instituts. I am also thankful for the friendly hospitality of the Internationales Wissenschaftsforum Heidelberg (personalized for me in Theresa Reiter and her staff).

Heidelberg, March 25, 2000, the last day of the *saṃskṛtavarṣa* (see p. 5)

A.M.

---

in the Mandākrāntā metre which he privately published in 1999.

I

INTRODUCTION

AXEL MICHAELS

Traditional Sanskrit Learning in Contemporary India

Among the English words that originated from India the term "pundit" figures prominently in journalism and fiction. It now mostly denotes an expert in commerce (particularily market swings or stock-exchange) or politics, though in previous British imperial usage it predominantly meant "a man learned in Sanskrit lore" and a Hindu law-officer (Yule/Burnell 1903: 740). In traditional India, it was *paṇḍita* ("learned") in its adjectival aspect that was more frequently used than the noun (for which other terms such as *śāstrī*, *ācārya*, *upādhyāya*, *guru* etc. were preferred).

The pandit as a scholar and teacher

Somebody called *paṇḍita* (cp. especially A. Aklujkar's paper, "Paṇḍita and Pandits", this volume) is not only well-educated (*vidvān*) he is, ideally, also characterized by wisdom, a great skill for memorization, an oral knowledge of the Veda(s) or one or several *śāstras*, a special tradition of writing, copying and excerpting texts (see G.C. Tripathi, this volume) and, last but not the least, by a certain kind of his personal relation to his student(s) or pupils. This special *guru-śiṣya-sambandha*, *-paramparā* or *-saṃvāda* (see Steinmann 1986 as well as the papers of J. Benson, B. Bäumer, M. Deshpande and M. Horstmann in this volume) is still the most effective form of teaching Sanskrit in India. The introduction of a dual system of Sanskrit education—i.e. at *pāṭhaśālās* and *saṃskṛta-vidyāpīṭhas* where Sanskrit is taught according to traditional methods and the English system at government schools, colleges and universities—contributed considerably to a decline of the traditional system.

The functions of a pandit in the traditional sense are manifold. He is a scholar, teacher, adviser, spiritual master, specialist and legal expert. He is a symbol of purity and identity for traditional Sanskrit scholarship, and Sanskrit is still highly valued due to its contribution to the cultural heritage of India, or its religious and spiritual features, even if the pandit is also sometimes criticized or ridiculed as an arrogant, unworldly figure or as somebody who wants to dominate non-Sanskritic groups.

In India it is believed that a traditional pandit should have a deep commitment to learning and teaching, a special charisma and sometimes even a sectarian initiation (*dīkṣā*, see Bäumer, this volume). As a matter of fact, a pandit quite often has an ascetic way of life, with restraints in food or sexual relations aiming at a balanced relationship between knowledge and personality similar to the life of holy men (*svāmī, jñānī, guru, sant* etc.).

Such spiritual and personal aspects to being a pandit are generally overlooked or denied in the West where a pandit was and is more respected for his vast learning and capacity of memorization rather than for his traditional wisdom, his preference for the aesthetical or spiritual value of Sanskrit, the stress on the unseen effects (*adṛṣṭaphala*) in the memorization of Vedic texts or the claims of the superiority of Sanskrit as the oldest and perfect language.

These different approaches to the acquisition and preservation of knowledge create an intercultural problem of "us" and "them", seen as a basic conflict between different approaches to truth, between religion and science, as exemplified by the scepticism of modern scholars when confronted with traditional Sanskrit scholarship and *vice versa* (cp. Bronkhorst, this volume). While Western methods allegedly focus on historical continuities, logic, facts, empirical methods, rational enquiry, coherence and order, or authorship, traditional scholarship often favours canonization, revelation, sacredness, inspiration, non-historical arguments and anonymity. However, this conflict is not limited to the West, for in India too pandits and professors have argued about the criteria for science and truth. The contributions to this volume by M. Horstmann, who demonstrates that tradition in India was not always limited to the śāstric heritage, and by Chr. Minkowski, who presents a conflict in astronomy between scriptural authority and observation, are especially telling in this regard.

The pandit in the modern educational system

While the history of the pandit is comparatively well documented (see Government of India 1958:11-26, Altekar 1934, Filliozat 2000, Aklujkar's first contribution to this volume) little is known in the West about his position in the contemporary educational system in India (cp. Mishra 1997). The following is an attempt to summarize its basic features (institutions, degrees, positions, specializations, syllabi, awards, projects etc.) which supplements the research on the Sanskrit tradition in *modern* India by the Sanskrit Commission (Government of India 1958, see below) and Victor van Bijlert, Corstiaan van der Burg as well as Saroja Bhate published in the volume "Ideology and Status of Sanskrit" edited in 1996 by Jan E.M. Houben. It should, however, be kept in mind that my rough overview disregards a great number of regional variations, local specialities and terminological differences.

The structure of Sanskrit learning in contemporary India is still unevenly affected by two historical developments: a) the dual educational system as mentioned above, b) the rise of the regional languages and the implementation of the so-called Three-Language Formula, which implies that every pupil in a Secondary School has to study his mother-tongue, English or another modern European language, and Hindi (for non-Hindi speaking areas) or another modern Indian language (for Hindi speaking areas). Both factors weakened the traditional system of Sanskrit learning considerably. The deterioration in Sanskrit education was intensified by the fact that the suggestion of the Sanskrit Commision that Sanskrit should be made a compulsory part of the curriculum at Secondary Schools was mostly ignored by the state governments of India. The *pāṭhaśālās*, on the other hand, were not able to adapt to the changing situation and generally remained isolated in the modern educational system.

However, even today Sanskrit is much more widespread in Secondary and Higher Secondary Schools in India than, for instance, Latin in public schools of contemporary Europe or North America. Sanskrit is taught in private and public Indian schools at all levels, from primary to post-graduate or doctoral level. Moreover, the new Government of India has launched various programmes to develop Sanskrit education and, indirectly, jobs for pandits. Thus, it declared the period March 18, 1999, to March 25, 2000, as a *saṃskṛtavarṣa* (Year of Sanskrit). It also has a special officer called Deputy Educational Adviser for Sanskrit in the Ministry of Human Resources Development. It provided financial assistance to Sanskrit magazines or for the felicitation of pandits on Independence Day (Bhate 1996:393) when fifteen Sanskrit scholars are awarded the Presidents Certificate of Honour (*rāṣṭrapatisammāna*) receiving a lifelong grant of Rs. 20 000 p.a.

The most important programme of the Government of India is, however, the Rashtriya Sanskrit Sansthan, which was established in October 1970 as an autonomous organization for the development, preservation and promotion of Sanskrit after an elaborate report of the "Sanskrit Commission" published 1958. This Commission—chaired by S.K. Chatterji and including seven more distinguished Sanskrit scholars, namely J.H. Dave, S.K. De, T.R.V. Murti, V. Raghavan, V.S. Ramachandra Sastry, Vishva Bandhu Shastri and R.N. Dandekar—observed the poor situation of Sanskrit at the level of *pāṭhaśālās* (see below) and Secondary Schools due to insufficient funding, incompetent teachers and disinterested students. It warned that traditional Sanskrit learning was rapidly disappearing. Nevertheless, traditional Sanskrit learning survived at different levels (see fig. 1) despite the fact that in general the pitiful situation of most public Sanskrit-teaching institutions remains the same as before.

To-date a qualified pandit can still be employed in various governmental and private institutions. Much teaching of Sanskrit takes place in thousands of private institutions mostly called *gurukula*, *pāṭhaśālā* or *ṭols*. To be sure, in present day India, the *gurukula* is mostly no longer embedded in the family setting of one's teacher, where the student was at the service of his teacher, but the methods of teaching and the personal bond between teacher and pupil still reflect the old days. It has mostly become an institutionalized

Fig. 1: Institutions of Sanskrit learning and English equivalents (cp. Fig. 2)

	ENGLISH SYSTEM	TRADITIONAL SYSTEM
School level	Primary education (class I-IV)	no equivalent (education in individual families or private coaching by local teachers, partly in *pāṭhaśālā*, *gurukula* systems etc.)
	Upper Primary (middle school, class V to VIII)	*pāṭhaśālā*, *gurukula* systems (Sanskrit school leading to *prathamā* level)
	Secondary education (class IX-X leading to High School)	*mahāpāṭhaśālā*, *vidyālaya*, *kalāśālā*, Sanskrit college (up to *pūrvamadhyamā*)
	Higher Secondary or Intermediate (Intermediate College class XI-XII)	dto. (up to *uttaramadhyamā*) leading to *viśārada*
College/University level	Graduation in B.A. (three years degree course in colleges)	*mahāvidyālaya*, *vidyāpīṭha* (mostly three years leading to *śāstri*)
	Graduation in M.A. (two years post-graduate course)	dto. (leading to *ācārya*, *śiromaṇi*, etc.)
	Postgraduate (Ph.D., D.Litt.)	*vidyāpīṭhas* and some Sanskrit universities award *vidyāvāridhi* or *vācaspati* degrees

form of teaching in which a significant change is the kind of remuneration for teaching. As a rule, Sanskrit teaching used to be free. It was a duty of the brahmin not only to daily recite the Veda (*svādhyāya*) but also to transmit his knowledge to other twice-borns. The teacher who asked for a payment was despised. The pandit received the service of his student, who generally lived with his guru, which included collecting of fire-wood and begging for daily meals. In this traditional *gurukula* system some pecularities of Sanskrit learning developed, e.g. the schools (*śākhā*, *caraṇa*) of recitation and thought, the teaching method by question and answer, the culture of writing commentaries on one's master's works, the mastering of certain *śāstras* by heart, etc. At the end of his studies the student was supposed to present to his master certain gifts (*dakṣiṇā*), in cases of princely students, which could include the gift of lands frequently mentioned in land grants and inscriptions.

The profession of a priest was and still is another form of earning his living for a brahmin who learned some Sanskrit. Many brahmins function as family priests performing the religious rites for their clients, and some are temple priests or reciters (*pāṭhaka*) in (Vedic) rituals. However, the position of a temple priest is often despised by brahmins due to its openess to all social groups and popularization of religious affairs, and such priests are generally not regarded as learned, i.e. pandits.

Most non-religious functions of a pandit, which were based on a system of patronage, have disappeared. In former times pandits could become paid court poets (*kavi*) composing eulogical works for the king and his state or works on other subjects of their choice and in the field of their learning. They could also be employed in the courts as legal advisers or judges (*dharmādhikārin*, see my other paper in this volume), ministers (*mantrin*) or school teachers (*upādhyāya*, *ācārya*). In the democratic system of contemporary India, only the latter profession still requires some qualification in Sanskrit though the diverse nomenclature in diplomas, degrees and titles (see fig. 2) hampered the employment of pandits from one region in another (Government of India 1958:30). Pandits can also obtain several posts in schools and universities such as—to mention only those in Sanskrit colleges and universities—*prācārya* (principal), *ācārya* (professor), *pravācaka* (reader), *pravaktā/prādhyāpaka* (lecturer), *adhyāpaka* (teacher), *kulapati/ kulaguru* (vice-chancellor) or *kulādhipati* (chancellor).

Until today many *pāṭhaśālās* used to be run by temples and monastic institutions (*āśrama*, *maṭha*) to which Sanskrit literature owes so much, but at present *pāṭhaśālās* are also sponsored by voluntary or governmental organisations. Thus, more than 4000 *pāṭhaśālās* are funded by the Rashtriya Sanskrit Sansthan or by the state governments respectively. There are also a number of Veda or Śāstra *pāṭhaśālās* concentrating on the recitation of the Veda or specific *śāstras* which are run by private organizations without any help from the government.

Most state governments fund schools where Sanskrit is either optional or compulsory even if it is sometimes no more than the recitation of *subhāṣita ślokas* or verses from the Bhagavadgītā. At an undergraduate level, Sanskrit is also taught at several hundred Ādarśa Mahāvidyālayas/ Śodhasaṃsthānas of which sixteen are supported by the Rashtriya Sanskrit Sansthan.

Higher Sanskrit education is organized in traditional Sanskrit colleges, sometimes called *vidyāpīṭha*, of which seven are run as Kendriya or regional Saṃskṛta Vidyāpīṭhas by the Rashtriya Sanskrit Sansthan, namely the Ganganath Jha Kendriya Sanskrit Vidyapeetha, Allahabad (U.P.), a research institute, Shri Sadashiv Kendriya Sanskrit Vidyapeetha, Puri (Orissa), Shri Ranvir Kendriya Sanskrit Vidyapeetha, Jammu Tawi (Jammu and Kashmir), Guruvayoor Kendriya Sanskrit Vidyapeetha, Trichur (Kerala), Kendriya Sanskrit Vidyapeetha, Jaipur (Rajasthan), Kendriya Sanskrit Vidyapeetha, Luck-

Fig. 2: Some Diplomas, degrees and titles in Sanskrit education and English equivalents (cp. Fig. 1)

ENGLISH SYSTEM	TRADITIONAL SYSTEM
School leaving certificate (class X or XII)	*prākśāstrī, upaśāstrī, viśārada*
B.A.	*śāstrī, snātaka, vidvān, tīrtha kovida, pāraṅgata*
M.A., M.Phil., M.Litt. etc.	*ācārya, vidvān, śiromaṇi, tilaka, mahopādhyāya*
Ph.D., D.Litt., etc.	*vidyāvāridhi, vācaspati, cakravartin vidyāmartaṇda*

N.B. This table presents only a rough idea of possible equivalents. It has to be emphasized that the lack of uniformity in nomenclature and uncertainty of equivalence with western degrees prevails.

now (U.P.), and Shri Rajiv Gandhi Kendriya Sanskrit Vidyapeetha, Sringeri (Karnataka). In all these *vidyāpīṭhas*, Sanskrit is recognized as medium of instruction, which is only rarely the case in non-Sanskrit universities.

Moreover, two former *vidyāpīṭhas* which were previously also run by the Rashtriya Sanskrit Sansthan, have gained the status of deemed universities: Shri Lal Bahadur Shastri Rasthriya Sanskrit Vidyapeetha at New Delhi and Rashtriya Sanskrit Vidyapeetha at Tirupati. In addition there are three Sanskrit universities in which Sanskrit is expected to be the medium of instruction: Sampūrṇānanda Saṃskṛta Viśvavidyālaya in Varanasi, Jagannātha Saṃskṛta Viśvavidyālaya in Puri and Kāmeśvara Siṃha Saṃskṛta Viśvavidyālaya in Darabhaṅga, Bihar. Finally, many universities in which English or a vernacular language is the medium of teaching have Sanskrit departments offering diploma or M.A. courses and doctorates in Sanskrit. In many *vidyāpīṭhas* and Sanskrit universities, students of Sanskrit can be trained as Sanskrit teachers becoming a *śikṣāśāstrī*, equivalent to B.Ed.

Furthermore, one finds research institutions which concentrate on preserving manuscripts, editing texts and publishing scholarly studies. In many of these institutions scholars are permitted for *vidyāvāridhi* (Ph.D.) level only. The most renowned research institutions are the Ganganatha Jha Kendriya Sanskrit Vidyapeetha in Allahabad, the Bhandarkar Oriental Research Institute and the Vaidika Saṃśodhana Maṇḍala in Pune or the Adyar Library of the Theosophical Society in Chennai. Many pandits have been employed in projects of such institutions, e.g. the project of An Etymological Dictionary of Sanskrit on Historical Principles of the Deccan College in Pune.

Finally, more and more voluntary or private institutions, e.g. the Lokabhāṣā Pracāra Samiti in Puri (slogan: *mātṛbhūmiḥ bhāratam, mātṛbhāṣā saṃskṛtam*), Saṃskṛta Bhāṣā Pracāra Samiti, Hindu Sevā Pratiṣṭhāna of Bangalore, etc., or various religious organizations (*devasthānas, maṭha* etc.) and trusts are organizing Sanskrit courses or support Sanskrit training institutions. Thus, the Tirumala Tirupati Devasthanam launched a scheme under which a father who teaches his son the Veda is given monthly financial support (Mishra 1997:7).

At college level, Sanskrit is sometimes a compulsory subject in the first year for students of arts and humanities, but more often not. The course of Sanskrit study as a main subject in the Sanskrit colleges is regularly divided into three stages with two or three years for each. The first stage is normally called *prathamā* or *praveśikā* (the feminine ending is referring to *parīkṣā*, "examination"). It often follows class X-XII of Higher Secondary School. However, if the equivalent of *prathamā* has been taught at the Higher Secondary School, the student can directly join the *madhyamā* level. After passing the *praveśikā* examinations the students can be called a *prākśāstrī* or *upaśāstrī*. Basically, the *prathamā* level implies the study of primary lessons with some Amarakośa portions and a few recitations.

The student is then eligible for the intermediate (*madhyamā*) courses at the Sanskrit colleges (*mahāvidyālaya, mahāpāṭhaśālā* etc.) in which the medium of instruction increasingly becomes Sanskrit. *Madhyamā* can also be subdivided in *pūrvamadhyamā* and *uttaramadhyamā*. On this level, the student is mostly trained in Pāṇini (usually through Siddhāntakaumudī), Kāvya, Sāhitya, Nāṭaka and some Alaṃkāraśāstra. The more the student progresses the more he is supposed to select one of the subjects mentioned below which are, however, not always offered. After the period of graduation the student receives the degree of a *śāstrī* or *viśiṣṭaśāstrī* which is equivalent to a B.A. degree. The title is generally preceded by the subject of specialization, e.g. *nyāya-śāstrī*.

After another two years of studies and further examinations, the student can obtain the title of an *ācārya*, equivalent to a M.A. The title of *ācārya*, which is sometimes regarded as equivalent to the other titles mentioned in fig. 2, normally has some specifications according to the main subject or specialization, e.g. *sāhityācārya*. After research and submitting a research thesis a student becomes a *vidyāvāridhi* or a *vācaspati* (equivalent to Ph.D.), and further a *cakravartin* (D.Litt.) which is somewhat equivalent to a German habilitation thesis. A student of Sanskrit at the non-Sanskrit universities can obtain M.A., M.Litt., M.Phil., Ph.D. or D.Litt. degrees in Sanskrit or Sanskrit literature as well as B.A.M.S. (Bachelor of Ayurvedic Medicine and Surgery) degrees. Several of the mentioned titles are not only official titles conferred by the Rashtriya Sanskrit Sansthan, the Government of India or other institutions but also titles conferred to somebody by some illustrious teacher or famous person, which then gained wide-spread acceptance. The term "pandit" is itself such a case. In some fields, there are special titles for the kind of specializations such as *nyāyatīrtha* or *vedāntasāgara. Tīrtha* is also a title awarded by the colleges run by the Calcutta Sanskrit Association (including the Sanskrit College at Calcutta), which is equivelent to *śāstrī* of Varanasi. However, it is of a little higher standard, being the highest title awarded by this institution. Appellatives like *dvivedi, caturvedi* or *tripāṭhi* are either traditional titles or family names.

Most educational institutions as well as a number of Sanskrit academies, associations, *sabhās* or *pariṣads* organize celebrations of Sanskrit Poets' days, lectures on specific topics, competitions in essay-writing (*prabandha pratiyogitā*), *śloka* competition (*antyākṣarī* or *ślokānta*), in which a student or scholar has to recite a *śloka* beginning with the last word of a *śloka* recited by a competitor, and *śloka* composition (*samasyāpūrti*), in which a student or scholar completes a *śloka* of which one line (*pāda*) is given. Some institutions issue certificates to the students who are successful at such events or the annual examinations. The best students can also win special awards and medals for their skills or behaviour (e.g. *vaktṛtvapadaka* or *sadācārapadaka*). Moreover, some institutions conduct *śāstrasabhās* or *vākyārthagoṣṭhīs* with special awards or *śāstrārthas* in which pandits can show their learnedness and verbal dexterity (Michaels forthcoming).

In the syllabi, the following subjects are common: *veda, purāṇa* and *itihāsa* (basically the two great epics Rāmāyaṇa and Mahābhārata), *vyākaraṇa* (grammar), *sāhitya* or *kāvya* (literature), *alaṃkāra* (literary aesthetics), *dharmaśāstra* (law), *rājaśāstra, arthaśāstra* or *nītiśāstra* (politics), *darśana* (philosophy)—sometimes subdivided into *advaitavedānta, viśiṣṭādvaitavedānta* and *mīmāṃsā, tantrāgama, nyāya, vaiśeṣika, yoga* or *sāṃkhya*—, and *bauddhadarśana* (Buddhism) or *jainadarśana* (Jainism). However, not all subjects are taught at each institution. Most common are the philosophical systems (*darśana*), *vyākaraṇa, dharmaśāstra, purāṇa* and *kāvya*. Some universities and colleges have separate departments for linguistics, where Sanskrit or Pāli classes are also held. Few such institutions offer specializations in modern subjects such as English or even computer science. Additionally, there are sometimes programmes of vocational training in *karmakāṇḍa* (ritual studies), *jyotiṣa* (astrology), *āyurveda*, manuscriptology etc.

The future of the pandit

Whatever the reasons, the traditional system of Sanskrit learning is suffering from a number of structural deficiencies. Thus, the tradition of writing commentaries has become very rare, the prescription of texts and syllabi as well as the uniformity of examinations at *pāṭhaśālās* has led to a deterioration in the standard of pandit scholarship (Government of India 1958:135), Vedic recitation and Buddhist or Jain scholarship are more and more neglected, and a narrowness of general knowledge of Sanskrit literature results from early specializations in certain fields. It, thus, must be asked what can be the future of the pandit in such an educational system.

The best training in Sanskrit studies does not mean that somebody is automatically called a pandit. For in India a pandit is only one scholar among many, e.g. *ācārya*, *svāmī*, *guru*, and the title "pandit" is not an official one. Moreover, traditional scholarship is often combined with training in Western methods and theories. Pandits are professors (see M. Deshpande, this volume, p. 119 and 124ff., A. Aklujkar, this volume p. 50 and Dutt 1994). One can even notice a kind of competition between the best forms of preservation and transmission of traditional knowledge, or between Sanskrit colleges and modern universities.

As mentioned, to be called a pandit, one must have a good education in Sanskrit as well as a good mastery of certain Sanskrit texts and a capacity to memorize them. However, it is not true that traditional Sanskrit scholarship is only an oral tradition (see, especially H. Falk and Chr. Minkowski, this volume). Although the Indian techniques of preserving texts by memorization (H. Falk, this volume) are undoubtly impressive, it is equally impressive that South Asia preserves a wealth of written text material (perhaps more than 20 million manuscripts and thousands of texts). Moreover, H. Falk aptly demonstrates in the present volume that there are indications of a revitalization of oral tradition from written texts.

Another feature of Sanskrit learning and scholarship is the intensive study of *śāstras* sometimes at the cost of a broader knowledge of Sanskrit literature. In this, the texts are studied line by line squeezing out all their grammatical and textual implications. This method has led to an unparalleled expertise as the Sanskrit Commission noted:

> "A Pandit, who devotes about 15 or 20 years to the study of a particular sastra or a group of allied subjects, generally becomes a master of his subject. His knowledge is precise and ready; there is no fumbling or hesitancy about him. He does not need notes, not even the book, for expounding the text." (Government of India 1958:136)

The future of the pandit is perhaps linked with some constituents of knowledge that cannot be obtained through Western methods which focus on abstraction, impersonal teaching, writing and reading. There is for instance the unparallelled focus on orality in traditional Sanskrit scholarship which implies a long history of personal contact with the teacher. To be sure, pandits do not object to the use of written and printed books but they also do not believe in books as the ultimate source of knowledge. They favour oral communication and presentation with its technical consequences for style and the form of texts, i.e. *sūtra* style, use of meters, repetitions etc. (see Falk 1990 and 1993, Filliozat 2000:85-102, Michaels 1996).

It might be the *dharma* of pandits in India and the West to preserve the memorization aspect of traditional Sanskrit learning not only because extensive memorization might have some yet undiscovered effects on the brain since it is, as a principle, not based on a separation of mind and body (see A. Aklujkar, this volume, p. 23 ff), but also because it is combined with a personal form of transmission of knowledge and learning. If it were only the memorization capacity of pandits that impressed the West, computers would partly do a better job (cp. Aklujkar, this volume, p. 43), but if it is acknowledged that such memorization is combined with the intimate relationship between teacher and student ensuring the continuity of a particular school of thought the pandit retains his uniqueness.

The life of the late S. Sharma Peri (1926-2000), as described by him, gives a moving account of the importance of this relationship between a guru and his student. I take the liberty of summarizing from his autobiography as presented in the conference paper which he left to me in manuscript form (see also Sharma Peri 1999).

Pt. Sharma Peri was born in the village Pedanandipalli Agraharam (Visakhapattanam District in Andhra Pradesh) which was donated to the Veda learning Brahmins two hundred years ago by the king of Madugula Estate. At the time of his birth, there were sixty Brahmin families in the village. Most of them were traditional families of pandits, learning and teaching the Vedas and the *śāstras*. In 1919, his grandfather and father managed a Sanskrit *pāṭhaśālā* in the village to transmit the basic knowledge of Sanskrit to the children. Up to the age of twelve his father was his *guru*. He learnt from him the Śabdamañjarī, the first *kāṇḍa* of the Amarakośa, the first nine cantos of the Raghuvaṃśa, the first seven cantos of the Kumārasambhava and the entire Meghadūta. The method of teaching adopted by his father was the following: The student had to read the *śloka* of the text to be studied. The father-teacher taught him how to split the *śloka* into different words. In the case of the compound words, he would explain how to compound the words and also the names of the different compounds. Then, he would explain the meaning of the entire *śloka* by way of putting questions and giving answers to them. All questions were asked in Sanskrit. At the end the meaning of the entire *śloka* was summarized. The *śloka* which was learnt today, had to be learnt by heart and repeated on the next day with the meaning before the father-teacher began to teach the next *śloka*.

At the age of twelve Pt. Sharma Peri was sent to Vizianagaram to the Mahārāja's Sanskrit college. He studied there for seven years mainly Sanskrit grammar along with other subjects such as Bhāravi's Kirātārjunīya, Māgha's Śiśupālavadha, Bāṇabhaṭṭa's Kādambarī, Daṇḍī's Daśakumāracarita. He got a certificate of *vyākaraṇavidyāpravīṇa* and was awarded a gold medal by the Andhra University, Visakhapattanam. He remembered the intimate relationship with his teacher:

> "Even in those seven years of my study at Vizianagaram, I had a very good *guru-śiṣya* relationship as we were only three students for learning grammar. I could go to my guru's house privately to learn the things I could not learn in the college hours."

From 1944 to 1947 he was offered a scholarship to study grammar in Varanasi at the Sanskrit university.

> "There were no benches for students and no chairs for the teachers, only a two metres long and one metre broad mattress with a one and half metre long round pillow for the teachers so that they could comfortably sit and a small mat for each student. We were only four students to learn the grammar at that time in the *Saṃskṛtamahāvidyālaya*. There also, I experienced really a nice *guru-śiṣya* relationship as the students and the teachers both lived within the compound of the university. The students lived in the hostels and the teachers lived in the quarters constructed for them separately. Paṇḍit Kāliprasāda Miśra who was my *guru* and the principal of the *Saṃskṛtamahāvidyālaya*, was also living in the same hostel where I lived. That was a good opportunity for me to have a good contact with him. I could often go to his residence and learn privately from him whatever I could not learn during the college hours. In that *Saṃskṛtamahāvidyālaya* there was a peculiar tradition which was unknown to me in the South. That was, whenever a student met his *Guru*, he had to touch the feet of the *Guru* with his right hand and with the same hand he had to touch also his [own, A.M.] eyes immediately."

Such personal relationships between teacher and student still exist in contemporary India, but especially in North India they have become an exception. All-in-all, the traditional system of Sanskrit scholarship with its most prominent figure, the pandit, and his broad-based knowledge and mastery of different branches is eroding, if not collapsing. Due to the decrease of the *gurukula* system, the future of the traditional pandit is greatly endangered and it will become increasingly hard to preserve the richness of Sanskrit. The pandit might become an anachronistic figure who will be admired but not sufficiently supported through the educational system. The reasons for this development are manifold. The most important one is perhaps that no real incentives are given any more for learning Sanskrit. Nor is there the social prestige of the past. The best students prefer technical sciences, medicine, commerce etc. to Sanskrit which has more and more the image of a low job-potential. As a consequence, low standards are increasingly noticed in Sanskrit studies. Thus, in many universities or Sanskrit departments, a thesis written in Sanskrit cannot be submitted any more. At school level, Sanskrit is increasingly left out of the curriculum. Due to the lack of adequate teachers many schools are not even able to offer Sanskrit classes though at the initiative of the Ministry of Human Resource Development, the Rashtriya Sanskrit Sansthan launched a programme, the *śāstracūḍāmaṇi* scheme, by which retired teachers or scholars of Sanskrit are appointed in the *vidyāpīṭhas* for a period of two years to train young scholars and students. Given the pessimistic over-all situation, the success of such programmes is doubtful.

However, in a few states—especially in Andhra Pradesh, Bihar, Gujarat, Orissa, Karnataka and Kerala (for Nepal see Pant 1979)—the situation of Sanskrit education gives some hope:

> "In Kerala, Gujarat and Bihar, students belonging to all castes and creeds are coming forward to learn Sanskrit. The number of students desiring admission into postgraduate courses is so large in Puri that admission is denied to quite a few applicants. In one or two places admission is given only to those who pass entrance test. Reason for these occasional encouraging situations are various. For instance, the Arya Samaj which is still dominating in Haryana is responsible for the encouragement of Sanskrit education in that province. In Andhra Pradesh and Kerala, students opt for Sanskrit because of a growing interest in the national culture as well as because of the awareness that the study of Sanskrit is helpful for strengthening the mother tongue. In Bihar, Sanskrit is regarded as a scoring and comparatively easy subject for those who want to pass the public service commission examination. The government policy in the remaining states is not very encouraging for Sanskrit because of the general misconception of Sanskrit as a language of particular caste and religion, because of ignorance about its greatness, as well as because of some political forces. For instance, it has been reported that recently the Uttar Pradesh government has taken the decision to introduce Urdu as a second language in the place of Sanskrit. This move is, according to political observers, motivated by the desires of the ruling party to ensure votes from the minority faction. In West Bengal the lack of modern outlook in preparing syllabi, the outdated method of teaching without creating any interest, and the utilitarian approach of the political leaders, are mentioned as the reason for the downfall in the status of Sanskrit education. Absence of an adequate number of teachers, of adequate library facilities, and of encouragement from the people are among the other reasons given for the general decline in Sanskrit education." (Bhate 1996:394-5)

Traditional Sanskrit scholarship and the pandit as its symbol might not survive in India, but the Sanskrit language will certainly be preserved, even if only in a modernized form and on a superficial level. There are indications of a popularization, simplification and vernacularization of Sanskrit: Sanskrit movies (the most famous being "Ādiśaṃkara" by G.V. Iyer), radio and TV broadcastings in Sanskrit, music cassettes and CDs with recitations of Upaniṣads, Bhagavadgītā or *stotras*, language courses in spoken Sanskrit (in a simplified form, for instance, offered by the Lokabhāṣā Pracāra Samiti) which aim, for example, at the omission of *sandhi*, of dual forms, the dropping of long compounds, the reduction of tenses and moods to present tense, one past tense, one future tense and the imperative, as well as a limited vocabulary (cp. Government of India 1958:221-223). Another trend seems to be that more and more (middle-class) women learn Sanskrit at universities and colleges. The diploma students at the Sanskrit College in Chennai, for instance, are overwhelmingly middle-class women who have discovered in themselves an interest in traditional culture. Some of them have already positions in Sanskrit departments which was a great exception in the older days. Moreover, there is an interesting modern Sanskrit literature (see Raghavan 1957, Upādhyāya 1973, Bhate 1996:397) which gives new perspectives into the pandits' traditional dilemma between orthodoxy and creativity (cp. Filliozat 2000:97 ff.). Finally, the Pandit Philosopher Project, sponsored by the Ford Foundation, could be mentioned as an attempt to bring together "traditional pandits and scholars in Western philosophy in order to establish a dialogue between ancient Indian philosophy and Western philosophy, and especially to revive the Indian tradition of philosophy" (Bhate 1996:396).

One of the most influential instruments of propagating and sustaining the study of Sanskrit are those institutions which have contributed to the politicization of religion that began already in the 19th century, mainly through the Arya Samaj (see van Bijlert 1996, van der Burg 1996 and Fisher-Tiné forthcoming). In present day India, it is the conservative Hindu parties which support Sanskrit schools and institutions to a large extent. Such a support for Sanskrit studies appears to go together with the acknowledgement, however reluctant, that older restrictions on who may or may not study Sanskrit texts can no longer be sustained in the current perilous state of Sanskrit scholarship. It seems to be a curious expression of this situation that Sahasrabuddhe, a cabinet minister of the Government of India, took her oath in Sanskrit. After all, she is supposed to come from a Dalit background, and it is told that she learned Sanskrit while she was sweeping the house of a pandit listening to his teachings. The pandit later taught her Sanskrit due to her keen interest. It is said that he was afterwards dismissed from the *paṇḍitasamāja* for this, but Sahasrabuddhe invited him to participate in her oath ceremony.

Thus, the present popularization and politicization of Sanskrit might not contribute to traditional scholarship, but it can contribute to a revitalization of an endangered language by broadening its usage such that it is no longer the exclusive preserve of traditional pandits. However, in this contemporary context it will be left to the pandit, among others, to remain that increasingly rare and admired figure which not only encompasses in itself a deep and polymathic knowledge of classical Indian thought and the richness of Sanskrit language and literature, but also preserves the intimate relationship between teacher and student as well as the memorization aspect of learning a language and texts.

ACKNOWLEDGEMENTS: I am very grateful to P. Aithal, A. Aklujkar, S. Das, S. Müller and G.C. Tripathi for reading drafts of this paper and offering many valuable suggestions.

REFERENCES

Altekar, A.S. 1934. *Education in Ancient India.* Varanasi: Indian Book Shop.

Bhate, Saroja. 1996. "Position of Sanskrit in public education and scientific research in modern India", in: Jan E.M. Houben (ed.), *Ideology and Status of Sanskrit*, 383-400.

Bijlert, Victor van. 1996. "Sanskrit and Hindu national identity in nineteenth century Bengal", in : Jan E.M. Houben (ed.), *Ideology and Status of Sanskrit*, 347-366.

Burg, Corstiann van der. 1996. "The place of Sanskrit in neo-Hindu ideologies: from religious reform to national awakening", in : Jan E.M. Houben (ed.), *Ideology and Status of Sanskrit*, 367-382.

Dutt, K.C. 1994. *Who 's who of Sanskrit Scholars 1991.* New Delhi: Sahitya Akademi.

Falk, Harry. 1990. "Goodies for India - literacy, orality, and Vedic culture", in: Wolfgang Raible (ed.), *Erscheinungsformen kultureller Prozesse.* Tübingen: Gunter Narr, 103-120.

———. 1993. *Schrift im alten Indien. Ein Forschungsbericht mit Anmerkungen.* Tübingen: Gunter Narr.

Filliozat, Pierre-Sylvain. 2000. *The Sanskrit Language: An Overview.* Varanasi: Indica Books.

Fischer-Tiné, Harald. forthcoming. *Der Gurukul Kangri und die Erziehung der Arya-Nation: Geschichte und Ideologie eines antikolonialen Bildungsexperimentes in British-Indien (1897-1922).* PhD. Diss., University of Heidelberg

Government of India. 1958. *Report of the Sanskrit Commision 1956-1957.* Delhi: Manager of Publications.

Houben, Jan E.M. (ed.). 1996. *Ideology and Status of Sanskrit. Contributions to the History of the Sanskrit Language.* Leiden, New York, Cologne: E.J. Brill.

Michaels, Axel. 1996. "Das Buch als Fundament von Religionen", in: P. Rusterholz and R. Moser (ed.): *Das Buch, gestern - heute - morgen.* Bern: Haupt, 111-142.

———. forthcoming. "Between Tautology and Contra-distinction: The Logic of Comparing in the Interreligious Debates of South Asia" (Ms.).

Mishra, K.K. (ed.) 1997. *Sanskrit Studies in India.* New Delhi: Rashtriya Sanskrit Sansthan.

Pant, Mahes Raj. 1979. *On Sanskrit Education.* Kathmandu: the author.

Raghavan, V. 1957. *Modern Sanskrit Literature.* Delhi: Sahitya Akademi.

Sharma Peri, Sarveswara. 1999. *Madvṛttāntaḥ katham atha ca me Jarmanīdeśavāsaḥ.* Marburg: the author.

Steinmann, Ralph Marc. 1986. *Guru-Śiṣya-Sambandha: Das Meister-Schüler-Verhältnis im traditionellen und modernen Indien.* Wiesbaden: Steiner.

Upadhyāya, Rāmjī. 1973. *Ādhunikasaṃskṛtasāhityānuśīlanam.* Delhi: Meherchand Lacchmandas.

Yule, Henry, and Arthur C. Burnell. 1903. *Hobson-Jobson: A Glossary of Colloquial Anglo-Indian Words and Phrases...* new ed. by W. Crooke. London: John Murray.

ASHOK AKLUJKAR

Paṇḍita and Pandits in History

History of the term paṇḍita

In the Indian tradition of word derivation, *paṇḍita* has been derived from the feminine noun *paṇḍā*. The paraphrase of *paṇḍā* given by Bhaṭṭoji Dīkṣita (Uṇādisūtra 1.111) is *buddhi* "waking up, realisation, intellect, intelligence". The dictionaries compiled by traditional scholars in the second half of the nineteenth century, namely Śabdārthacintāmaṇi (p. IIIA.25), Śabdakalpadruma (p. III.20) and Vācaspatya (p. V.4203), are more specific. They explain *paṇḍā* with *tattva-viṣayiṇī buddhi* "a mental state or cognition concerning reality, knowledge pertaining to truth", *tattvānugā buddhi* "an intellectual state that follows (= seeks or is based on) reality",[1] *nirṇayātma-jñāna* "a cognition in which a determination (about the true nature of something) is made", *vedojjvalā buddhi* "understanding illumined by the Veda".[2] A Jain paraphrase quoted by Siddhāntashāstrī (p. II.657), on the other hand, is *ratna-traya-pariṇatā buddhiḥ* "a mind or an intellect mature with respect to the three jewels (of Jainism, namely, *jñāna* 'knowledge', *darśana* 'insight, correct view' and *cāritra* 'morally sound conduct')." Although there are thus variations in the glosses, it is evident that *paṇḍā* is something like "wisdom", "realisation (in the sense of coming to know what something really is)" or the faculty that makes such states possible, namely, the "intellectual faculty" or "intelligence".

As a noun *paṇḍā* is derived from the root *paṇḍ*, but it is possible that the root has not actually given rise to the noun and has been postulated only to account for the noun, since it is not independently attested.[3] Even if we were

1 Ascribed to Hemacandra in the specified entry of Śabdakalpadruma.

2 Probably these dictionaries were following older sources, of which they have specified only Hemacandra.

3 *paṇḍ* is given as *paḍ* or *paḍi* in certain Dhātupāṭhas as, for example, in *Pāṇinīya Dhātupāṭha* 1.301: *paḍi gatau*, 10.74: *paḍi nāśane*. The difference is due to the derivation process presupposed, that is, due to technical reasons, rather than real; *paḍ* becomes *paṇḍ* at the appropriate stage in deriving forms from it; similarly, *i* of *paḍi* is dropped when the derivation is underway. Most other Dhātupāṭhas other than the Pāṇinīya list the first root, namely 1.301, as *paṇḍ* (Palsule 1955:79). The reading of the second as *paḍi* is not uniform; the variations *pasi* and *paśi* are found. Probably the variations constitute the older or genuine reading; *pas* / *paś* seems to have existed in the sense *nāśana*, not *paḍ*. The *paṇḍ* → *paṇḍā* link is not stated by Pāṇini but is attested in some commentaries on the Uṇādisūtra, a supplement to Pāṇini's own rules. It is found under *ñamantāḍ ḍaḥ*, numbered variously as 1.107, 1.109, 1.113 and 1.114 in the available edns. Śvetavanavāsin's and Rāmabhadra Dīkṣita's commentaries do not include *paṇḍā*, but Bhaṭṭoji Dīkṣita's does.

to assume that not to be the case, the meanings *gati* "moving, accessing" etc. assigned to *paṇḍ* are too general to help us with a better understanding of *paṇḍā*, and, through it, of *paṇḍita*.

There are good grounds to suppose that the great Sanskrit grammarian Pāṇini (not later than 5th century B.C.) was familiar with the word *paṇḍita*, although the word itself or its common derivatives such as *pāṇḍitya* "wisdom, scholarship" do not appear in his Aṣṭādhyāyī. As will be established below, *paṇḍita* and *pāṇḍitya* occur in literature that is usually viewed by specialists as coming from a pre-Pāṇinian period. Moreover, the Gaṇapāṭha under Pāṇini 2.1.40 (*saptamī śauṇḍaiḥ*) and 5.1.123 (*varṇa-dṛḍhādibhyaḥ ṣyañ ca*) lists the word *paṇḍita*. It is unlikely that both listings could be later additions. Besides, they do not occur toward the end of the *gaṇas*, 'lexeme classes', as later additions generally do.[4]

The high probability that Pāṇini derives *paṇḍita* from *paṇḍā* (in the sense "having the property called *paṇḍā*, possessing intelligence") would further make it unlikely that Pāṇini was not familiar with *paṇḍita*. Aṣṭādhyāyī 5.2.36 (*tad asya saṃjātaṃ tārakādibhya itac*) is usually cited as authority in the traditional derivation of *paṇḍita*. The *tārakādi* lexeme class mentioned in this *sūtra* includes *paṇḍā*. No valid reason has been put forward to cast doubt either on the authenticity of the *sūtra* with its attendant lexeme class or on the tradition's view that this specific *sūtra* be pressed into service to derive *paṇḍita*.

The modern historically oriented linguistic approach has gone beyond Pāṇini primarily in suggesting a connection of *paṇḍita* with a hypothesized *prajñita* (and thus of *paṇḍā* with *prajñā* "knowing ahead, insight, wisdom") or in suggesting a connection of *paṇḍita* with a hypothesized Indo-Iranian word *pandā* (with dental *n* and *d* and hypothesized on the basis of New Persian *pand* meaning "counsel, good advice").[5] Under the first possibility, a process of prakritization which changed *prajñita* to *paṇḍita* (or, first, *prajñā* to *paṇḍā*) needs to be assumed, while, under the second, one needs to concede that spontaneous retroflexion has taken place. The first would take at least certain aspects of prakritization to a period not later than that of the Śatapatha-Brāhmaṇa (or Bṛhadāraṇyaka-Upaniṣad), while the latter would increase the probability that the word *paṇḍita* existed even in Old Indo-Aryan (cf. Burrow 1971:541-542).

Neither of the consequences just mentioned would cause any fatal damage to the results of historical linguistics considered valid in our time. However, it should be recognized that both the modern etymologies of *paṇḍita*

4 Given the evidence of *sūtra* 5.1.123, Pāṇini was probably aware also of the abstract noun *pāṇḍitya* derived from *paṇḍita*.

5 Other etymologies were proposed, and, at one time, a borrowing from the Dravidian family of languages was also suspected (cf. Mayrhofer vol. II/1963:196-198; vol. II/1996:70-71). However, the totality of evidence suggests that these other explanations of the origin of *paṇḍita* need not now be seriously entertained.

are not superior to Pāṇini's probable etymology in logical strength. There is at least one unexplained factor and hence some leap of faith in all the three derivations. While in the Pāṇinian derivation the non-occurrence of *paṇḍā* as an independent vocable leaves an element of uncertainty, in the explanation resting on prakritization the non-attestation of the "*jñ : ṇḍ*" change leaves a logical gap, and the explanation allowing "spontaneous" cerebralization contains an implicit admission that a requirement of historical linguistics, namely that the causes of a sound change be specified, cannot always be met. Yet, when it is noticed that there is a convergence in the three derivations (*paṇḍita* is traced to a word meaning "intelligence, discerning thought"), that the word has close relatives in separate sources of evidence (*paṇḍā* in Pāṇini's lexeme classses, *prajñā* in Indo-Aryan and *pand* in New Persian) and that the early usage of *paṇḍita* intimates connection with the meaning associable with all the relatives, we may assure ourselves that we are on the right track. We do not get the satisfaction of having come up with a totally satisfactory etymology, but at least we do not do violence to the positive and mutually independent evidence that is available in our sources.

To the extent of the convergence mentioned in the preceding paragraph, the Pāṇinian derivation has anticipated the modern etymologies. There are, however, subtle differences in the process of derivation which are interesting.

Modern linguists have pointed out the similarity of the hypothesized *prajñita* with the attested word *saṃjñita*. There is a suggestion in their discussions that the common past participial suffix *-ita* behaves unusually in *saṃjñita* and that the base preceding *-ita* should be taken to be a denominative root *saṃ* + *jñā*, rather than the feminine noun *saṃjñā* (Mayrhofer vol. II/1963:196-198; vol. II/1996:70-71). Pāṇini (5.2.36) may be said to have noticed the unusual semantics of the formation, although his manner of identifying the unusualness and accounting for it is different (his examples are also more numerous than those of modern linguists). He derives *tārakita*, *puṣpita*, *paṇḍita*, etc. from the nouns *tārakā*, *puṣpa*, *paṇḍā* etc., respectively. To that extent, his procedure is close to the modern procedure which operates with the denominative notion. However, he postulates a separate suffix *-itaC* (= *-ita*), distinct from the past participial suffix *-Kta* (= *-ta* or *-ita*), and specifies that *-itaC* is attached to a noun in the *tārakādi* class, when what *tārakā* ("star") etc. stand for happens to be, that is, becomes a feature of, another item (e.g., *nabhas* "sky"). Thus, *tārakitaṃ nabhaḥ* means "the sky in which stars have come about, the starry sky". It can be used as an adjectival phrase as the translation indicates, but its use even as a complete sentence ("The sky is starry", "Stars have appeared in the sky") is possible, since in Sanskrit a complementation like *asti* ("is"), used as a copula, can always be supplied.

The word *paṇḍita/prajñita* may, then, be taken, at least in the present state of our knowledge, to have originally meant "one endowed with *prajñā*, one characterized by the ability to discern, that is, by intelligence".[6]

A similar determination of the core meaning of *paṇḍita* is reflected in two types of statements coming from the pandits themselves. In the first type, *paṇḍita* is paraphrased with *śāstrajña, vidvas, vipaścit, doṣajña, kovida, budha, manīṣin, prājña, prajñila, saṃkhyāvat, kavi, dhīra, vicakṣaṇa, dūra-darśin, dīrghadarśin, viśārada, vidagdha, kṛtsni/ kṛṣṭi*—all implying investigation, analysis etc. (cf. Śabdārthacintāmaṇi p. IIIA.25, Śabdakalpadruma p. III.20, and Vācaspatya p. V.4203). The other type of statements defines *paṇḍita* in verses or prose sentences. Examples of relatively well-known verses are:

> *niṣevate praśastāni, ninditāni na sevate /*
> *anāstikaḥ śraddadhāna etat paṇḍita-lakṣaṇam //*
> "He involves himself with recommended (actions). He does not involve himself with (actions) that are censured. He is not a non-believer (in a higher reality) and has faith (or trust in what he has learned). This is the mark (or definition) of a paṇḍita."[7]
>
> *na paṇḍitāḥ sāhasikā bhavanti. śrutvāpi te saṃtulayanti tattvam /*
> *tattvaṃ samādāya samācaranti. svārthaṃ prakurvanti parasya cārtham //* (Dhanaṃjaya, Daśarūpaka 4.26)
> "Pandits do not act rashly. Even after hearing something, they weigh and determine the truth. Having accepted the truth, they act [and] accomplish their own interest as well as that of others."

Over its long career, *paṇḍita* can be said to have undergone two interesting changes of meaning. On the one hand, it has moved from a meaning such as "intelligent, one who knows (*jñā*) ahead (*pra*) of most others" to developing a strong association with "a person with impressive memory, one who retains much in his mind or brain". On the other hand, from a neutral meaning such as "a person with *prajñā*, a person capable of prognosis (in a literal sense)", which could be reconciled with having spiritual insight, *paṇḍita* has come to mean "one who simply teaches or repeats the texts he has learned from others", "one who lacks insight into the ultimate philo-

---

6 Other less commonly encountered derivations recorded in the Śabdakalpadruma etc. are: *paṇḍayā anugataḥ* "followed by, that is, equipped with paṇḍā"; *pāpād ḍīnaḥ* "one who has swiftly distanced himself from *pāpa* or sin"; *paṇḍyate tattvajñānaṃ prāpyate 'smāt* "the one from whom knowledge of reality is acquired". The first is not different from the older Pāṇinian derivation in essence. The second, having the appearance of a folk-etymology, should more appropriately be viewed as an attempt to capture the core of the meaning of the term rather than as an attempt to etymologize.

7 The Śabdakalpadruma informs us that the verse comes from Cintāmaṇi, which should be the compiler's abbreviation for Hemacandra's Abhidhānacintāmaṇi, but I have not been able to find the verse there.

sophical truth", "one who is inferior to the *sants*[8] and *gyānīs* (or *jñānins*)".[9] This latter development too emphasizes the memorization aspect and, to that extent, is not far removed from the first development. Alternatively, we could say that a deflation of the "intelligence" element has occurred in both the developments.

That *paṇḍita* initially stood for "one prone to investigation and making sense" is borne out, in addition to the etymological discussion above, by the earliest occurrences accessible to us:[10]

> *tasmād brāhmaṇaḥ*[11] *pāṇḍityaṃ nirvidya bālyena tiṣṭhāset. bālyaṃ ca pāṇḍityaṃ ca nirvidyātha muniḥ. amaunaṃ ca maunaṃ ca nirvidyātha brāhmaṇaḥ* // (Bṛhadāraṇyaka 3.5.1 = Śatapathabrāhmaṇa 14.6.4.1)

---

8 The word *sant* can be explained in many ways. For our present purpose, a rendering like "a person who is absolutely devoted to God", "a devotional mystic" or "a saintly individual" would suffice.

9 The *gyānīs* or *jñānins* are those who have seen the ultimate truth, the self-realised ones.

10 Like many early Upaniṣadic passages, the following passages can be translated variously. The intended meaning is not always so clear as to enable us to reject certain other translational possibilities with absolute certainty. I have tried to render the passages by taking the context into consideration and by consulting the better of the translations accessible in print, but I will not take up space by giving explanations of why I set certain translations aside. Olivelle 1998 contains succinct accounts of the variations.

11 A variant *paṇḍitaḥ* is found for this word in the Mādhyaṃdina recension. Although editors have generally preferred *brāhmaṇaḥ*, probably as a lectio difficilior and as a reading accepted in the earliest available commentary, namely Śaṃkara's, it should be noted that the structure of the passage favours *paṇḍitaḥ*. The passage clearly advises that *pāṇḍitya* should give way to *bālya*. Therefore, *paṇḍita* should be the presumed starting point. Also, since to be a Brāhmaṇa, a truly spiritual person, is envisaged as the outcome, *brāhmaṇa* should not be the starting point. One can, of course, accommodate *brāhmaṇaḥ* as a reading in the first sentence by taking it to mean "*brāhmaṇa* in the worldly or conventional sense of the word, a person *expected* to pursue knowledge and spiritual progress". However, there is no indication in the passage or its context to the effect that we should think of a lower Brāhmaṇa initially and then of a higher or true Brāhmaṇa. It is possible that *brāhmaṇaḥ paṇḍitaḥ pāṇḍityaṃ* ... was the older reading, that some redundancy was perceived in the phrase *brāhmaṇaḥ paṇḍitaḥ* (a Brāhmaṇa was generally a *paṇḍita*, and vice versa) and that while the Mādhyaṃdina recension eliminated the redundancy by dropping *brāhmaṇaḥ*, the Kāṇva achieved the same result by dropping *paṇḍitaḥ*.

Śaṃkara, in his commentary on the Bṛhadāraṇyaka, takes even the first *brāhmaṇaḥ* as standing for *brahmavit*, the higher or true Brāhmaṇa, and consequently interprets the key words of the remaining sentences very differently from the way I have interpreted them: *pāṇḍitya* as *ātma-vijñāna* "knowledge of the true self", *nirvidya* as *niḥśeṣaṃ viditvā* "having known thoroughly", *bālyena* as *jñāna-bala-bhāvena* "with the strength of the knowledge (of the true self, which knowledge transcends the ordinary means-and-result relationship)", *mauna* as *anātmapratyayatiraskaraṇasya paryavasānaṃ phalam* "the culmination resulting from excluding the experience of things that are not the true self". While this interpretation is consistent in itself, it involves importation of a number of ideas not specifically stated in the context and assignment of an unusual meaning to *nir+vid*.

"Therefore, a Brāhmaṇa (or *paṇḍita*; note 11), becoming disinterested in the state of a *paṇḍita*, should aspire to abide in a child's (simple, nondiscriminating) state. Further, having become disinterested in both the state of a child and the state of a *paṇḍita* (i.e., when he is consciously cultivating neither state), [he becomes] a person given to silence (or quietening of the mind). Then, becoming disinterested in both silence and its opposite (i.e., when he is consciously cultivating neither the quietening nor the activating of the mind), [he becomes] a [true] Brāhmaṇa."

Here the direct contrast with the state of a child and the indirect contrast with the state of a *muni* (a meditative person or sage) indicates that the *paṇḍita* envisaged in the statement is one who is capable of and involved in judgmental knowledge. This inference is further supported by the larger context of the statement. That context speaks of *eṣaṇās* "worldly aspirations", which invariably involve judgment about what is good and what is bad, based on acquisition and analysis of much information.

atha ya icched duhitā me paṇḍitā jāyeta, sarvam āyur iyād iti, tilaudanaṃ pācayitvā sarpiṣmantam aśnīyātām. īśvarau janayitavai. atha ya icchet putro me paṇḍito vigītaḥ samitiṃgamaḥ śuśrūṣitāṃ vācaṃ bhāṣitā jāyeta, sarvān vedān anubruvīta sarvam āyur iyād iti, māṃsaudanaṃ pācayitvā sarpiṣmantam aśnīyātām. īśvarau janayitavai // (Bṛhadāraṇyaka 6.4.17-18 = Śatapathabrāhmaṇa 14.9.4.16-17)
"Now, one who wishes that a daughter be born to him who would be a *paṇḍitā* and who would live a full span of life, should, having got rice with sesame seeds cooked, eat (that rice)—he and his wife should eat that rice—along with clarified butter. (He and his wife are then) able to give birth to (such a daughter). Now, one who wishes that a son be born to him who would be a *paṇḍita*, who would be variously praised,[12] who would be admitted to councils,[13] who would be a speaker of words (that others) would like to hear, who would recite all the Vedas [and] who would live a full span of life, should, having got rice with meat cooked, eat (that rice)—he and his wife should eat that rice—along with clarified butter.[14] (He and his wife are then) able to give birth to (such a son)."

Quick grasp, distinction in expressing thoughts, and sense of what is proper in society and the assemblies are evidently seen in the preceding citation as qualities one can expect from a *paṇḍita*. Thus, intelligence and discretion

---

12 That is, praised for many reasons or in diverse manners. Another possible translation: "especially praised, praised distinctively over and above the others".

13 Literally, "one who would go to councils—attend council meetings". The connotation could be, as Śaṃkara's paraphrase with *pragalbha* suggests, of boldness or of not being shy with respect to public speaking.

14 This may not mean that clarified butter be mixed with the rice prepared—be a part of the same morsel. In some parts of India milk products are not mixed with meat dishes.

must have been viewed as parts of the meaning of *paṇḍita*. The passage prescribes two different rice preparations and connects a public profile with the *paṇḍita* status of only the son. Therefore, a difference between the understanding of a daughter as *paṇḍitā* and the understanding of a son as *paṇḍita* is likely to have existed. But, there is no indication that the difference pertained to intelligence or judgment.[15]

> *sa grāmād grāmaṃ pṛcchan paṇḍito medhāvī gandhārān evopasaṃpadyeta. evam evehācāryavān puruṣo veda //* (Chāndogya 6.14.2)
> "That one (the man released away from Gandhāra, his place of residence), inquiring in one community after another,[16] being *paṇḍita*, [and] retentive (of the information given to him), will approach Gandhāra itself. Exactly thus does in this world a person having (the benefit of) a teacher come to know (who he really is)."

The juxtaposition of *paṇḍita* with *medhāvin* "one with a retentive faculty of the mind" is especially worth noting in this last passage. In it, the person concerned is assumed to be intelligent enough to inquire properly or in an informed way (with a clarification of what has happened to him, where he wishes to go etc.) and to understand the advice given to him.[17] In other words, resourcefulness and ability to see through a situation reasonably quickly are most likely to be the qualities the author of the passage had at the back of his mind when he used the word *paṇḍita*.

That the meaning component "intelligence" implicit in *paṇḍita* was neutral as to which kind of knowledge it would lead to, academic or spiritual, and could easily be associated with spiritual knowledge is borne out by the following Bhagavadgītā statements:

> *gatāsūn agatāsūṃś ca nānuśocanti paṇḍitāḥ /* (2.11cd):
> "The paṇḍitas do not mourn either the dead or the living."
>
> *yasya sarve samārambhāḥ kāmasaṃkalpavarjitāḥ /*
> *jñānāgnidagdhakarmāṇaṃ tam āhuḥ paṇḍitaṃ budhāḥ //* (4.19):
> "The knowledgeable ones call him a *paṇḍita* whose undertakings are in their entirety free from desire and purpose and whose actions have been burnt up in the fire of knowledge."

---

15 Commentator Śaṃkara's clarification of how a daughter could be viewed as *paṇḍitā* is: *duhituḥ pāṇḍityaṃ gṛha-tantra-viṣayam eva, vede 'nadhikārāt* "A daughter's being a *paṇḍita* is possible only with respect to the technique of (running a) household, since she would be ineligible to study the Veda". The state of affairs articulated by Śaṃkara may or may not go back to the Vedic times.

16 Alternatively, the phrase could mean "inquiring in the earlier community he encounters what the next village in the direction of his destination would be".

17 Śaṃkara paraphrases *paṇḍitaḥ* with *upadeśavān* "one who possesses—holds on to—the instructions" and *medhāvī* with *paropadiṣṭa-grāma-praveśa-mārgāva-dhāraṇa-samarthaḥ* "capable of understanding the way of entering (his own) village/community—the way taught by others". This is a reversal of the meanings I have assigned to the two words, but it too retains the distinction of meanings.

> *sāṃkhya-yogau pṛthag bālāḥ pravadanti, na paṇḍitāḥ /* (5.4ab):
> "Only the simpletons put forward the view that Sāṃkhya and Yoga are separate, not the *paṇḍitas*."
>
> *vidyā-vinaya-saṃpanne brāhmaṇe gavi hastini /*
> *śuni caiva śvapāke ca paṇḍitāḥ samadarśinaḥ //* (5.18):
> "The *paṇḍitas* see the same thing in a Brahmin endowed with wisdom and education, in a cow, in an elephant, in a dog and in a person eating the most polluting food."[18]

One should also recall in this context the Jain tradition of using the term *paṇḍitamaraṇa* "death of a paṇḍita" when the occasion is to speak of the voluntary nonviolent death of a spiritually excelling person (cf. Settar 1989: 95, 97, 101-102, 118-120, 130-131, 140-141). The Jain definitions and grammatical derivations of *paṇḍita* also leave no doubt about the presence of knowledge, enlightenment and ethical behaviour as components of the meaning of *paṇḍita* (cf. Siddhāntashāstrī p. II.657).

In the last one thousand years, however, two seemingly contradictory phenomena, despiritualization and desecularization, have occurred in the case of *paṇḍita*. The medieval and modern occurrences of *paṇḍita* do not place spiritual qualities centre-stage. They place academic or academic type of proficiency at the core of its meaning. This is borne out both by the attempts to remind people about what the word *paṇḍita* should mean, as well as by statements sharply distinguishing a pandit from a bhakta "devotee" or a *gyānī* (*jñānin*) "(true) knower, a person who has realised who he really is". A pandit's academic expertise is viewed as not only useless for enlightenment and release from *saṃsāra* but also as an impediment to the latter two. Disapproval is expressed of his wasting time on pursuits that bring no spiritual benefit. We read in Kabīra, for example:

---

18 As other relatively early occurrences of *paṇḍita* the following may be cited with the help of Vishva Bandhu's Vaidikapadānukramakośa: Śaṅkhalikhitadharmasūtra 219: *uṣṇam annaṃ dvi-jātibhyaḥ śraddhayā vinivedayet / anyatra phala-puṣpebhyaḥ pānakebhyaś ca paṇḍitaḥ //*. Āpastambadharmasūtra 1.23.3 (= 1.8.23.3 on p. 40 in Bühler's edition): *doṣāṇāṃ tu vinirghāto yoga-mūla iha [→ °mūlo hi?] jīvite / nirhṛtya bhūtadāhīyān kṣemaṃ gacchati paṇḍitaḥ //*. Viṣṇudharmasūtra 82.30: *brāhmaṇāpasadā hy ete kathitāḥ paṅkti-dūṣakāḥ / etān vivarjayed yatnāc.chrāddha-karmaṇi paṇḍitaḥ //*. Māṇḍūkīśikṣā 16.13: *ācāryāḥ samam icchanti, pada.cchedaṃ tu paṇḍitāḥ / striyo madhuram icchanti, vikruṣṭam itare janāḥ //*. Nāradīyaśikṣā 1.3.13 (= Māṇḍūkīśikṣā 16.13 as above), 2.3.11: *svaryuvo devayuvaś cārati devatātaye / cikitiś cukrudhaṃ caiva nāvagṛhṇanti paṇḍitāḥ //*. (Vishva Bandhu also lists Hiraṇyakeśidharmasūtra 1.6.11 and Yājñavalkyaśikṣā 2.84. The former should be similar to the Āpastambadharmasūtra passage. The latter I have not been able to locate.) These passages presume the same understanding of *paṇḍita* as the passages translated above, namely that a *paṇḍita* is primarily a discriminating and informed person, which qualities may enable him to make spiritual progress. For this reason, as well as because they are relatively late, I will not explicate them further.

Dohā:
pothī paḍhi paḍhi jagamu.ā paṇḍita bhayā na koya /
eka ākhara pī.ū kā paḍhe sa paṇḍita hoya //
"Reading a book again and again,
no one becomes a pandit in this world.
He is (truly) a pandit
who reads (even) one syllable of (God's) love."

Ramainī 34:[19]
paḍhi paḍhi paṃḍita karai caturā.ī /
jina muktī mohi kahu samujhā.ī //
kaha.ṃ base puruṣa kauna so gā.ūṃ /
so paṃḍita samujhāvahu nā.ūṃ //
cāri veda brahmai nija ṭhānā /
mukti ke marma unahu nahiṃ jānā //
"Read, read, pandit, make yourself clever.
Does that bring freedom?
Kindly explain.
Where does the supreme being dwell?
In what village?
Pandit, tell his name.
Brahmā himself made the Vedas,
but he doesn't know the secret of freedom."

Śabda 40:
paṃḍita bāda badai so jhūṭhā / ...
nara ke saṃga suvā hari bolai, hari pratāpa nahiṃ jānai /
jo kabahīṃ uḍi jāya jaṃgala ko, tau hari surati na ānai //
binu dekhe binu darasa parasa binu, nāma liye kā ho.ī /
dhana ke kahe dhanika jo hovai, tau niradhana rahata na koī //
The pandits' pedantries are lies. ...
The parrot gabbles "God" like a man
but doesn't know God's glory.
When he flies off to the jungle,
he'll forget God.
If you don't see, if you don't touch,
what's the use of the name?
If saying money made you rich,
nobody would be poor. ..."

Śabda 53:
kahaiṃ kabīra hama ḍāti pukārā,
paṃḍita hoya so la.i bicārā //
Kabīra says, I go on shouting
and the pandits go on thinking."

A verse quoted in Śabdārthacintāmaṇi (p. IIIA.25), furthermore, reads:

---

19 The following translations from the Ramaini and Śabda sections of Kabīra's Bījaka are quoted from Hess-Singh 1983.

> *nātaḥ parataraṃ loke kvacid āścaryam adbhutam |*
> *putradāragṛhāsaktaḥ paṇḍitaḥ parigīyate ||*
> "There is no greater, unprecedented, miracle in the world than (the phenomenon) that a person attached to progeny, wife and house is praised around as a *paṇḍita*."[20]

Some evidence of despiritualization is furnished also by the employment of *paṇḍita* in the context of performing arts such as music and dancing. In asserting this, I do not wish to imply that performing artists do not have spiritual experiences or cannot make spiritual progress through their art. Some of them do practise art as yoga, worship etc. and do seem to get results that are at least similar to those of what we principally understand as activities of yoga, worship etc. However, in the field of performing arts *paṇḍita* is not reserved only for such artists. It is commonly applied to all artists who aim at entertaining and earning a living. To that extent, a despiritualization of the word may be said to have occurred. Sometimes this is revealed by the fact that if a performing artist comes to be known primarily for his spiritual stature, the epithet *paṇḍita* appearing before his name is replaced by epithets such as *sant* or *svāmin*.

A distancing of *paṇḍita* from spiritual wisdom may be said to have occurred also in the use of the term to refer (a) to *vaidikas* or *vedapāṭhakas* "those who specialize only or primarily in reciting the Vedas", (b) to *arcakas* or *pujārīs* "those who are engaged in temple service, particularly image worship", and (c) to almost any propagator of Sanskrit.

The extreme of the apparently opposite change to desecularization is seen in the use of *pandit* for the Hindus of Kashmir. This use covers all Hindus regardless of whether they can be considered to have distinguished themselves

---

20 (a) The source of the verse is not specified. The word *silhake* which appears after the verse does not give its source but adds another meaning of *paṇḍita* (through confusion with *piṇḍāta* which also means "incense, olibanum"?).
(b) Mr. Narhari Narayan Bhide (= Narahari Nārāyaṇā Bhiḍe) was the Sanskrit teacher who may be said to have changed my life. Once, after I had become aware of how much precious knowledge he had given to me, there was some reason why I had to get in touch with him by writing a letter. Thinking that the ordinary honorific *śrī* or *śrīyuta* was inadequate in the case of such a knowledgeable person constantly in pursuit of knowledge, I wrote "Pandit N.N. Bhide" in the address section of my letter. I received a reply by return post in which Bhide sternly advised me not to attach the label "pandit" to his name. Quoting a line from Sant Tukārām, he asserted that pandits were *tuccha* "of no consequence, worthy of neglect" and what mattered was development of the self. Note that this came from a person who knew the Gītā passages quoted above by heart, who learned German and French, struggling with the hard life of an Indian highschool teacher and with several family problems, although receiving a diploma in German or French was not going to bring any worldly benefit to him. Nor was Bhide's dislike of the title "pandit" for himself based on a dislike of any person bearing that title and known to him.

from their co-religionists in being proficient in some branch of knowledge.[21] Its coming into being is exceptional. Nothing similar to it is known to have occurred with respect to other parts of India. It represents a strong association of pandit with a specific religious group. In the earlier period, however, a pandit could be Brahmanical, Jain or Buddhist in persuasion.[22] Evidence that learned Buddhists were included in the pandit category is furnished by the attestation of "Paṇḍita Jitāri", "Paṇḍita Durvekamiśra", "Paṇḍita Aśoka" etc. in the colophons of manuscripts. Among the Jains, *paṇḍita* has been used as an honorific, freely and naturally, in print as well as speech, before the names of Sukhlal Sanghavi, Nathuram Premi, Pannalal Soni, Mahendra Kumar etc. in modern times. Because almost all the surviving early Jain works have been written by monks, who had other designations with which the use of *paṇḍita* would have been either superfluous or awkward, one would expect it to be difficult to find early examples. Yet one finds them at least from the 12th century A.D. (*Paṇḍitayati*, *Paṇḍitārya* etc. in Settar 1989:59 fn 77, 89-90). Moreover, the (relatively recent?) practice of attaching *panyāsa* before the names of monks indicates that the use of the related word *paṇḍita* could not have been unusual in the earlier times.

---

21 The explanations I have been able to get of how this development came about are not as complete as I would have liked them to be. Basically, they are two, implicit and explicit in Sender 1988:43 and Madan 1989:xxii-xxii: (a) Due to historical developments, the major among which was conversion to Islam through coercion, only learned Brahmins, who, on the whole, offered stiffer resistence, were left as Hindus in Kashmir. Since they were already known as *paṇḍitas*, the term *paṇḍita* became co-extensive with the term *Hindu*. (b) One of the Brahmins who had emigrated, Jai Ram Narain Bhan, reportedly asked the Mughal ruler Muhammad Shah (1719-49), whom he served with distinction, that the honorific *pandit* be used for his compatriots. The ruler granted the request. The honorific, originally used appropriately for learned persons, came to be applied to all Kashmiri Hindu emigrés. Explanation (a) expects us to imagine either that most of the emigration from Kashmir took place after only the Brahmins were left unconverted or that the designation current in Kashmir was somehow later extended to those who had already left Kashmir. On the other hand, explanation (b) requires that an assumption be made that the title *paṇḍita* was somehow carried back from the emigrés to the Hindus (= Brahmins) who had remained in Kashmir.

See Madan 1989:16-20 and Sender 1988:9-46 for an historical overview of the situation of Hindus in Kashmir.

22 Surprisingly, *panyāsa* (variations: *pannyāsa*, *paṃyāsa*) is not recorded in the Sanskrit, Prakrit, Hindi and Gujarati dictionaries I could consult. It is, however, attested as the following randomly collected citations will establish: *asya saṃśodhane jaināgama-pravīṇānāṃ muni-vara (paṃnyāsa) śrīmad-ānanda-sāgara-mahāśayānāṃ* ... (p. 5 of the Upodghāta written by Muni Lalitavijaya to his edition of Haribhadra's Samyaktvasaptati, vol. 35 of Śreṣṭhi Devacandra Lālabhā.ī Jainapustakoddhāra Series, Mumbai, 1916), [Hindi:] ... *muni-rāja (saṃprati panyāsa-pravara) śrī Śubhaṃkara-vijayajī mahārāja ke sātha* ...in the Prakāśakīya (publisher's preface) by Bhā.īlāla Ambālāla Śā to the edition of Hemacandra's two Dvātriṃśikās under the title Dvātriṃśikādvayī, probably published somewhere in Gujarat in Vikramasaṃvat 2015.

In response to the point of the preceding paragraph, the following objection may be raised. Since Brahmanical, Jain or Buddhist traditions did not think of themselves as religions in that early period,[23] the secular nature of the early use of *paṇḍita* is not proved by the fact that the word was applied to scholars in all three traditions.

The secular nature, it is, true, is not directly or positively proved by the specified usage. However, we can at least deduce that the kind of religious (in our sense of the term) organization, mode of religious practice and body of authoritative texts a person preferred had no bearing on whether *paṇḍita* would be used as an honorific for him if he happened to be a learned intellectual. He was not denied that honorific and considered fit for some other honorific because of such "religious" considerations. The probability that terms related to *paṇḍita* were current even in the Iranian community (see above) would also indicate that the dominant considerations in the application of *paṇḍita* were non-religious. Later, however, distinctions such as *ustād* for a Muslim specialist and *paṇḍita* for a Hindu specialist emerge. The evidence clearly suggests that *paṇḍita* was not thought to be appropriate for a learned man who did not follow Brahmanical, Jain or Buddhist mode of religious life. To this extent, the neutrality with respect to religious aspects that the earlier usage had is lost. Of this loss, the Kashmiri application represents an extreme in the sense that it removes even the requirement of scholarship or expertise from *paṇḍita* without taking a similar step with respect to terms like *ustād*.[24]

---

23 The notion "religion" is a relatively recent importation in Indian life, despite the probably unsurpassed variety of (what we would call) religious activities in that life.

24 It is interesting that in modern India when both Muslimhood and proficiency in Sanskrit can be attached to a person, there is no resistence—at least no resistence of which I am aware—to considering the person a pandit. In contemporary Maharashtra, Pandit Gulam Dastgir Birajdar (Mumbai) is reasonably well-known. I have heard his speeches in Sanskrit rarely but I have heard them from his student days to his middle age. The organizers of Sanskrit Day ceremonies etc. nowadays routinely introduce him as a pandit, and the audiences not only do not mind but welcome such an introduction. This indicates that at present association with the Sanskrit heritage is a weightier criterion of pandithood than affiliation with Hindu religion. The trend toward such a development can be traced at least to the beginning of the twentieth century, when Pandita Ramabai was not deprived of her title *paṇḍitā* even after she converted to Christianity. It is still too early to conclude, however, that a Muslim scholar of Sanskrit is commonly referred to as pandit. The fact that the number of such scholars is very small and most of them teach in Western-style educational institutions makes it almost impossible to have an adequate sample to test the possibility.

In the present context, it should also be noted that the "ustad : pandit" distinction in the field of performing arts is nowadays occasionally deliberately ignored in the efforts to promote Hindu-Muslim harmony and the more well-known title "pandit" is applied even to a Muslim performing artist. This phenomenon has not as yet become as widespread as the phenomenon of referring to a Parsee or Zoroastrian musician or dancer as pandit.

The despiritualization-desecularization development, probably an indirect result of the arrival of Islam on the Indian subcontinent, has increasingly created the image of the pandit as a diehard conservative. His effort to save what he thought was his *dharma* ("cultural duty") largely took place in a context in which he was unable to display the sense of a larger mission that characterized many Brahmins of an earlier period of Indian history. He became increasingly incapable (a) of explaining why his mode of thinking and behaving was what it was and (b) of adapting to the new circumstances *without losing the philosophy behind his mode.* As an actor without articulation, so to say, he was perceived more and more as an oddity—a relic from the past. To quote Kabīra again, we have statements like the following (Śabda 41):

> *paṇḍita dekhahu mana meṃ jānī* /
> *kahu dhauṃ chūti kahāṃ se upajī, tabahiṃ chūti tuma mānī* //
> *nāde biṃdu rudhira ke saṃgai, gharahī meṃ ghaṭa sapanai* /
> *asṭa kamala hoya puhumī āyā, chūti kahāṃ se upajai* //
> "Pandit, look in your heart for knowledge.
> Tell me where untouchability came from,
> since you believe in it. Mix red juice, white juice and air—
> a body bakes in a body.
> As soon as the eight lotuses are ready,
> it comes into the world.
> Then what's untouchable?"

However, there were exceptions among (the Brahmins and hence) among the pandits. Also, they were the ones who usually had the necessary learning and, therefore, the means to think through the changing world. So we see a phenomenon that appears contrary to conservatism. Most of the attempts at adjustment with alien religions or at social reform were either initiated or carried out by the pandits. Many of them took seriously the widely known remark *yaḥ kriyāvān sa paṇḍitaḥ* contained in Mahābhārata Vanaparvan, appendix 32.47:

> *paṭhakāḥ pāṭhakāś caiva ye cānye śāstra-cintakāḥ* /
> *sarve vyasanino mūrkhā. yaḥ kriyāvān sa paṇḍitaḥ* //
> "Readers, preachers and any others thinking about the *śāstras*—all are excessively attached fools. He who is a man of action is (alone) a (real) *paṇḍita*."[25]

---

25 There was regional variation in the matter, with the pandits of Varanasi generally tending to be conservative in matters of social reform (cf. Upādhyāya 1983:138-142) and those of Bengal generally displaying liberal tendencies in the same sphere (cf. Sinha 1993:v-vi). However, prominent pandits at neither place remained uninvolved in social and political issues. They could have possibly done more, but one should not forget that the changes that came with Islam and the Europeans were very different in nature, speed and magnitude from any changes that might have come about because of the arrival of

Pāṇḍitya *today*

After these historical observations which have a sense of certainty about them because they are grounded in philology and examination of literary evidence, I will offer a few observations that are impressionistic in nature, based on my general reading in Indology. The main intention in offering them is to provoke discussion and help in the process of bringing greater specificity to the research on pandits.

Very soon after the possibilities to make a living through learning, teaching etc., shrank considerably for the pandit in the Islamic period[26] of Indian history, the "Macaulay" policy of imparting higher education in English was instituted (1835 A.D.). That so much of the panditic tradition still survives despite nearly a thousand years of (first) largely hostile and (then) largely indifferent environment in many parts of India is mainly an indication of how strong and widespread the tradition must have been at one time. It would be unjustifiable (and insensitive) to infer from the tradition's survival that the pandit's suffering was not long and serious.[27] To say this is not to deny that

---

the Yavaṇas, Hūṇas, Śakas etc. Life and livelihood had become precarious. Older organizations had been destroyed or weakened. Earlier channels of communication had been eliminated or disrupted.

26 By the phrase "Islamic period" I mean to convey only that there was an influential political presence of powers subscribing to Islam—that Islam became a factor to reckon with in many walks of Indian life. I do not mean to imply that Islam prevailed over all of India or that non-Muslims did not shape the cultural processes.

27 (a) In the otherwise useful accounts contained in Shukla 1969 and Sharma 1976, there is no attempt to determine what the condition of Sanskrit learning was before the impact of the East India Company rule began to be felt on the channels of education. The former begins with the assumption that Sanskrit did not face any decline and its condition was as robust as in ancient India. This assumption is not only made without offering adequate justification, it is extremely unlikely to be correct, given the many clear accounts of political upheavals that we have from both Hindu and Muslim sources and the fact that almost all the centres of Sanskrit learning that Shukla lists were either relatively small or belonged to areas relatively free from Muslim domination. Sharma, too, does not see the need to determine particularly the nature of Sanskrit learning surviving in spheres of direct Muslim political influence in order to be able to evaluate properly the ideas of Indians and Europeans concerning education. As already indicated, I prefer to take into account what was probably lost along with what survived and do not see any need to doubt that the custodians of Sanskrit learning suffered extensive losses for several centuries in succession over large areas of India, both as individuals and in terms of learning resources such as manuscripts.

(b) One day my teacher Professor S.D. Joshi was telling me about his teachers. When he came to mentioning Shankarshastri Marulkar, he suddenly choked up with tears. For several minutes he could not speak. The reason was that he suddenly remembered Marulkar's last days and could not control his grief. Through Vasudevshastri Abhyankar, Ramshastri Godbole, Bhaskarshastri Abhyankar, Nilakanthashastri Thatte and Vaidyanath Paygunde, Pandit Marulkar belonged to the *vidyāvaṃśa* of the great Nāgeśabhaṭṭa (cf. Abhyankar 1954:101, 1960:Preface pp. 6-7). He was versatile to the extent of being entrusted with the responsibility of editing several texts for the

some patronage to panditic learning continued even under the Muslim and European governments or that there were no pragmatic and/or genuinely liberal Muslim and European rulers. The loss the pandits had suffered was, however, on the whole, so serious that they could not recover from it successfully even in the respites and opportunities they got in between.

As a consequence of Islamic and European dominations of parts of India, among possibly other things, the pandits, as a group, have lost their earlier ability to be innovative and to influence the course of society on a large scale, although their situation in the periods of European domination was, on the whole, much better than their situation in the periods of Islamic domination, although they were the ones who tried most to regain the lost ground and although they fared better than most other groups in Hindu society. They succeeded in getting jobs and progressing materially than most other Indians, but in the process they ceased to be pandits, either totally or to a significant extent. Their education gave them a head-start in a rapidly and profoundly changing world that the industrial revolution and colonial expansion brought about. They also contributed much to the new world, but the process ultimately left them ineligible to claim the old descriptive designations.

One striking piece of evidence of loss of leadership ability as a pandit in the earlier or full sense of the term is that even after so many centuries of retreat there is no forum of pandits which is mindful of the new political and economic realities and which has a feasible strategy for turning things around.[28] Yes, the pandit is found to some extent in Indian national political parties, national religious organizations and national learned societies,

---

Ānandāśrama Sanskrit Series. He was a dedicated and skilled teacher. Yet during the last few years of his life he had nothing but two small pots left in his possession, which he used to cook rice and dal. What occurred to Joshi as he thought of Marulkar was that one day even these pots were stolen and Marulkar had no means left even to prepare his food.

In Varanasi, I have heard the story of a pandit who was so frustrated with the devaluation his great learning had suffered that on his death bed he told his wife to make his funeral pyre out of the manuscripts he had inherited and collected. It is probable that this disturbing directive was at least partially carried out as it expressed one of his last wishes.

Stories according to which manuscripts are offered to Gaṅgā on the death anniversaries of scholars may also owe their origin, in part, to such feeling of rejection felt by the pandits.

28 I do not wish to leave the impression that the situation summed up in this sentence has come about suddenly. There is evidence to the effect that pandits have fought back, at least in some parts of India, valiantly, diplomatically and by pooling their resources together. That they did not succeed in Sultanate Kashmir or that their success in Vijayanagara did not last beyond approximately 130 years does not mean that they have always been unable to come together and settle upon a course of action appropriate to the times.

as well as in regionally active agencies created for specific purposes such as preservation of *pāṭhaśālās* or creation of Sanskrit universities. The efforts of various governments within India to preserve Sanskrit may also be due to his participation in these bodies. Yet, as far as I know, there is no organization of pandits which has a pan-Indian basis, which has periodically taken stock of the "new world" with a sense of realism, and which has discussed possible strategies. Some Sanskrit and Prakrit scholars are making valiant, dedicated and innovative efforts to solve the general and specific problems of Sanskrit and Prakrit studies. Yet no non-governmental or widely effective structures—structures going beyond the individuals and individual organizations, working in unision for the pandit up to the national level—have emerged. Whether it was the effect of policies carried out under the name of Islam or of the stroke of Macaulay's prejudiced pen, the traditional scholars in India have been suffering from the effect without having an opportunity to assess it collectively and on a sustained basis. They have been responding to it in a piecemeal fashion and on the basis of a limited perception of the change. Even the findings of the Sanskrit Commission, appointed by the Government of India in 1956, have reached very few of them. They are not known to have demanded follow-up studies. They are still dependent on government initiative and sponsorship of religious bodies and the increasingly weaker Brāhmaṇa-Sabhās (or *saṃghas*). There has been no "collective psycho-analysis" that may enable them to see widely and repeatedly where they are and why they are where they are even as a special group among the Hindus or Brahmins. They have generally remained in a reactive mode and not attempted to become masters of their destiny in a collective way.

For the last several hundred years, incisive and creative panditic scholarship has *mainly* survived in those areas of India which were not strongly affected by Islam.[29] In the areas dominated by Islam, the panditic tradition has largely lost the cutting edge and has been reduced to a retaining or preserving role. South India (including Maharashtra), Rajasthan, Nepal and parts of Bengal have produced the largest number of creative pandits.[30] Even

---

29 These areas, it should be remembered, do not correspond to the provinces of modern India. Generally, they were much smaller. Politically and culturally, they aligned with Islam to differring degrees and in different ways. One should not be unmindful of the internal variation in Indian Islam.

30 One interesting indication of the emphasis on creativity in south Indian scholarship is found in Narayana Pillai (1951:Introduction p. 14). Pillai mentions the custom in the Payyūr family that for the father's *śrāddha* the sons were expected to bring a new work of theirs dealing with Mīmāṃsā. The Payyūr family of Kerala made significant contributions to the *śāstras* from the fourteenth century onwards.

In addition to the easily accessible evidence in the works produced during the Yādava and Vijayanagara dynasties and in the works of Mallinātha, we have many instances of impressive original scholarship in Rajasthan, south India and Bengal that one comes to know only after a study of scattered research publications. To mention only the few

in Varanasi, the most well-known centre of Sanskrit scholarship in north India, the area noticeably but not uniformly affected by Islam, the invigorating *pāṇḍitya* has mainly come from south Indian and Bengali pandits. In effect, Varanasi has functioned both as a magnet attracting some of the best pandits from all parts of India (especially if they were inclined toward devotion and/or asceticism) and as an island preserving traditional Hindu learning in a sea of Muslim political influence.[31] Upādhyāya 1983 is the most extensive account of Varanasi's Sanskrit scholarship that is available to us in a published form.[32] In reading it, one does not fail to notice the preponderance of pandits from Maharashtra, from further south (especially Andhra) and from Bengal, among those who have written works that strike us as extraordinary because of the learning evident in them or because they give a different direction to a particular *śāstra* or line of religious thinking. Just to cite a few examples, the following figure in pp. 25-74 of Upādhyāya's account as residents of Kashi/Varanasi: (a) from Maharashtra: Rāghavabhaṭṭa, the extent of whose amazing learning is well-captured in Gode 1936, Nīlakaṇṭha, the most well-known commentator of the Mahābhārata, Nāgeśabhaṭṭa (also known as Nāgojibhaṭṭa), a polymath known particularly for his command of Pāṇinian grammar, and Nandapaṇḍita, an authority in Dharmaśāstra; (b) from Gujarat: Bhāskararāya, without whom the deeper significance of devotional Tantric texts would have been lost to us; (c) from Āndhra: Rāmacandra, author of the first known Brahmanical rearrangement of Pāṇini's Aṣṭādhyāyī that extends the Aṣṭādhyāyī's applicability to cover some new usages, and Bhaṭṭoji Dīkṣita, author of Siddhāntakaumudī that changed the way of studying Pāṇini for centuries to come; and (d) from Bengal: Madhusūdana Sarasvatī, a formidable defender of Advaita Vedānta. In Upādhyāya's pages dealing with the British period of Indian history there are even more examples, suggesting that the ratio of extraordinary pan-

---

that I can easily recall, Nāgarājarāva 1995 contains an excellent illustration of what the calibre of south Indian scholarship was even in the late 19th century; Gode 1944 adds much to the information that Bhattacharya 1944 gives on Ānandapūrṇa Vidyāsāgara, a Goa scholar who attempted textual criticism of the Mahābhārata in the 14th century.

31 It seems plausible that several Hindu political powers of late medieval India made a deliberate effort to maintain Varanasi as a statement of what they valued in their culture.

32 (a) I learned from Prof. Bettina Bäumer that a survey of pandits in Varanasi prepared by Vaidyanātha Sarasvatī exists in an unpublished form. I do not know what its scope and approach are. Although Upādhyāya's work is not as precisely worded as one would have liked (it could have used the services of a good editor) and shows a tendency to be emotional and hyperbolic (sometimes quite understandable, given that the memories of some of the pandits still shape the thinking of pandits in Varanasi), it contains a mine of information collected with much effort. We are fortunate that Upādhyāya saw so many generations of pandits in Varanasi and decided to write down the information that would, otherwise, have been lost.

(b) A short but important contribution on Bengali scholars at Varanasi is Bhattacharya 1945.

dits who hailed from outside Uttar Pradesh to those who belonged to Uttar Pradesh probably went up.[33]

With the large-scale loss of political and religious patronage, the *pāṇḍitya* in those *śāstras* which have a greater need of material resources and empirical observation has been waning for many centuries. Architecture, metallurgy, dramaturgy etc. have been losing ground at least from the beginning of the second millenium A.D. Even grammar has survived mainly in the field of Sanskrit and, to a much lesser extent, in the field of Prakrit and Pāli. The tradition that created many Sanskrit and Prakrit grammars shrank after the production of a few Apabhraṃśa grammars to such an extent that it could produce only skeletal and isolated descriptions of the early phases of modern Indian languages. Scholarship concentrated on only those *śāstras*, such as philosophy, grammar and poetics, which did not need the regional languages or anything more than pen and paper and which could be cultivated in a relatively changeless context. Of the traditions of knowledge with a significant empirical element, Dharmaśāstra and Āyurveda fared relatively better because of their immediate practical utility (one could not simply stop using them), but they too do not give the impression of having prospered through experimentation and innovation to the same extent as in the earlier period. Compendia and digests came to dominate the scene, except where the British sought the input of the pandits and other educated Hindus on social issues (*satī*, widow remarriage, child marriage etc.) and possibly health issues.

At present, the best panditic scholarship and the strongest lines of transmission of traditional *śāstra* knowledge probably survive among the Jain *sādhus*, in whose case the older patronage and protection pattern has been preserved more than in the case of Brahmanical and Buddhist scholars and the dependence on governments has never been as important a factor as in the case of the latter two. Brahmanical *pāṇḍitya* is in the doldrums. Attempts to maintain it have been made and are being made, but there has been a very serious decline in its quantity as well as quality.[34] Traditional Buddhist scholarship, after having been increasingly pushed to the East and the South of the subcontinent by the advent of Islam, has virtually disap-

33 In addition, Upādhyāya mentions several prominent authors of late medieval Sanskrit literature, who stayed in Varanasi while completing specific works.

34 The pandits themselves have been acutely aware of the loss of quality. Modern Sanskrit literature, in particular, contains several poems and essays bemoaning the loss. One short example would be the following composition attributed to Rudradeva Tripathi: *gatā veda-vidyā, gataṃ dharma-śāstraṃ, gataṃ re, gataṃ re, gataṃ re, gataṃ re / īdānīntanānāṃ janānāṃ pravṛttiḥ subante tiṅante kadācit kṛdante //* "Gone is the knowledge of the Vedas. Gone is Dharmaśāstra. These things have indeed gone—definitely disappeared. What the people nowadays work at is declension or conjugation, (maybe) once in a while, primary derivates!"

peared from the Indian heart lands after the fourteenth century. It survives in certain respects in Tibet and Sri Lanka and, in a form frequently difficult to separate from the channels of Brahmanism, in Nepal. The Jain panditic tradition too has shrunk in terms of magnitude and variety, but it seems, on the whole, to be faring much better than its Brahmanical counterpart. Jainism still makes it possible for its *sādhus* to devote themselves almost exclusively to scholarly pursuits. It does not require of them that they deliver sermons or participate in communal religious activities. Unlike the contemporary Brahmin pandits, the Jain *sādhus* do not have to attempt acquisition of knowledge while seeking the means to support themselves, although, because of their frequent movement from one place to another, they do not have easy access to libraries. However, the stronger resolve that a monk's life requires also makes the *sādhus* generally more resolute in studying, editing etc., particularly, the important texts of their own rich tradition.

Until a few decades ago, Indian scholarship in *śāstra* texts excelled. It was as impressive as Western[35] achievements in setting the Veda in a larger historical ccntext. One did not find many Western scholars who could comprehend a Sanskrit philosophical or grammatical text with the ease with which a pandit comprehended it.[36] In the last thirty years or so, however, the gap in comprehension has been narrowed to a point at which its elimination seems a distinct possibility. The production of better learning resources (more translations, more specialized dictionaries, concordances, indices etc.) and increase in the number of bright youths who have studied with pandits have taken place in the West at about the same time India has been increasingly failing to attract bright students to humanities in general and to Sanskrit-Prakrit studies in particular and has been letting its libraries deteriorate. It would not be false to say that at present more original, sound and helpful work in Indian philosophy is being done outside India than in India. Even the Japanese, who, because of the peculiarities of their language, have a serious handicap in mastering a language like Sanskrit and the Western languages in which most of the research concerning Sanskrit

35 I use the term "Western" for want of a more convenient term and without making a value judgment. I should not be understood in a very rigid geographical or temporal sense.

36 Bhashyāchārya 1905:28 contains one of the early statements finding the preparation of Western professors of Sanskrit good enough for handling Purāṇic Sanskrit, but not for the *śāstra* Sanskrit of the Śābarabhāṣya, Śāṅkarabhāṣya, Tattvacintāmaṇi etc. The statement is made on the basis of a lecture of R.G. Bhandarkar delivered in Bombay in 1878 after his return from Europe. Without Professor Albrecht Wezler's chance discovery of Bhashyāchārya's 29-page booklet and thoughtful procuring of a copy of it for me, I would not have been able to discover this piece of information. The title of the booklet, *The Age of Patañjali*, is incapable of revealing that it contains a pandit's criticism of Western scholarship.

takes place, are now successfully tackling traditions such as that of Navya Nyāya on the basis of the original Sanskrit texts—an impressive and welcome achievement that could not have been predicted even three decades ago. On the other hand, more and more Indian philosophers are writing about Indian philosophy on the basis of English translations and without adequate knowledge of Sanskrit and without access to the latest research in the field.

What the pandits accomplished has, on the whole, been a glorious achievement in preserving access to the past, in effecting social change through evolutions rather than disruptive revolutions and in making contributions to the development of human ideas. Yes, there were (and there are) a few false pandits, narrow-minded pandits, short-sighted pandits, even socially harmful pandits. Nor is it the case that the pandits have always made decisions that served the interests of the community that supported them and thus improved the chances for their long-term survival. But the pandit as an institution has, on the whole, rendered invaluable service to humanity. Wihout them, the great treasure of human experience and wisdom that Sanskrit and Prakrit literature is would not have come down to us. Without letting us know, they have made available to us a channel of globalization by preserving past heritage and the ways of enriching it. That is why their disappearance is being noticed even outside India with a sense of concern, which was generally not the case five or six decades ago.

ACKNOWLEDGEMENTS: I wish to thank Professor Madhav M. Deshpande, whose comments led me to improve this essay in light of Burrow 1971, Professor Albrecht Wezler and Mr. Michael Dodson, who read the semi-final draft carefully, and the authorities of the Alexander von Humboldt Stiftung, which supported my research during 1998-99.

REFERENCES

BIBLIOGRAPHIC NOTE: The publications in which a focus on collecting historical information about the pandits can be said to exist are the following and the ones mentioned in them: Abhyankar 1954, Upādhyāya 1983, Sinha 1993, and Bhatt 1995. Of these, Upādhyāya's and Sinha's are the most informative books from the point of view of lives of pandits (although they concentrate, understandably, on the regions Kashi-Varanasi and Bengal, respectively). In addition, there is much more information about the pandits scattered in prologues and epilogues of the works written by the pandits, in Sanskrit periodicals, and in hundreds of research articles written on individual scholars—practically in all of Indological literature. To the extent the thoughts expressed in the essay required, I have added to this information, but without making such addition my major aim. The stories I have told of the pandits incidentally serve also to preserve for posterity some panditic lore that is not, as far as I know, recorded in books.

Kalla 1985, Madan 1965 and 1989, and Sender 1988 deal with Kashmiri pandits. The aim of Bhatt 1995 is the same to a considerable extent. However, it also contains many accounts of the pandits in the sense primarily intended here: "traditionally trained Sanskritists and Prakritists adept in belles lettres (*kāvya*) and literature of knowledge (*śāstra*, Veda etc.)". Sharma 1976 discusses what happened to these pandits in a particular period but does so as an overview only, not by reconstructing the lives of individual pandits or their communities. A few generalizations concerning the situation of pandits in a specific period are indirectly present also in Shukla 1969.

Abhyankar, Kashinath Vasudev. 1954. *Prastāvanākhaṇḍa* [seventh volume added to the six volumes of Vāsudevaśāstrī Abhyankar's Marathi translation of Patañjali's Mahābhāṣya]. Poona: Deccan Education Society. [Marathi].

Bhatt, S. (general ed.). 1995. *Kashmiri Pandits: a Cultural Heritage*. New Delhi: Lancers Books.

Bhashyāchārya, N. 1905. *The Age of Patañjali*. Madras: The Theosophist Office, Adyar.

Bhattacharya, Dineṣh Chandra. 1944. " Vidyāsāgara's commentary on the Mahābhārata", *Annals of the Bhandarkar Oriental Research Institute* 25:99-102.

———. 1945. "Bengali scholars at Benares", *Indian Historical Quarterly* 21:91-97.

Bhaṭṭoji-dīkṣita. *Vaiyākaraṇasiddhāntakaumudī with Vāsudevadīkṣita's Bālamanoramā commentary and Jñānendrasarasvatī's Tattvabodhinī commentary*. (eds.) Caturvedi, Giridhara-śarman; Parameśvarānanda-śarman. Vols. 4. Second edn. 1949-51. Delhi etc.: Motilal Banarsidass.

Bṛhadāraṇyaka Upaniṣad: see Olivelle.

Burrow, T. 1971. "Spontaneous cerebrals in Sanskrit", *Bulletin of the School of Oriental and African Studies* 34:538-559.

Chāndogya Upaniṣad: see Olivelle.

Dhanaṃjaya. *The Daśarūpaka of Dhanaṃjaya with the Commentary Avaloka by Dhanika and the Sub-commentary Laghuṭīkā by Bhaṭṭanṛsiṃha*. (ed.) Venkatacharya, T. Madras: Adyar Library and Research Centre. 1969.

Gode, P.K. 1936. "Date of Rāghavabhaṭṭa, the commentator of Kālidāsa's Abhijñāna Śākuntala and other works—last quarter of the 15th century (1475-1500 A.D.)", *The Calcutta Oriental Journal* 3.6:177-184. Reprinted in *Studies in Indian Literary History*, pp. I. 429-436. Bombay: Singhi Jain Shastra Sikshapith, Bharatiya Vidya Bhavan. 1953.

———. 1944. "New light on the chronology of the commentators of the Mahābhārata", *Annals of the Bhandarkar Oriental Research Institute* 25: 103-108.

Hess, Linda; Sukhdev Singh. 1983. *The Bījak of Kabir*. San Francisco: North Point Press. [Hindī. See Siṃha below.]

Kalla, Aloke K. 1985. *Kashmiri Pandits and Their Diversity (a Socio-demo-genetic Profile)*. Delhi: B.R. Publishing Corporation.

Madan, T.N. 1965. *Family and Kinship. A Study of the Pandits of Rural Kashmir*. London: Asia Publishing House. Second enlarged edition 1989. Delhi, etc.: Oxford University Press.

Mayrhofer, Manfred. 1956, 1963, 1976, 1980. *Kurzgefasstes Etymologisches Wörterbuch des Altindischen*. Vols. 4. Heidelberg: Carl Winter. Universitätsverlag. Indogermanische Bibliothek. II. Reihe. Wörterbücher.

———. 1992, 1996. *Etymologisches Wörterbuch des Altindoarischen*. Heidelberg: Carl Winter Universitäts Verlag.

Nāgarājarāva, H.V. 1995. "Paiṅgānāḍu Gaṇapatiśāstriviracitā 'Guru-rāja-saptatiḥ' ", in: *Ānanda-bhāratī: Dr. K. Krishnamoorthy Felicitation vol., Saṃskṛtavibhāga*, pp. 15-20. (eds) B. Channakeshava; H.V. Nagaraja Rao. Mysore: D.V.K. Murthy for the Dr. K. Krishnamoorthy Felicitation Committee. Mysore: Krishnamurthipuram.

Narayana Pillai, P.K. (ed.) 1951. *Jaiminīyasūtrārthasaṃgraha of Ṛṣiputra Parameśvara*. Trivandrum: University of Travancore.

Olivelle, Patrick. 1998. *The Early Upaniṣads. Annotated Text and Translation*. New York, Oxford: Oxford University Press.

Palsule, Gajanan Balkrishna. 1955. *A Concordance of Sanskrit Dhātu-pāṭhas (with Index of Meanings)*. Poona: Deccan College Postgraduate and Research Institute.

Rādhākāntadeva (or Rādhākāntadeva Bāhādura) et al. 1886-1893?. *Śabdakalpadruma*. Vols. or kāṇḍas 5. Calcutta: [Probably published by Rādhākāntadeva himself]. Publication years for the vols are specified as Śaka 1808, 1811, 1813, 1814, 181 (the last digit was not printed in the copy of the original edition accessible to me). Photographic reprint 1: Varanasi: Chowkhamba Sanskrit Series Office. 1961.

Śaṃkara. *Bhāṣya (commentary) on the Bṛhadāraṇyakopaniṣad*. Third edition of saṃvat 2014 (= 1957/1958 A.D.). Gorakhapura: Gītā Press.

Śaṃkara. *Bhāṣya (commentary) on the Chāndogyopaniṣad*. Third edn of saṃvat 2013 (= 1956/1957 A.D.). Gorakhapura: Gītā Press.

Sender, Henny. 1988. *The Kashmiri Pandits. A Study of Cultural Choice in North India*. Delhi etc.: Oxford University Press.

Settar, S. 1989. *Inviting Death. Indian Attitude towards the Ritual Death*. Leiden etc.: E.J. Brill.

Sharma, Narinder Kumar. 1976. *Linguistic and Educational Aspirations under a Colonial System. A Study of Sanskrit Education during British Rule in India*. New Delhi: Concept Publishing Company.

Shukla, Hira Lal. 1969. *Macaulay and Sanskrit Education*. Raipur, M.P.: Ālok Prakāshan.

Siddhantashastri, Balchandra. 1972-79. *Jainalakṣaṇāvalī; Jaina Pāribhaṣika Śabdakośa (an Authentic Descriptive Dictionary of Jaina Philosophical Terms)*. Vols. 3. Delhi: Vir Sewa Mandir.

Siṃha, Śukadeva. *Kabīrabījaka*. Ilāhābāda: Nīlābha Prakāśana. 1972.

Sinha, Samita. 1993. *Pandits in a Changing Environment: Centres of Sanskrit Learning in Nineteenth Century Bengal*. Calcutta: Sarat Book House.

Sukhānandanātha, Brāhmāvadhūta. 1864-1885. *Śabdārthacintāmaṇi*. Vols 8 (= 4 bhāgas, each divided into *a* and *ba*). Udaya-pura: Sajjana-yantrālaya/Vājapeyi-Baṃśīdhara. Reprint 1991-92. Jaipur: Printwell. The reprint gives the date of the original publication as 1860, which must be approximate. The first volume, bhāga 1*a*, gives the date of its publication as Vikramasaṃvat 1921 (= 1863/1864 A.D.) and p. 1040 of the last volume, bhāga 4*ba*, informs us that the printing was finished in Vikramasaṃvat 1942 (1884-85 A.D.).

Tārānātha Tarkavācaspati. 1873-1884. *Vācaspatyam / Vāchaspatyam*. Photographic reprint 1962. Vols. 6. Varanasi: Chowkhamba Sanskrit Series Office.

Upādhyāya, Bala-deva. 1983. *Kāśī kī pāṇḍitya paramparā: kāśīstha saṃskṛta vidvānoṃ ke jīvana-carita evaṃ sāhityika avadānoṃ kā prāmāṇika vivaraṇa*. Vārāṇasī: Viśvavidyālaya Prakāśana. Hindi.

II

Roles and Functions

ASHOK AKLUJKAR

The Pandits from a *piṇḍa-brahmāṇḍa* Point of View

"It is sad to see the number of great Śāstrīs, distinguished no less for their humility and modesty than for their learning and intelligence, diminish year after year, and to feel that with them there is dying away more and more of that traditional learning which we can so ill dispense with in the interpretation of the enigmatic works of Hindu antiquity, but it appears to me all the more to be the duty of both Native and European Sanskrit scholars to save as much as can still be saved, and to fix in writing what in less than half a century will otherwise be irreparably lost." Franz Kielhorn 1874:xxiv-xxv

Introduction

In Sanskrit poetry, when a poet wishes to convey a scene of battle, commotion, density etc., he frequently uses highly compounded language abounding in the repetition of certain sounds considered to be relatively harsh. The consonants *ṇ* and *ḍ* commonly find his favour in such contexts. Paṇḍitarāja Jagannātha, for example, writes thus in praise of a hero who finds himself in the thick of a battle:

dor-daṇḍa-dvaya-kuṇḍalī-kṛta-lasat-kodaṇḍa-caṇḍa-dhvani-
dhvastoddaṇḍa-vipakṣa-maṇḍalam atha tvāṃ vīkṣya madhye-raṇam /
valgad-gāṇḍiva-mukta-kāṇḍa-valaya-jvālāvalī-tāṇḍava-
bhraśyat-khāṇḍava-ruṣṭa-pāṇḍavam aho ko naḥ kṣitīśaḥ smaret //.[1]

"Two clublike arms.
A big shining bow bent to a circle's shape.
A piercing pervading sound.
A host of weapon-brandishing enemies devastated.
Seeing you thus in the middle of the battle,
which king will not think of the wrathful Arjuna:
His swift[2] Gāṇḍiva bow,
shooting forth a torrent of arrows.

---

1 Rasagaṅgādhara, *ānana* 2, example of the figure of speech *smaraṇa*. In Jagannātha's Prāṇābharaṇa (also known as Jagadābharaṇa), the first quarter of the verse ends with *caṇḍāśuga* "terrifying arrows"; cf. Paṇḍitarājakāvyasaṃgraha p. 114.

2 (a) Some commentators of the Rasagaṅgādhara (Nāgeśa p. 286, Kedāranātha Ojhā p. 153) take *valgat* in the sense *manohara* "attractive" or *sundara* "beautiful". Madanamohana Jhā takes it as meaning *vācāla* "making much sound, resounding". The latter is appropriate to the context and can be supported by usage to some extent (cf. Monier-Williams under *valg*). The other possibility which I have adopted in my translation above is based on the fact that the dictionaries associate *valg* more commonly with the sense "jump, spring, flutter". This specification of meaning on their part agrees with

Rings of flames dancing Śiva's dance of destruction.
The Khāṇḍava forest crumbling to the ground."[3]

Although there is an alliteration of *ṇ* and *ḍ* in the title of this paper, my intention is not to present a battle. It recognizes that a crisis of survival of the pandits, about which most of the world unfortunately does not seem to care, exists, but it does not go into a delineation of the crisis. Instead, it tries to address the underpinnings, mostly sociological and philosophical, of the pandit phenomenon and to explain why they may resurface, although the possibility of their resurfacing appears remote at this stage.

The second clarification I should provide is about the expression *piṇḍa-brahmāṇḍa* in the title; *piṇḍa* means "body", and *brahmāṇḍa* stands for "all creation". In Sanskrit religio-philosophical literature, *piṇḍa* and *brahmāṇḍa* are used as a pair to speak of everything from an individual to all the creation around him.[4] Frequently, the thesis of the contexts in which the words are used is *yat piṇḍe tad brahmāṇḍe* "what exists in the individual body (*piṇḍa*) exists also in cosmos (*brahmāṇḍa*)". I am, however, using the expression only to suggest that my thoughts in the present essay will range from the pandit's body to what is viewed, at least by some thinkers, as fundamental to all creation. In other words, the intention behind using the phrase *piṇḍa-brahmāṇḍa* is to suggest that I am going to be daring (or foolish) and to take a holistic (or sweeping) approach and consider the pandit as an individual linked to the whole *saṃsāra*.

Finally, three minor clarifications: (a) To the extent the thoughts to be expressed in the essay will require, I will refer to the names of some pandits and will also narrate briefly a few stories revealing how we think of

---

the meaning *gati* "movement" recorded for *valg* in the Cāndra Dhātupāṭha (the Pāṇinīya Dhātupāṭha lists *valg* without meaning).

(b) In a verse like the following *valg* could mean either "sound" or "move": *keṣāṃcid vāci śukavat, pareṣāṃ hṛdi mūkavat / kasyāpy ā hṛdayād vaktre valgu valganti sūktayaḥ //* "They exist in speech, as of a parrot, in the case of some. They exist in the heart, as of a person who cannot speak, in the case of some others. Only in the case of a (rare) person here or there, do good sayings move (or resound) charmingly from the heart to speech." (Vallabhadeva, Subhāṣitāvali 143).

3 Jagannātha has been treated by some historians of Sanskrit literature as the last great or real representative of the classical period. It is true that the classical ideal of combining sharp *śāstra* scholarship with high poetic talent in oneself (*kāvyeṣu komala-dhiyo vayam eva nānye, tarkeṣu karkaśa-dhiyo vayam eva nānye* "A delicate mind for poetic compositions—that's me, no one else. An adamantine mind for logical compositions—that's me, no one else.") is realised in Jagannātha in an impressive way. Although there have been others who have been called *Paṇḍitarāja* "King of pandits" or "Lord of scholars", subsequent to him, no one has acquired the pan-Indian fame he has. Appropriate to the present context, one can also view him as the prime example of the predicaments the pandits have faced and the weaknesses they have displayed when culturally alien rulers came to dominate significantly large parts of India.

4 However, *piṇḍa* and *brahmāṇḍa* do not seem to occur commonly as members of a *dvandva* or copulative compound as in my title.

the pandits. These stories are intended mainly as illustrative of my observations and as suggesting that a particular line of thinking cannot entirely be wrong. I do not view them as substitutes for a comprehensive collection of evidence. (b) The close and long-standing relation between the Brahmin and the pandit makes it inevitable that many of my thoughts on the pandit will be applicable to the Brahmin too. I will not, however, always mention the parallels explicitly. Also, several of the strengths the pandits have and several of the problems they face are of a piece with those of Hinduism. I will leave this connection too to the imagination of the reader. (c) The ground for my *piṇḍa-brahmāṇḍa* approach will be provided by three of our current dominant associations with the notion "pandit". As the other essay of mine in this volume will indicate, these associations have not always been there—at least not in exactly the same form, but they are fairly common in our times albeit not always explicitly stated. Their statements will be followed by discussions on the type of philosophy of individual life and the world which lies behind them, which made the pandit phenomenon possible and which can be consigned to the junkyard of ideas only if we choose to think superficially.

Associations with "pandit"

About the middle of the 1980's, Professor Michael Hahn visited the University of British Columbia to deliver a lecture. During an informal exchange of thoughts over tea and coffee following the lecture, Professor Hahn presented before me and a few other colleagues his vision of what computers would do for Indology. Indologists had then just begun to evince sustained professional interest in computers. After describing how computers could be used to store several texts and retrieve information from them swiftly, Professor Hahn quipped "We will not need the pandits' help then!" A question popped out of my mouth even before I realised that I had opened it: "Will there be any pandits left to help?"

In 1992, Professor Robert P. Goldman came to India with a video camera with the intention of filming the pandits in action. When he asked me if I could suggest the names of some truly impressive pandits whom he could interview and capture on the film, I could not come up with more than two or three names, all of them belonging to pandits close to or beyond their seventies![5] This may be due to my limited knowledge of traditional scholarship in India. After all, I have now spent most of my life outside India, visiting only

5 In his e-mail of 9 July 1999, Professor Goldman kindly supplied the following information to me, which I reproduce with some abridgement: "The videorecording of pandits that I did was done in various parts of India (Pune, Varanasi, Karnataka, and Calcutta) in 1992. I interviewed and recorded a variety of scholars in various disciplines and of various degrees of learning etc., asking them to speak (in Sanskrit) mostly about their own lives and the conditions under which they had entered the world of Sanskrit schol-

a few small parts of it whenever I had the opportunity. It is also possible that the standard I was implicitly applying was too high, set by whatever little I was fortunate to observe of Pt. Rajeshwar Shastri Dravid (Varanasi/Kashi), Pt. Shivaramakrishna Shastri (Deccan College, Pune), and Pt. Shriniwasa Shastri (Deccan College, Pune), not to mention the pandit teachers with whom I was fortunate enough to study a few basic texts. However, in view of what I hear from many of my knowledgeable colleagues, I am inclined to discount these possibilities. I consider it almost certain that a true pandit is now an extremely endangered species.

In the account of my exchange with Hahn, in several floating stories and in the statements Indologists make about the pandits, it is assumed that a pandit is characterized by memorization or near-memorization of a number of traditionally valued texts, either of a particular branch or of several branches.[6] If the latter is the case, a pandit becomes more respectable as, for example, Raghunath Sharma of Varanasi, in recent memory was. We also expect a pandit to be capable of teaching advanced students. If a pandit further displays the capability to solve the problems of interpreting texts previously unsolved by specialists, to integrate the thoughts expressed in various texts, or to advance a received line of thought, he, understandably, becomes an especially respected member of his class.[7] Rajeshwar Shastri

---

arship in their youth. These men, often quite elderly, included the late Pattabhirama Shastri, Baladeva Upadhyaya, Shivaji Upadhyaya, Herambanath Shastri, Pandharinath Galagali Shastri, the late Shrinivas Shastri and a number of others."

6 My teacher Mr. N.N. Bhide was fond of telling the story of Bhaṭṭajī-śāstrī Ghāṭe (also spelled "Bhatji Shastri Ghate"), a pandit in Nagpur (who, I guess, lived in the late nineteenth and early twentieth centuries). Ghāṭe's area of expertise was Pāṇinian grammar. If someone asked him a question relating to grammar, Ghāṭe would almost always simply point to the books and handwritten copies stacked on wooden planks fixed to the walls of his *agnihotra* area and advise the inquirer to take down a particular volume and look up a particular part or page for the answer he (the inquirer) was seeking. He would not feel the need to consult the volumes before formulating his answer. If questions pertaining to *śāstras* other than grammar were put to him, Ghāṭe would most of the time modestly say, "I know only grammar." Yet, when he was cajoled into writing a commentary on Bhavabhūti's Uttararāmacarita, he wrote it without opening any book and by citing several authorities outside the grammatical literature.
Ghāṭe's commentary Bhāvabhūtārthabodhikā has been published as a commentary by Jayakṛṣṇa (probably Ghāṭe's personal name), together with an English translation of the Uttararāmacarita, notes and introduction by Vinayak Sadashiv Patvardhan. The Catalogue of the India Office Library, vol. II, part I (revised edition, 1957), p. 2831, lists the second edition under the call number 21.D.19 as published by the Induprakāśa Press of Bombay in 1909. I have so far not been able to consult the work for confirmation of any of the aspects of the story given above.

7 The more impressive among such pandits may receive designations such as *Mahāmahopādhyāya*, *sarvatantrasvatantra* and *paṇḍitarāja*. They may also be appointed as *āsthānavidvas* "court pandit", *sāndhivigrahika* "minister for peace and conflict, minister for external relations" etc.

Dravid and Badrinath Shukla can be cited as recent examples. However, it can be seen that in all such gradations the ability to command the contents of texts without being required to consult the texts' written or printed forms to any significant extent remains an irremovable part of our understanding of the pandit.[8]

A common misconception entertained even by some educationists who devise the teaching policies for our primary schools and highschools is that memorization is an impediment to creative thought. We occasionally also hear the talk of not burdening the students' minds with the information they could easily get from printed and electronic sources when the need arises. It is presumed, without any real evidence as far as I know, that retention and creation of thought are causally unrelated activities.[9] Besides the practical convenience of not having to consult the sources of one's knowledge again and again,[10] no significant benefit is usually attached to memorization. It is not clear to me why the possibility that the capabilities of the brain itself, particularly the grasping capabilities, may change through extensive memorization over a long period is discounted. Individuals who learn several languages frequently report that they found each succeeding language easier to learn. If this could scientifically be proved, it behooves us all the more that we take a kinder view of memorization. Furthermore, as we do not find the phenomenon of biological inheritance—the child acquiring certain instincts and capabilities from the parents—problematic, we should not discount "off-the-cuff" the possibility that a tradition of memorization main-

---

8 In other words, an intimate and wide connection with the older Indian way of preserving knowledge, coupled with an ability to impart that knowledge, is at the core of what *paṇḍita* means to us. The use of the term in performing arts also points in the same direction. It is based on the elements (a) of study in the presence of a teacher outside the Western-style academic institutions that have become common in South Asia and (b) of oral retention.

The above observation, however, does not imply that pandits do not build personal libraries, do not prepare manuscripts and editions, or do not make a significant contribution to the preservation and deciphering of manuscripts. Their association with reading, writing and printing is also close. Their distinction from "Western" and "westernized" scholars consists in the *manner* in which they relate to these latter activities.

9 (a) Perhaps in the case of learning a language such a presumption is not made. In that context, specialists in language learning may have accepted that retention of vocabulary etc. is instrumental in the generation of thought.

(b) Professor Wezler has kindly drawn my attention to Assmann 1999:11-13, in which a broad overview of Western attitudes to memory as an art or skill is found. He has also rightly emphasized in our discussions that the Western educational tradition has in the past shown awareness of the importance of memorization.

10 The Indian tradition was widely aware of the convenience in containing the information in mind and thus controlling it. One of the commonly repeated sayings is: *pustakasthā tu yā vidyā para-hasta-gataṃ dhanaṃ / kārya-kāle samutpanne, na sā vidyā, na tad dhanam //* "Knowledge existing in books and (one's own) wealth in the hands of someone else—when the need arises, it is not knowledge, it is not wealth."

tained in a family over several generations may eventually lead to children with superior intellectual equipment.[11] Also, if intelligence is primarily the ability to detect swiftly the structures present in a situation—to find the organizing principle, to see order in chaos, to make sense of something that was not presented to the senses with instructions for interpretation—does it not seem plausible that memorization, which forces one to concentrate on structures, will habituate a person to search for structures and gradually increase his ability to identify them? In our contemporary science and medical treatments etc., we try to find as many causes in matter—to ground our explanations in the material world—as we can, keeping the intractable and intangible "mental" out, but we do not seriously pay attention to the possibility that the mental may be changing the matter and that how the mental or brain of the present is developed may hold implications for the brain matter of the future. As Michele Demarais has kindly informed me, some Western scientists and philosophers (e.g. Patricia and Paul Churchland, Antonio Damasio, Paul Martin, Joseph LeDoux) have begun to probe the "mental vs. physical" distinction as a primary problem. However, the dominant tendency is still to confer upon the separation of mind and body, made for the sake of convenience in analysis and description, the status of an unchanging and unchangeable physical fact. The philosophy that gave rise to the pandit does not seem to do so.[12]

In addition to memorization, a strong association with the "pandit" concept is that a pandit is a Hindu (in a broad sense of the term)[13] scholar or

---

11 Many instances of extraordinary scholarship continuing in the family line are recorded in accounts such as those in Upādhyāya 1983. The only account known to me in which the concepts "pandit" and "genetic history" come together is Kalla 1985. However, in it, the term *pandit* stands for Kashmiri Hindus. Because of this wider and exceptional meaning (see p. 26 of my other essay in the present volume), it does not deal with as controlled a sample as the testing of the possibility suggested here would require. Whether it is a valid study and can still be used to draw indirectly relevant conclusions is something I cannot decide, for I have no competence in the areas concerned.

12 The recommendation of memorization implicit in the preceding lines should not be construed as a recommendation of indiscriminate memorization. Services of the knowledgeable members of society should indeed be used to decide what the younger generations should memorize. The society also needs to develop the appropriate genres of literature. The Indian tradition developed them, especially in the form of the *sūtra* and *kārikā* literature.

13 This broad sense of "Hindu" includes all religions of Indian origin. (Although it can be and has been used for unpleasant purposes, one cannot deny that it exists in historical records and has also served positive purposes.) In the present context, "Hindu" serves mainly to distinguish the pandit from a Muslim learned man. Not all experts who have remained largely impervious to the influence of Western (particularly British and more recently American) education and who are engaged in the preservation and cultivation of traditional branches of learning are pandits. Non-association with the Arabic-Persian heritage and association with the Sanskrit-Prakrit heritage constitute a widely recognized element in the notion of a pandit.

expert who is primarily educated in non-Western or non-Western-style institutions of higher learning.[14] A deeper layer in this *parisaṃkhyā* ("through exclusion") understanding of the pandit consists of a judgment regarding the presence of sense of history. It is frequently assumed that pandits are not engaged in historical research as their Sanskritist-Prakritist counterparts in the Western and Western-style institutions are.[15] In fact, one gets the impression that, according to some, the pandits are incapable of carrying out true historical research. They are generally not expected to engage in the kind of teaching and research that professors of Sanskrit and other Indological subjects do—to account for things historically or to express themselves in a language other than Sanskrit. Something in their education is seen as preventing them from studying things diachronically or with a detachment expected of a historian. They are, at least implicitly, thought of as prone to cultivating knowledge with faith or in an eternalistic mode.[16] It is not that

---

14 (a) This element in our understanding obviously holds good only for the last 250 years or so, but primarily for the last 150 years—roughly from the time of the founding of the University of Calcutta in 1858 when Western-style education began to be directly available to Indians.

(b) Out of practical necessity, the element identified here rests on not attaching much value to indirect and non-formal exposure to Western education—on not taking seriously the possibility that the traditional scholars who came into contact with the early Europeans beginning with the seventeenth century A.D. learned some new ways of handling knowledge. Is it not likely, for example, that Kavindrācārya Sarasvatī's *pāṇḍitya* was affected, however minutely, by his meetings with Burnier (Gode 1945, 1954; Upādhyāya 1983:75-76)? Of course, it is. But we generally play down the inroads the exposure to the West has been making in the pandit territory and pretend as if there is no gradation in the change the pandit has undergone over the centuries. For the sake of simplicity, we posit the pandit as an un-Western scholar occupied with the business of handed-down knowledge in India.

(c) A similar consideration should be extended to pandits in the pre-Western days of Indian history. They too must have changed over the course of time and geography.

15 (a) Creativity or originality, if expected of a pandit, is primarily expected in terms of exposition, unearthing of information, and piecing together of related statements and indications in various texts (including the *kośas*). In exposition, the novelty is not expected to arise out of a text-critical activity based on manuscript research or out of a delineation of historical change, although it may occasionally so arise. The implicit assumption is that novelty will come about synchronically and without a change in the text which receives the explanation.

(b) In addition to absence of training in the method of historical research, it is possible that the rendering of the term "research paper" with *śodha-nibandha*, *saṃśodhana-nibandha* etc. in Sanskrit and other Indian languages had a delimiting effect on the kind of papers pandits read in Indological conferences or contribute to volumes of Indological research. Since the primary association of *śodha* is with "cleaning, purification", the pandit participants might have thought that restating the thought of ancient texts in a clear or defensible manner constitutes research and thus the historical dimension of the Indological enterprise might have eluded them.

16 (a) The phenomenon is related to colonialistic assumptions, to the creation of tagged "pandit" positions in Indian colleges and universities and to the holding of separate

exceptions to this general understanding are not admitted,[17] but it is also accurate to say that the general understanding just stated very much prevails.

In our academic world and cultural life obsessed with history, the association just outlined leads to a devaluation of the pandit's scholarship, consciously or unconsciously, just as some other things associated with traditional India are devalued. It cannot be a coincidence or merely a sign of the low economic status of the pandits that when non-Indian scholars or Indian scholars producing Indological works in the non-panditic, Western mode acknowledged the help they received in the completion of their research projects or books, the pandit was overlooked or got a short shrift, especially in the early days of Indology.[18] At the hands of a Whitney, he would also become an object of criticism if he happened to have written a commentary giving a nonhistorical explanation of something for which a historical explanation was possible. He was thought to be good only as an informant or as an exponent of the traditionally received explanation.[19] A greater affinity was felt with someone who could operate on the historical

---

paṇḍita-pariṣads in the sessions of the All-India Oriental Conference, World Sanskrit Conference etc., but it is probably not fully explained by all these things taken together. (b) I should not be understood as holding that Western scholars, as a rule or almost always, handle the historical method well. Some of the objections to their way of reconstructing history expressed or indicated in Bhashyāchārya (1905:25-29) still remain valid (although, ironically, the same publication is also a clear instance of a pandit's very imperfect grasp of the complexities of carrying out historical research and of his proclivity to faith).

17 (a) There is unlikely to be any disagreement that the following scholars, for example, first trained in the panditic tradition, have given evidence of being able to handle the historical method: S. Kuppuswami Sastri, S.D. Joshi, K.S. Arjunwadkar, Parameswara Aithal, and Rewa Prasad Dviwedi. Their research does go beyond *śodha* or *pariṣkāra* of what is stated in the *śāstras* etc. Particularly impressive is the case of Kuppuswami Sastri. He provided instruction in historical linguistics and ultimately became such a prominent figure in reconstructing the histories of Kāvya-śāstra, Vedānta etc. that an institute dedicated primarily to historical research was justifiably given his name.
(b) One can easily detect various degrees of success in historical research in the scores of introductions contributed by pandits to the editions of Sanskrit and Prakrit texts and in the papers in Sanskrit written by pandits in journals, conference proceedings etc.

18 Notable exceptions exist. Recently, acknowledgements have become more common, although one cannot be certain that all the help received from the pandits is unreservedly acknowledged.

19 Occasionally, pandits have responded to the devaluation of their learning by pointing out the lack of "real" learning in modern university-fostered scholarly publications. The modern poet Rudradeva Tripaṭhī, for example, is said to have written: *bhūmikā-paṇḍītāḥ kecit kecit phuṭ-noṭa-paṇḍitāḥ / repharans-paṇḍītāḥ kecid bhavanty evaṃ tu ḍākṭarāḥ //* "Some are introduction-scholars (they simply write introductions to volumes consisting of research papers written by other scholars). Some are footnote-scholars (they create an aura of scholarship by giving one footnote after another). Some are reference-scholars (they attach a long list of titles of books). Thus, they become doctors (Ph.Ds and D.Litts)."

plane or wave-length. The contribution a scholar with a historical bent of mind made to a scholarly undertaking was more readily appreciated.

Franz Kielhorn was one of the early European scholars who had an extensive contact (1866-1881) with the pandits at a young age and in an area (Pune-Mumbai) which had many excellent pandits specializing in a *śāstra* of which very few Europeans had any command at that time. He wrote the memorable remarks quoted at the beginning of this essay. One cannot see any exploitative colonialist attitude in them or fault them for lacking feeling. Just before making them, Kielhorn also wrote the following: "But with all the valuable help afforded by these works [= the commentaries of the Paribhāṣendu-śekhara], I should hardly have been able to accomplish my task, had I not been assisted in it by my learned friends and colleagues, Cintāmaṇi Śāstrī Thatte, Ananta Śastrī Pendharkar and the late Viṭṭhala Rāva Gaṇeśa Paṭavardhana. There is not a page, I might almost say, not a line in my whole translation the contents of which have not been submitted again and again to their criticism, and though I have honestly tried to form my own opinion and to judge independently in every difficulty, though I am ready to bear the blame for any errors and inaccuracies which I cannot hope to have escaped altogether, yet it would be wrong not to acknowledge here the great and invaluable benefit which I have derived from the learning and intelligent discussion of my fellow-teachers."

But even with the collegial attitude, great regard, sympathy and historical imagination he had in the case of the pandits, individually the pandits were not at as high a position in Kielhorn's eyes as someone who was more proficient in the historical approach than in śāstraic learning. As we have seen, he does mention by name the traditional scholars who were well-established in the public eye as his teachers, but he does not feel the need to mention individually his assistants in the demanding project of editing Patañjali's Vyākaraṇamahābhāṣya. Because he returned to Germany in 1881 before the second and third volumes of his Mahābhāṣya edition were published (respectively in 1883 and 1885), the pandits might not have helped him all the way, but it is hardly likely that at least the first drafts of these volumes were not ready when Kielhorn left India.[20] His work could scarcely have been possible without their initial assistance and explanations. Furthermore, they had to be learned at least to the extent of being able to understand the advanced texts of the intricate Pāṇinian grammatical tradition. Yet in the prefaces of the first two volumes of Kielhorn's edition, there is no mention of any assistants. The first is dedicated to Albrecht Weber and the second to the principal and professors of Deccan College. Toward the end of the preface

20 The Preface to the first volume of the first edition leads one to conclude that most of the text to be printed was ready with Kielhorn in some form and he was waiting mainly for it to be published. The second edition of 1892 contains no change in the Preface.

to the third volume, we find the following statement: "The Mahābhāṣya may be said to be composed in the form of a series of dialogues, and there can be no doubt that its meaning is best brought out by oral discussion among scholars versed in the science of grammar. For this reason I have often regretted that I was obliged to prepare the greater portion of the text of this edition far away from those friendly Paṇḍits, to whom I owe a deep debt of gratitude for all they have taught me; but most of all do I regret that I have not been able to discuss my difficulties with that Indian scholar who has contributed more than any other towards a right understanding of the Mahābhāṣya, and to whom I dedicate this volume as a small token of my sincere admiration and friendly regard."

Kielhorn's 'that Indian scholar' was Ramakrishna Gopal Bhandarkar. One can doubt Bhandarkar's greatness as a scholar only at the risk of being ridiculed. However, his published contribution toward understanding the Mahābhāṣya itself is relatively small—considerably smaller than his contributions to other areas of Indology.[21] It helps us in determining the historical context of the Mahābhāṣya (specifically the author's date, place). It is important for this reason and as evidence of Bhandarkar's keen eye and good judgment. But it can hardly equal what Ananta-shastri Pendharkar and others must have contributed by explicating the text of the Mahābhāṣya (Bhandarkar too had learned grammar from Pendharkar). Yet, Kielhorn was clearly more impressed by Bhandarkar, who approached Sanskritic studies with a historical bent of mind, than by any of his *śāstrīs*. He dedicated the third volume to Bhandarkar and suggested that the way Bhandarkar explored the Mabhābhāṣya was the right way. He did not feel the need to state specifically that there were others who helped him in the Mahābhāṣya project or to name them individually.

Also revealing is the phenomenon that once a pandit becomes reasonably known as a researcher writing in a language other than Sanskrit and on historical themes, the honorific "pandit" preceding his name generally falls off and is replaced by "Doctor", "Professor" etc. as may be possible.[22]

Now, what should be our reaction to this situation? Just as it would be better if more and more pandits acquired the capability to write as historians (without losing their existing strengths), we need to rethink—we need

---

21 Kielhorn's wording "who has contributed more than any other towards a right understanding of the Mahābhāṣya" rules out the possibility that he intended to refer to the help he privately got from Bhandarkar in understanding the Mahābhāṣya. The wording presupposes that Bhandarkar's contribution is public knowledge.

22 In the recent past, it has become common for pandits appointed in Indian institutions of higher learning to teach, almost exclusively, in the language of their region. More and more pandits in north India are doing their writing in Hindi, albeit of a highly Sanskritic kind: In the latter respect, the gap between pandits and professors is smaller in northern India than in some other parts of India.

to adjust our glasses with respect to—the importance we attach to history. Historical truth needs to be brought down by a few notches in our scheme of values. The high status we have accorded it, as if it were the same as scientific or philosophical truth, is contributing to creation of much misery in the world. Ancient Indians may not have had a word for "history" in our sense of the term, but they were obviously wise when they created a trend that played down past factual differences. Without a devaluation of historical knowledge as a norm for conducting the affairs of society, there would not have emerged in India a transcendence of names of individual gods, religious practices etc., and a generally tolerant composite culture would not have come into existence at an early date. Social harmony seems to have carried greater weight for the thinkers of ancient India. They seem to suggest pursuit of happiness as a more important value than pursuit of historical truth. This does make the work of persons like us difficult and inconvenient, for, one way or the other, we, as Indologists, are reconstructing history or contributing to its reconstruction. However, our selfish professional considerations should not be allowed to get the better of our sense of social responsibility and our awareness of the historian's limitations. We should see that while we may not imitate the pandit's disinterest in history (which, incidentally, is not total or unqualified), we can at least meet him half-way by distancing ourselves from the persons who read more than justified certainty in our reconstructions and make history the overriding consideration in dealing with social divisions and areas of tension. We should also acknowledge that devaluation of history as a factor in our life is conducive to assigning a more important role to myths, which add colour to literature, ritual etc. and which, if properly used, can be very helpful in maintaining good social institutions. Rationality and attachment to facts is not meant for and cannot indeed be maintained for all aspects of life.[23]

Restrained, self-sacrificing behaviour is the third element we commonly associate with the kind of pandit I have in mind here. Restraint in food (what, when and how he eats it) and restraint in sexual relations are prescribed for and are usually practised by the traditional scholar of Sanskrit, Prakrit etc.

---

23 This, however, necessitates, that those charged with the responsibility of conveying truth must not feel tempted to take liberties with it for the sake of personal gain. (The constant exhortations to the Brahmins to free themselves from considerations of personal gain may, among other things, be due to this factor in the intellectual atmosphere of ancient India.) Secondly, the devaluation of historical truth should not be understood as absence of a sense of history. Although little historical information has been preserved in India in some respects, I am not convinced that there were no attempts in early India to preserve what we would call historical information.
Absence of historical awareness in the sense of denying what actually happened is also not a part of my suggestion that history not be assigned the importance that is assigned to it at present in many societies of the world.

The general reaction of a modern Western or Westernized individual to this kind of behaviour—if at all he thinks about it—is to treat it as a kind of quaint relic left over from a superstitious period of human history. "One of these days these men will progress from religion to true scientific, rational thinking, just as they progressed from nature worship to religion" is the hope his anthropology inspires in him in his moments of intellectual generosity. Here too, he does not realise the irony that, while he has been trying to locate the bases for behaviour in something that can be handled impersonally—in matter or material objects, the pandits' behaviour is sending a signal of close relation between matter and mind and between matter and society and that this signal could be good for human beings, possibly all creatures.

In the modern "scientific" man's compartmentalization of life and insistence that a specific correlation be proved between factor f1 and its consequence c1 in such a manner that everybody could verify the correlation if he or she wished to, a large chunk of human behaviour is either left out of investigation or consigned to the realms of religion, sociology, history etc. in such a way as to obscure its probable relevance for life here and now. The "scientific" man may admit that a pandit provides a good model for society, just the way a minister or priest provides in many religions, when he does not behave as he wishes or demonstrates the benefits of reducing consumption. Many medical practitioners and psychologists nowadays even translate specific self-imposed behaviours of religious or spiritual practitioners in general secular terms and recommend their acceptance, if not fully in a qualified way or in certain situations. Yet our scientific community has not, as yet, displayed, at least on a large scale, the open-mindedness of investigating specifically the elements in the restrained behaviour of a pandit or Brahmin. The benefits that may accrue from determining, even in probabilistic terms, the relationship between this behaviour and its effects are thus lost. That a sportsman or boxer is advised to refrain from sexual contact in the days preceding his day of performance is reported as lore from the field of sports, but because we may not be able to establish a relation between retention of semen and superior performance in the arena in such a manner that some other "objective" person may be able to verify it—because we have become reluctant to run the business of society on the basis of probability (see pp. 54 below)—we do not allow this lore and the thinking that may be behind it to become a basis of our social policy.[24] If we do not ridicule it, we are content to leave it as a matter of individual preference or

24 With this may be contrasted the following observation about pre-modern India made by Gopinath Kaviraj (1987:67-68): "It is an article of universal acceptance in this country that *Bindu* (essence of the physical body in the form of *Vīrya*, *Śukra*, or seminal fluid), *Vāyu* (the intra-organic vital currents) and *Manas* (mind or the principle of thinking) are closely related to one another, so that by restraining any one of them the remaining two may be easily held in check."

interesting ethnological curiosity. Again, we do not realise the irony that, on the one hand, we try to provide more and more material basis for things of the mind, but, on the other hand, prevent a probable material basis from being linked with a thing of the mind.[25]

Reading through the lives of Jain monks of recent times, I have been struck by the intellectual achievements many of them registered subsequent to their initiation and after long periods of restrained behaviour, even though they did not come from a highly educated family, did not belong to the Brāhmaṇa *varṇa* or evince a particular attachment to pursuit of knowledge in pre-initiation days. I admit I cannot prove it to everyone's satisfaction, but I do suspect a correlation between their panditic performance and their acceptance of a mode of living that at least partially resembles the one recommended for a Brahmin pandit.

Consider also the practical advantages to society, other than the ones coming through growth of knowledge, of the restrictions enjoined upon the pandit. The restrictions bring the pandit close to a *yogin* or a religious figure.[26] He is seen by the society as making a sacrifice of the comforts and

---

25 The discussion of extraordinary capabilities of cognition mentioned in Yoga frequently takes place on the assumption that such capabilities are a matter of faith (instances of God's or guru's grace) or are mysterious (inexplicable) psychic phenomena. Such discussion rightly leads to rejection of the very notion of extraordinary capabilities or to strong scepticism regarding them on the part of "rational" or "scientific" thinkers. But it should be noted that the explanation for such capabilities given in the theoretical works of *yoga* is, to a considerable extent, quite down-to-earth and basically materialistic: (a) Repeated effort enables an aspirant to perceive what he could not perceive before, just as a person aspiring to be a jeweller learns to see, through apprenticeship, the positive and negative features of jewels which he could not see before. (b) A particular mode of living, including *yama-niyama-āsana-prāṇāyāma* etc. and dominated by *saṃyama* "restraint" heightens the abilities of the senses.

26 There seems to have prevailed in India a world view according to which any activity that involved restraint of the senses was seen as enhancing the spiritual stature of a person. The Bhagavadgītā (4:28) lines *dravya-yajñās tapo-yajñā yoga-yajñās tathāpare / svādhyāya-jñāna-yajñāś ca yatayaḥ saṃśita-vratāḥ //* ("Some sacrifice with substances, some with abandonment of comforts, some with discipline (of body and mind), some with study of the scriptures and some with knowledge. Men practising restraint have strict vows.") have helped in creating such an ethos in India, particularly among the Brahmins, for centuries. The widened notion of sacrifice, therefore, probably played a significant role in running the business of society.

The Bhagavadgītā praise of *jñāna-yajña* has been understood as a praise of dispassionate pursuit of worldly knowledge as it has been understood as a praise of spiritual, liberating, knowledge. Teachings like *brāhmaṇena niṣkāraṇaṃ ṣaḍaṅgo vedo 'dhyeyo jñeyaś ca* ("A Brahmin should study and come to know the Veda with its six ancillaries with no (worldly) motive in mind") are naturally seen as conforming to the Gītā prescription of *karmayoga* and hence as leading to spiritual enhancement.

Upādhyāya (1983:26-27, 68, 70-716 etc.) gives several examples of pandits who were thought of as special persons in spiritual terms and who, in turn, tried to live up to such reputations.

pleasures that commonly attract men. The society, in turn, becomes more inclined to sacrifice some of its resources for him. The burden on the government treasury is reduced. Pursuit of knowledge does not depend entirely on the personal preferences of some administrator or minister. Objectives that seem to have little or no practical or immediate benefit to society can be pursued. Search for academic knowledge and search for spiritual knowledge are not artificially kept apart.[27] A scholar need not contend with a "publish or perish" mentality or feel inhibited by department labels and walls. He can carry out his inquiry as far as his capabilities and resources allow him, without feeling overly constrained by compartmentalization of knowledge.

A subpoint in what I have observed above regarding the restrained, self-sacrificing behaviour of pandits should be explored further, for it leads us, I believe, to a deeper understanding of what made the pandit phenomenon possible. In speaking of reluctance to run the business of society on the basis of probability, I was obviously not asserting that we do not at all run the business of society on the basis of probability. Much of our management of social issues and processes is, in fact, determined by considerations of probability: we set up a curriculum because we think it will probably be useful to most students; we do not allow certain offenders to come out of jails because we think they will probably repeat the offences, and so on. My point rather is that the area between what is amenable to laboratory testing and that which, because of its very nature, cannot be tested in a laboratory or can be tested only to a limited extent, remains an unutilized or severely underutilized territory in our present outlook of the world. The dominant attitude toward an item falling in this intermediate area is "wait until it is verified in the laboratory" (cf. the state of affairs in psychology). Now, the effort to separate the variables present in a situation and to split a problem into several subproblems that can be individually studied for specific correlations is fine in itself. That is what a scientific approach should attempt. However, the effort tends to be construed in such a way as to overlook (a) the possibility that the discovery of scientific truth could be a process rather than a fixed destination to reach and (b) the possibility that it may not be desirable to postpone all decisions until the destination is reached. Furthermore, in the area with which we are concerned, the experiments, if carried out rigorously, do not ultimately take us beyond a relationship between two material entities, regardless of the expressions the authors of the experiments may employ to describe them. (They leave the larger ques-

---

27 Thus, the incentive to scholarship comes in terms of social recognition—a special social status not economic in nature. Educational establishments have to earn their support from the government as well as the citizenry, but not by demonstrating that they are making direct contributions to the material welfare of the society. It is enough for the society to know that they are providing models of limited consumption and pursuit of knowledge and are creating positive forces for the natural and cosmic order.

tion of "mind" unexplored, unless the researcher thinks of mind as nothing but a complex of material entities, as is essentially the case in psychiatry in which specific mind-substances are controlled by specific physical substances.) Alternatively, if the experiments are not carried out so rigorously and an intrusion of other variables is allowed, they do not yield results that other researchers can universally replicate and accept. Consequently, very little is actually achieved beyond what natural sciences achieve in the laboratories, and the attitude of uncertainty regarding the in-between area is not dislodged. The in-between area remains open for claims and counterclaims arising out of different experiments. As probabilities suggested by reasonably controlled and reasonably large samples do not inspire confidence—because such probabilities are not thought to be good enough, making recommendations based on them that would apply to the entire society or to specific groups within it is considered inappropriate. The choice is left to the individual, and, until he becomes a member of a group as a consequence of his behaviour, the recommendations are generally not proffered.

The situation in traditional India was very different in this regard. An individual was primarily considered to belong to a group (we do not have to get into the issue of how this belonging was determined). Generalizations regarding groups were freely and frequently aired (we do not have to get into the issue of how these generalizations were arrived at). The notions of *varṇa*, *karman* and *punar-janman* ("reincarnation, rebirth") were almost universally accepted.

The pandits are usually placed in those social classes (Brahmin, monk) which are expected to engage in ascetic actions. It is thought that good *karman* of past lives, particularly disciplined behaviour, gives them superior minds.[28] They are expected to behave in accordance with the norms for their social class, if they wish to go ahead in that class or to attain the still higher *varṇa*-less (*mokṣa* or *nirvāṇa*) state. Thus, *varṇa* "social class (defined in a specific way)", *karman* "action", and *punar-janma* "rebirth" are the associations related to the surface-level associations I have discussed. They are especially related to my first and third dominant associations: memory and restrained behaviour.

---

28 Good deeds or observance of religious vows on the part of parents is frequently indicated to be the cause; cf. the accounts of the birth of Abhinavagupta (Pandey 1963:6-8), Nārāyaṇabhaṭṭa (the author of Tristhalīsetu etc.; Benson in this volume) etc., which are widely separated in time and region but agree in attaching special importance to ideal religious conduct on the part of the parents. The number of cases in which the authors of surviving works praise their fathers (sometimes the mothers too) for learning as well as conduct is also quite high. But such good *karman* on the part of parents does not rule out past good *karman* on the part of the pandit to be born, for it is that *karman* which should logically make him (and not someone else) eligible to be born as a child of a particular couple. A pandit is thus similar to a *yogabhraṣṭa* (Bhagavadgītā 6.40-44).

Conclusions

The preceding exploration suggests that the kind of pandit I have been discussing here is possible only under a philosophy of human body and mind and of the world that is significantly different from the dominant philosophy of our times. A logical consideration of the notion of reincarnation I have attempted elsewhere (Aklujkar 2000) further suggests that the "reincarnation-*karman-varṇa*" complex existing in this "body-mind-world" philosophy has not been vanquished for ever and its re-emergence is not impossible, although it seems improbable at present.

The Sanskrit universities and colleges and the religious establishments in the Indian subcontinent are trying to keep the pandit alive, but the odds are heavily against his gaining the necessary political and economic clout and against the governments' and religious establishments' success in stopping the forces that may ultimately eliminate him. He has come to be too closely associated with a minority, whose value is not only being questioned and challenged but which is seen as an oppressor in several parts of India (with some truth in the allegation). To make matters more difficult, through the centuries of Muslim and British rule and nearly two centuries of an educational system that inculcates a different (not necessarily bad) way of looking at the affairs of the world, the minority itself has lost contact with its past. In particular, it is generally incapable of reactivating the devices that enabled it to manage change and challenges in the past and to be able to lead the community in such a manner as to preserve traditional religious and educational institutions. There is thus the serious problem of whether the present-day Brahmins will be able to lead the society, even if they were given a chance, in such a manner as to create an environment in which panditic knowledge would survive and prosper.

It also needs to be realised in this context that the problem of the survival of the pandit has a global dimension. Society still needs individuals having the pandit minds in the sense that it will always require the guidance of scholars and experts. But apart from this general global dimension, there is a specific global dimension that is more immediately related to the issue of the pandits' continuance as an institution in our social life. Unless the value of humanistic research, particularly of the philological component of it, is increasingly recognized in the rich countries of the world, not only the pandits of the Sanskritic-Prakritic tradition, but the pandits of many other traditions of the world, as well as the modern specialists of languages, literatures etc. stand in danger of serious diminution, if not extinction.

All this means that, unless there is a fundamental rethinking of the dominant ideas of our time—unless there is a change in the philosophy of life dominant in our age, any efforts made to maintain the panditic type of scholarship will be "band-aid" solutions. The pandit is possible as a phenomenon only on the background of a host of other factors that extend from human body to how creation is viewed. A true pandit can be a product of only a certain kind of *piṇḍa-brahmāṇḍa* theory. The elements of that theory generally find no favour with the influential theoreticians of our time.

If our current and otherwise laudable ideas of equality, individual freedom, justice, historical truth and scientific proof are circumscribed or modified *by common consensus* in practice[29]—if they do not come in the way of recognition of excellence and of granting *qualified and balanced* privileges to certain classes of individuals and if the separation of body and mind dominant in our present educational, medical, scientific etc. practices is reduced, we might have a new pandit class. It may not be confined to Sanskrit or India. It may be global in its spread. Until such a class emerges, however, the pandit will primarily live in the twinkle seen in the eyes of a Sanskritist when he meets a Sanskritist from a culturally different part of the world and finds that he can discuss a very subtle problem of textual interpretation or philosophy with this other "being" despite the differences in their upbringing—that unbeknownst to them, a bond exists between them; that they stood on the same platform even before they turned to each other and their eyes met.

ACKNOWLEDGEMENTS: I wish to thank Professor Robert P. Goldman of the University of California (Berkeley) for the specifics he promptly provided of the video recordings he made of the speeches and teaching sessions of certain prominent pandits (see note 5). Professor Madhav M. Deshpande's comments brought home to me the need to consult Kielhorn 1874. This consultation has resulted in a significant improvement of the parts in which the justly esteemed scholar is mentioned. Further help in this respect came from Dr. Roland Steiner. He obliged me much by providing the publication details of Kielhorn 1874 with impressive precision and fullness, when I had access only to the 1960-62 reprint of that publication. I am also thankful to the authorities of the Alexander von Humboldt Stiftung for their support during 1998-99, the year in which this essay was written. Like many of my other research writings in that year, this one too has benefitted much from Professor Albrecht Wezler's "Rat und Tat". Finally, it is my pleasure to acknowledge the help I received from Michele Desmarais, Michael Dodson and Muktak Aklujkar in catching typographical errors and realising the possibilities for better wording.

REFERENCES

Aklujkar, Ashok. 2000. "Reincarnation revisited rationally", Forthcoming in the D.H.H. Ingalls Memorial Volume of the *Journal of Indian Philosophy*.

Assmann, Aleida. 1999. *Erinnerungsräume. Formen und Wandlungen des kulturellen Gedächtnisses*. Munich: Verlag C.H. Beck.

---

29 Democracy brings several advantages to society, but it also has a levelling effect and potential to kill the growth of excellence. Even the political cultures that took the ideal of equality in the strongest possible form had to make provision of special privileges to scientists, doctors, professors etc. in order to maintain and promote excellence.

Bhashyāchārya, N. 1905. *The Age of Patañjali*. Madras: The Theosophist Office, Adyar.

Gode, P.K. 1945. "Some evidence about the location of the manuscript library of Kavīndrācārya Sarasvatī at Benares in A.D. 1665", In the edition of *Jagadvijayacchandas* by C.Kunhan Raja, pp. XLVII ff. Bikaner. Reprinted in *Studies in Indian Cultural History*, vol. III [= P.K. Gode Studies Vol. VI], pp. 71-76. Poona: Bhandarkar Oriental Research Institute.

———. 1954. "Bernier and Kavīndrācārya Sarasvatī at the Mughal Court", In *Studies in Indian Literary History*, pp. II. 364-379. Bombay: Singhi Jain Shastra Sikshapith, Bharatiya Vidya Bhavan. 1954. [The preceding source informs us that originally the paper was published in *Annals of S.V. Oriental Institute, Tirupati*, 1.4:1-16. I have been unable to find out the year in which the specified journal issue appeared.]

Jagannātha, Paṇḍitarāja. 1958. *Paṇḍitarājakāvyasaṃgraha (Complete Poetic Works of Paṇḍitarāja Jagannātha)*. Ed. Sharma, Aryendra. Hyderabad: Osmania University, Sanskrit Academy.

———. *Rasagaṅgādhara*. (a) ed.: Bhaṭṭa Mathurānātha Śāstrī. Bombay: Nirṇayasāgara Press. Kāvyamālā Series. Sixth edition 1945. Reprint Delhi: Motilal Banarsidass. 1983. (b) ed., commentator: Madana-mohana Jhā. Varanasi: Chowkhamba Vidyabhawan. Vidyabhawan Sanskrit Granthamala 11. Vols 3. 1969. (c) ed., commentator: Kedāranātha Ojhā. Varanasi: Sampurnanand Sanskrit Vishvavidyalaya. Vols 3. 1981.

Kalla, Aloke K. 1985. *Kashmiri Pandits and Their Diversity (a Socio-demo-genetic Profile)*. Delhi: B.R. Publishing Corporation.

Kaviraj, Gopinath. 1987. *Notes on religion and philosophy*. Ed. Gaurinath Sastri. Varanasi: Sampurnanand Sanskrit University Press. [This is a collection of reprints of much older articles that does not specify when and where the articles were originally published.]

Kielhorn, Franz or Kielhorn, Lorenz Franz. 1874: see Nāgeśabhaṭṭa and Patañjali.

Nāgeśabhaṭṭa. *Paribhāṣenduśekhara*. (a) Ed., expl. Lorenz Franz Kiehlhorn. *The Paribhāṣenduśekhara of Nāgojībhaṭṭa*. Part I: the Sanskrit Text and Various Readings. Bombay: The Indu Prakash Press. Bombay Sanskrit Series 2. 1868. (b) *The Paribhāṣenduśekhara of Nāgojībhaṭṭa, edited and explained by F. Kielhorn. Part II: Translation and Notes*. Bombay: The Indu Prakash Press (7, 9) / Government Central Book Depot (12). Bombay Sanskrit Series 7, 9, 12. 1871-1874. (c) Second edition with revisions and addition of Tattvādarśa commentary by Vasudev Shastri Abhyankar. (Ed.) K.V. Abhyankar. Parts 2. Poona: Bhandarkar Oriental Research Institute. 1960, 1962. [My references are given according to the second edition.]

Pandey, Kanti Chandra. 1963. *Abhinavagupta: an Historical and Philosophical Study*. Second edition, revised and enlarged. Varanasi: Chowkhamba Sanskrit Series Office.

Patañjali. *Vyākaraṇa Mahābhāṣya*. (ed.) Kielhorn, Franz. Vols 3. Bombay: Government of Bombay, Department of Public Instruction. 1880, 1883, 1885. Second edition revised 1891/1892, 1906, 1909. Same publisher. Third edition revised by K. V. Abhyankar. 1962, 1965, 1972. Poona: Bhandarkar Oriental Research Institute. [Photoreprint of the first edition: Osnabrück: Otto Zeller Verlag, 1970.]

Upādhyāya, Baladeva. 1983. *Kāśī kī pāṇḍitya paramparā: kāśīstha saṃskṛta vidvānoṃ ke jīvana-carita evaṃ sāhityika avadānoṃ kā prāmāṇika vivaraṇa.* Vārāṇasī: Viśvavidyālaya Prakāśana. (Hindī).

Vallabhadeva. Subhāṣitāvali. (ed.) Peter Peterson; Durgāprasāda. Bombay: Bombay Sanskrit and Prakrit Series 31. Second edition edited by Raghunath Damodar Karmarkar. Poona: Bhandarkar Oriental Research Institute. 1961.

AXEL MICHAELS

The Pandit as a Legal Adviser: *rājaguru, rājapurohita* and *dharmādhikārin*

Introduction

Jan Heesterman (1957:226) calls the relationship between the king, the upholder of the *dharma* (see Gonda 1969, Derrett 1976, Heesterman 1985:108-27), and his priest (*purohita*) a "marriage-like bond". Indeed, the union of both is demonstrated not only in the share of the Vedic sacrifice or in royal coronation rituals,[1] but even more so in the share of jurisdiction. Penance and penalty, *prāyaścitta* and *daṇḍa*, priest and king were two different but interdependent realms—sometimes having a cumulative effect (Gampert 1939:251, Lingat 1973:234), at other times not. Thus, it has been observed that "the classical legal systems of India substitute the notion of *authority* for that of legality [sc. in Western juridicial systems, A.M.]" (Lingat 1973:258). Hindu law is to a great extent natural and customary law and as such much more dependent on the opinion and authority of the qualified interpreter in comparison to the positive law in Western societies.

It was, of course, the learned and traditionally educated Brahmin who advised the king on matters of Hindu law and the interpretation or application of the Dharmaśāstra, though in many cases it remained the king's prerogative to execute the law. However, the status of the Brahmin as a legal adviser was claimed and competed for by, at least, three learned Brahmin pandits: the royal chaplain or royal *paṇḍita* preceptor (*rājaguru, rājapurohita*), the *paṇḍita* minister (*pradhāna, āmātya, mantrin*) and the *paṇḍita* judge (*dharmādhikārin* etc.).

In this paper I shall try to demonstrate how the status of the pandit as a functionary in religious matters at courts in India and Nepal is challenged by his involvement in the executive. My focus is on the late 18th and the 19th century, more specifically I compare (a) the pandit and *dharmādhikārin* in the Śukranīti and at the courts of the Marāṭhas, (b) the pandit in the Company's law, and (c) the *dharmādhikārin* in the Rāṇā administration and the Nepalese Mulukī Ain of 1854. My point is that the pandit was employed not only as a learned authority of traditional legal systems but also to help the king to remove or "digest" the evil of his subjects. As the example of the *dharmādhikārin* in Nepal will make clear, a pandit sometimes only had to be a Brahmin. In other words, the more penance became penalty, the

1 For Nepal, see Witzel 1987:415-167.

lower the status of the pandit. [I am aware that this point contrasts with D. Quigley's (1993) recent criticism on Heesterman. However, this is not the place to elaborate on these issues (see Michaels 1998:208-214 for a critique of Quigley)].

The pandit in the Śukranīti and at the courts of the Marāṭhas

According to the Dharmasūtras, the king cannot decide upon religious matters alone, especially if penances (*prāyaścitta*) are involved. He has no legislative power. In the period of the Dharmasūtras, the king therefore formed a kind of advisory board or council for jurisdiction in socio-religious conflicts: the *pariṣad* or *samiti* of Brahmins (Lingat 1993:14-16, Kane 1974: 966-975), which became more and more responsible for the rules of good and right conduct (*ācāra*), the law of transactions (*vyavahāra*), the expiation of sins (*prāyaścitta*) and even for the king's order (*rājaśāsana*), i.e. for most parts of jurisdiction. This institution remained basically untouched until the 19th century. Such benches of learned Brahmins can be found, for instance, in the form of *brahmasabhās* in the judicial system of the Marāṭhas:

> "The Brahmasabha is generally noticed in connection with holy places such as Nasik, Paithan, Punatamba, Karhad, Kolhapur, Mahabaleshwar, Wai and Pandharpur. It was composed of the local learned Brahmins like *Vaidik*, *Pandit*, *Mimamsak* (well-versed in the science of interpretation), *Jyotishi*, *Puranik* and others. The head of the Brahmasabha was known as the *Dharmadhikari* (the Public Censor) and enjoyed the *Watan* of *Dharmadhikara*, by virtue of which he was authorised to decide the suits coming under *Achara* (right religious conduct), *Vyavahara* (Hindu Law), *Prayaschitta* (religious expiation) with the help of the Brahmasabha.
> The main judicial function of the Brahmasabha however seems to be to give advice in matters referred to them by the *Majlis*, or the government officer and to try the cases of social and religious offences. It was looked upon as a body of experts having jurisdiction over personal and canon law cases. The awards of the Brahmasabha are generally supported by quotations from the Sanskrit Law Books pertaining to the points raised." (Gune 1953:65 f., cf. also pp. 110 and 112)

The Dharmasūtras do not agree on how many members such a council should have,[2] but they agree that learnedness and moral quality are more important than number of members. A single qualified Brahmin could be enough to proclaim *dharma* and *ācāra* provided he is qualified by his brahminhood, good conduct (*sadācāra*, *śīla*) and learnedness (*śiṣṭa*, *paṇḍita*); the latter is basically characterized by command of the Veda and knowledge of the Dharmaśāstra.[3] The *longue durée* of these characteristics can

---

2 See, for example, BaudhDhS I.1.1.9 or Manu XII.113-114; Lingat 1993:15.

3 See, for example, the definition of a *śiṣṭa* in BaudhDhS I.1.1.5-6 or ĀpDhS I.7.20.8; cf. also Thieme 1957:60-62 and Wezler 1985:8 f.

also be seen in similar prerequisites for the legal adviser in the Śukranīti, a text from the 19th century, which stated that the pandit should first consider which traditionally and contemporary observed *dharmas* are related to the people, which rules were mentioned in the *śāstras*, which ones are now opposed, and which of them contradict the customary law (*lokaśāstra*) and then advise the king in such a manner that he will be granted prosperity (*sukha*) in this life and hereafter:

> *vartamānāś ca prācīnā dharmāḥ ke lokasaṃśritāḥ* /
> *śāstreṣu ke samuddiṣṭā virudhyante ca ke 'dhunā* //
> *lokaśāstraviruddhāḥ ke paṇḍitas tān vicintya ca* /
> *nṛpaṃ saṃbodhayet taiś ca paratra ha*[4] *sukhapradaiḥ* //
> (Śukra II.99-100)

For this purpose, says the Śukranīti, a *paṇḍita* has to be honest and unprejudiced (see Kumar 1975:44).

While in some places—including Nepal (see *infra*)—the royal (family) priest (*purohita, rājaguru*) remained the main adviser for the king in religious matters up until the 19th century, he was in many kingdoms and governments supplanted or supplemented from within the cabinet of ministers by a special *paṇḍita* minister (Altekar 1977:169, Kane 1973:126). In general, such experts did not—as in the case of the *rājaguru*—occupy a hereditary post. However, they held the status of a minister or high officer and, more importantly, they were directly involved in the executive.

Both *purohita* and *paṇḍita* ministers are regarded as supporters of the kingdom,[5] but the *purohita* is basically a priest, spiritual preceptor and teacher (*guru*) to the king, while the *paṇḍita* minister is basically a juridical functionary. To be sure, the *purohita* often had a number of political and administrative duties such as jurisdiction in cases where penances had to be meted out, or supporting the king and his soldiers in war by, for instance, consecrating the weapons, elephants and horses in the state army. Therefore, one sometimes finds the *purohita* listed among the ministers (*āmātya, mantrin*; cf. Śukra II.69-70), but "according to most authorities he played a role that was pre-eminently religious" (Kane 1973:119).

In the Śukranīti, the *paṇḍita* is listed among the ten advisers (*prakṛti*) of the king.[6] It has been convincingly argued by P.V. Kane, L. Gopal and others that this list had as its model Shivaji's council of eight ministers (*aṣṭapradhāna*), and the model for the *paṇḍita* minister was the *paṇḍitarāo*, one of the most influential *pradhānas* in Shivaji's cabinet (Altekar 1977:172, Gune 1953:111, Kane 1973:106, and 1974:972, Gopal 1978:40). Jadunath

---

4 conj. *paratreha*.

5 AitBr 40.2 calls the *purohita* a *rāṣṭragopa* ("protector of the kingdom"), and the Śukranīti calls him a *rājarāṣṭrabhṛt* ("supporter of the king and the kingdom"); cf. Kane 1973:117 f.

6 Śukra II.141-3.

Sarkar describes his duties as follows:

> "The ecclesiastical head (Persian *Sadr* and *Muhatasib* joined together, Marathi *Pandit Rāo* and *Dānādhyaksha*): It was his function to honour and reward learned Brahmans on behalf of the king, to decide theological questions and caste disputes, to fix dates for religious ceremonies, to punish impiety and heresy, and to order penances, &c. He was Judge of Canon Law, Royal Almoner, and Censor of Public Morals combined." (Sarkar 1961:362)

Kane, quoting G.C. Vad's Marāṭhī collection of Sanads and Letters,[7] describes the work of the *paṇḍita* minister in similar words:

> " 'The jurisdiction of the Paṇḍitarao [i.e. *paṇḍita* minister, A.M.] extended over all religious matters [*dharmādhikāra*, A.M.], he was to examine and decide disputes about dharma and adharma, he was to honour the śiṣṭas (respectable persons) on behalf of the king, was to make his signature expressing his approval of the writings (decisions) about ācāra, vyavahāra and prāyaścittas (made by learned brāhmaṇas). He was to superintend and carry into immediate execution gifts, propitiatory rites (for the king)'. This shows that even in matters of prāyaścitta (penance for lapses and sin) the final control rested with the Paṇḍitarao, who used to send doubtful matters to learned brāhmaṇas at holy places like Wai, Nasik, Karad for their opinions and accept them. There are letters which show that Paṇḍitarao convened meetings of learned brāhmaṇas and with their approval declared prāyaścitta in the case of a brāhmaṇa who had been forcibly converted by Mahomedans and who was thereafter restored to caste" (Kane 1974:972).

As can be easily seen from the functions of the *paṇḍitarāo*, who was also called *nyāyaśāstrī* (Gune 1953:111), the main duty of a *paṇḍita* minister was to ensure that the work of the government was in accordance with the *dharmas* and the Dharmaśāstra. This is also true for similar posts in different governments, and quite often it is expressed in the names and titles of the *paṇḍita* minister in which *dharma-* builds the first part of a compound word. Examples are Aśoka's *dharmamahāmātra*, the *dharmāṅkuśa* of the Rāṣṭrakūṭas (I.A. XVIII:230), the *dharmapradhāna* of the Cedis[8] or the *dharmādhikārin* (or °*-adhikaraṇika*, °*-adhikaraṇin*) mentioned in various documents from Bengal, Maharashtra and Nepal.

The term *dharmādhikārin* is also found in the Matsyapurāṇa which mentions the following qualifications:

> *samaḥ śatrau ca mitre ca dharmaśāstraviṣāradaḥ /*
> *vipramukhyaḥ kulīnaś ca dharmādhikaraṇo bhavet //* (215.24)

7 Gune (1953:111) also quotes from the same work published 1913 in Poona, which unfortunately, I did not have in my hands; he refers to vol. 4, p. 123 ff.

8 E.I., vol. II, p. 309: *mahādharmādhikaraṇika* in a Benares copper plate of king Karṇadeva, 1042 A.D.

> "Equal to enemy and friend, experienced in the Dharmaśāstra, best of the Brahmins and from a good (or Kulīna?) family should the *dharmādhikaraṇa*[9] be."
>
> *dharmādhikāriṇaḥ kāryyā janā dānakarā narāḥ /*
> *evaṃvidhās tathā kāryyā rājñā dauvārikā janāḥ //* (215.29)
> "Charitable men should be made (i.e. employed as) *dharmādhikārins*, in the same way as such people are made gate keepers."

It seems that in most cases the *dharmādhikārin* functioned as a supervisor or superintendent in religious affairs, more specifically as a judge or juridical functionary, especially in Nepal. As such the *dharmādhikārin* is also mentioned as a caste functionary (M.C. Regmi 1979:137) and the religious preceptor of certain castes in North India "whose duty it is to fix the punishment and who, in Garhwal, at any rate purifies the out-caste for readmission to caste" (Hutton 1969:98 quoting E.A.H. Blunt, *The Caste System of Northern India*).

The pandit in the 19th century, thus, was often not only a learned adviser or priest, but also a functionary in juridical affairs. His status was not only based on the authority of brahminhood and knowledge of the Veda, but also on his social standing in political and civil matters. In short, if the *paṇḍita* Brahmin of the Dharmasūtras had authority, the *paṇḍita* minister or judge in the 19th century had both authority and power.

The pandit in the Company's law

The traditional authority of learned Brahmin jurists was also of great value to the Muslim and even more the British rulers. In the Company's Law, the term *paṇḍita* became a kind of title for "professors of the *śāstra*, in view of their Vedic learning" (Derrett 1968:230), who despite the fact that the depth of their learning varied considerably, were needed all over India.

As has been demonstrated by J. Duncan M. Derrett in his seminal article "The British as Patrons of the Śāstra" (1968), on which the following is based, it was fixed in the famous Administration of Justice Regulation of April 11th, 1780, initiated by Warren Hastings, that the opinions (*vyavasthā*) of pandits were necessary in cases on listed subjects, such as inheritance, marriage, caste rules or religious matters and institutions (Derrett 1968:232 f.). Hastings knew that pandits in the courts of the Marāṭhas or other small independent states were highly esteemed as legal advisers. He arranged not only for a proper training of the pandits for the Company's service but also employed and paid them as judges for certain cases.

---

9 It is difficult to decide whether *dharmādhikaraṇa* is a technical term in this context and whether it denotes the office or the person. According to V.S. Agrawala (1963:293-4) the *dharmādhikaraṇin* is the "Incharge of [the department of] Justice or Dharmādhikaraṇa".

However, the British law courts in India did not feel comfortable with their dependence on Brahmin pandits. They could not understand the Sanskrit texts themselves, were suspicious of the alleged corruption of the Brahmins, and the rules and principles of Hindu law always remained strange to them since they were not applicable in the legal system of British law. From the very beginning of the Company's rule in India, the need for translations and special legal compilations was felt. Already in 1775 eleven pandits submitted a law digest which Hasting had ordered, the Vivādārṇavasetu ("Bridge across the ocean of litigation") or Vivādārṇavabhañjana ("Breakwater to the ocean of litigation"). The text was soon translated into Persian and subsequently into English under the title "A Code of Gentoo Laws, or, Ordinations of the Pundits" by N.B. Halhed in 1776 (with reprints in 1777 and 1781); a French translation by J.B.R. Robinet appeared 1778 and a German by R.E. Raspe was published 1778 in Hamburg under the title "Gesetzbuch der Gentoo's, oder Sammlung der Gesetze der Pundits, nach einer persianischen Übersetzung des in der Schanscrit-Sprache geschriebnen Originales" (see Derrett 1968:240).

Despite William Jones' efforts to change Hindu law into codified law, from which neither the pandits nor the Company's judges could deviate, and which would give certainty to jurisprudence, despite several newly compiled law digests and texts such as Jagannātha's Vivādabhaṅgārṇava or the Mahānirvāṇatantra, the Company could not find what they were used to and what they also wanted to find in Hindu law: clarity, accuracy, certainty, uniformity and finality. Hindu law remained the law of different social groups, regions and schools. For the British it was too customary, too natural, too religious. After some time they were so desperate that they even compiled their own digests of Hindu law. What Colebrooke noted on the 3rd of May, 1800, seems to be characteristic of the situation of the British administration in India: "After the experience I have had, that no Pandit is capable (or adapted by his habits of thinking) to compile a digest in the form I require, I must now seriously set about compiling it myself. I shall take the arrangements of this compilation for the basis; because the public have, no doubt, more confidence in them than in me" (quoted from Derrett 1968:251 n. 2).[10]

The British apparently required the pandits in order to rule over India, they supported and employed them, encouraged them to write or compile new law texts, a new *śāstra*, but these texts had little practical influence (Derrett 1968:269). As it were, the relationship between the pandits and the British rulers was always full of misunderstandings and suspicion, since

---

10 See also the letter of Sir W. Jones to Ld. Teignmouth, 1907: "I can no longer bear to be at the mercy of our pundits, who deal out Hindu law as they please; and make it at reasonable rates, when they cannot find it ready made" (quoted in Hobson-Jobson 1886, s.v. *pundit*).

"what the British really required was hardly within the pandit's power to supply" (ibid.). As a consequence, the influence of the pandits as legal advisers declined more and more. The pandits lost both authority and power. The principle of legality overruled the principle of legal authority.

The dharmādhikārin *in Nepalese law*

The situation in the independent states such as the Hindu kingdom of Nepal was rather different. The Nepalese rulers also required pandits as legal advisers, but they did not mistrust them, they were not irritated by discrepancies in or the impracticability of Hindu law, they were not morally shocked by rules regarding widow burning or child marriage. One could therefore assume that the status of the pandits as legal advisers in Nepal must have been much higher than in British India. After all, Nepal used to declare herself a *puṇyabhūmi*, the only pure and meritorious Hindu kingdom left, after the conquest of India by the Muslims and the British. However, a close look at the available sources makes it clear that this, in fact, was not the case.

One of the most prominent and powerful Brahmins at the courts of Nepal was the *dharmādhikārin* whose position was created by the Śāha kings in the late 18th century. The *Mulukī Ain* of 1854, Nepal's most important legal source,[11] does not define the term *dharmādhikārin*. In accordance with most Nepālī sources it uses the form *dharmādhikāri* or °-*ī* or *dharmādhikāra*.[12]

Scholars who have worked on the Śāha- or Rāṇā-periods, have translated the term *dharmādhikāri(n)* differently: "chancellor" or "owner of justice" (Hamilton 1819:102), "judge" (also *nyāyadāsa*) (J.C. Regmi V.S. 2036:207), "owner of justice" (M.C. Regmi 1979:136), "righteousness officer" or "enforcer of morals" (Whelpton 1992:11), "chief criminal judge" (H.N. Agrawal 1976:7). However, the term is exclusively used for persons involved in religious jurisdiction.[13]

In the pre-Rāṇā period (i.e. before 1846, when Janga Bahadur Rana became Prime Minister), the *rājagurus* had the highest position in the legal administration of the palace. The official title for them was *guru paṇḍita rāja śrī ... paṇḍita-jyu* (Kumar 1967:92, Sen/Mishra 1951:Doc. 20, p.48 and 149). The chief of *rājagurus* was sometimes called *dharmādhikāri* (ibid.), who also acted as the (chief) judge. There could be more than one *rājaguru*, but only one *dharmādhikārin*. This is evident from a *pajani list* (Kumar 1967:92, Adhikari 1984:316)—a list of affirmation or dismissal, respectively, regarding the status of all employees in the palace—

11 For an introduction into the various editions and manuscripts of the *Mulukī Ain* see Michaels 1994a:1213-1218.

12 See especially the use in the MA 1945.

13 The term *dharmādhikārin* also appears as a family name in Benares: see Sen/Mishra 1951:128 n.14 and Benson, this volume, p. 106.

dated of V.S. 1901 Pauṣa *baḍi* 3 (December 27, 1844) which contains all the personnel of the palace when Mathabar Singh Thapa (1843-45 A.D.) was *mukhtiyār* or Prime Minister. In this list, eight *rājagurus*, among them the *dharmādhikārin*, and four *purohitas* are mentioned. It is likely that the *rājapurohitas* had been concerned with the religious and ritual affairs of the royal family such as giving religious advice, performing *pūjā* in the palace, arranging for the *rites de passage* (*saṃskāra*) etc., whereas the *rājagurus* had been mainly spiritual and legal advisers.

It is likely that the Śāha dynasty established the post of the *dharmādhikārin* already in Gorkhā, i.e. before they conquered the Kathmandu valley, eventually through a direct influence from Maharashtra since Marāṭhas, known as Marahaṭṭas, migrated to West Nepal in the 18th century. Thus it is mentioned in the Divya-Upadeśa of king Pṛthvī Nārāyaṇa Śāha, who ascended the throne of Gorkhā in 1743, and the thrones of the three kingdoms of Kathmandu, Patan and Bhaktapur in 1768/69, that a *paṇḍita* should work in every court to control the decisions in accordance with the Dharmaśāstra (Stiller 1989:45 and 63). Moreover, it is stated in the colophon to three chapters (*parvan*) of a *Mahābhārata* manuscript, copied Śaka 1659 Caitra *śukla* 10 (1737 A.D.):

> *mahārājādhirājakumārayuvarājaśrīśrīśrīman nṛpa Pṛthvī-Nārāyaṇa-mahādevājñayā likhitam idaṃ pustakaṃ śrī-Mokṣe-śvara-Śarmaṇā dharmādhikāraṇena.* (quoted from Panta 1988:793)
>
> "(....) by the command of crown-prince Pṛthvī Nārāyaṇa Śāha this book was copied by Dharmādhikāra [sic!] Śrī Mokṣeśvara Śarman."

Finally, the Gorkhārājavaṃśāvali mentions that during the time of Rāma Śāha (1614-1636 A.D.) the work of the *dharmādhikāra* (sic!) as well as that of the personal clerk (Nep. *khardārī*) and cook (Nep. *bhānsyā*) was given to Arjyāl Brahmins.[14]

The duties of the *dharmādhikārin* are described as early as 1811[15] by Colonel William Kirkpatrick:

> "The Dharma-Udhikar is the chief criminal judge whose business is to pronounce sentence in all cases cognizable by the tribunal, in which he presides on the part of the Rajah, by whom, however, such sentence must be approved before it can be carried into execution." (Kirkpatrick 1811:201)

14 *dharmādhikāra khardārī bhānsyā kāma arjyāllāī baksanu bhayo* (*Gorkhārājavaṃśāvalī*, p. 792).

15 For another early document of the *dharmādhikārin*, see *Regmi Research Collection* 39:302 ("Royal order regarding expiation for the offence of taking water from the hands of Gaines"), dated Śrāvaṇa baḍi 10, 1867 (1810 A.D.).

Even more precise are the notes of Brian Hodgson, the British Resident in Nepal from 1833-1843:[16]

> "Eating with those with whom you ought not to eat; sexual commerce with those between whom it is forbidden; drinking water from the hands of those not entitled to offer it—in a word, doing anything from negligence, inadvertence, or licentiousness by which loss of caste is incurred, renders the sinner liable to the censure of the *dharmadhikari*. He must pay the fine called Gao-dan [*godāna*] to the *dharmadhikari*, who will cause him to perform the prayaschitta [*prāyaścitta*]. In such matters only has the dharmadhikari concern." (Hodgson 1880:114)

The duties of the *dharmādhikārin* have been regulated in the Mulukī Ain of 1854 (ch. 89, of which I am currently preparing a critical edition with an English translation). According to this code, the main duty of the *dharmādhikārin* is to prescribe expiation (*prāyaścitta*) and grant rehabilitation (*patiyā*) in cases where somebody has been inflicted with impurity so that persons who have accidentally or unknowingly (Nep. *bhor*) been polluted by sexual or commensal contacts with impure persons, including spouses and other family members, can get a partial or full re-admission to their caste. For this purpose the *dharmādhikārin* could issue a writ of rehabilitation (Nep. *purjī*).

The Nepalese historian J.C. Regmi notes, on the basis of documents, that court cases were decided by officers working as judges (Nep. *ḍiṭṭhā*, *bicārī*) and then given to the *dharmādhikārin*. Only after he had signed the decision it was declared in the court (J.C. Regmi 1979:207). However, in cases of caste rehabilitation it was compulsory for the *dharmādhikārin* to first receive a formal letter (Nep. *lālmohor*) from the king or the Prime Minister; otherwise he could be fined and dismissed (MA 1854, ch. 89, § 4). This means that the *dharmadhikārin* often did not decide the cases himself but only confirmed them.

The *dharmādhikārin* could also delegate his duties to local officers and landlords who had tenurial authority over certain areas:

> "The under judges, in every part of the kingdom excepting the formed districts, hold their appointments from him, and in most cases they require the seal of his confirmation to render the judgements they pass valid." (Kirkpatrick 1811:201)[17]

The documents and the texts from Nepal show that the post of the *rājaguru/dharmādhikārin* was one of the most influential posts in the royal administration. In mid-19th century, the *rājaguru* seems to have been "an official

16 For a biography of B. Hodgson see Hunter 1896.

17 For a list of these officers and representatives of the *dharmādhikārin*, see MA 1854, ch. 89, §§ 51, 54 and 60; cf. also Höfer 1979:196.

whose rank and influence may be considered as second only to the Minister" (Cavenagh 1851:55).

According to the list of *signatores* (Nep. *tapasīl*) of the preamble of the Mulukī Ain of 1854, the juridical hierarchy in the Rāṇā period, which is also expressed at state banquets or other ceremonial occasions, is the following:[18] At the top was the king as the supreme executive authority in a formal sense (he is, however, not mentioned in the *tapasīl* of the Mulukī Ain). The *de facto* ruler was the Prime Minister who considered himself as the prime representative of the king. Next in the hierarchy were the brothers of Janga Bahadur Rana and other close relatives, who kept military ranks. Then followed the Minister (Nep. *kājī*) Raṇa Śer Śāha, after whom three pandits are listed, the *rājaguru*, the *dharmādhikhārin* and the *rājapurohita*, namely *śrī guru rājapaṇḍita śrī dharmādhikāra* Vijaya Rāja [Pandey] *paṇḍitjyu*, *śrī guru rājapaṇḍita śrī* Nagendra Rāja *paṇḍitjyu*, and *purohita* Tīrtha Rāj *paṇḍita* (MA 1854 p.3). The high position and the great power of the *rājaguru/dharmādhikārin* can also be estimated by the fact that a special army (*baḍagurujyu-ko palṭan*) was stationed to guard his house; it still exists and shows up at certain festivals, e.g. the Gaṅgāmāijātrā (Michaels 1994:190).

It would, however, be wrong to overestimate the power of the *dharmādhikārin*. In the pre-Rāṇā period, the king continued to be the supreme authority in such matters since important cases were decided or confirmed by him (J.C. Regmi V.S. 2036:207), and in the Rāṇā time the Prime Minister could always interfere in the decisions (see MA 1945, ch. 5 § 28). He could, for instance, suspend the decisions of the courts and even disregard the written law, considering himself as a "law unto himself" (Kumar 1967:85). It is true that most cases were not decided by the king or the Prime Minister but by various courts of justice (*adālat, amāli, bhārādāri kausal, aḍḍā, kacāhari*) which included the *dharmādhikārin* as a judge. In some cases, however, the Prime Minister interfered in the court decisions during his audiences.

Moreover, in major decisions such as degradation or capital punishment, or if the Ain was found to be at variance with common practice (*ainmā vihorā namilnyā kurā pariāyā bhanyā*), the courts of justice had to contact the Court Council (*bhārādāri kausal*) set up by Janga Bahadur Rana after his return from England in order to compile the first Mulukī Ain. It consisted of 230 noblemen including all the senior Rāṇās, royal priests (*rājaguru*), royal collaterals (*chautariyas*) and many civil and military officers (MA 1854, ch. 35, § 11, see also Höfer 1979:196 n. 15). Interestingly, Brahmins formed only a minority of thirty in the *bhārādāri kausal* or Court Council. The majority consisted of *kṣatriyas*: 31 dignitaries belonging to the Rāṇā family,

18 See Kumar 1967:99 f. for a similar ranking.

4 Śāhas from the royal *ṭhākuri* caste, and more than 10 members of various Chetri castes (Gaige 1975:166 and Höfer 1979:42).

The influence of the nobility on the Mulukī Ain is also evident in the special treatment given to the Mecyā caste (MA 1854, ch. 89, § 49, see Höfer 1979:100 f.), from which many of their servants were recruited, the special juridical function of the Prime Minister (MA 1945, ch. 5, § 28), or the exceptional treatments of soldiers (MA 1854, ch. 89, §§ 7, 25-26). The influence of the Brahmins on the Mulukī Ain of 1854 can be seen in certain special measures to prevent the contamination of their caste status. Thus, persons claiming falsely the rank of a *brāhmaṇa* were punished (ibid., §§ 44-45), and the precautions against the lower Jaisī Brahmins (ibid., § 69) may also be seen as a sign to protect the pure status of the Upādhyāya Brahmins.

Further, the influence of the Dharmaśāstra on the Mulukī Ain of 1854 is not evident as far as direct quotations from Dharmaśāstra or Nibandha texts are concerned. Nowhere are such texts used as a reference. Rules and principles from the Dharmaśāstra are only indirectly applied, since religious matters had to be decided by Brahmins. Moreover, the terminological influence of Western and Islamic law (Whelpton 1992:218; Höfer 1979:41), which is especially strong in the Mughal terminology of land revenue and taxation, is also comparatively weak. It still remains to be worked out to what extent written law books had been used in the Court Council, but *prima facie* the Mulukī Ain seems to be more a codification of customary law than a deductive application of Hindu and Islamic law. It seems to be the case that the work of the *dharmādhikārin* under such circumstances did not need to be facilitated by references to already existent law books. The pandit was not asked, as in British India, to use classical law books referring to the authority of the Veda or to produce new ones. He had to decide according to the customary law of the country, applying Hindu law principles of penance and religious behaviour, but he did not have to be a very well-learned pandit.

If the authority of the *dharmādhikārin* was limited by the *rājaguru*, and if his power was limited by the Rāṇā aristocracy, what, then, constitutes his high rank? As it were, the *dharmādhikārin* in Nepal was not indispensable because of his learnedness and advice, his knowledge of Sanskrit, his spiritual or priestly functions, or even his juridical functions since most cases were decided by non-Brahmin judges or the Prime Minister himself. Rather, the *dharmādhikārin* was required in cases of heavy social impurity, for prescribing expiation. For this work he merely had to be a Brahmin, who alone can take away the evil of the king's subjects. The Mulukī Ain makes it very clear that a certificate of *patiyā* cannot be issued without prior punishment (MA 1854, ch. 89, § 5; MA 1945, ch. 5, § 1). Only if persons unknowingly accept food from an impure or degraded person, can *patiyā* be granted without a punishment or fine (MA 1854, ch. 89, §§ 56-59, 63-64, 56). Thus punishment is regarded as a necessary but not sufficient infringement. In cases of social impurity, penalty has to be supplemented by expiation, and for this a Brahmin is necessary because it is only he who can digest the evil implied.[19]

For this work, the Brahmin had to be compensated. Along with a writ of expiation the fees and fines (Nep. *dastur, godān*) charged by the *dharmādhikārin* constituted a considerable source of income not only for the state budget but also for the *dharmādhikārin* himself. According to the Divya-Upadeśa the income obtained through fees, called *dharmadāna*, was used by the king[20] for religious works such as donations to temples, building rest houses or offerings to ascetics since such money was considered to be "evil", but the charges for rehabilitation (*patiyā*) were considered as constituting the salary (*khaṅgī*) of the *dharmādhikārin* (J.C. Regmi V.S. 2036:207). What Kirkpatrick notes may therefore be true:

> "The Dhurmadhun [*dharmadāna*], or fees of this department [i.e. the office of the *dharmādhikārin*], are said to be very great, and I have reason to think that it is principally on this account, that the farming governors usually stipulate for the privileges of commissioning their own officers of justice." (Kirkpatrick 1811:201)

According to Hamilton (1971:102), the fees given as expiation (*prāyaścitta*) for the neglect of rituals in the pre-Rāṇā time were shared equally by eight persons: king, tax collector, *dharmādhikārin*, and five Brahmin clans (Pāṇḍe, Panta, Āryals, Khanal and Agnidaṇḍa). It would be highly unusual to find a budget for such penalties issued by the *dharmādhikārin*. However, given the fact that the offences mostly concerned everyday behaviour (eating, taking water, sexual intercourse etc.), one may estimate that it amounted to a considerable sum, as was already assumed by William Kirkpatrick:

> "Most offences, according to the Dhurma Shaster [*dharmaśāstra*] (which is the foundation of the civil code of Nepaul), being punishable by amercement, and the catalogue of crimes of this description being extremely long, it is easy to conceive that such penalties constitute a considerable source of emolument." (Kirkpatrick 1811:201)

Moreover, in the Gorkhā and Rāṇā governments, it was the right of the *dharmādhikārin* to collect a certain tax from each household, known as *dān* (Kumar 1967:92, Rana 1995:129). In the pre-Rāṇā period this was at the rate of one *anna* (4 *paisā*) per annum from each household. Another tax levied by the *dharmādhikārin* is called *cāndrāyaṇa* because it could be taken as a substitute for a so-called *cāndrāyaṇa-vrata* ("vow of the course of the

---

19 See Michaels 1997 and 1998:218-221 (with further references) for a more detailed treatment of the lengthy discussion on the Indian theory of gift-giving.

20 Stiller 1989:64 f., Wright 1966:162: The (Buddhist) merchants from Patan trading in Tibet had to be purified after their return by the abbot (*naike*) of five monasteries (*vihāra*) in order to be re-admitted to their caste, "but the fees should go to the Raja".

moon"). This is an old expiation vow (cf. Gampert 1939:53-55 *et passim*), by which evil-doers in Nepal basically take an increasing and decreasing amount of food for one month—in accordance with the course of the moon. According to the Bhāsāvaṃśāvali (II, p. 63), king Siddhinarasimha Malla (1619-1661 A.D.) performed this vow by increasing the given amount of his food intake from one handful (*muṭhī*) of rice to one *pāthi* (= 80 handful)[21] and vice versa.

A further source of income for the *dharmādhikārin* was the fine which was levied for killing a cow. According to Dineś Rāj Pant (V.S. 2043:514-5), one third of that fine, called *brahmādaṇḍa*,[22] was given to the *dharmādhikārin*.

All these fees and fines were given to the *dharmādhikārin* in compensation for a crime or loss of purity. Thus, we can conclude that the *dharmādhikārin* in 19th-century Nepal had more power than authority, and that his power too was based on his brahminhood and his capacity for "eating" and digesting the evil caused by impurity rather than a power based on learnedness and an impeccable character. The king and the state participated in this form of Hindu indulgence but it was only the Brahmin *dharmādhikārin* who could transform, as Heesterman (1964:4) would have it, *pāpman* into *śrī*.

Conclusion

The pandit as a legal adviser can be priest, minister or judge. The status, authority and power of these functionaries depend on historical, regional and political circumstances. In the Dharmaśāstra, the pandit is a legal adviser with comparatively high authority but little power. In the Śukranīti and 19th-century Maharashtra, the pandit is a minister with both power and authority that he shares with his pandit fellows in the *brahmasabhā*. In the Company's law, the pandit initially had great authority and power but lost both soon after being employed as a judge. In Nepal, the pandit was a chief judge with a power that was constantly endangered by impurity that had to be compensated.

In short, if one were to speak of a marriage-like bond between king and the Brahmin, it certainly was a polygamous one. In India too, the marriage between "church" and king or state was far from being harmonious. On the contrary, both quarrelled about supremacy and both did not really want to sully their hands. The Brahmin pandit as a legal adviser was trapped in between because he wanted to have both power and authority. As a Brahmin, he was confronted with the ascetic ideal of staying outside of the world, as an adviser of the king he was asked to stay at the centre of power, but as a pandit he had the option of doing both. Perhaps it was such a troubled pandit who composed the following *śloka*:

---

21 8 *māna* = 1 *pāthi*; 1 *māna* = 10 *muṭhī*.

22 In Maharashtra the same term was used for any expiative fee: see Gune 1953:110 ff.

dharmārtham yasya vittehā varaṃ tasya nirīhatā |
prakṣālanād dhi paṅkasya śreyo nasparśanaṃ nṛṇām || (Böhtlingk 1870-73: No. 3117)

"Even though a man might desire money in order to do good deeds, it is still better for him to have no desires at all. It is better not to touch the mud at all than, having touched it, to wash it off."[23]

REFERENCES

1. TEXTS

AitBr	*Aitareyabrāhmaṇa.* Das Aitareya Brāhmaṇa - mit Auszügen aus dem Kommentar von Sāyaṇācārya (...) ed. by Theodor Aufrecht. Reprint Hildesheim/New York: Georg Olms Verlag, 1975 [¹Bonn 1879].
BhV	*Bhāṣāvaṃśāvalī,* [Part 1:] Ed. by Nayanātha Pauḍela. Kathmandu: Nepāla Rāṣṭriya Pustakālaya, V.S. 2020; [Part 2]: ed. Devīprasāda Laṃsāla. Kathmandu: Nepāla Rāṣṭriya Pustakālaya, V.S. 2033.
I.A.	*Indian Antiquary*
E.I.	*Epigraphia Indica and Record of the Archaeological Survey of India,* ed. E. Hultzsch et al., Calcutta: Office of the Superintendent of Government Printing.
Gorkhārājavaṃśāvalī,	ed. by D.R. Pant, *Gorkhāko Itihāsa,* vol. 4, Kathmandu: D. R. Pant, V.S. 2050.
Hobson-Jobson	Henry Yule and A.C. Burnell: *Hobson-Jobson. A Glossary of Colloquial Anglo-Indian Words and Phrases....* Calcutta & Co.: Rupa (reprint, 1st. ed. 1886).
Matsyapurāṇa	*Matsyamahāpurāṇam.* Ed. by Puṣpendra Śarman. Delhi: Mehar-Candra Lachamandas, 1984.
MA	Mulukī (Ain)
1854	*Śrī 5 Surendra Bikram Śāhadevakā Śāsanakālamā Baneko Mulukī Ain.* Ed. by Śrī 5-ko Sarkāra [H.M.G.]. Kathmandu: Kānūna tathā Nyāya Mantrālaya [Ministry of Justice], V.S. 2022 [1965 reprint].
1945	*Ain.* Ed. by Śrī 5-ko Sarkāra [H.M.G.]. Kathmandu: Kānūna tathā Nyāya Mantrālaya [Ministry of Justice], V.S. 1945 [1888] and V.S. 1961 [1905].
Manu	*Mānavadharmaśāstra,* ed. V.N. Mandlik. Bombay: Nirṇaya Sāgara Press, 1933.
Sen/Mishra	*Sanskrit Documents being Sanskrit Letters and other Documents preserved in the Oriental Collection at the National Archives of India.* Ed. by Surendranath Sen and Umesha Mishra. Allahabad: Ganganatha Jha Research Institute, 1951.

23 See also Śataślokena Paṇḍitaḥ no.65.

Śataślokena Paṇḍitaḥ	Sarveswara Sharma Peri (comp.), *Śataślokena Paṇḍitaḥ. By Learning Hundred Verses one Becomes Wise*. Marburg: the author, 1982.
Śukra	ed. by Rāmacandra Govinda Śāstrī, Allībāga: Satya-sadana, n.d. *The Śukranīti*, transl. by Benoy Kumar Sarkar. 2nd. ed. New Delhi: Oriental Books Reprint Corp., 1975 (1st ed. 1914).
Wright	Daniel Wright (ed.), *History of Nepal - translated from the Parbatiyā by Munshī Shew Shunker Singh and Pandit Shrī Gunānand*, Cambridge: University Press, 1877 (reprint, 3rd ed., Calcutta: Ranjan Gupta, 1966).

2. SECONDARY LITERATURE

Adhikari, Krishna Kant. 1984. *Nepal Under Jang Bahadur 1846-1877*. Kathmandu: Buku.

Agrawal, Hem Narayan. 1976. *The Administrative System of Nepal*. New Delhi: Vikas Publishing House.

Agrawala, Vasudeva S. 1963. *Matsya Purāṇa: A Study*. Ramnagar, Benares: All-India Kashiraj Trust.

Altekar, A.S. 1977. *State and Government in Ancient India*. Delhi: Motilal Banarsidass (reprint of 3rd ed., 1958).

Böhtlingk, Otto. 1870-73. *Indische Sprüche*. 3 Vols. Petersburg: Kais. Akademie der Wissenschaften (reprint 1966).

Cavenagh, Orfeur. 1851. *Rough Notes on the State of Nepal: Its Government, Army and Resources*. Calcutta: W. Palmer.

Derrett, J. Duncan M. 1976. "Rājadharma", *Journal of Asian Studies*, vol. 35.4: 597-610.

———1968. "The British as Patrons of the Śāstra", in: id., *Religion, Law and the State in India*. London: Faber and Faber, 225-273.

Gaige, F. 1975. *Regionalism and National Unity in Nepal*. Berkeley etc.: University of California Press.

Gampert, Wilhelm. 1939. *Die Sühnezeremonien in der altindischen Rechtsliteratur*. Prague: Orientalisches Institut.

Gonda, Jan. 1969. *Ancient Indian Kingship from the Religious Point of View*. Leiden: Brill.

Gopal, Lalanji. 1978. *The Śukranīti: a Nineteenth Century Text*. Varanasi: Bharati Prakashan.

Gune, Vithal Trimbak. 1953. *The Judicial System of the Marathas*. Poona: Deccan College (Deccan College Dissertation Ser.; 12).

Hamilton Francis (Buchanan). 1971. *An Account of the Kingdom of Nepal* (1819). New Delhi: Manjushri Publishing House (reprint).

Heesterman, Jan C. 1957. *The Ancient Indian Royal Conservation*. The Hague: Mouton.

———. 1964. "Brahmin, Ritual, and Renouncer", *Wiener Zeitschr. für die Kunde Süd- und Südostasiens* 8: 1-31 (also in: id., *The Inner Conflict of Tradition. Essays in Indian Ritual, Kingship, and Society*. Chicago and London: The University of Chicago Press, 1985:26-44).

———. 1985. "The Conundrum of the King's Authority", in: id., *The Inner Conflict of Tradition. Essays in Indian Ritual, Kingship, and Society.* Chicago and London: The University of Chicago Press, 108-27 (first published in: J.F. Richards (ed.), *Kingship and Authority in South Asia,* Madison 1978:1-27).

Hodgson, Brian H. 1971. *Essays on the Languages, Literature and Religion of Nepal and Tibet together with further Papers on the Geography, Ethnology and Commerce of those Countries.* London: Trübner and Co., 1874 (reprint Varanasi: Bharat, 1971).

———. 1880. *Miscellaneous Essays Relating to Indian Subjects.* 2 Vols. London: Trübner and Co.

Höfer, Andràs. 1979. *The Caste Hierarchy and the State in Nepal - A Study of the Muluki Aiṅ of 1854.* Innsbruck: Universitätsverlag Wagner (Khumbu Himal, 13/2).

Hunter, William Wilson. 1991. *Life of Brian Houghton Hodgson, British Resident at the Court of Nepal.* New Delhi, Madras: Asian Educational Services (1st ed. London 1896).

Hutton J.H. 1969. *Caste in India.* Bombay: Oxford University Press (reprint).

Kane, P.V. 1973. *History of Dharmaśāstra.* Poona: Bhandarkar Oriental Research Intitute, vol. III, 2nd ed.

———. 1974. *History of Dharmaśāstra.* Poona: Bhandarkar Oriental Research Institute, vol. II, 2nd ed.

Kirkpatrick, William. 1975. *An Account of the Kingdom of Nepal* (1811). Reprint: Asian Publication Services.

Kumar, Satish. 1967. *Rana Polity in Nepal - Origin and Growth.* London: Asia Publishing House.

Lingat, Robert. 1993. *The Classical Law of India.* Transl. by J.D.M. Derrett. New Delhi: Munshiram Manoharlal (reprint, 1st publ. Berkeley: Univ. of California Press, 1973).

Michaels, Axel. 1994. *Die Reisen der Götter. Der nepalische Paśupatinātha-Tempel und sein rituelles Umfeld.* Bonn: VGH Wissenschaftsverlag.

———1994a. "The Legislation of Widow Burning in 19th-Century Nepal. Edition and Translation of the Chapter *Satijānyako* of the Mulukī Ain", *Asiatische Studien* XLVIII.4:1213-1240.

———. 1997. "Gift and Return Gift, Greeting and Return Greeting in India. On a Consequential Footnote by Marcel Mauss", *Numen* 44: 243-69.

———. 1998. *Der Hinduismus. Geschichte und Gegenwart.* Munich: C.H. Beck Verlag.

Panta, Dineśa Rāja. V.S. 2043 (1986). *Gorkhāko Itihāsa,* vol. 2. Kathmandu: D.R. Panta.

———. V.S. 2045 (1988), *Gorkhāko Itihāsa.* vol. 3. Kathmandu: D.R. Panta.

Quigley, Declan. 1993. *The interpretation of Caste.* Oxford: Clarendon Press.

Rana, Pramode Shamshere. 1995. *Rana Intrigues.* Kathmandu: R. Rana.

Regmi, Jagaddīśa Candra. V.S. 2036 (1979). *Nepālko Vaidhānika Paramparā.* Kathmandu: Tannerī Prakāśana.

Regmi, Mahesh Candra. 1979. "The role of the Dharmadhikar", in: *Regmi Research Series,* 11.9.

Sarkar, Jadunath. 1961. *Shivaji and his times.* 6th ed. Calcutta: M.C. Sarkar & Sons (reprint, 1st ed. 1919).

Stiller, Ludwig. 1989. *Prithivinarayan Shah in the Light of Dibya Upadesh*. Kathmandu: Himalayan Book Centre (reprint, 1st ed. Ranchi 1968).

Thieme, Paul. 1957. "The interpretation of the learned", in: *Felicitation Volume presented to S.V. Belvalkar*. Benares, 47-62.

Whelpton, John. 1983. *Jang Bahadur in Europe*. Kathmandu: Sahayogi Press.

———1992. *Kings, Soldiers and Priests: Nepalese Politics and the Rise of Jang Bahadur Rana, 1830-1857*. Kathmandu: Ratna Pustak Bhandar.

Wezler, Albrecht. 1985. "Dharma und Deśadharma", in: H. Kulke and D. Rothermund (eds.), *Regionale Traditionen in Südasien*. Wiesbaden: Franz Steiner Verlag, 1-22.

Witzel, Michael. 1987. "The coronation rituals of Nepal - with special reference to the coronation of King Birendra (1975)", in: N. Gutschow and A. Michaels (eds.), *Heritage of the Kathmandu Valley*, Sankt Augustin: VGH Wissenschaftsverlag, 415-167.

Wright, Daniel: see 1. Texts.

CHRISTOPHER Z. MINKOWSKI

The Pandit as Public Intellectual: The Controversy over *virodha* or Inconsistency in the Astronomical Sciences

The future of Sanskrit learning

The question of the future of traditional Sanskrit scholarship raised in this collection of studies revolves around an assumption something like the following: that modern, technocratic, American-style social and cultural forms are going to prevail and dominate, sweeping away, among many other things, traditional Indian learning. If it seems safe to assume an ever-technologizing future, then the question posed to us amounts to this: to what extent can other forms of being intellectual inherited from the past, even the deep past, adapt themselves to a technocratic future, or carve out an alternative space for themselves?

The implication of the question is that scholars of Sanskrit literature, especially "traditionally trained" scholars, now find themselves in historical circumstances that have an impact on the sort of work they can do. Put this way the point might seem obvious, but it is not often stated as a starting place for intellectual inquiry, as opposed to a complaint in the hallways and offices of the university department/faculty/seminar. Yet should we suppose that scholars today are in a radically different situation from scholars in the past? Is it only pandits at the close of the 20th century who are subject to historical processes? One way to answer a question about how the Sanskrit learned will fare in the future, is to consider how they fared in the past. It would be unsafe to assume that learned *śāstrīs* of the past lived out their intellectual lives according to patterns that did not change for all the centuries that precede our own.

One valuable result of this colloquium would be the beginning of a more comprehensive attempt to understand the history of the Sanskrit literati: to map out the relationship of scholarship and scholars to larger historical trends, social, economic, political, and to reexamine what we mean by "traditional scholarship". Is there in fact such a thing, in the sense of an unchanging, extrahistorical scholarly tradition?

Such a study would be in keeping with recent trends in Indian historiographical writing in English. Historians associated with these recent trends have stressed a concern with articulating the "agency" of actual individuals, as opposed to articulating timeless structures and "mentalities". Of all the outcomes of the "post-orientalist" critique of the last few decades, this at least is a point easily granted: that the authors of Sanskrit texts were men living in South Asia in particular historical moments, who were subject to their historical contexts at least to some extent as they wrote their work; and that recovering an understanding of their historical context would enhance our understanding of the meaning and significance of their work.

And yet, having granted the point, we must also point out that the attempt to reconstruct the historical position of the authors of Sanskrit literature is not trivial to accomplish. This is because of the historical depth of the literature, which extends into the deep past, beyond the period for which we have good data for doing history, even intellectual history. It is also because there are attitudes and practices active in Sanskrit literature that run counter to a focus on historicizing individual "agents", and that are even designed to resist such historicism.[1] For example, one regularly sees the intentional effacement of the individual author from certain texts, which are instead attributed to great authors of the past, or to legendary sages, semidivine beings, or deities.

Given the obvious yearning of the Sanskrit world of letters to construct for itself a discursive universe that transcends the vicissitudes of history, given that the Sanskrit literatus actively seeks to enter this extrahistorical, non-localized imaginative world in reading and writing Sanskrit, to what extent is it meaningful to talk about the impact of his own times upon his work?[2] Certainly for authors in the remote past, for whom the sum of what we know about them is what they tell us in their works, the difficulties for historiography loom large. If, however, we turn attention to the more recent past, where the historical data is better, it becomes more feasible to attempt to understand the work of learned *śāstrīs* against their historical background.

I wish to discuss here some scholars active at the beginning of the 19th century, at a time when Sanskrit pandits came into direct contact with the growing imperial presence of the British. It is in this period that some pandits emerged, or rather reemerged, to become public intellectuals of a sort. The ways in which *śāstrīs* participated in the great transformations of 19th century India is a vast topic with many overarching narratives. Here I will focus on a particular controversy that attended what might be called the Indian version of the Copernican revolution, and consider the work of a handful of Indian astronomers who participated in the transformation of cosmological knowledge. Before I introduce the main characters and texts that I am presenting today, I need to give some general background of the historical situation of the schools of thought involved, and also some immediate background of the historical situation of the innovators whose works provoked the controversy.

1 See, e.g. Pollock 1989.

2 For that matter, have we been convinced that historical forces are constitutive of authorial intention in any literature in any age or place?

Purāṇas[3]

The Purāṇas are consistent in presenting a model of the cosmos in which the earth is a flat horizontal disk in a vertical, egg-shaped universe, in which there are seven heavens above and seven underworlds below. Mount Meru stands at the center of this disk, and above Meru are suspended a series of wheels, with the Sun, Moon, *nakṣatras*, Mercury, Venus, Mars, Jupiter, Saturn, and the Saptarṣi stars, in that order, riding on them. Above the Saptarṣi is the pole star. The rising and setting of the Sun, Moon, *nakṣatras* and planets is explained by the enormous height of Mt. Meru, behind which in their circular rotations above us the celestial bodies are blocked from our sight.

Viewed from above, the disk of the Earth is made up of seven concentric continents with seven intervening oceans. The central continent with Meru at its center is called the Jambūdvīpa, which is surrounded by the salt ocean. The southernmost portion of Jambūdvīpa is the location for the land of Bhārata. As far as distances are concerned, Mt. Meru is 84000 *yojanas* high, Jambūdvīpa is 100,000 *yojanas* in diameter, the Bhāratavarṣa is 9000 *yojanas* in extent, while the disk of the earth as a whole, including all seven continents and seven oceans, and what lies outside them, is 50 crores or 500 million *yojanas* in diameter.

As Kirfel demonstrated, this account of the cosmos is found in a number of Purāṇas and can be traced to a common source, which Pingree has argued was probably completed in the latter half of the 2nd century AD (Kirfel 1954:7-49; Pingree 1990:275).

Siddhāntas

In the Siddhāntic model of the cosmos the earth is a fixed, nonrotating sphere at the center of a series of internesting spheres on which the sun, moon, and the various planets and stars revolve around the earth. In this model the planets are ranged above the earth in this order: Moon, Mercury, Venus, Sun, Mars, Jupiter, Saturn, and all the Stars. In this model the diameter of the earth is calculated to be about 1600 *yojanas*, with a circumference of about 5000 *yojanas*. This is the model articulated already in the Paitāmahasiddhānta of the 5th century, and it is the model taken up in all other astronomical Siddhāntas in India, regardless of their other differences (Pingree 1990:276-78).[4]

---

3 The following account of Purāṇic and Siddhāntic models is a brief summary of views that follows very closely the work of Pingree 1990. See also Minkowski, forthcoming.

4 Note however that the astronomers of the Āryapakṣa assume the circumference of the earth to be distances in the vicinity of 3300 *yojanas* (Pingree 1978: 591, 593, 597, 609).

The Siddhāntic model makes a better explanation available for celestial phenomena such as the rising and setting of the sun, moon, planets and stars, the eclipses of the Sun and Moon, the variation in length of the day through the course of the year, and the waxing and waning of the Moon.

Virodha?

It certainly appears to us that there are important inconsistencies between the Purāṇic and Siddhāntic cosmologies: to begin with in one the earth is flat, while in the other it is a globe; in one it has a huge size, while in the other it has a manageably small size. As far as we know, however, their mutual inconsistency passed largely undiscussed until the mid-9th century, when the astronomer Lalla turned to a critique of the Purāṇic model in his Siddhānta, the Śiṣyadhīvṛddhidatantra. Lalla did attempt to accomodate some elements of the Purāṇic model to the globular earth of the Siddhāntas: Mt. Meru is made the axis inside the earth on which the earth revolves; all the other oceans and continents of the Purāṇic model are assumed to be south of the equator; and the power that drives the internesting spheres is still the Pravaha wind, which is the force that makes the planets and stars revolve around Meru in the Purāṇic model.

Nevertheless Lalla explicitly rejected the improbable Purāṇic assertions that eclipses are caused by Rāhu; that night is caused by Meru blocking the Sun; that the Moon wanes because the gods are drinking the Soma in the moon; that the Moon is higher in the heavens than the Sun is; and that the earth is flat and rests on a support. These criticisms are repeated in later Siddhāntas, especially in Bhāskara II's very influential work, the Siddhāntaśiromaṇi, of the 12th century (Pingree 1990:279).[5]

Avirodha?

At some point, *śāstrīs* began to attempt to further reconcile the cosmological inconsistencies pointed out by Lalla and subsequent astronomers. The beginnings of this intellectual trend are difficult to locate, but are certainly evident in Sūrya's astronomical work of the 1530s, the Siddhāntasaṃhitāsārasamuccaya. The twelfth and final chapter of the text is devoted to *jyotiḥśāstrapurāṇavirodhaparihāra*, that is, removing the contradiction between the Jyotiḥśāstra and the Purāṇas.[6]

---

5 See Siddhāntaśiromaṇi, Golādhyāya, Chapter 3 (Bhuvanakośa).

6 The text is as yet unedited and unpublished. Details of MSS of this text in CESS A6, (forthcoming). Sūrya Paṇḍita from Pārthapura on the banks of the Godāvarī, was the son of Jñānarāja, author of the Siddhāntasundara, from whom he might have derived his interest in *avirodha*. On the author and text (Sarma, K. 1950): (Dikshit 1969, 2:144-45).

In the 1680's in Benares, Nīlakaṇṭha, the commentator on the Mahābhārata, wrote an independent work on the subject of noncontradiction, the Saurapaurāṇikamatasamarthana.[7] Nīlakaṇṭha was not an astronomer, but he probably drew on the work of astronomers alive in Benares in his day, especially Kamalākara Bhaṭṭa.[8]

In the 1720's, Kevalarāma, the Jyotiṣarāya in the court of Amber, was commissioned by his lord, Sawāī Jaisingh, the celebrated astronomer-king, to write an independent work on the subject of noncontradiction, the Bhāgavatajyotiṣayor Bhūgolavirodhaparihāra (Pingree 1997).[9] This work was expanded by Nandarāma Miśra in the 1780's in Kāmakavana in southern Rājputānā.[10]

All of the works attempted in one way or another to demonstrate the non-contradiction between the Purāṇic and Siddhāntic models. For reasons of space I cannot discuss all the details of their arguments, and will confine myself to some general comments.[11] Aside from Nīlakaṇṭha the authors of these works were predominantly astronomers. Nevertheless they wrote primarily as defenders of Purāṇic authority and validity.[12] The general approach of the argument is that faced with an apparent contradiction between Siddhānta and Purāṇa, the Purāṇa overrules the Siddhānta in its authority claim.[13] This approach, therefore, relies on the hermeneutical stance toward sacred texts as *pramāṇa* found in the Mīmāṃsā and Vedānta, but as extended in later periods to include the *pramāṇa* of *aitihya*, or truth revealed by the Itihāsas and Purāṇas.

Since the Purāṇas must be true, therefore, it is in their proper interpretation, and in the proper construal of the Siddhāntas, that contradictions can be removed. Typically it is asserted that the Siddhāntas describe only some limited part of the real, Purāṇic world, or else that they describe some al-

---

7 It has the alternative title of Paurāṇikajyautiṣam. Nīlakaṇṭha developed ideas he had already expressed in his commentary on the Bhūkhaṇḍavinirmāṇaparva of the Mahābhārata (Minkowski, Forthcoming).

8 Especially his Siddhāntatattvaviveka. Kamalākara in turn was probably influenced by the work of his father, Nṛsiṃha Daivajña, in particular his magisterial commentary on the Siddhāntaśiromaṇi, the Vāsanāvārttika.

9 For MSS see CESS A2, p. 63; A3, p. 23; A4, p. 63, and A5 p. 54.

10 The text is entitled Goladarpana or Bhūgolakhagolavirodhaparihāra. CESS A3, p. 128-30; A5, p. 156.

11 An edition of these latter works, with translation and notes is in preparation.

12 It was especially the Bhāgavata Purāṇa that Kevalarāma and Nandarāma were concerned to validate.

13 However, there are some authors who say that the ontological status of the two genres of texts is equivalent, both falling in the category of smṛti, and that therefore the way to determine the truth of them is entirely on the grounds of comparison with our own reason and experience. It was a common strategy of defenders of Jyotiṣa astronomy to find the authority of their texts not in their reasonableness or persuasive argumentation, but rather in divine authorship (Pingree 1978b:315, 328-30).

ternative, and less actual world, or that the Siddhāntic model is simply a convenient fiction, not literally believed even by the astronomers, but useful for making calendars and calculating the relative latitudes and longitudes of places in our local range of knowledge.

Why did these *avirodha* texts appear? Why was it astronomers who began to write them? Why did they write them in the historical moment that they did? So far no one has attempted an explanation of the appearance of the *avirodha* literature. It seems plausible to look to such historical factors as the rise of Bhāgavata worship and the towering importance of the Bhāgavata Purāṇa in the Moghul period; the patronage by Rajput princes, with the blessings of the Moghuls, of Braj / Mathurā as a religious site, and Vārāṇasī as an academic center; the rise also of the Maratha confederacy as alternative patrons of Brahminical religion and learning; and the presence in the Moghul cultural sphere of Islamicate models of cosmology and astronomy, which are explicitly discussed by some of the astronomers mentioned above, Kamalākara and Kevalarāma, for example, and which would exert a pressure on, or imply a critique of, internally conflicting indigenous cosmologies.[14]

The immediate background

The immediate background of the manuscripts I wish to discuss is the *sabhā*, or intellectual circle of Lancelot Wilkinson.[15] Wilkinson had been appointed the British Political Agent to the court of Bhopal sometime before 1829, and continued there until his death in 1841. The Agent's residence was located in the nearby town of Sihore, and attached to the residence was a school, which Wilkinson made into a Sanskrit school with a special emphasis on the study of the astronomical Siddhāntas. Wilkinson was interested in the Siddhāntas, whose serious study, he felt, had largely vanished by the beginning of the 19th century. In addition to learning Sanskrit and Jyotiḥśāstra himself, he promoted the study, edition and publication of various Indian astronomical texts.[16] Wilkinson believed that the best way to introduce the modern Copernican system of astronomy to learned Indians, especially to the whole class of Indian astronomer / astrologers, was through the medium of Sanskrit, and in particular through the instrumentality of the Siddhāntic model of the cosmos. Since the Siddhāntas already rejected much of the Purāṇic cosmology, Wilkinson reasoned, and since they already made use of many of the necessary principles of geometry, trigonometry, and arith-

14 For discussion of the last factor see Pingree 1978b and Pingree 1996.

15 The information in these paragraphs about Wilkinson, Bāpudeva Śāstrī and Subbāji Bāpū is drawn from the following sources: Sarma, S. 1995-6, Young 1997, Dvivedi 1933:118 ff. See also Prakash 1996.

16 For example Sastri and Wilkinson 1861. Further works are listed in Sarma, S. 1995-6.

metic, it would be a short step to move from the Siddhāntic to Copernican scientific models, which could be presented in a way that would not alarm the whole class of Jyotiṣa paṇḍits (Wilkinson 1834).

The two most talented of the *śāstrīs* in Wilkinson's *sabhā* were Nṛsiṃhadeva Śāstri, a Citpāvan Brahmin from Ahmadnagar district, known as Bāpudeva Śāstri (CESS A4:241; Dvivedi 1933:126-29; Dikshit 1969:300-01), and the subject of my interest today, Subbāji Rāmacandra Śāstrī, also known as Subbāji Bāpu, a Telugu speaking Brahmin of Chandrapur in Berar who had been in Wilkinson's employ since the 1820's.

In 1836, Subbāji wrote a text in Marāṭhī called the Siddhāntaśiromaṇiprakāśa (or Śiromaṇiprakāsa,) "Light on the Siddhāntaśiromaṇi", which was published in lithograph form in Bombay under the auspices of Wilkinson (Young 1997:251). A version in Hindi was produced and published by Oṃkāra Bhaṭṭa, another paṇḍit in the Sihore *sabhā*.[17] Since these texts so particularly fulfilled one of the ideals of the Asiatick Society, namely to revive ancient Indian learning as a vehicle for advancing European visions of scientific and social progress, a special prize was awarded to Subbāji and Oṃkāra Bhaṭṭa at the 1837 meeting of the Asiatick Society in Calcutta.[18]

I have not yet located a copy of the Siddhāntaśiromaṇiprakāśa, but a summary of some of its arguments appears in an article by Young, who lays out the cultural-historical context in which the debate to be discussed today occured (Young 1997:251-53). I have also been able to examine a copy of the Hindī version of the argument by Oṃkāra Bhaṭṭa, the Bhūgolasāra.[19] In brief, the Śiromaṇiprakāśa assesses four different astronomical models: the Purāṇic, the Siddhāntic, the Jaina, and the 'English.' Subbāji and Oṃkāra endorse the English heliocentric model as the correct one. The earth is a globe with the continents located where they are found by modern sailors and explorers, who are seen as the pioneers of a modern, observation-based scientific geography. In general there is a certain awe of the English for their observational instruments and exploratory zeal. At the same time the title itself suggests the sense of continuity and revival of the Siddhāntic view, which Subbāji sees as basically in conformity with modern scientific models. Both Subbāji and Oṃkāra regularly cite the Siddhāntas as a basic and reliable source for arguments about such things as the reason for the days getting longer and shorter, the reason we know the earth is a globe, and so on. The Purāṇas are cited occasionally when they accord with the mod-

---

17 Bhūgolasāra, or Jyotiṣacandrikā. Reprinted in 1840 and 1881 by the Agra School-book Society. Also reprinted in 1841 with an English title page: A Comparison of the Puranic and Siddhantic Systems of Astronomy with that of Copernicus.

18 A pair of engraved silver inkstands. See Macnaghten 1837.

19 Thanks to Gillian Evison of the Indian Institute Library, Oxford, I was able to obtain a copy of the 1881 printing. Note that the success of the text is suggested by its numerous reprintings.

ern scientific view, but they generally come in for harsher treatment. The Purāṇic geography of the flat earth with its seven concentric oceans and continents is explicitly rejected. Yet Subbāji and Oṃkāra are careful to reject only those features of the cosmology that are demonstrably at odds with the English scientific model. And there is no question of these authors rejecting their basic faith in Vedic and Purāṇic theology. What is most striking about these works is the high valuation that they give to reasoning from direct observation, especially as aided by techonologically advanced instruments, and the corresponding devaluation, within the sphere of what is observable, of textual authority.

With this as preliminary, then, I wish to turn to the three texts of this study.

The three texts

Reaction to Subbāji's publication was immediate. Yajñeśvara Sadāśiva Roḍe, also known as Bābā Joshi Roḍe, a Puṇe Deśastha Brahmin, wrote a text in 67 verses called the Avirodhaprakāśa, "Light on Non-contradiction", which was a reply to, and refutation of, Subbāji's Śiromaṇiprakāśa (CESS A5:318-19; Diksit 1969:299-300). There is one known manuscript of this text, held in the RORI Alwar.[20]

The text of the Avirodhaprakāśa is more widely available than this single, difficult to reach MS might suggest, because it was published by Subbāji, together with a rejoinder to Yajñeśvara, a text called the Avirodhaprakāśa viveka, the "Analysis of the Avirodha-Prakāśa" in 65 verses. The Avirodhaprakāśa and the Avirodhaprakāśaviveka were published in lithograph form in Bombay in 1837, again under the auspices of Wilkinson, along with a commentary by a pupil of Subbāji's whose name was also Rāmacandra (Subbāji 1837). There are numerous copies of this lithograph available in collections in India and also in England. Since Subbāji's reply to Yajñeśvara appeared in 1837, we must assume that Yajñeśvara's work, the Avirodhaprakāśa, must have appeared in the interval between Subbāji's works, and hence must also date to 1836 or 1837.

The rapid speed of the exchange between the *śāstrīs* continued, for Yajñeśvara in turn responded in a text of 72 verses called the Virodhamardana, the 'Crushing of Contradiction,' of which there are two known manuscripts, one in Jaipur, the other in Baroda.[21] Yajñeśvara accompanied this text with a commentary in which he dates the work to 1837.

20 RORI (Alwar) 2682 = Alwar 1715. 4 ff. copied in Saṃ 1912 = 1855 A.D. The MS described in Kielhorn 1874 (XXIII 2), is in fact a copy of the lithograph, as the date, foliation, and ownership show. The same owner also is listed as owning a copy of Avirodhaprakāśaviveka with the date and foliation of the lithograph.

21 Jaipur Museum 205. 16 ff. with Marāṭhī autocommentary. Copied in Saṃvat 1894 = A.D. 1837. Baroda 10846. 26 ff. with Sanskrit autocommentary. Copied in Śaka 1763 = 1841 A.D.

Avirodhaprakāśa

Yajñeśvara's purpose in the Avirodhaprakāśa is twofold: to show that there is no contradiction between the Siddhāntic and Purāṇic models, and to show that the European Copernican model is invalid.

To accomplish the first goal, Yajñeśvara adopts two intertwined strategies: he proposes new explanations of points of difference between the two models, and he asserts that the two models have different purposes and scopes of application. His challenge is to explain the apparent inconsistencies in geographical and astronomical models. As for geography, the small earth of 5000 *yojanas* in circumference assumed by the Siddhāntakāras is explained as being only a subsection of the Purāṇic *bhūmaṇḍala*; in fact it is a subportion of Bhāratakhaṇḍa which measures about 2000 *yojanas* on its longest side and 5000 *yojanas* in circumference (AP vss. 3-6).

Moreover, even this small earth is flat. What of the old Siddhāntic argument in favor of the spherical earth based on the fact of the progressive elevation of the northern or southern pole stars for people traveling north or south? And what about the reports of sailors who have sailed around the earth, returning to the point where they began? Yajñeśvara replies that there is only one pole star, in fact situated above the Himālayas, with the southern pole star being only a reflection of the northern one in the southern ocean (AP vss. 13-17). And as for the reports of circumnavigation, Yajñeśvara explains these as resulting not from sailing around the spherical earth, but from sailing around the circular salt ocean that surrounds the abovementioned subportion of the Bhāratakhaṇḍa (AP vs. 25).

The other great inconsistency between Purāṇic and Siddhāntic cosmologies has to do with astronomical models. Yajñeśvara takes up the order of the planets and the explanations of eclipses, which differ between the Purāṇas and Siddhāntas. Yajñeśvara maintains the Purāṇic order of the planets, basically arguing from scriptural authority. As for the Siddhāntic explanation of eclipses, which would be impossible if the moon were higher than the sun and if the moon did not orbit a spherical earth, Yajñeśvara proposes an ingenious explanation that what appears to be the moon at the time of a solar eclipse is in fact the head of Rāhu, which has the same size as the moon. Rāhu is suspended from the wheel of the *nakṣatras* in such a way that his head hangs down to the level of the sun and blocks the sun's light from time to time, while meanwhile his body will block the light of the moon from time to time. Hence, Yajñeśvara reasons, the Siddhāntas' predictions of eclipses can be used without rejecting the Purāṇic order of the planets (AP vss. 39-51). Appeal to scriptural authority also explains the phases of the moon as a filling and emptying of Soma.

In order to show that the Copernican and Siddhāntic models are in disagreement, Yajñeśvara focuses on the features of the Copernican model not found in the Siddhāntas. Thus the basic notion that the earth spins on its axis and rotates around the sun are non-Siddhāntic, Yajñeśvara points out, and so is the doctrine that gravitation is the force causing planets to move in their orbits, and so is the doctrine that every star is a sun with its own planetary system, including planetary satellites, and living beings inhabiting each planet. Furthermore the old concessions to the Purāṇas found in the Siddhāntas, the placing of the 6 other oceans in the southern hemisphere, the positing of Yamakoṭi and the other cities of the global quadrature, and so on, are rejected by European astronomy (AP vss. 24, 26-32).

For Yajñeśvara, this discrepancy between Siddhāntic and Copernican models reflects badly on the Copernican model. After all, the Siddhāntas are authored by gods and sages, while the European model is invalid for Yajñeśvara, because it is not supported by any scripture, because it depends on an overvaluing of perception or observation, and because, after all, it is the work of *mlecchas*, whose arguments are only designed to deceive people (AP vss. 32, 66).

In the end, however, there are points where the two Indic systems do not coincide, as for example in the absolute size of the earth, and in the order of the planets above the earth. Thus Yajñeśvara ends by asserting that the two Indian systems have different purposes and scopes. So that while the Purāṇas are making true statements about the cosmos as a whole for the purpose of communicating the majesty of the Lord God, the Siddhāntas have adopted a model which is limited in scope to local phenomena, and whose purpose is merely for the generation of *pañcāṅgas* (AP vss. 61-65).

Now, while Yajñeśvara's arguments are on their face reactionary in nature, it is worth noting three things: Yajñeśvara understands the Copernican model and does not reject it out of incomprehension—indeed nearly a third of even his basic text is devoted to a description of the European model in some detail; many of his proposals are in fact his own innovations, and so he cannot be taken to be following a preexisting course; and further, his general proposal that the Siddhāntas and the Purāṇas must be understood as providing different models concerned with different kinds of truth can be understood in various ways, as a variation of the modernizing attitude, in which religious views of the past are removed from the arena of scientific inquiry and made metaphorical, or as an extension of the Vedāntic stance toward different levels of truth with different scopes of operations, or as an accommodation via the latter to a context that demands the former.

Avirodhaprakāśaviveka

Subbāji Rāmacandra replied to Yajñeśvara in his Avirodhaprakāśaviveka, which he published in 1837.[22] Subbāji cites lengthy passages from the

22 Subbāji says in his preface in Marāṭhī that he has given the full text of Yajñeśvara's work

Avirodhaprakāśa in the body of his own work, and then subjects them to extended criticism. His polemical strategy to invalidate Yajñeśvara's arguments incorporates a variety of techniques, including appeals to reason, to perception and to scriptural authority. Subbāji can show that Yajñeśvara is self-contradictory, in that Yajñeśvara maintains in one place that there is no contradiction between the Siddhāntas and Purāṇas, while in another place he appears to imply a criticism of the Siddhāntic view, and at the end even asserts a fundamental difference in scope and purpose between them, as mentioned above (APV vss. 6-8).

Subbāji can further argue that Yajñeśvara's innovative proposals that are intended to reconcile differences between the two models are in fact innovations supported by neither, and are therefore themselves exterior to, and not authoritative for, the schools of thought they purport to defend. In particular Subbāji can cite the Vedas and Purāṇas against Yajñeśvara when it comes to his explanation of eclipses. Subbāji also reads the Vedas against Yajñeśvara in such a way that the Siddhāntic explanation for the phases of the moon can be made consistent with the Purāṇic one (APV vs. 47-52).[23]

Thus Subbāji has not rejected the authority of scriptural sources, but he does assert that *pratyakṣa* or observation is a legitimate means of gaining knowledge in its own right, and indeed, Subbāji at the close of his work does assert that even the statements of the *śruti*, when unsupported by logic and observation, can be wrong (APV vs. 63).[24]

Subbāji again points out the improbable nature of the standard features of the Purāṇic cosmology. He also shows how in physical terms Yajñeśvara's proposals about the pole star do not work. Since, finally, the Siddhāntas are quite clearly designed for more than making *pañcāṅgas*, Yajñeśvara's conclusion that the two models have different scopes and purposes must be rejected, and hence the *virodha*, or contradiction between them has not been resolved. The implication of this is that the Purāṇic model is simply incorrect.

One final point on which Subbāji exercises a particularly effective argument is Yajñeśvara's suggestion that the astronomy of the Europeans should be rejected simply because it is the product of foreigners. This was a battle that the Indian astronomers had fought before,[25] and Subbāji repeats the ar-

---

before his own so that objective people can read both works and come to a reasoned conclusion about who is correct, but the tenor of Subbāji's text makes it clear that he has no doubt about what a reasonable person will conclude.

23 See especially Rāmacandra's commentary.

24 *nyāyopabṛṃhito no cec chrutipakṣo 'pi duṣyati / śāstrapratyakṣaduṣṭe syāt kalpane katham ādaraḥ.* His commentator, Rāmacandra, however, softens the shock of this statement, by showing that passages in the philosophical *śāstras* already argue that the statements of the *śruti* do not overrule direct perception when it comes to accurate knowledge of the physical world.

25 See for example the regularly cited verse of Varāhamihira, Bṛhatsaṃhitā 2, 14: *mlecchā*

guments about how the possibility of divine insight or revelation cannot for fundamental reasons be limited to Bhāratavarṣa. But he adds a further argument from orthodox Brahminical philosophical literature, in which seeing differences between people, instead of seeing sameness, is deplored (APV vss. 57-61).[26]

Virodhamardana

Yajñeśvara replied within a few months with the Virodhamardana and its commentary. For reasons of space I shall give only a summary. The Virodhamardana is approximately the same text as the earlier Avirodhaprakāśa, but with some *pādas* and lines replaced or inserted, so that the later text is five verses longer than the earlier one.[27] The changes to the text are exactly at places where it was criticized by Subbāji.

The most notable change is that the attempt to invalidate the views of foreigners as foreigners is dropped. Instead Yajñeśvara concedes that the foreigners' model might be useful, but asserts that it does not refute the truth of the Purāṇas (VM vs. 68).[28] Yajñeśvara moves more toward applying the layers-of-truth model inherited from Vedāntic and other Indian philosophical traditions as a way of differentiating the nature of astronomical truth from Purāṇic truth.[29]

On the other hand, Yajñeśvara's defence of the Purāṇic order of the planets by appeal to his own ideas of the nature of Rāhu is kept intact. Elsewhere adjustments are less than total. The argument that the southern pole star is a reflection in the waters is quietly omitted. Instead it is just the great distance that prevents one from seeing the north star as one sails south.

In general Yajñeśvara stands by his explanations, and has a number of aspersions to cast on those who have criticized him, those who have the presumption to call themselves knowers of Jyotiṣa, as he makes clear at the end of his autocommentary.[30]

Indeed the Virodhamardanaṭīkā constitutes the real sustained reply to the Avirodhaprakāśaviveka. Space does not permit a full consideration here

---

hi yavanās teṣu saṃyak śāstram idaṃ sthitam / ṛṣivat te 'pi pūjyante kiṃ punar daivavid dvijaḥ //

26 The commentator is able to cite, among other texts, Bhagavadgītā 5.12: *vidyāvinayasampanne* etc.

27 The following verses and verse halves are replacements: 1, 2, 5cd, 11ab, 17abc, 26, 27, 28, 67cd, 69, 70. The following verses and verse halves are additions: 13cd, 19cd, 25ab, 36ab, 39cd, 57cd, 58cd, 69, 72.

28 *naitāvatā purāṇoktata(t)tvabādho bhaved iti / parilekhādi yan mlecchaiḥ kṛtaṃ tad api yujyate //*

29 e.g. vs. 58 in its revised form: *ity āgamādisiddho 'rtha āstikair durapahnavaḥ / vyavahārārthakalpena vastvārthānām abādhanāt //*

30 In the first concluding verse of the *ṭīkā* he calls them *jñānalavadurvidagdhapurusa-* and *jyotirvitpadalipsu-*.

of this densely argued work, but it is in this *ṭīkā* that Yajñeśvara demonstrates his more than passing comprehension of the Copernican model that he seeks to reject. He also reviews some of the attempts at establishing *avirodha* advanced in preceding centuries. Certainly he knows of the views that Nṛsiṃha discusses in his Vāsanāvārttika on the Siddhāntaśiromaṇi.[31]

Conclusion

Three points by way of conclusion: First there is the sheer speed of this flurry of literary activity, with four texts and countertexts being composed, published, circulated, and replied to in the space of less than two years—a pace faster than many exchanges of letters to the editor of learned journals today. Then again these "pamphlets" were produced in various languages, beginning with Marāṭhī, then Hindī and English, and finally Sanskrit with Marāṭhī. The format of publication was itself various, with Wilkinson's paṇḍits having their works lithographed and "mass produced", while Yajñeśvara's were copied by hand. It is possible that Sanskrit texts had circulated at great speed in earlier periods,[32] but in this context the speed is perhaps itself an indicator—as are the differential choices of languages and the availability of lithography—of the growing impact of the colonizing and modernizing presence on the Sanskrit intellectual establishments.

Second, the aftermath of the controversy: what became of the efforts of Wilkinson and his circle of pandits? In his own writing Wilkinson depicted his pandits as embattled, and bemoaned the stiff opposition to his project emanating from "the learned in Poona, Nagpore, Oojain, Sagar, and Benares."[33]

He further complained that the Gosāīns of Mathurā had placed a "bann of excommunication against all who study the Siddhantas, and Astronomy" (Young 1997:253). Richard F. Young interprets Subbājī's later writings, especially his Laghutaṅka rejoinder to the caste-bashing Vajrasūcī, and his Mataparīkṣāśikṣā—a reply to John Muir's critique in Sanskrit of Hindu religious and cultural ideologies—as a climbing down from the strong form of endorsement of European notions of science, modernity and progress found in the Siddhāntaśiromaṇiprakāśa and Avirodhaprakāśaviveka (Young 1997:258-63). Furthermore, Young considers that the Sihore Siddhāntas

---

31 See Nṛsiṃha's comments on Siddhāntaśiromaṇi II.3.51, pp. 357-59 in the Sampūrṇānand edition. Nṛsiṃha completed this text in 1621. Yajñeśvara's comments appear on folios 11r - 12v.

32 There are examples of Sanskrit texts circulating at great speed in early periods. See Pollock (forthcoming) for examples, among them the speedy translation and circulation of the Persian Yūsuf o Zulekhā in the 15th century.

33 Cited by Young from Wilkinson's preface to his edition of the Gunitadhia (*Gaṇitādhyāya*) of the Siddhāntaśiromaṇi (Young 1997:253).

project died along with Wilkinson when Wilkinson succumbed to an early death in 1841, while "real" science education in the later 19th century left the Siddhāntas behind (Young 1997:263).[34]

This is not entirely true: Wilkinson's other chief protegé, Bāpudeva Śāstrī, went on to teach both Indian and European astronomy at the Benares Sanskrit College beginning in 1841. Bāpudeva published voluminously in Sanskrit and English, and promoted a modernization of Indian astronomy and the knowledge of European astronomy in India. It was his pupils and intellectual descendants, including Sudhākara Dvivedi, who dominated the intellectual scene in Benares for at least the rest of the century.[35] It could be said that via the pandits in Benares Wilkinson had a long term impact on the growth, in Indian intellectual movements, of an accommodation of science and scientific rationality which still enabled holding on to the context of traditional Sanskrit learning.

Furthermore, the controversy was still remembered among Indian astronomers for the rest of the century, even if not entirely accurately.[36] The histories of Sudhākara Dvivedi and S.B. Dikshit take note of the exchange between Yajñeśvara and Wilkinson's *sabhā*. Their accounts present a different picture of what happened by comparison to what Wilkinson recorded. In Sudhākara Dvivedi's Gaṇakataraṅginī, "Brief Lives of Indian Astronomers", he records a correspondence between Wilkinson and two pandits of Benares about this *virodha / avirodha* controversy.[37]

It becomes clear from these letters, and from Sudhākara's account of them, that Wilkinson was actively promoting the acceptance of Subbājī's work and sending copies of the Avirodhaprakāśa and Avirodhaprakāśaviveka around to expert pandits in hopes of gaining acceptance for them. It is also clear that at least some paṇḍits in Benares, far from mounting a resistance couched on orthodoxy, were quite worried about angering Wilkinson. After all Wilkinson was able to secure positions for pandits he favored, for example at the Benares Sanskrit College.[38]

---

34 I reproduce Young's use of quotation marks around the word "real." See also the review of Wilkinson's proposal in the JASB of 1834 in the Calcutta Review 1 (1844):286-90.

35 Their impact on the Sanskrit world of letters in Benares and its satellites could be traced through a study, as yet to be done, of the Sanskrit journal, the *Pandit*, in which the problems of "tradition vs. modernity" or perhaps "hybridity" are discussed in an open, published forum. In the first volume of the Pandit, (1866/67), pp. 32-35, 82-84, for example, there are articles by Bāpudeva and his pupil Govindadeva that continue the Wilkinsonian project of interrelating the accounts of the Siddhāntas and modern science.

36 Sudhākara Dvivedi, for example, considers the Avirodhaprakāśaviveka to be a reply to Nīlakaṇṭha's work, not Yajñeśvara's (Dvivedi 1933:123).

37 See the letters of Durgāśaṅkara Pāṭhaka and Lajjāśaṅkara to Wilkinson (Dvivedi 1933:119, 123-24).

38 Bāpudeva Śāstrī got his position there in 1841 as a result of Wilkinson's patronage;

Thus the portrait of this exchange as a dichotomous clash of modern and English, yet foreign and colonizing, science versus traditional and indigenous, yet reactionary and antirational, scholarship is already confused by the varying accounts of the events and their aftermath. It is further confused by the fact that Yajñeśvara, at the time of writing the Avirodhaprakāśa and the Virodhamardana, was also in the employ of the British, teaching at the Poona Sanskrit College. Then again, Yajñeśvara left his position, or perhaps lost it, in 1838, the year after the exchange of pamphlets at the time that Thomas Candy took over administration of the Poona Sanskrit College (Dikshit 1969:176-77).[39] Then again, what is the evidence, aside from Wilkinson's mention of it, that the Gosāīns of Mathurā were in the habit of pronouncing "banns of excommunication" in the 19th century?

Third, I began with a general argument for reading the work of Sanskrit authors in their larger historical context, and suggested that the 19th century presents to us for this purpose the lure of the recent past, a time when contextualizing information about individual authors and their contexts is more readily available. In this light, the exchange between Wilkinson and his paṇḍits and Yajñeśvara and other 'traditional' astronomers can be studied in some detail and can be seen as part of the great transformation that overtakes India in the 19th century.

What is the role of the pandits and *śāstrīs* in the history of this modernizing transformation? What influence does this transformation have on the intellectual life of the *śāstrīs* and pandits? The foregoing discussion shows some examples of ways in which the Sanskrit literati adopted positions in relation to the modernizing or westernizing intellectual currents flowing in the period. Furthermore, at least two general points are supported by the preceding evidence. First, the Sanskrit astronomers of the modern period inherited intellectual traditions that were historically contingent, the result of ongoing debate, internal development, and reaction to external influences. Furthermore, as Young has already argued (Young 1997:264-69), the Sanskrit *śāstrī* was in fact capable of functioning as a public intellectual, even in the 19th century, engaging from his own position the modernizing scientific teachings that were spreading around him. This latter point is not a trivial one if one considers the historiography of the 19th century, and the role accorded to learned Brahmins in it.

Lajjāśaṅkara also taught there; for others supported by Wilkinson, such as Sevārāma Śarma, see Dvivedi 1933.

39 Candy is cited there as having characterized Yajñeśvara as "very intelligent and learned, but a very bigoted champion of the mythological doctrine." To make matters more interesting, the letters of Durgāśaṅkara and Lajjāśaṅkara nevertheless suggest that Yajñeśvara was in direct correspondence with the Sihore Sabha, and indeed agreed with Wilkinson in rejecting the work of Nīlakaṇṭha. For more on the Poona Sanskrit College or Poona Hindu College see Madhav Deshpande's article in this collection of essays.

For in one common version of that history, the learned traditions in Sanskrit that continue from the deep past are depicted as a traditional heritage whose main purpose is to underpin a static social and religious structure.[40] In another recent rendering the learned traditions in Sanskrit are only one of many features of a pre-Colonial past that are occluded from view by the colonial experience, elements of a past not knowable or recoverable except in the distorted form they gain at the hands of orientalists and other agents of empire.[41] But surely it is not edifying to take the Sanskrit learning of the past as an unchanging body of conclusions and stances that are largely unconscious of contemporary events, whether this be a virtue or a vice. The Brahmins, given the dubious distinction of then being the hereditary custodians of this tradition, can appear in the history of the century only as they emerge or escape from their traditional world, or as they help orientalists learn about or 'imagine' it. Elsewhere in Indian history, 'traditional Brahmins' would be condemned to appear only in such generic circumstances as when they are deployed to the countryside *en masse* by rulers to 'Brahminize' lands being converted to a village-style agricultural economy, almost as if they were a species of beneficial, exotic plant or insect.

As a way of concluding this talk, then, a consideration of *virodha* and *avirodha*, or inconsistency and consistency should be thought off. Are inconsistencies present in an intellectual tradition even when no one is aware of them? Is consistency produced only by those who seek to find it? As I have mentioned, the problem of consistency / inconsistency in cosmological accounts had already been 'theorized' in the 8th century. The problem had emerged from its settled state into active theorizing again in the 16th century, well before the British had asserted colonial / imperial power. It is in the language of *virodha* and *avirodha* that both Wilkinson's circle and Yajñeśvara choose to carry out their cosmological clash. Why?

We need to think further about this question, but I would suggest that the orientation toward logic and argumentation this language calls up provided a common ground for the two competing models. For Yajñeśvara, talk of *avirodha* and *virodha* activated the inherited methods of interpretation, argument and proof, which he hoped to use to remove the glamour of the European scientific method. For Subbājī and Wilkinson, talk of *virodha* and

40 This account of the role of Brahmins has many reincarnations. Even a very recent work such as Bose and Jalal 1997, which is very much aware of every development in Indian historiography and the pitfalls that are faced, makes use of the term "brahmanical" exclusively in the following phrases: "brahmanical orthodoxy", "brahmanical social orthodoxy", "neo-brahmanical orthodoxy", "the high brahmanical tradition", and "brahmanical ruling ideology". I can find no definition of what "brahmanical" means except that it has to do with legitimation of power.

41 The literature asserting the "invention of Indian tradition" by "colonial discourse" is now extensive and well known. See for example, Inden 1990.

avirodha activated the inherent instabilities of the Brahminical cosmology, which they hoped to fragment and reassemble.

ACKNOWLEDGEMENTS: It is an honor to be asked to participate in a conference devoted to felicitating Dr. Parameswara Aithal. I have many fond memories of studying with Aithal Mahodaya on a DAAD (German Academic Exchange Service) grant in Heidelberg in 1993, and also at the Indian Institute Library in Oxford. We have met at various conferences, and we have corresponded over the years. I am grateful to him for the benefits I have always received from his knowledge, and also from his personal qualities, especially his powerful work ethic and his balanced sense of what is important in academic work. I congratulate him on his successful career in Heidelberg. The body of work he has produced is of unique value, proceeding as it does from his double training and double knowledge.

My thanks to Mrs. S. Sahasrabuddhe and the curators of the Sanskrit MSS collection at the Ānandāśrama in Poona; to R.I. Nanavati, curator of the Sanskrit MSS collection at the Oriental Institute, Baroda; to Y. Sahai, curator of the Palace Museum in Jaipur; to Gillian Evison, curator of the Indian Institute Library, Oxford; to Peter Scharf, Brown University, and to the DHIRC, Columbia; all of whom provided invaluable help in obtaining copies of manuscripts and of rare books in preparing this paper. My thanks as always to David Pingree, Brown University, for extensive help with bibliography, and for commenting on several drafts of this paper. I am grateful to Asmita Hulyalkar for her help with reading some of the relevant passages in Marāṭhī. Thanks also to Saurabh Dube, Thomas Trautmann, and to the participants at the Aithal Colloquium, for comments and suggestions.

REFERENCES

1. Sanskrit Texts

Bhāskara. *Siddhāntaśiromaṇi*, ed. Muralīdhara Caturvedī 1998, with *Vāsanāvārttika* of Nṛsiṃha Daivajña. Vāraṇasī: Sampūrnānand Saṃskṛta Viśvavidyālaya.

Kamalākara Bhaṭṭa. *Siddhāntatattvaviveka*, ed. K.C. Dvivedī 1996. Vārāṇasī: Sampūrnānand Saṃskṛta Viśvavidyālaya.

Lalla. *Śiṣyadhīvṛddhidatantra*, ed. C.B. Pandey 1981 as *Śiṣyadhīvṛddhidam*. Vārāṇasī: Sampūrṇānand Saṃskṛta Viśvavidyālaya.

Nīlakaṇṭha Caturdhara. *Saurapaurāṇikamatasamarthana*, ed. Indunātha Śarma 1989 as *Paurāṇikajyautiṣam*. Varanasi: Sampūrṇānand Saṃskṛta Viśvavidyālaya.

Varāhamihira. *Bṛhatsaṃhitā*, ed. Sudhākara Dvivedi 1895-97, with commentary of Bhaṭṭotpala. 2 vols. Benares: E.J. Lazarus.

2. Secondary Sources

Bayly, C.A. 1988. *Indian Society and the Making of the British Empire*. Cambridge: Cambridge University Press.

Bose, Sugata and Jalal, Ayesha 1997. *Modern South Asia: History, Culture, Political Economy*. Delhi: Oxford University Press.

CESS, see Pingree 1970-1994.

Dikshit, S.B. 1969. *History of Indian Astronomy*. Translated by R.V. Vaidya. 2 vols. Delhi: Director General of Observatories.

Dvivedi, Sudhākara. 1933. *Gaṇakataraṅgiṇī*. Benares: B.K. Shastri.

Halbfass, Wilhelm. 1988. *India and Europe: an Essay in Understanding*. Albany: State University of New York.

Kielhorn, F. 1874. *Catalogue of Sanskrit MSS Existing in the Central Provinces*. Nagpur.

Kirfel, Willibald. 1954. *Das Purāṇa vom Weltgebäude*. Bonn: Selbstverlag des Orientalischen Seminars der Universität Bonn.

Macnaghten, W. H. 1837. in: *Proceedings of the Asiatic Society*, May: 401-402.

Minkowski, C. Forthcoming. "Nīlakaṇṭha's Cosmographical Comments in the Bhīṣmaparvan", *Purāṇa*, forthcoming.

Pingree, David. 1970-1994. *Census of the Exact Sciences in Sanskrit, series A*. (=CESS) 5 volumes, (volume VI forthcoming). Philadelphia: American Philosophical Society.

———1978. "History of Mathematical Astronomy in India", *Dictionary of Scientific Biography*, vol. 15:533-633. New York: Scribner's.

———1978b. "Islamic Astronomy in Sanskrit", *Journal for the History of Arabic Science* 2:315-330.

———. 1990. "The Purāṇas and Jyotiḥśāstra: Astronomy", *Journal of the American Oriental Society* 110.2:274-80.

———. 1996. "Indian Reception of Muslim Versions of Ptolemaic Astronomy", in: F.J. & S.P. Ragep (eds.), *Tradition, Transmission, Translation*, 471-85. Leiden: E.J. Brill.

———. 1997. "Paurāṇic versus Siddhāntic Astronomy", in *English Abstracts, Xth World Sanskrit Conference*, 318-19. Bangalore: Rashtriya Sanskrit Sansthan.

Pollock, Sheldon 1989. "Mīmāṃsā and the Problem of History in Traditional India", *Journal of the American Oriental Society* 109.4: 603-10.

———. Forthcoming. "Sanskrit Literary Culture in History".

Prakash, Gyan 1996. 'Science Between the Lines', in: S. Amin & D. Chakrabarty (eds.), *Subaltern Studies IX*: 59-82, Delhi: Oxford University Press.

Sarma, K. Madhava Krishna 1950. "Siddhānta-saṃhitā-sāra-samuccaya of Sūrya Paṇḍita", *Siddha-Bhāratī* 2:222-25.

Sarma, S.R. 1995-6. "Sanskrit as Vehicle for Modern Science: Lancelot Wilkinson's Efforts in the 1830's", *Studies in History of Medicine and Science* XIV.1-2:189-99.

Sastri, Bapu Deva and Wilkinson, Lancelot. 1861. *The Surya Siddhanta or An Ancient System of Hindu Astronomy Followed by the Siddhānta Śiromaṇi, Translated into English with Extensive Explanatory Notes, by Pundit Bapu Deva Sastri § Lancelot Wilkinson*. Bibliotheca Indica 32. Calcutta: Asiatic Society.

Subbāji. 1837. *Avirodhaprakāśaḥ. Avirodhaprakāśavivekaś ca*. Bombay. Wilkinson, Lancelot 1834. "On the Use of the Siddhāntas in the work of Native Education", *Journal of the Asiatick Society of Bengal* 3:504-19.

Young, Richard F. 1997. "Receding from Antiquity: Indian Responses to Science and Christianity on the Margins of Empire", *Kokusaigaku-Kenkyu* 16 (*Meiji Gakuin Ronso* 595):241-74.

III

Traditions and Biographies

BETTINA BÄUMER

Tantric Pandits in Varanasi: A Brief Survey

Varanasi, Banaras or Kashi has a long tradition of Tantra in its various branches, with a number of followers: textual scholars, ritual practitioners and yogīs. This is not the place to give a history of the tantric tradition in Varanasi. I only intend to present some of the most influential pandits of Tantra in Varanasi in the last 30 years[1] and to describe the present situation of tantric scholarship.

This paper certainly does not pretend to be a complete survey of the pandits of Varanasi representing the tantric traditions.[2] I am mainly interested to elaborate on the question of the relation between theory and practice, and the changes that may occur or have already occurred in our present age.

Anybody familiar with Tantra and/or with the pandit traditions of Varanasi will immediately take the name of Mahāmahopadhyāya pandit Gopināth Kavirāj (1887-1976). I may quote a short account of his life from the Centenary Volume entitled Navonmeṣa, published in 1987:

> "Pandit Gopinath Kaviraj, who has become a legendary figure in the field of Indological studies, was born in a Bengali Brahmin family on 7th September, 1887 in the District of Dhaka, in Bangla Desh.
> Being a posthumous child, after having passed through many vicissitudes he passed his B.A. examination from Maharaja's College, Jaipur with academic distinctions. The final phase of his education started at Varanasi in 1910 under the loving care and guidance of Dr. Arthur Venis, the then Principal of Government Sanskrit College and got the M.A. degree in Sanskrit in 1913, standing first in order of merit.
> At the instance of Dr. Venis he was soon appointed Librarian of the famous Saraswati Bhavan Library and whole-heartedly started his career of research. From now on for the next 62 years he remained uninterruptedly and deeply engrossed in dissemination of knowledge till he left his body on 12th June, 1976 in the holy city of Varanasi itself.
> He delved deep into the so far unexplored wealth of learning and got published about seventy-two books which opened for all a new horizon in the field of Indological studies and research. He discovered in most of his studies completely new meanings and shed new light not

1 This paper is my tribute and an act of gratitude to the pandits of Varanasi, my gurus, collaborators and friends since 32 years.

2 Prof. B.N. Saraswati has made an almost complete survey of the pandits of Varanasi under the Anthropological Survey of India with a questionnaire from which one can extract the scholars on Tantra. These questionnaires have not been published but are available for scholars at N.K. Bose Foundation, Varanasi.

> only on different branches of philosophy, but also on Ancient Indian History, Epigraphy, Kashmir Śaivism, Buddhism, Jainism, Christian mysticism and Sufism as well, which are considered to be the invaluable guide to academic and spiritual research for generations to come.
> For 23 years he served the Sanskrit College, Varanasi first as Librarian and subsequently as Principal, till he voluntarily retired in 1937 in order to devote himself fully in his life-long pursuit of spiritual studies and intense *sādhanā* under the guidance of his Guru, the great Yogi Visuddhanandaji of Varanasi.
> The Government of India conferred upon him the title of Mahamahopadhyaya in 1934, Coronation Medal in 1937 and the title of 'Padmavibhushana' in 1964. Many an Indian University honoured itself by bestowing upon the great personality various degrees and certificates of honour.
> Gifted through divine grace with a prodigious memory and rare *prajñā*, Pt. Gopinath Kaviraj became a name to reckon with. He was indeed a rare combination not only of uncommon erudition but also of singular Yogic experience."

The greatness of Gopinath Kaviraj lay in the fact that he combined in himself on the one hand traditional scholarship and a critical and historical indological approach, and on the other hand scholarship with spiritual practice and achievement. He received the indological training from Arthur Venis, and the Yogic training from Swami Viśuddhānanda. He himself was not only teaching in the traditional way, but he also practiced tantric Yoga. In fact, most of the scholars on Tantra in Varanasi today are his students or disciples in varying degrees.

Gopinath Kaviraj (1965) also wrote about the pandit tradition of Banaras from the 13th to the 18th centuries.

It is also to a great extent the merit of Gopinath Kaviraj—after Arthur Avalon/Sir John Woodroffe—that Tantra has been washed clear of its negative associations of magic and sex and has been raised to the status of a serious subject of research. He has drawn the attention of the scholars to the rich literature of Tantra which was to a great extent unknown or forgotten.[3] Besides, he contributed greatly to the re-discovery of Kashmir Śaivism outside Kashmir.

In close association of Gopinath Kaviraj I have to mention Ācārya Rāmeśvara Jhā, a Mithila pandit, who was a great authority on *vyākaraṇa* and was then drawn to Kashmir Śaivism after his meeting with Swami Lakshman Joo in Kashmir, from whom he took initiation.

Thakur Jaideva Singh, who may not be called a pandit in the traditional sense, neither by caste nor by his original training, was a disciple of all the three, Gopinath Kaviraj, Rāmeśvara Jhā, and especially in the last years

---

3 Cf. Tantrasaṅgraha, Varanaseya Sanskrit Visvavidyalaya, several volumes.

of his life of Swami Lakshman Joo in Kashmir with whom he studied the Śaiva texts which he translated into English. He was thus an important scholar who published and made known by his translations the Kashmir Śaiva tradition which he received from his three gurus. He, too, had taken initiation into the spiritual practice of the tradition.

An important living disciple of Ācārya Rāmeśvara Jhā is Prof. K.D. Tripathi, Professor and for a long time head of the Department of Āgama and Dharmaśāstra in Banaras Hindu University (B.H.U.) Though he has not published much, he is an authority in Bhartṛhari, in Nāṭyaśāstra and Abhinavagupta.

Among the disciples of Gopinath Kaviraj I should also mention Pt. Hemendra Nath Chakravarty, who is a Śākta by family tradition, but was drawn towards non-dualistic Kashmir Śaivism from dualistic Nyāya-Vaiśeṣika.

All the above mentioned pandits belong to one group which we could call the *paramparā* of Gopinath Kaviraj. I want to mention two more *paramparās* before coming to the present situation and a general reflection on the tradition.

Swami Hariharānanda Karapātrījī was one of the most influential *saṃyāsīs* in Varanasi in recent times. It was his aim to preserve and revive the pure tradition of Hinduism in its various aspects. I need not go into his importance as a religious teacher and author. But he also revived the practical tradition of Śrīvidyā in Varanasi, and some of the present practitioners and gurus are his disciples, mainly Sītārām Kavirāj.

But another, less spectacular, more discrete and authentic representative of the Śrīvidyā tradition is pandit Baṭuknāth Śāstrī Khiste, born in 1919,[4] of a family originally from Maharashtra but settled since several generations in Varanasi. His case is particularly interesting since he belongs by family tradition to the unbroken lineage of Bhāskara Rāya. His father M.M. Pt. Nārāyaṇa Śāstrī Khiste, who was also a great Sanskrit scholar, was at the same time his guru. Pt. Baṭuknāth Śāstrī Khiste's field in teaching was literature and he is himself a great poet in Sanskrit, but his spiritual tradition is Śrīvidyā. Apart from his literary activities he has also written on Bhāskara Rāya, and he is a truly traditional authority on the Śākta Sampradāya. He has been offered a felicitation volume entitled *Unmīlanam*.[5]

An important Tantra Conference took place at the Saṃskṛta Viśvavidyālaya in 1965 (Tantra Sammelana). Swami Pratyagātmānanda Sarasvati, one of the most reputed tantric scholars of the age, a poet, a versatile scholar, the great collaborator of Arthur Avalon, who was at that time known as Pramatha Nath Mukhopadhyay, had been the chairperson of the conference.

---

4 He died in January 2000 in Varanasi.

5 *Unmīlanam, Batuknath Shastri Khiste Abhinandan Granth*, ed. by S.P. Vyas, Varanasi, Praśānt Prakāśan, 1998.

It was a landmark in bringing the most important tantric scholars together, in an effort of presenting a pure, traditional, undistorted image of Tantra. One of the highlights was the presence of the Ācārya of Kashmir Śaivism, Swami Lakshman Joo, who came from Srinagar and spoke on *Kuṇḍalinī Vijñāna Rahasya* in Sanskrit.[6]

From the examples I have given emerges the following picture of the tantric tradition as reflected in the Indian microcosm that is Varanasi: on the one hand there is an unbroken tradition continuing in a mostly hidden way. Since we are here concerned with the pandit tradition, I am not including the ritual practitioners and yogīs or saṃyāsīs in this discussion. They represent the practical tradition of Tantra as associated with certain temples, deities and *maṭhas*, but they have not contributed to the literature or scholarly discussion. On the other hand there is a certain need for revival, and thirdly there is an effort to purify the tradition of Tantrism from its decadence and tainted image by giving more emphasis on a scholarly study of the texts. This goes along, certainly not by chance, with a re-discovery of Kashmir Śaivism. In all this, Gopinath Kaviraj played the most crucial role, and even today he is continually referred to as the authority.

This brings us to the present situation of tantric studies in Varanasi. Again, we find three levels of the study of Tantra which are sometimes separate, sometimes overlapping in the same person. There are the pandits who are strictly studying and editing the texts. The foremost, also as far as publications are concerned, is pandit Vraj Vallabh Dvivedi who has edited a number of tantric texts and is very conversant with them. The second are the modern scholars, mostly those teaching at B.H.U., such as Kamalakar Mishra, Sūrya Prakāsh Vyās, Kamalesh Jha, Kailashpati Mishra, L. N. Sharma and others, and in Sampūrṇānanda Saṃskṛta Viśvavidyālaya, pandit Paramahaṃsa Miśra, Dr. Shitala Prasad Upadhyāya, and the third are the practitioners.

After the premature death of Prof. R.C. Dvivedi of Jaipur, a Trust was established in Varanasi in 1997 named "Ācārya R.C. Dvivedi Bhāratīyavidyā Pīṭha" (Institute of Indology), under the leadership of Dr. Sūrya Prakāsh Vyās of B.H.U. which is since then organizing regular *tantra goṣthis*. The effort was to bring together all the tantric pandits and scholars of Varanasi for an exchange of ideas and information of ongoing work, but in a deeper sense to revive the tradition of tantric scholarship in Varanasi and to encourage young scholars of Sanskrit to take up this study with a view to preserve the tradition. Pandit Khiste as the senior tantric (Śākta) pandit inaugurated the first Goṣṭhi and in the first few meetings every pandit or scholar had not only to speak about his work, but also on his relationship with the tradition,

6 The papers of the Conference were published in Sanskrit in: Sārasvatī Suṣamā Vārāṇaseyasaṃskṛtaviśvavidyālaya Patrikā, 20/1 (Samvat 2022 = 1965).

the *guru paramparā* and the spiritual aspect of this relationship. These presentations and the following discussions revealed the basic questions before the pandits and therefore before the tantric tradition:

1. to preserve the tradition in the face of the danger of its dying out,
2. to bring the studies of Tantras up to the scholarly level,
3. to be aware of the relationship between theory and practice in the context of Tantra.

The main question which emerged and which gave rise to lively discussions was, whether one could promote tantric studies without being initiated into the spiritual practice. The Tantras constantly stress the importance of initiation by a competent *guru* of the traditional line in order to understand the text. Can we demand this of modern scholarship? And how can one discriminate who is in the authentic tradition? All kinds of misuses are possible and are constantly happening by pretending *gurus*. But the injunction of the Tantras cannot be bypassed easily. The ideal is therefore an authentic combination of theory and practice, as in the case of Pt. Gopinath Kaviraj, Swami Lakshman Joo and Ācārya Rāmeśvara Jhā. But in the absence of such genius the study of the Tantras has to go on. This dilemma is one of the most fascinating aspects of the tantric tradition which will continue to occupy the minds of the pandits and of indologists.

REFERENCES

Kaviraj, Gopinath. 1965 (2nd edn. 1998). *Kāśī kī Sārasvat Sādhanā*. Patna: Bihar Rāṣṭrabhāṣā Pariṣad.

———. 1963 (2nd edn. 1978). *Tantric Vāṅmaya men Śākta dṛṣṭi* (Hindī). Patna: Bihar Rāṣṭrabhāṣā Pariṣad.

———. 1972. *Tantric Sāhitya*. Lucknow: Hindi Samiti.

———. 1987. *Notes on Religion and Philosophy*. Edited by Gaurinath Sastri, Varanasi: Sampurnanand Sanskrit University.

———. 1987. *Navonmeṣa*. Mahamahopadhyaya Gopinath Kaviraj Commemoration Volume. Vol. IV (English). Varanasi: Mata Anandamayi Ashram.

———. 1986. *Arcā Smṛtiḥ*: M.M. Gopinath Kaviraj. Varanasi: Mata Anandamayi Ashram.

———. *Sarasvatī Suṣamā*. Vārāṇaseya Saṃskṛta Viśvavidyālaya Patrikā (Sanskrit). 1965 (Saṃvat 2022), 20/1. Editor: Baldev Upādhyāya (issue containing the papers of the Tantra Conference).

Upadhyaya, Baldev. 1983. *Kāśī kī pāṇḍitya paramparā*. A comprehensive historical account of the Sanskrit Pandits of Varanasi... (1200 - 1980). Varanasi: Viśvavidyālaya Prakāśan.

Vyas, Suryaprakash. 1998. *Unmīlanam* (Sanskrit and Hindī). M.M. Pandit Baṭuknāth Śāstrī Khiste Abhinandan Granth. Varanasi: Praśānt Prakāśan.

JAMES BENSON

Śaṃkarabhaṭṭa's Family Chronicle: The *Gādhivaṃśavarṇana*

In 1912 Haraprasad Shastri published a short article in Indian Antiquary entitled "Dakshini Pandits at Benares", in which he discussed the contributions to Sanskrit literature made by a small number of families from South India who lived and wrote in Benares from the 16th century (Shastri 1912:7-13). The article became somewhat famous, and its introduction is perhaps worth quoting at some length:

> "Benares is in Northern India, yet the Paṇḍits of the South have the greatest influence there, and this influence they are not only exerting at the present moment but have exerted for centuries past...If anyone examines the manuscripts available at Benares, and these count by thousands and tens of thousands, he will be struck not only by the enormous quantity of modern Sanskrit literature but also by the fact that most of this was written at Benares, and by Paṇḍits from the South, specially by a few distinguished families of Mahārāshṭra brāhmaṇs...The great Paṇḍit, who infused southern ideals at Benares in all matters relating to Hindu life and Hindu religion in preference to northen ideals current in Kanauj, Kāśī, Mithilā and Bengal, was Nārāyaṇ Bhaṭṭa, an intellectual giant who not only wrote a vast number of Sanskrit works but organised the colony of Southern Brāhmaṇs at Benares, travelled far and wide and founded a family of Paṇḍits who hold their preeminence even up to the present moment. An authentic history of Bhaṭṭa Nārāyaṇa's family is likely to clear much of the obscurity in which the history of Sanskrit literature during the Muhammadan period is now involved. Rao Sahib Viśvanātha Nārāyaṇ Māṇḍalik has done a great service by publishing in his edition of the Vyavahāra-mayūkha a genealogy of this family. But genealogy is not history, and it is well known that historical works are very rare in India. Though histories are rare, biographies of historical persons rarer, and biographies of scholars rarer still. In the present case we have got a history of this family written by a distinguished member of the family themselves (sic). The work is entitled Gādhivaṃśānucharitam and the author is Śaṃkara Bhaṭṭa, the second son of Nārāyaṇa Bhaṭṭa and a man as distinguished in learning as his father. By the courtesy and good offices of my late lamented colleague Mahāmahopādhyāya Govinda Śāstrī of Benares, I have a copy of that work made for me. The first leaf is missing and the work comes abruptly to an end. It is full of inaccuracies and omissions. The abrupt closing does not detract much from its historical value, for in

> the last chapters, Śaṃkara was indulging in grief over the loss of a promising nephew, but the loss of the first leaf is a serious one as it prevents our seeing the real founder of the family" (Shastri 1912:7).

Shastri then proceeds to report the main outline of the narrative of Śaṃkara's Gādhivaṃsānucarita, the Bhaṭṭa family chronicle, listing the names of family members, students, and texts, both composed and taught, and describing events, travels in Mahārāṣṭra and its environs, and the final migration to Benares. He adds to the story a certain amount of background information, filling in details taken from other sources. This accounts for the greater part of the short article, which then continues with a fairly cursory glance at other southern scholars and ends with the list of the seven families "that swayed the Hindu Society at Benares during the last four hundred years", namely, the 1) Sesha, 2) Dharmādhikārī, 3) Bhaṭṭa, 4) Bhāradvāja, 5) Pāyaguṇḍe, 6) Chaturdhara, and 7) Puntamkar familes (Shastri 1912:13). Unfortunately, Shastri's outline does not always make clear which events are actually found in his copy of the manuscript and which he has supplied, either from other sources or simply as plausible suppositions.

The text and its history

Shastri's account of Śaṃkara's work has frequently been cited by scholars writing on various members of the Bhaṭṭa family. Among others, P.V. Kane refers to it at length in the introduction to his edition of the Vyavahāramayūkha, a book written by Śaṃkarabhaṭṭa's son Nīlakaṇṭhabhaṭṭa (Kane 1926:v ff.), and in his "History of Dharmaśāstra" (Kane 1975:903 ff.). Pandit V. Krishnamacharya, one of Pandit Aithal's predecessors at the Adyar Library, refers to it in his catalogue of *mīmāṃsā* and *advaita vedānta* manuscripts at the Adyar Library (Krishnamacharya 1952:46) and in his article on rare commentaries on Pārthasārathi Miśras Śāstradīpikā (Krishnamacharya 1947:257 ff.), one of which, the Prakāśa, was written by Śaṃkarabhaṭṭa. In more recent times, Richard Salomon cites Shastri's article in his 1985 edition of Nārāyaṇabhaṭṭa's Tristhalīsetu (Salomon 1985:xxiv ff.), as does Pandit Aithal's student Klaus-Werner Müller in his 1992 translation and study of Nārāyaṇabhaṭṭa's Antyeṣṭipaddhati (Müller 1992:15). It seems that the Sanskrit text of Śaṃkara's work has never been published. The "New Catalogus Catalogorum" refers only to Shastri's original article, but gives no information about manuscripts (Raghavan 1949-, Vol. V:348).

Nine years before Shastri drew attention to Śaṃkarabhaṭṭa's family chronicle, Kāntanāthabhaṭṭa referred to the work in his own version of the family's history, the Bhaṭṭavaṃśakāvya. Kāntanātha was a 19th to 20th century member of the Bhaṭṭa clan employed in the Sanskrit College at Mirzapur by G. Thibaut, a native of Heidelberg who served as superintendent of Sanskrit Studies in the United Provinces. In his Hindi introduction, Kāntanātha claims that he felt induced to write his work after seeing Mandalik's brief account of his family (Mandalik 1880:3 ff.), which Shastri referred to in his quote given above, and a copy of the Gādhivaṃśavarṇana, presumably the same work referred to by Shastri as the Gādhivaṃśānucarita.[1] The Bhaṭṭavaṃśakāvya was published by the Nandakādambinī Press in Mirzapur in 1903. On the basis of this work, but using other sources as well, J.R. Garpure drew an elaborate family tree of the Bhaṭṭa family for his 1924 edition of Nīlakaṇṭhabhaṭṭa's Vyavahāramayūkha (Gharpure 1924:ii ff.). Kāntanāthabhaṭṭa appears in Gharpure's chart as Bhaṭṭa number 85 (followed only by his younger brothers Kṛṣṇa, Rāma, and Nārāyaṇa, Bhaṭṭas 86, 87, and 88), and his famous ancestor Nārāyaṇabhaṭṭa as Bhaṭṭa number 5. Kane makes reference to Kāntanātha's Bhaṭṭavaṃśakāvya in his "History of Dharmaśāstra" (Kane 1975:906), as does M. Krishnamachariar in his "History of Classical Sanskrit Literature" (Krishnamachariar 1984:784).

I do not know if the 1903 edition of Kāntanātha's poem found a home in any western library—I have not found it in Britain—but in 1983 the work was edited and published by Shiva Shankar Tripathi. In his preface, Tripathi states that in 1980 he had written an article in the Hindi weekly *Dharmayug*, Bombay, on Gāgābhaṭṭa, the great-grandson of Nārāyaṇabhaṭṭa and great-nephew of Śaṃkarabhaṭṭa who had officiated at Shivāji's coronation. He goes on to say that the article, which mentioned the existence of a copy of Kāntanātha's work in the Bharatiya Manisha Sutram in Allahabad, excited such interest in Sanskrit lovers, who then wrote him letters of appreciation, that he felt obliged to publish it (Tripathi 1983:21). This book too failed to find a home in British libraries, but is securely placed in numerous American universities.

But old libraries sometimes do have old books, and by good fortune a manuscript of Śaṃkarabhaṭṭa's Gādhivaṃśavarṇana arrived at the Bodleian Library in Oxford in 1909 with the collection purchased in Benares and donated to the library by Chandra Shum Shere, prime minister of Nepal.[2] The only other manuscript of the work which I have located is in the Sarasvatī Bhavana in Benares.[3] This was used by Kumudranjan Das in his book Raja Todar Mal, and Das refers to it at a passage we will consider below.

The text preserved in the Oxford and Benares manuscripts is often difficult, though Shastri's characterization of his own copy of the Gādhivamśānu-

---

1 This account of Kāntanātha's introduction is taken from Kane 1975:906.

2 MS Chandra Shum Shere d.438(6) ff. 2-17. No date.

3 *A Descriptive Catalogue of Sanskrit Manuscripts acquired for and deposited in the Sanskrit University Library (Sarasvatī Bhavana) Vārāṇasī during the years 1791-1950, Vol. XI, Sāhitya MSS*, No.42254, pp. 170-71. I obtained a copy of this manuscript just before this article went to press, but after initial study it seems to me likely to be a copy of the Oxford manuscript.

carita as "inaccurate and full of omissions" would not be appropriately applied to it.[4]

Unfortunately, Kāntanāthabhaṭṭa's 1903 composition does not offer us much help in understanding the text. A relatively small number of verses from the first half of the Gādhivaṃśavarṇana, before Śaṃkarabhaṭṭa begins to lament his great personal loss and the general calamity of human existence, find an echo, or even direct copy, in the modern work, but the latter does very little to elucidate difficult readings in the older text. In spite of these difficulties, it is possible on the basis of the manuscript to give a fuller account of the Bhaṭṭa family chronicle than Shastri could in 1912.

The contents

As in Shastri's copy, the first folio of the Oxford and Benares manuscripts is missing. The narrative begins at verse 9 with Rāmeśvarabhaṭṭa, the father of Nārāyaṇabhaṭṭa and the grandfather of the author Śaṃkarabhaṭṭa, attaining fame in the south. Kāntanātha lists Rāmeśvara's ancestors, in chronological order, as 1) Nāganātha, 2) Cāṅgadeva, and 3) Govinda, a genealogy confirmed by the colophon of Nārāyaṇabhaṭṭa's Vṛttaratnākaravyākhyā,[5] and says that the first of these settled in Paiṭhan.[6] Śaṃkara tells us that Rāmeśvara, who is the major character in his work, had all sorts of personal virtues, was learned in various *śāstras*, and wrote a *kāvya*, the Rāmakutūhala, which rivalled the Naiṣadīyacarita of Śrīharṣa. He seems to have set out on his own career when an "excellent ascetic" (*uttamayati*) became the head of a local college (*maṭha*) in Paiṭhan and started to give poor teaching. Rāmeśvara went west, about 80 miles, to the village called Samgamner (Saṃgamanera), to found his own establishment with a number of students. There, at the Pravarā river, he set up a Rāma *liṅga* and, as the text says, set people on the Vaiṣṇava path (*vaiṣṇavamārga*). Meanwhile the Nizām Shāhī king appointed one Zafar Malik (Japharamalika) to high office, and one of Zafar's officers, Viṣṇupanta, told Zafar about Rāmeśvara. It is not stated which Nizām Shāhī ruler this was, but possibly it was Burhān Nizām Shāh, who succeeded his father Malik Ahmad, the founder of the Nizām Shāhī dynasty in Ahmadnagar, in 1508. These were grandson and son of Tīma Bhat, a *brāhmaṇa* convert who originally came from Pathri, about 70 miles east and south of Paiṭhan (Haig 1928:398). In the Gādhivaṃśavarṇana, Śaṃkara

4 Shastri quotes directly from his text of the Gādhivaṃśānucarita only twice in his article, and, as far as I have seen, once elsewhere, namely, in his catalogue of *vedic* manuscripts in the Asiatic Society of Bengal (Shastri 1923:375). The few differences between his quotations and the text of the Gādhivaṃśavarṇana seem likely to be scribal errors.

5 Krishnamacharya, Pandit V. ed., *Descriptive Catalogue of Sanskrit Manuscripts in the Adyar Library*, Vol. VI., No. 778. See also Krishnamacharya 1947: 259.

6 *Bhaṭṭavaṃśakāvyam*, 1. 5-8.

tells us that the sole son of Zafar Malik was suffering from leprosy (*kuṣṭha*), and found no relief either from his attractive youth or, it seems, from his new garden. Considering his wealth nothing but misery, the son determined to worship the deity on the hill called Saptaśṛṅga (Seven-peaked) or to commit suicide by throwing himself from it. Identifying this site, D.C. Sircar writes, "Saptaśṛṅga is again a famous place to the north of Nasik. The image of the eighteen-armed goddess of this place is 12 feet high" (Sircar 1960:106). The name does not seem to be widely attested in Sanskrit. The only instances I have seen are in Sircar's text of the Śaktisaṃgamatantra,[7] and, following Sircar's note, in a quotation cited by P.K. Gode from the Vaidyajīvana (Gode 1941:449), a medical treatise by Lolimbarāja, a Mahārāṣṭrian writer of the 17th century who married a beautiful Muslim girl and became a devotee of Saptaśṛṅga Bhavānī when she died. The Imperial Gazetteer though provides a full account of the site, from which the following description is taken:

> "The shrine of the goddess, known as Mahishāsur Mardini or Saptashringanivāsini, is in a cave at the base of a sheer scarp, the summit of which is the highest point of the hill. Not far from the bathing-place is a precipice known as the Sit Kade, which overhangs the valley about 1,200 feet; from this rock human sacrifices are said to have been formerly hurled; a kid is now the usual victim...A large fair lasting for a week, and attended by about 15,000 pilgrims, is held on the full moon of Chaitra (April). On the occasion of the fair the steps leading to the shrine are crowded with the sick and maimed, who are carried up the hill in hopes of a cure."[8]

Zafar Malik's son did not need to make the trip, since he was told, presumably in a dream, that if he ate Rāmeśvara's leftovers, his body would heal. The next day various officials related this to Rāmeśvara, but he said that only if he received consent in a dream would he agree to participate in the scheme to heal the young man. He did, and after 21 attempts the disease and its scars disappeared. Everyone, the students, Zafar Malik, his foreigners (*mlecchas*), women, children, and the lowly (*hīnaloka*) all gained confidence in Rāmeśvara's power.

The second *sarga* (chapter) begins with the Nizām Shāh receiving the news, considering it with his ministers, and sending a messenger to Rāmeśvara asking for an audience. He urges the messenger to act with caution and tact, so as not to rouse Rāmeśvara's powerful and potentially deadly wrath. A letter with gold writing is sent. Zafar Malik meets the messenger as he arrives and the two proceed on foot. Rāmeśvara rejects the request, and the letter is sent back. No reason is given. This worked out well for Rāmeśvara, since Zafar Malik became devoted to him, in spite of Rāmeśvara's rebuke

---

7 At 3.7.56. This text is included in Sircar 1960.

8 *Imperial Gazetteer of India*, Vol. XXII, p. 80. The Gazetteer states that the hill is "otherwise, but wrongly, called Chattar-singh or the 'four-peaked' ".

of the king. Zafar Malik ordered his officials to provide Rāmeśvara with a year's free food. They agreed, kept their word, and the *brāhmaṇa* became carefree, entrusting all the household duties to his wife. She was devoted to him and attractive, and gave birth to a daughter. The girl was given in marriage to a Vaiṣṇava of good family, Sakalakala Mahlāri, and the two of them had two sons.

Meanwhile, Rāmeśvara continually expounded the meaning of the Bhāgavatapurāṇa in the evenings, just after dinner, and the best people were not denied attendance. On hearing the exposition of the 10th chapter (where Kṛṣṇa's birth and childhood exploits are described), Rāmeśvara's wife herself became anxious, and told him that she could not be happy without a son. When he heard that, he too became desirous of the same thing, and was confident that Rāma would provide it. The next morning he tended his fire and promised his wife they would perform a pilgrimage (*yātrā*) to Kolhapur (Kolāpura) to see the goddess Lakṣmī there in order to get the son. The *sarga* ends with the introduction of a fantastic episode as Śaṃkara explains that a ghost (*bhūta*) has taken possession of the virtuous daughter of Rāmeśvara's neighbor.

The third *sarga* begins with the girl hearing Rāmeśvara recite the Bhāgavata at his home. The ghost realizes that Rāmeśvara recognizes him, and so he describes his current condition, taking over the voice of the girl. He says that hearing the Bhāgavata has relieved him of his sin and that Rāmeśvara will get a son. Specifically, he asks Rāmeśvara to perform his funerary rites (*antyeṣṭi*) and burn the blanket he lives in. The ghost will protect Rāmeśvara from tigers etc. on his pilgrimage to Kolhapur. Once Rāmeśvara arrives in Kolhapur and performs the funerary rites, the ghost will be conceived as his son. However, the boy will suffer from consumption (*yakṣman*) and in his fourth year must be taken to Dvarka (Dvārāvatī) to see Kṛṣṇa. He will be cured by Kṛṣṇa, initiated in the following year, and then, in his eighth year, be brought to Benares to live life as a householder. His fame will be enormous, he will have ample progeny, and he will die at a ripe age, never to return.

The girl then faints, quickly revives, asks her father what happened, and shrinks with embarrassment. Rāmeśvara now determines to visit his family deity (*kuladevatā*) at Kolhapur in order to get a son, and sets off with his entire household. Along the way they employ a guide who, in a forest, warns them that a leopard might be approaching and leads them off to hide. A bit further ahead, he points out that a bird call signals that a tiger is nearby. Still further along, a fearsome snake sees them and hisses. That night the ghost tells an astonished Rāmeśvara that he had assumed the form of the guide and the bird so as to guard him from dangers.

The fourth *sarga* finds the party camped near the city going about routine chores, while Rāmeśvara, who has settled his students in the camp (*śibira*) for their protection, goes out to attend to nature's duties. A great snake hisses at him and he faints from fear. The snake then circles around him, but the ghost then appears and casts away the snake using a stick. The students, anxious at the delay, find him and revive him. The ghost comes out of the blanket, makes an *añjali* gesture, and tells him that since he saved him from the giant snake he, Rāmeśvara, should help him cross over the ocean of misery. Rāmeśvara promises to perform the ghost's funerary rites, and the latter disappears again into the blanket. Immediately they reach Kolhapur (Śrīpura), Rāmeśvara burns the blanket and performs the funerary rites (*antyeṣṭi*), and the ghost begins to grow in the womb of Rāmeśvara's wife. She, in turn, thinks her son will attain the summit of all literature, and so, putting aside any other desire, wants to go to that city which is distinguished by knowledge and rich with countless scholars. Rāmeśvara perceives her wish, and, eager to see Kṛṣṇarāja's city very quickly, sets out to visit his fabulous assembly. In other words, they go to Vijayanagar, ruled by Kṛṣṇadevarāya (1509-29).

There Rāmeśvara and his wife stay with a childhood friend, the *rājaguru* Tatsat Kṛṣṇabhaṭṭa. She manages to overhear scholarly discussions from within the house, and, with no other thoughts, delights in the fullfillment of her longings. Kṛṣṇabhaṭṭa and others tell Kṛṣṇarāja (i.e., Kṛṣṇadevarāya) that a great scholar has arrived, but that he, Rāmeśvara, has no desire to see him. Kṛṣṇarāja answers that he will himself go to the assembly and greet Rāmeśvara as the latter arrives. This happens, and after Kṛṣṇarāja praises Rāmeśvara himself, he announces that he has at last found a worthy recipient for the great gift of elephants. He then proclaims that a public festival is in order.

In the first verse of *sarga* five Rāmeśvara hears this, recalls that accepting the gift of an elephant is prohibited, turns away from Kṛṣṇarāja, and, at dawn, leaves town for Samgamner, accompanied by his approving wife. A single verse looks back at Vijayanagar, where everyone is unhappy, and at the king, who, as long as he lived, never found a comparable recipient for his elephants.

Samgamner, by contrast, compares favorably with the cosmos from the powerful luster of its famous resident, and, just as various female deities had begotten famous sons, so did Rāmeśvara's wife, in the month of Mādhava of the *śaka* year 1435 (i.e. 5 April to 5 May, 1513).[9] The boy, Nārāyaṇa, was afflicted by consumption (*yakṣman*). Rāmeśvara remembered what the ghost had said, namely, that he had to be taken to Dvarka for a cure, and so the family made the trip accompanied by Rāmeśvara's pupils. Śaṃkara does not describe the arrival at Dvarka, but simply says that once there,

---

9 Kāntanātha gives the date as the tenth *tithi* of the bright fortnight of Rādhā, *vikrama* 1570, which corresponds to April 15, 1513 (Bhaṭṭavaṃśakāvya 1.38).

Rāmeśvara, worried about his son, took some pleasure in teaching Nārāyaṇagūrjara both Śeṣa's (i.e., Patañjali's) Mahābhāṣya and Sureśvara's Vārttika (on Śaṃkarācārya's Bṛhadāraṇyakopaniṣadbhāṣya) for six months. Meanwhile, the god Kṛṣṇa took pity on Rāmeśvara, telling him in a dream that two men would come with medicine for his son, and that he should also accept some rice. He then told a doctor to prepare some medicine and bring it to Rāmeśvara's son. Finally, he told a merchant to bring rice along with other items. The two men came the next morning, and also for the following 20 days, and at the end the boy was cured. The god Kṛṣṇa also arranged for the tonsure of Nārāyaṇa, an act Rāmeśvara remembered having agreed to the ghost to undertake as soon as the boy was healthy. His wife, on account of her being a woman, according to the text, was actually worried about how to acquire the proper implements. Kṛṣṇa told a worshipper of his in a dream to give these to Rāmeśvara, which he did. So Rāmeśvara then performed the initiation on the five year old Nārāyaṇa, established the tradition of teaching the Mahābhāṣya and Sureśvara's Vārttika, set up his student Nārāṇayagūrjara, and went back to his own city, presumably Paiṭhan. The citizens were thrilled to see him, and he taught his son all the *smṛtis*, the *veda*, and the six auxillary texts (*aṅgas*).

Sarga six begins with Rāmeśvara and his household going to Benares (Kāśī). On route a second son is born, Śrīdhara, and at Benares a third, Mādhava. At Benares Rāmeśvara arranges the marriage of all three. Śaṃkara then lists Rāmeśvara's students at Benares, starting with a Konkan, Anantabhaṭṭa Cittale. Two excellent ascetics (*yativaryavarau*) follow, Dāmodara Sarasvatī and Mādhava Sarasvatī, who travelled far and became famous. Then comes Maheśa Ṭhakkura, who the text says composed the difficult Pakṣadharīpracāra.[10] Then comes Govinda Dvivedi, from Gujarat, who, along with Rāmeśvara's son Śrīdhara, became proficient in the Mahābhāṣya. Next are mentioned Ācāryabhaṭṭa and his son Viśvanātha, who became famous teachers of vedānta in the south. Śaṃkaramiśraśarman, from Kānyakubja, is then mentioned as the author of a commentary on the Gītagovinda (the Rasataraṅgiṇi). Lastly, the text refers to still other unnamed students from a list of various regions of India, and in the next verse Rāmeśvara and his wife die.

The rest of the *sarga* narrates the achievements of the author's father, Nārāyaṇabhaṭṭa. He learned *śruti*, *smṛti*, and the six *darśanas* directly from his father, and composed the Tristhalīgamanasetu, along with other *nibandhas*. The lord of Utkala invited him to debate with the easterners, and after a month he established the supremecy of the southern schools.[11]

---

10 Maheśa Ṭhakkura wrote a *Darpaṇa* commentary on Pakṣadhara Miśra's Āloka on Gaṅgeśa's Tattvacintāmaṇi.

11 *yaś cotkareśvara samīritapatrapūrvavijñāpanād grahaṇavīkṣaṇanirṇayārtham/*
prācyair vivādam aniśaṃ pravidhāya māsaṃ śrīdākṣiṇātyamatam ūrjitatāṃ nināya//

In an assembly called by Toḍaramala he defeated all the Maithila and Gauḍa scholars, starting with Vidyānivāsa. Shastri writes:

> "At a Śrāddha ceremony at Dehli in the house of Toḍar Mal, he worsted in disputation all the Paṇḍits of Gauda and Mithilā with Vidyānivāsa at their head...the point at dispute was one of vital importance to modern Brāhmaṇism. The ancient Rishis declare that at the performance of Śrāddha, live Brāhmaṇs are to be fed with the cooked food offered to the manes. Bengal holds that this is impossible in the Kaliyuga as there are no Brāhmaṇs worthy to feed. And so they feed symbolical Brāhmaṇs (Brāhmaṇs made of *kuśa* grass). The southern people hold that the injunctions of the Śāstras should be respected, and live Brāhmaṇs are to be fed." (Shastri 1912:9-10)

In his book Raja Todar Mal, Kumudranjan Das similarly says, with reference to the Benares manuscript of the Gādhivaṃśavarṇana, that "During a *śrāddha* ceremony Nārāyaṇa Bhaṭṭa subdued the paṇḍits of Mithila and Gaur who had assembled at the Rāja's house (Das 1979:214)." Not having seen Shastri's copy of the Gādhivaṃśānucarita, it is impossible to judge this interpretation. Although effegies of *kuśa* grass are certainly specified for *śrāddhas* in the event that *brāhmaṇas* are not available, I have not yet seen any references to the dispute mentioned by Shastri. The Oxford and the Benares manuscripts suggest a different issue: "this argument was about the prohibition of meat (offering) at a *śrāddha* in the Kali age" (6.14.d: *śrāddhe kalau palaniṣedhavivāda eṣaḥ*).[12] Among the various texts attributed to Nārāyaṇabhaṭṭa, the New Catalogus Catalogorum lists a Calcutta manuscript of the Kaliśrāddhemāṃsadānavicāraḥ (Rāghavan 1949-, Vol.X:71), in which, judging from the published extract, Nārāyaṇa opposed those "whose tongues are eager for the juice of meat" (*māṃsarasalolupara-sana*).[13] Could *pala*, which means meat or straw, have been taken by Shastri somehow to refer to straw *brāhmaṇas*?

Returning to the Gādhivaṃśavarṇana, the poem names Brahmendra Sarasvatī and Nārāyaṇa Sarasvatī, and then makes a reference to other similarly great ascetics (*yatis*), all of whom were Nārāyaṇa's pupils. It then says that Nārāyaṇa composed a text known as the Dharmapravṛtti in the south, but as the Prayogaratna north of the Vindhyas.[14] In Shastri's account it looks

---

6.13. (*cotkareśvara* Oxford; *coktareśvara* Benares; *cottareśvara* Shastri) In a similar passage (3.22) the Bhaṭṭavaṃśakāvya has *utkalādhīśvara* (which is adopted above).

12 *dillīśvarākhilamahākaraṇādhikāriśrīṭoḍarasya samitau ca jigāya sarvān/ vidyānivāsamukhamaithilagauḍavindūn śrāddhe kalau palaniṣedhavivāda eṣaḥ//* 6.14.

13 *A Descriptive Catalogue of Sanskrit Manuscripts in the Library of the Calcutta Sanskrit College*, Vol. II, No. 462, p. 417.

14 *dharmapravṛttir iti dakṣiṇataḥ prasiddhāṃ cakre samastabudhasaṃśayanāśaśastrīm/ vindhyottare vyavahṛtāṃ tu budhaiḥ prayogaratnākhyayā nikhilasaṃskṛtipaddhatiṃ yaḥ//* 6.16. Shastri quotes this verse in the form given here in his catalogue of *vedic* manuscripts in the Asiatic Society of Bengal (Shastri 1923:375).

as though these were two separate works (Shastri 1912:10), but Kane has already questioned the claim that Nārāyaṇa could have written the extant text Dharmapravṛtti, which was written by someone with the same name (Kane 1975:907). Śaṃkara then states that Nārāyaṇa brought about the greatness of Nṛsiṃhāśrama, Upendrāśrama, and Madhusūdana Sarasvatī. He set up his sons, gave his house to a devotee of Hari named Nṛsiṃha, gave hundreds of gold coins to *brāhmaṇas*, saw his sons' sons and died, never to return.

The seventh *sarga*, which is the last to offer historical information about the Bhaṭṭa family, begins with the names of Nārāyaṇabhaṭṭa's three sons, Rāmakṛṣṇa, Śaṃkara, and Govinda. According to the text, the first taught Trimmalabhaṭṭa, wrote *nibandhas* including the *jīvatpitṛkṛtyanirṇīti*, a commentary on the Aśvistuti in the Mahabhārata, and a *paddhati* on the śatāsyapaṅktyānanakoṭihoma etc.[15] He died at 52, having taught and set up his three sons Dinādhinātha, Kamalākara, and Lakṣmaṇa. Nārāyaṇa's youngest son, Govinda, had four sons, taught the first two of these, Lakṣmīpa and Vināyaka, along with groups of various students, and then died at 48. He had served his mother from birth, and followed her on her death to continue doing so.

Five verses syntactically joined (*kulaka*) then account for the life of the author. He renounced travel (i.e. was a *kṣetrasaṃnyāsin*), and, having learned the Kāśikā, taught *kaumārilamīmāṃsā* to Mallāribhaṭṭa, Bhaṭṭojī Dīkṣita, other scholars and other ascetics (*yatis*), his eldest son Dāmodara, and his next two sons, Nṛsiṃha and Nīlakaṇṭha. He writes that his eldest son (*jyeṣṭhasuta*) was honored by the king, earned lots of money, was well established, handsome, fortunate, rich, and devoted to his parents. Śaṃkara then concludes this passage by stating that he experienced a loss. I think this may refer to the death of his son Dāmodara, but the text is unclear to me.[16] At this point the poem turns from its historical narrative to describe

15 I am not certain what this refers to. A *śatānana* is a type of *koṭihoma*. The Catalogue of Sanskrit Manuscripts in the North-Western Provinces, V, p. 56, lists a Koṭihomaśatamukhādiprayogapaddhati by Rāmakṛṣṇabhaṭṭa.

16 The *kulaka* is as follows:
śrīśaṃkarākhyas tv atha madhyamo yaḥ sa kṣetrasaṃnyāsy adhigatya kāśikām/ mahlāribhaṭṭādikavindubhaṭṭojīdīkṣitārādhyamukhāṃs tathā parān/9/ yatīṃs tathā jyeṣṭhatanūjadāmodaraṃ ca kaumārilaśastrapāragam (*°śāstragaṃ paraṃ* Benares)/ *kṛtvā nṛsiṃhaṃ ca tato 'nujaṃ tatkaniṣṭham antyam sutanīlakaṇṭhakam/10/ adhyāpayan* (*adhyāpya* Benares) *jyeṣṭhasutena rājamānyena bhūridraviṇarjakena* (*°draviṇārjanakena* Benares) *ca/ labdhapratiṣṭhena surūpabhājā saubhāgyayuktena bahuvyayena ca/11/ bhaktena pitror api jaiminīyaśāstraṃ* (*jaiminīyaṃ śāstraṃ* Benares) *tathā 'dhyāpya bahūṃs tu śiṣyān/ kṣīrābdhirāmaṃ tv abhayaṃkarākhyaṃ bālaṃ sadāsāryakaviśvanātham/12/ dāntyopanāmānam atha dviputryāṃ* (*dviputrāṃ* Benares) *nṛharyupākhye tv atha siddhanāthe/ ṣaḍvarṣadeśīyam athā 'dyaputraṃ vivāhya muktena viyogam īyivān/13/*

the grief of the parents. The lament for the dead son is sharp and direct. At one point Śaṃkara says that the parents have reached the age of 68. A few verses are then partially illegible, but he then says that his wife died and that learned good friends tried to console him. The *sarga* concludes with a number of verses on the frailty of human existence. The colophon names the *sarga* "*bhrātṛsutaśokāpanoda*" "removal of the grief for *bhrātṛsuta(s)*" from which, possibly, Shastri assumed that Śaṃkara was grieving for the loss of a nephew. Although the compound "*bhrātṛsuta*" could certainly mean "nephew(s)", it could also, I think, be taken as a *dvandva* meaning "brother(s) and son(s)" the order of the items following the order of the narrative.[17]

The eighth and ninth *sargas* describe the degradation, futility, and misery of each succeeding stage of life, starting from the moment of conception. Although the theme is common and the references learned, the accumulation of these direct and often bitter statements makes a forceful impression. Śaṃkara finds relief, eventually, in the refuge offered by the god Hari and he rebukes himself for not turning to him earlier in life. The ninth *sarga* ends with a verse disclaiming any merit in his humble praise of the god, since "neither the goddess of speech herself, nor even the whole of the triple world, transforming itself into the preceptor of the gods, could, as long as they lived, complete the job of writing out your (i.e. Hari's) virtues, using the peak of the Himalaya as chalk and the sky as a board."[18]

The great figure in the poem is the author's grandfather, Rāmeśvarabhaṭṭa. The first eight verses are missing from the two manuscripts, but already in the ninth verse the author tells us that Rāmeśvara attained celebrity in the south, so there was hardly space to say much about his ancestors. In

---

There are difficulties here and I am uncertain of the interpretation. Could it be that Śaṃkara experienced the loss of Dāmodara after the latter had taught various pupils and arranged the marriage of his first son, a boy not yet six? Dāmodara is known to have at least one son, Siddheśvarabhaṭṭa. Only two works of Dāmodara are known, a *pariśiṣṭa* on his father's Dvatianirṇaya, and a Kalivarjyanirṇaya. Śaṃkara refers to the first (cited in Kane's Introduction to the Vyavahāramayūka, p. xii). The second is recorded as complete in 16 folios as No. 3076 in the Asiatic Society of Bengal (Shastri 1925:1044). Alternatively, but I think less likely, Śaṃkara may be referring to the death of his own first son (*ādyaputra*), Raṅganātha, whose name is known from the works of Nīlakaṇṭha. See below.

17 I confess I am not sure about this interpretation.

18 *likhec ced vāgdevī gaganaphalake tvadguṇagaṇaṃ*
svayaṃ yāvajjīvaṃ himaśikharināmnyā khaṭikayā|
trilokī vā sarvāpy amaragurubhāvaṃ gatavatī
tadāpy antaṃ yāyān na khalu mama kā tatra gaṇanā|| 9.55.

At this point the manuscripts present a Durgādevībhūjágaprayāta (*devīstotra*) in 15 verses and a Raghunāthāṣṭaka, both composed by Śaṃkara. They then introduce a "yamakaśobhipadyāṣṭaka", and the Benares manuscript concludes at the point where the text continues, illegibly, on the reverse side of the final folio of the Oxford manuscript.

the text as we have it, Rāmeśvara alone works miracles, as in his curing of Zafar Malik's son and his liberation of the ghost. He refuses an audience with the Nizām Shāhī king and the gifts of Kṛṣṇadevarāya. When he is rewarded by Zafar Malik he can, for a year, be rid of cares, but he is sympathetic to his wife, undertaking the pilgimage to Kolhapur and the further trip down to Vijayanagar mainly for her, and likewise he is anxious for their sick son, travelling to Dvarka for his cure. He shows concern for his students on the dangerous route to Kolhapur. The narrative suggests that migrating to Benares was itself his great deed, though this is not stated explicitly.

The depiction of the adult life of Nārāyaṇabhaṭṭa is, by contrast, rather thin, and happens in just 13 verses. His books, students, and generosity are about all there is. Certainly there is no mention of the famous deed later attributed to him, namely, the restoration of the Viśvanātha temple in Benares, which he was said to have requested from the Muslim lord as a reward for relieving a serious drought.[19] However, Śaṃkara says that the *liṅga* set up by Rāmeśvara at Samgamner conferred a benefit on the faithful similar to that conferred at the site of Viśveśa in Benares, which could conceivably be taken to refer to the great story about Nārāyaṇa. His authorship of famous works on pilgrimage and funerary rites, the Tristhalīsetu and the Antyeṣṭipaddhati, might in some way have been connected, in the mind of his son Śaṃkara, with Rāmeśvara's pilgrimage to Kolhapur which brought about Nārāyaṇa's conception, and with the funeral rites for the ghost who in fact became Nārāyaṇa, but of course that can not be known. In any case Nārāyaṇa's *Antyeṣṭipaddhati* is not mentioned in the Gādhivaṃśavarṇana.

Śaṃkara does not spend much time describing his own generation. That his younger brother Govinda was especially attached to their mother stands out in an otherwise fairly routine account. Obviously it would have been extremely satisfying to have learned something more from the text about Śaṃkara's student Bhaṭṭojī Dīkṣita, who infused his great grammatical text, the Śabdakaustubha, with discussions of *mīmāṃsā* doctrine.

It is not clear how much biographical information Śaṃkara may have written in his other works, since only two of these have been published. His known works on mīmāṃsā include the Mīmāṃsābālaprakāśa,[20] the Mīmāṃsāsārasaṃgraha,[21] the Prakāśa (on the Śāstradīpikā), the Nirṇayacandrikā, and the Vidhirasāyanadūṣaṇa, and, on *dharmaśāstra*, the Dvaita-

---

19 See Altekar 1937:45 ff. Altekar (p. 48) cites the Dānahārāvalī of Divākarabhaṭṭa, Nārāyaṇabhaṭṭa's grandson: *Srīrāmeśvarasūrisūnur abhavan nārāyaṇākhyo mahān/ yenākāry avimuktake suvidhinā viśveśvarasthāpanā* (India Office Catalogue of Sanskrit Manuscripts, Part II, p. 547). He suggests that Śaṃkara wrote his family chronicle when he was 30 or 35, before his father had the temple rebuilt, but, as shown above, Śaṃkara records his father's death and refers to himself as 68.

20 *Mimāṃsābālaprakāśa*. 1902. Chowkhamba Sanskrit Series, Vol. 16.

21 *Mīmāṃsāsārasaṃgraha*. 1904. Chowkhamba Sanskrit Series, Vol. 17.

nirṇaya (or Dharma-), and the Dharmaprakāśa (or Sarva-). Kane has pointed out that Śaṃkara gives his mother's name as Pārvatī in the last of these works.[22]

It is clear though from the Vyavahāratattva, a work on *dharmaśāstra* written by Śaṃkara's son Nīlakaṇṭha, that Śaṃkara had four sons. In the colophon to that work Nīlakaṇṭha refers to himself as the younger brother of Raṅganāthabhaṭṭa, Dāmodarabhaṭṭa, and Nṛsiṃhabhaṭṭa, the order here presumably following that of the brothers.[23] Elsewhere in the text Nīlakaṇṭha refers to his eldest brother (*jyeṣṭabhrātṛ*) Dāmodarabhaṭṭa.[24] Shastri and Kane have suggested that Raṅganātha had died early, before Śaṃkara wrote the family history. In any event, it seems that Śaṃkara chose not to record the name of this son.[25]

REFERENCES

Altekar, A.S. 1937. *History of Benares*. Benares: The Culture Publication House, Benares Hindu University.

Catalogue of Sanskrit Manuscripts in the North-Western Provinces, V. 1880. Allahabad.

Das, Kumudranjan. 1979. *Raja Todar Mal*. Calcutta: Saraswat Library.

A Descriptive Catalogue of Sanskrit Manuscripts acquired for and deposited in the Sanskrit University Library (Sarasvati Bhavana) Varanasi during the years 1791-1950, Vol. XI, Sāhitya MSS. 1964. Varanasi: Sanskrit University.

A Descriptive Catalogue of Sanskrit Manuscripts in the Library of the Calcutta Sanskrit College, Vol.II. 1898. Calcutta: Printed by J.N. Banerjee and son.

Gharpure, J.R., (trans.) 1924. *The Vyawahāramayūkha (A treatise on positive law)*, Part II. Bombay.

Gharpure, J. R. (ed.). 1925. *The Nīti Mayūkha by Bhaṭṭa Nīlakaṇṭha*. The Collection of Hindu Law Texts, Vol. XIX.

Gode, P.K. 1941. "Lolimbarāja and His Works", *Indian Culture*, Vol. VII, No.4. Calcutta: Indian Research Institute.

Haig, Wolseley. (ed.) 1928. *Cambridge History of India*, Vol.II. Cambridge: Cambridge University Press.

Imperial Gazetter of India, Vol. XXII. 1908. Oxford: Clarendon Press.

Kane, P.V. (ed.). 1926, *Vyavahāramayūkha of Nīlakaṇṭha Bhaṭṭa*. Poona: Bhandarkar Oriental Research Institute.

---

22 Kane 1926:x. Kane quotes the India Office Catalogue of Sanskrit Manuscripts, Part III, No. 1564, p. 482.

23 *iti śrīmīmāṃsakaśaṃkarabhaṭṭātmajaraṅganāthabhaṭṭadāmodarabhaṭṭanṛsiṃha bhaṭṭānujanīlakaṇṭhakṛtavyavahāratattvaṃ samāptam*. Text given in Kane 1926: Appendix A, p. 973. An identical list of the four brothers appears in the the colophon to Nīlakaṇṭha's Nītimayūkha (Gharpure 1925:67).

24 *eṣāṃ kalivarjyāvarjyādiviveko smajjyeṣṭhabhrātṛbhaṭṭadāmodarakṛtakalivarjyanirṇayād avaseyaḥ*. Cited by Kane 1926:xiii.

25 I hope to publish before long an edition and translation of the Gādhivaṃśavaraṇa.

———. 1968, 1975. *History of Dharmaśāstra*, Vol.I, 2nd ed. Poona: Bhandarkar Oriental Research Institute.

Krishnamachariar, M. 1937. *History of Classical Sanskrit Literature*. Madras: Tirumalai-Tirupati Devasthanam's Press, Madras. Reprint. 1984. Delhi: Motilal Banarsidass.

Krishnamacharya, Pandit V. 1947. *A Descriptive Catalogue of Sanskrit Manuscripts in the Adyar Library, Vol. VI, Grammar, Prosody and Lexicography*. Madras: The Adyar Library.

———. 1947. "Two Rare Commentaries on the *Śāstradīpikā*", *Adyar Library Bulletin*, Vol. XI, Part 4, pp. 257-262.

———. 1952. *A Descriptive Calalogue of Sanskrit Manuscripts in the Adyar Library, Vol. IX, Mīmāṃsā and Advaita Vedānta*. Madras: The Adyar Library.

Mandalik, Viśvanāth Nārāyaṇ (ed. and trans.). 1880. *The Vyavahāra Mayūkha* (of Nīlakaṇṭha Bhaṭṭa). Bombay: Printed at the Education Society's Press, Byculla.

Müller, Klaus-Werner. 1992. *Das Brahmanische Totenritual nach der Antyeṣṭipaddhati des Nārāyaṇa Bhaṭṭa*. Stuttgart: Steiner.

Rāghavan, V. et al. (ed.). 1949-. *New Catalogus Catalogorum*. Madras: University of Madras. Revised ed. 1968-.

Salomon, Richard (ed. and trans.). 1985. *The Bridge to the Three Holy Cities, Nārāyaṇa Bhaṭṭa's Tristhalīsetu*. Delhi: Motilal Banarsidass.

Śaṃkarabhaṭṭa, *Mīmāṃsābālaprakāśa* (ed.). Mukundaśāstri Aḍakara. 1902. Kāśī.

———. *Mīmāṃsāsārasaṃgraha* (ed.). Lakṣmaṇa Śāstri Draviḍa. 1904.

Shastri, Hariprasad. 1912. "Dakshini Pandits at Benares", *Indian Antiquary*, Vol.41, pp. 7-12.

———. 1923. *A Descriptive Catalogue of Sanskrit Manuscripts in the Government Collection Under the Care of the Asiatic Society of Bengal, Vol. II, Vedic Manuscripts*. Calcutta: The Asiatic Society of Bengal.

———. 1925. *A Descriptive Catalogue of Sanskrit Manuscripts in the Government Collection Under the Care of the Asiatic Society of Bengal, Vol. III, Smṛti Manuscripts*. Calcutta: The Asiatic Society of Bengal.

Sircar, D.C. 1960. *Geography of Ancient and Medieval India*. Delhi: Motilal Banarsidass.

Tripathi, Shiva Shankar. (ed.). 1983. *Bhaṭṭavaṃśakāvya* by Kāntanātha Bhaṭṭa. Allahabad: Bhartiya Manisha Sutram.

MADHAV M. DESHPANDE

Pandit and Professor: Transformations in the 19th Century Maharashtra

During my school years in Pune, I came in contact with a variety of Sanskrit teachers. Some of these teachers were addressed as Pandit or Shastri, others as Professor. In their general use, these terms categorized people's perceptions of a person's identity. For instance, among my teachers, Pandit Vāmanaśāstrī Bhāgavat was never addressed as Professor, and Professor Mohan Dhadphale was never addressed as Pandit. However, there were other personalities in Pune who seemed to be included in both of these categories, e.g. Professor S.D. Joshi was called Panditji, and Professor K.V. Abhyankar was called Mahāmahopādhyāya and Śāstrī. Thus, while the terms Pandit, Shastri, and Professor may prototypically represent memberships in markedly different categories, these categories nonetheless have overlapping areas. In my Preface to "Pāṇinian Studies, Professor S.D. Joshi Felicitation Volume", I have briefly traced the transformation of S.D. Joshi from a Pandit to a Professor. In my presentation today, I would like to trace this transformation in the 19th century broadly in the region of Maharashtra, and more specifically in the city of Pune.[1]

Maharashtra, before the takeover of Pune by the British forces in 1818, was a major center of traditional Sanskrit scholarship. From the Dharmaśāstra author Hemādri to the grammarian Nāgeśa, Maharashtra produced illustrious Sanskrit scholars. Especially beginning with Nāgeśa, the unbroken transmission of grammatical scholarship in *guru-śiṣya* lineages can be traced in Maharashtra to this day, and I myself have felt proud to have had teachers like Professor S.D. Joshi[2] who belonged to *guru-śiṣya* lineages going back to Nāgeśabhaṭṭa. While the charts of these lineages provided by Kielhorn[3] and K.V. Abhyankar[4] indeed give a sense of continuity of the tra-

1 For some general accounts of education, and Sanskrit education in particular, in the 19th century Pune, see: Bhate 1996, Walimbe 1974. For detailed accounts of Sanskrit traditions and their transformations in the region of Maharashtra, see: K.V. Abhyankar 1954, Kelkar 1915, and Dandekar 1972. For an enlightening discussion of patronage for languages and literature during the Peshwa period, see Dadoba Pandurang (1865, Introduction).

2 S.D. Joshi studied with his uncle Maheśvar Śāstrī Joshi, who was a student of Śaṅkar Śāstrī Mārulkar. Among Śaṅkar Śāstrī's teachers was Vāsudev Śāstrī Abhyankar, who, as explained later, is in direct line of Nāgeśabhaṭṭa's disciples.

3 *Paribhāṣenduśekhara*, Pt. II, Preface, p. xxv.

4 K.V. Abhyankar 1954:99-101. The chart shows only one European name, i.e. Kielhorn, as the student of Anantashastri Pendharkar, and Bhandarkar as Kielhorn's student.

dition of Sanskrit learning in Maharashtra, these charts by themselves do not provide us any indication of the profound transformation in this tradition of learning which occurred in this region over the past two hundred years.

Before the coming of the British rule to Pune, the Marathi Brahmins were not only known for their Sanskritic learning, but they were also deeply involved in political, military, administrative, and financial occupations. While Brahmins like Hemādri in the role of ministers were known from the days of the Yādava rule in the 13th century, their importance in Maharashtra steadily grew under the rule of the Peshwas, the Brahmin prime ministers of the successors of the famous Maratha king Shivaji. Referring to this period, the Viśvaguṇādarśacampū (verses 133-152) of Veṅkaṭādhvarin presents a fascinating pros-and-cons argument about the Maharashtrian Brahmins. They have now abandoned the study of the Vedas and are flocking to study Persian in order to serve the Muslim rulers of the region. On the positive side, they are also given the credit for having protected and preserved Hindu religious traditions under very difficult circumstances. This variety of pulls on the lives of Brahmins in the region is seen in many ways. The Brahmin Peshwas, who were the de-facto rulers of the region, had to act in a Kṣatriya mode, and this tension is illustrated in the story of Rāmaśāstrī Prabhuṇe (the judge) and Mādhavarao Peshwa. Because of being busy with Brahmanical rituals, Mādhavarao found less time to pay attention to administrative and military duties. Rāmaśāstrī is believed to have admonished him that if he wanted to spend his time in these rituals and neglect his royal duties, he might as well renounce his Peshwa office and go and live in Banaras (see: Telang in Ranade. 1900:132-3).

Under the Peshwas, the Brahmins not only prospered in administrative and military roles,[5] the Peshwas offered substantial financial inducements

---

5 Ranade (1915:350) says: "One other general feature, which distinguishes the first period under Shivaji and Shahu from the period which followed the establishment of the Peshwa's power at Poona, relates to the fact that while most of the great military commanders in the earlier period were Mahrattas, with the notable exception of the Peshwas themselves, the men who rose to distinction in the latter half of the century were, for the most part, Brahmins." Ranade goes on to provide details of the roles Brahmins played under the Peshwas and the privileges they acquired for themselves (pp.351-2): "The Brahmins at this time came to regard themselves as a governing caste with special privileges and exemptions, which were unknown under the system founded by Shivaji. The Konkanastha Brahmin Karkoons, who had the monopoly of all the Secretariat or Daftar offices, and received respectable salaries, obtained the privilege of having their goods exempted from Custom duties and ferry charges when they imported grain and other goods from outside ports and places. The Brahmin land-holders in the Kalyan Prant, and also in Maval, had their lands assessed at half or lower rates than were levied from other classes. In criminal courts, the Brahmins had always enjoyed the exceptional privilege of exemption from the extreme penalty of the law, and even when they were confined in forts, they were more liberally treated than the other classes. Besides these advantages, they had the monopoly of the charities freely bestowed by the state

for the propagation of Sanskrit scholarship.[6] Each year, in the month of Śrāvaṇa, the Peshwas distributed Dakṣiṇā to a large number of Brahmins who gathered in Pune.[7] The tradition of annually distributing Dakṣiṇā to Vaidikas and Shastris was initiated by the Maratha king Shahu's commander Dābhāḍe. This was subsequently taken over by the first Bājīrao Peshwa. The amount of Dakṣiṇā distributed by him in 1736 is said to have been Rupees 16,354. With the expansion of the power of the Peshwa, this amount increased by 1758 to Rupees 1,800,000. We are told that in the year 1770, the Peshwa distributed Dakṣiṇā in Pune to 39,912 Brahmins who had come from all parts of India, north and south. They were rewarded according to the level of their accomplishments in the Vedas and Śāstras. Besides this distribution of Dakṣiṇā by the Peshwas, many other Maratha chiefs gave patronage to traditional learning which flourished in several other centers like Vai, Paithan, Nashik, and Pandharpur, besides Pune.[8] The Sanskrit education was provided by learned individuals at their homes, and there was little institutional structure available during this period. There is substantial evidence of the movement of students and scholars between the regional centers in Maharashtra and the transregional centers like Banaras.

In the November of 1817, the British forces defeated the army of the 2nd Bājirao Peshwa in Pune and the governance of the region passed into the hands of Mountstuart Elphinstone. He was the British resident at the Peshwa court before their fall and knew the region very well. In its declaration of February 11, 1818, the British East India Company assured the population of the region that there will be no interference in the religious and cultural life of the people. In the March of 1818, Mountstuart Elphinstone called an assembly of the local people in Pune and, like the Peshwas he replaced, he distributed Dakṣiṇā to the Brahmin Shastris and Pandits.[9]

---

on this class in consideration of their sanctity. The record which relates to the time of Bajirao II bears ample testimony to the extent of the abuses which followed this indulgence. The Dakshana charity, started with a view to encourage learning, became a grant generally to all Brahmins, and Poona became a centre of a large pauper population. As many as 30 to 40 thousand Brahmins were fed for days together at state expense at the great festivals with the costliest viands." For a recent analysis of the rise of Brahmins under the Peshwas, see Gordon 1993:185.

6 See: *Vedaśāstradīpikā*, Preface, p. 1; Ranade (1900:58-59) for the history of Dakṣiṇā.

7 Ranade 1915:373.

8 Grant Duff (1826, Vol. III, p. 355) says: "The great Mahdoo (= Madhava) Rao confined the donations principally to poor Bramins, whose proficiency in science and mythology entitled them to distinction; and the rewards were conferred in proportion to their acquirements, moral conduct, and sanctity. During the reign of the second Bajee Rao, though a portion was always reserved as the reward for learning, it degenerated into an indiscriminate distribution, dictated by the superstitious idea of feeding and bestowing on Bramins, as an atonement for sin."

9 Grant Duff (1826, Vol. III, pp. 355-6) says: "Many poor Bramins, however, had become greatly dependent on this charity, and therefore to have stopped it at once would have been inconsistent with the humane munificence which pervaded every act of the

However, there was not going to be a mere continuation of the old ways under the new rule of the British. In 1824, Elphinstone announced his policies regarding the education of the people of the region. This included the following:[10]

1. To improve the teaching methods in schools and to increase their number.
2. To provide textbooks to vernacular schools.
3. To encourage the lower classes of the society to make use of the educational facilities.
4. To publish books in the regional languages.
5. To open schools for a western-style education and to encourage people to make use of the western education in English.

Thus, with the coming of the British rule, the concept of education, at least for the Brahmins of the region, suddenly acquired broader dimensions. Beside the continuation of traditional Sanskrit education, the Brahmin community, now under the British auspices, was pulled into both the new dimensions: vernacular education and English education. The Bombay Native School Book and School Society was established in 1823. It aimed at the spread of education in the local vernacular, Marathi, and also in the preparation and publication of textbooks in Marathi for these schools. The first government school in Marathi opened in Bombay in 1818, while a similar school opened in Pune in 1824.

The last Peshwa, Bajirao, used to distribute 500,000 Rupees per year as Dakṣiṇā to Brahmin Pandits and Vaidika reciters. After the takeover by the British, Elphinstone sought approval from the Company authorities to spend 200,000 Rupees per year for educational purposes.[11] Initially he decided to offer grants to Brahmin scholars who were experts in traditional Sanskrit and Vedic scholarship and in the "more useful" fields like those of Dharmaśāstra and Mathematics. He appointed William Chaplin to oversee the proper utilization of the Dakṣiṇā funds.

British government in the conquered territory; but to have continued that promiscuous alms to all Bramins, who chose to collect at Poona for the purpose, would have been a wasteful, and in many respects a useless and pernicious expenditure. It was at first therefore bestowed under certain limitations; the portion assigned to men of learning was duly distributed; and that the benefit to the country might be rendered more essentially important, as the donations at the Dukshina were circumscribed, a Hindu college was instituted at Poona, where the minds of the youth might acquire such instruction in their own way, as they are disposed to receive in mathematics, astronomy, medicine, & and pains were taken to erase from their elementary books of ethics such principles of morality as have a dangerous or a doubtful tendency."

10 For a detailed discussion of these developments, see: Walimbe 1974, Jog 1965:28 ff.

11 Walimbe 1974:9 ff.

The Poona Hindu College (known locally as Pune Pāṭhaśālā) was established on October 7, 1821, at the annual expense of 15,250 Rupees.[12] There were ten classes and a hundred students. The school aimed at teaching those areas of Sanskrit scholarship which were of some contemporary utility, and also to eventually provide for the western-style education for those who desired such education. A concurrent desire on the part of the British authorities was to "preserve the attachment of the learned Brahmans who had suffered severely by the change of Government, and who had considerable influence over the feelings and conduct of the people at large."[13] With this added purpose, William Chaplin insisted on the appointment of Brahmin teachers even in those areas which were deemed to be of no contemporary practical utility. This school thus taught the subjects of Nyāya, Dharmaśāstra, Vyākaraṇa, Jyotiṣa, Alaṃkāra, Vedānta, Āyurveda, besides Ṛgveda and Yajurveda. All these subjects were taught in traditional ways, and the British officials had only nominal supervision.

Pandit Rāghavācārya was the principal of this Poona Hindu College. Many major figures of this period like Krishnashastri Chiplunkar were students at this school. Until 1837, only traditional Sanskrit subjects were taught in the traditional way, and there was no teaching of English. In the June of 1830, eighteen graduates of this school were awarded prizes totaling 920 Rupees. In 1837, Major Candy was appointed to supervise this school. He introduced the teaching of English. Around this time, many private schools, both missionary schools and native schools opened up in Pune and other centers. These schools gradually led to the spread of education in the vernacular as well as English, besides the traditional Sanskrit education. One of the major difficulty in vernacular education was the lack of trained teachers and the lack of appropriate textbooks in Marathi. Elphinstone encouraged the translation of English books into Marathi. Preparations of textbooks in Marathi was one of the goals of the Native School-book and School Society. It was felt that this task could be done better by English-educated Indians who would transmit the information contained in the English textbooks to their vernacular audiences. The government spent a large amount of 97,233 Rupees from 1826 to 1830 on books prepared and published in vernaculars like Marathi, Gujarati, and Kannada.

---

12 Walimbe (1974). Grant Duff (1826, Vol. III, p. 356) says: "Though the institution of the college which was committed to Mr. Chaplin was at first regarded with some signs of distrust, before the end of 1822 there were one hundred and forty-three Bramins, students or candidates for admission, even before fit teachers for all the branches had been found." Choksey (1976:98) quotes Chaplin's own opinion of Brahmins and their learning: "All their worldly learning (loukeeka viddeea = *laukikavidyā*) consists in the reading of old letters, set forms of correspondence and book-keeping. Their spiritual learning (or vaidyak vidya?) is acquired from the study of the Vedant, Vyakarana, Natuk, the Purans, the Dharmashastra, Jotish or astronomical treatises, the Vadiyak Shastra or treatise on medicine and the Kawe-grunth."

13 Cited in Walimbe 1974:10.

The Marathi Brahmin community was significantly involved in all these developments. Marathi Brahmin Pandits were also working hand in hand with Captain Molesworth on the preparation of a Marathi-English Dictionary, and with figures like Major Candy in the preparation of textbooks in Marathi.[14] Here the Brahmin Pandits were exposed to English education, and they transferred the new contents and the new methods to the vernacular education.[15] For example, Krishnashastri Chiplunkar, a graduate of the Poona Hindu College, prepared a Marathi book on political economy. Bhaushastri Petkar wrote a Marathi book on the history of Greece. Shrikrishnashastri Talekar translated an English book on the history of Rome into Marathi, while Vishnushastri Pandit translated a work on the history of England. Most of the individuals involved in the process of translation of western materials into Marathi were Marathi Brahmins.

In 1851, the Poona Hindu College and government English schools were integrated and a new institution, Poona College, was set up, which eventually branched into Poona College, Poona College School, and Normal School. While English professors taught subjects like English literature, mathematics, and physics, Krishnashastri Chiplunkar[16] was the head of the Sanskrit divisions in all the three branches. He was also appointed as the Assistant Professor for Marathi, one of the first few Marathi persons to hold the western title of Professor. But there were other Pandits like Nīlakaṇṭhaśāstrī Bhaṭ (*dharmaśāstra*), Dhoṇḍaśāstrī (*vyākaraṇa*), Nṛsiṃhācārya (*nyāya*), and Nārāyaṇaśāstrī (*alaṃkāra*) who taught at these schools, but were not given the title or salary of a Professor. In 1859, Dr. Martin Haug was appointed as the first European professor for Sanskrit in Poona College. In 1860, the Deccan College was set up in Pune for higher education, and in the same year the Elphinstone College opened in Bombay. These institutions played a major role in the intellectual and cultural transformation of Brahmins in Maharashtra, as they constituted the majority of students.[17]

Now I would like to take a closer look at how these political and institutional changes affected the lives of particular individuals.

Bāḷśāstrī Jāmbhekar

Bāḷśāstrī Jāmbhekar[18] was perhaps the most prominent Marathi Brahmin figure in the beginning of the British rule in Maharashtra. He was born in 1810 in Konkan in the village of Pomburle. His father was a learned priest and taught his son the Sanskrit poetry. But with the insistence of Mr. Bapu Chatre, another prominent Brahmin, Bāḷśāstrī began to study English. Dur-

---

14 For details, see: Jog 1965:31 ff; Pinge 1960:107 ff; Potdar 1922:15 ff.

15 Walimbe (1974:12).

16 For the details of Krishnashastri Chiplunkar's life, see: Puranik 1992: 17-26.

17 Seal 1971:89.

18 For the details of Balshastri Jambhekar's life and work, see: Potdar 1922:31 ff and Shejwalkar 1977:309 ff.

ing the day, he used to go to the English school, while he would study the Siddhāntakaumudī in the evening. After finishing his education in 1828, he was appointed as an assistant professor in the Elphinstone School in Bombay to teach mathematics. He was fully trained in the traditional subjects of Sanskrit logic and grammar, and now as the first Indian person to be appointed Professor he became very famous. Besides mathematics, he was deeply interested in subjects like history and chemistry. He translated into Marathi an English work on "the object, advantages and pleasures of knowledge". He has published books in Marathi on grammar, geography, ethics, a Marathi translation of the ritual of Sandhyā, and Marathi translations of a number of English works. From 1841, his articles began to appear in the journal of the Bombay Royal Asiatic Society. He knew Marathi, Sanskrit, English and Latin very well, and had working knowledge of Hindustani, Gujarati, Bengali, Kannada, and Persian. He is the first important Sanskrit Pandit of modern Maharashtra who became a transmitter of Western ideas and themes to Marathi audiences, and a traditional pandit to transform himself into a modern scholar.

Krishnashastri Chiplunkar and Vishnushastri Chiplunkar

This transformation of a Sanskrit pandit into a modern scholar was not a simple and easy change. This can be seen in the lives of Krishnashastri Chiplunkar and his illustrious son, Vishnushastri Chiplunkar, whose writings transformed Marathi into a powerful modern language.[19] Krishnashastri was born in Pune in 1824. For the first fourteen years, he studied Veda recitation. Then he intensively studied Sanskrit poetics, logic, and Dharmaśāstra with a famous scholar of the day, Pandit Moraśāstrī Sāṭhe at the Poona Hindu College which was set up by Elphinstone in 1821. When Krishnashastri was studying at this institution, he was the best among his classmates and was given the title "Bṛhaspati" by his teacher, Moraśāstrī Sāṭhe. Such excellence in Sanskrit scholarship was still of no practical use in earning a good living, which only English education could offer. Moraśāstrī himself began studying English at a late age, and also inspired Krishnashastri to do the same. At the age of 25, Krishnashastri began his English education at the Poona Hindu College, where an English-education wing was opened, besides the older Sanskrit wing, by Major Candy. He became a favorite student of his English professors. In 1852, he was appointed "translator exhibitioner", and soon he was given the post of assistant pro-

---

19 For the details of Krishnashastri and Vishnushastri Chiplunkar's life, see: Puranik 1992. Shejwalkar (1977:171) offers a critical review of the contributions of Balshastri Jambhekar and Vishnushastri Chiplunkar and argues that while the first worked to create a modern civil society, the latter worked to promote Brahmanization of Marathi and Maharashtra. On the whole, Shejwalkar (177 ff.) also offers a strong critique of the role of Brahmins in the interpretation of Marathi history as well.

fessor of Marathi at the Poona College. Besides translating Sanskrit works like Meghadūta into Marathi, Krishnashastri wrote a number of works on topics like economics.[20] However, Krishnashastri's transformation from being a Sanskrit pandit to a modern professor came with a cost. S.S. Puranik (1992:25) says:

> "The sad thing is that the same English-education which helped him attain material prosperity also completely uprooted his religious faith. The traditional branches of knowledge which he had so assiduously studied in his younger days were thrown aside in his mature age. Because of the arguments from rationalists like Mill, Darwin, and Huxley, the tower of his religious faith came down crashing. As a result of the English-education, he became a committed atheist."

Krishnashastri Chiplunkar's son, Vishnushastri, rose to even greater prominence in Maharashtra. Vishṇushastri was born in Pune on May 20, 1850. After his home-based education till he was 7 years old, Vishnushastri was sent to the Infant School, a relatively modern institution at that time. Thereafter he went to a series of English, Marathi, and mixed schools, and finally passed his high school matriculation in 1865. His memorization ability was excellent, both for Sanskrit and English materials. He studied Sanskrit at the Poona high school with Krishnashastri Vaijapurkar, who was appointed as a Shastri at the high school. In the January of 1866, Vishnushastri joined the newly opened Deccan College for further education. When Vishnushastri joined the Deccan College, there were European professors like Wordsworth, Oxanham, and Kielhorn, besides the Indian teachers Kerunana Chatre and Anantashastri Pendharkar.

When Kielhorn was appointed as Professor of Sanskrit at the Deccan College, he was very young. But he continued his own intense study of Sanskrit with the local Pandits, among them Anantashastri Pendharkar at the Deccan College. The local students felt that the Shastri knew far more Sanskrit than the Professor.[21] Anantashastri was himself directly in line from the great Nāgeśabhaṭṭa, and was famous for his scholarship in the field of Sanskrit grammar. The students at the Deccan College compared the different styles of teaching of Professor Kielhorn and Anantashastri Pendharkar. Kielhorn would not, and could not, teach a class if he left his books at home. On the other hand, Anantashastri never needed to hold a book in

---

20 Krishnaṣhastri's modern approach is evident in his essays on Marathi grammar (1971).

21 For a negative reaction of Vishnushastri Chiplunkar to Kielhorn, see Vishnushastri Chiplunkar 1891:11. A detailed criticism of the appointment of European professors in Pune and the stature and salary granted to them is found in N.C. Kelkar 1915:39 ff. Kelkar refers to a 1881 article in the Times of India by K.T. Telang on the same issue. He does not mention a specific date, but summarizes Telang's criticisms of European professors in Pune. He refers to similar comments by Bhandarkar and Ganganath Jha. The disparity in salary was a particularly touchy issue.

his hand, and hence while teaching his class he would do other things with his hands, such as cutting the betal nuts. While Kielhorn was studying with Anantashastri at the same institution, he was the Professor and Anantashastri was appointed as a Shastri, and there was a big gap in the salaries paid to Professors and Shastris. This created great tensions among the Professors and Shastris, and Anantashastri, we are told (Puranik 1992:34-35), was so displeased that he would often not pay much attention to his teaching duties. The students themselves made fun of the old-fashioned Shastris. In his introduction (Vijapurkar 1963:7) to the collected articles of Professor V.G. Vijapurkar, M.G. Deshpande reports that when the Deccan College was inaugurated in Pune in 1860, the British authorities intended to offer instruction in Marathi. However, the students insisted that they be taught in English. M.G. Deshpande refers to the chapter titled "The Early Curriculum" in J. Nelson Fraser's book Deccan College 1851-1901 for this debate.

Among his Indian professors, Vishnushastri respected Professor Kerunana Chatre who taught mathematics and astronomy. Among modern Indian professors of his generation, Professor Chatre was known for his observational work in astronomy. However, like Krishnashastri Chiplunkar, the movement toward modernity had conflicted his mind. Puranik (1992:36) reports that with his rationalism, Chatre was no longer convinced about the existence of God, and yet he would unfailingly recite the Viṣṇusahasranāma each day before going to bed, because his grandmother had asked him to do so. Puranik (1992:36) further narrates a conversation between Mr. Anna Saheb Patwardhan and Professor Chatre. When Patwardhan mentioned to Chatre that his recitation of the Viṣṇusahasranāma will lead him to spiritual liberation, Chatre responded that he was not convinced of the existence of God. However, he was going to continue his recitation of the prayer, just in case God did exist. If God did exist, He would be pleased with his prayer, and if He did not exist, it was no big loss!

Trained under such teachers, Vishnushastri Chiplunkar developed into an avid reader of English, Marathi, and Sanskrit materials which were available both at his home and at the library of the Deccan College. He read the works of Greek, Roman, and European historians, literary works of Shakespeare and Milton, and the writings of Macaulay, Addison, and Johnson. He was particularly impressed with the works of Johnson and Macaulay, and in his own writings (collected in his Nibandhamālā), he praises these authors profusely for their vision, insight, and industry. He believed that the English literature reflected the irrepressible desire for freedom, spotless patriotism, and limitless love of learning on the part of the English people, and he called English education "the milk of the tigress". It was this milk of the tigress, the English education, that transformed his outlook and methodology. Without losing his love for the local traditions and patriotism, he openly admired the new ways offered by the English education. This "new outlook" is seen on every page of Vishnushastri's Nibandhamālā, which covers a wide range of literary, religious, historical, linguistic, and political topics. As an example of this "new outlook", I would like to refer to his long articles published in the magazine Śālāpatraka on the Sanskrit authors Kālidāsa, Bhavabhūti, Bāṇa, Subandhu, and Daṇḍin. These essays are a demonstration of the "new methodology" (*navī paddhati* in his words).[22] Each essay begins with a discussion of the date of the respective poet, followed by a description of his works, and ending with a selection of beautiful extracts from the works of this poet. Vishnushastri says:

> "There is little tradition of discussing the good and bad features of poetry in India. Topics such as the true nature of poetry and its connections with the modes of human mind have been appropriately discussed in hundreds of works in the English language, as it has not been done in Sanskrit. The works of Sanskrit poets are filled with treasures of astonishing beauty and relish. But how do our contemporary Pandits appreciate this? This can been seen from their commentaries. Even in the commentaries of great scholars like Mallinātha, we do not find anything but literal meanings of words and a discussion of grammar. We do not find there the sort of indications of poetic beauty as seen in the works of English literary critics."[23]

From Bhavabhūti's works, Vishnushastri endeavors to derive conclusions about his personal life experiences. It was through this "new outlook" derived from his English education that Vishnushastri attempted to resuscitate the love of things Indian among his readers by using a supercharged form of analytical and incisive Marathi prose. D.V. Potdar, in his important work Marāṭhī Gadyācā Iṅgrajī Avatār ("Anglicized Appearance of Marāṭhī Prose", 1922:5 ff), appropriately points out that the Marathi prose produced from the beginning of the English rule in Maharashtra till the appearance of Vishnushastri's works was marked with a secondary "translatory" form and had non-native inspiration.[24] In Vishnushastri's writings, the English education has been fully internalized to lead to the emergence of indigenous analytical approaches.

The contribution of institutions like the Deccan College to this transformation of the Poona Brahmins cannot be overemphasized. Most major figures of the period from the Brahmin community in Maharashtra have gone through these institutions and have been transformed by them in some significant way. Among such figures must be counted persons like Lokamānya B.G. Tilak, his mentor Professor Shridhar Ganesh Jinsiwale, (An-

---

22 These essays are collected in Vishnushastri Chiplunkar (1891) under the title Saṃskṛtakavipañcaka.

23 Vishnushastri Chiplunkar 1891:12.

24 For a similar conclusion, see: Ranade 1915:24 ff, and Jog 1965:44.

nasaheb) Vinayak Patwardhan, (Āhitāgni) Shankar Rajwade, and many others. While in the early part of the 19th century, the old Sanskritic tradition of teaching lived on in the Poona Hindu College, it was slowly combined with English education with the emergence of the Poona College under Major Candy. With the emergence of the Deccan College, there seems to have been a new separation of the traditional Sanskritic education and the new European style education. The traditional Sanskritic education was no longer part of the government-supported institutions, and it had to find its own expressions in the emergence of institutions like the Sanskrit Pāṭhaśālā and the Vedaśāstrottejaka Sabhā. But the Deccan College remained the premier institution of modern education in Pune until the emergence of the Fergusson College in 1885. This bifurcation of the traditional Sanskritic education and the Western education continued into the 20th century Pune.

Shridhar Ganesh Jinsiwale

Shridhar Ganesh Jinsiwale (my great-great-grand-mother's brother, and the first Professor of Sanskrit in my family) was born in 1852 at Ujjain.[25] After his Upanayana, his father Ganeshpant taught him the daily Brahmanical rituals of Sandhyā, Brahmayajña, Saurasūkta, and other recitations of prayers. In Ahmednagar, he was admitted to an English high school. An avid reader, he would sit reading under a public lamp-post near a local mosque late into the night. After 5 years of English high school at Ahmednagar, he went to Pune for higher education in 1868. After his matriculation in 1868, he was awarded three scholarships by the government which allowed him to join the Deccan College, where he was awarded a personal scholarship by its principal, Professor Wordsworth. At that time, besides Professor Wordsworth, Professor Kielhorn also taught at the Deccan College, and so did Kielhorn's own teacher, Anantashastri Pendharkar, as the chief Shastri. Even while living at the Deccan College, Jinsiwale maintained his daily Brahmanical rituals and recited the Bhāgavata-Purāṇa daily. At this college, his interests deepened in the area of literature, history of the world, and politics. In 1873, he passed his B.A. in the subjects of Logic and Moral Philosophy, and in 1876 he passed his M.A. in History and Philosophy. In 1873, he became a Fellow at the Deccan College. In 1878, he was appointed Professor of Sanskrit at the Wilson College in Bombay. As a Fellow at the Deccan College, he taught B.G. Tilak for some time.

While maintaining his personal Brahmanical life-style, Jinsiwale underwent a tremendous personal transformation. He was fully familiar with world history and modern Sanskrit scholarship of the day, and had aquired a personal collection of over 3000 books. I have his personal diaries for the

25 For the details of Jinsiwale's life, see: Gadre 1903.

year 1882, where I see notations for the purchase of books almost on every page. It was this opening up of his mind which made him question some of the deeply held traditional doctrines such as the *apauruṣeyatva* of the Vedas. There are many reports of his public speeches and debates with various religious figures, where he would openly question this traditional doctrine,[26] and advocate a more rational understanding of the Vedas. In the atmosphere of the late 19th century Pune, such a rejection of the *apauruṣeyatva* was not quite politically correct, and it made him unpopular with the local conservatives. His own pupil, B.G. Tilak, was in agreement with Jinsiwale on this issue, and yet Tilak would take a rather non-committal position in public debates, since he perceived it to be counter-productive to his political causes.

On the other extreme was Vinayak (popularly known as Annasaheb) Patwardhan who graduated from the Deccan College in 1868 and then pursued his education in medicine and law. At the Deccan College, Patwardhan developed deep affection for his professors like Kerunana Chatre and Wordsworth. Aprabuddha, Patwardhan's biographer, reports (1926:21) his interactions with Professor Kielhorn. Kielhorn had just joined the Deccan College, and in one of his classes he said that a certain Sanskrit word was obsolete. Patwardhan, with his traditional Brahmanical background, got up and told Kielhorn: "There is no such thing as obsolete in Sanskrit." This argument worsened into a nasty debate and finally the principal of the college, Professor Wordsworth, had to intervene. With his exposure to the Deccan College, Jinsiwale could no longer believe in the traditional doctrine of the *apauruṣeyatva* of the Vedas, while Patwardhan, holding on to the traditional Brahmanical conceptions, fought with his western mentors, without yielding his own ground.

Lokamānya B.G. Tilak

Lokamānya B.G. Tilak, though normally considered to be conservative in comparison with his reformist contemporaries like G.G. Agarkar, is also a prominent example of a personality transformed through English education. Tilak was born in 1856 in Ratnagiri, where he inherited the tradition of Sanskrit learning from his father. He entered the Deccan College in 1873 for higher education, received his B.A. in 1876, and his LL.B. in 1879. As N.R. Inamdar (1983:xxvi) remarks: "Tilak was a child of the renaissance as much as Raja Rammohan Roy, Ranade and Agarkar from his own region. Like his co-workers in the Congress and predecessors and other contemporaries like Vishnushastri Chiplunkar, Tilak had internalised the essence of Western civilization through English education." A vivid picture of Tilak's life as a graduate student at the Deccan College is found in the memoirs left by

---

26 Gadre 1903:29; Rajwade 1980:387.

his classmate Krishnarao Sharangapani of Baroda (Bapat 1925:609-617). The Brahmanical life-style of students at this western-style institution is described by Sharangapani (Bapat 1925:611): "We had in our club students all sitting with silken cloths at dinners, several of them being of orthodox bent of mind performing their Sandhyas and reading Bhagavadgita. Mr. Tilak of course was one of those who used silken cloth at dinner." At the same time, "Tilak was a close reasoner, his method of study being analytical" (Bapat 1925:615).

We are not concerned here with Tilak's political career. But his scholarly publications such as the Gītārahasya, The Arctic Home in the Vedas, and Vedic Chronologies and Vedāṅga-Jyotisha attest to his bold departures from the norms of traditional interpretation of these subjects. The Gītārahasya shows him debating with Śaṅkara, not just using traditional modes of argument, but essentially from an entirely new mode of textual and contextual criticism of the Bhagavadgītā and the Mahābhārata. Referring to Tilak's Gītārahasya, M.R. Jayakar says (S.B. Bapat, 1925:650): "His work on the Bhagavad-Gita has, within my knowledge, shocked many an orthodox scholar, and I knew a scholarly Mīmāṃsaka who considered it a sacrilege even to touch Mr. Tilak's work on the Bhagavad-Gītā. In that book Mr. Tilak carried to a finish, but with a scholar's originality, his tendency towards hard constructive criticism. ... Many times this was done irreverently, but the irreverence arose from a search after higher truth, unfettered by claims of loyalty or orthodoxy." Many instances of Tilak's debates with traditional Sanskrit pandits are recorded by S.B. Bapat (1925).

Tilak's works on astronomy and Vedic pre-history were perhaps his most original contributions. In his Preface to The Arctic Home in the Vedas (p. v), Tilak cites with approval Max Müller's statement emphasizing the need to broaden the study of the Vedas to include many branches of humanistic and physical sciences, and comments: "But alas! it is not given to us to move in an atmosphere like this, and small wonder if Indian students are not found to go beyond the stage of passing the examinations. There is not a single institution in India ... where one can get all up-to-date information on *any* desired subject, so easily obtainable at a seat of learning in the West." In the Introduction to his Vedic Chronology and Vedāṅga Jyotisha (p. 11), Tilak explains his departure from the ways of the traditional pandits:

> "The Vedic texts collected by Weber were not unknown to our old Pandits and the rate at which the equinoctial points retrograded is also so accurately recorded in the ancient astronomical Siddhāntas, that those who would not give any credit for accurate observations to the Hindus ... are obliged to account for it. ... But it was a fixed article of faith with these Pandits that the Vedas were *anādi* (beginning-less) being handed over orally from generation to generation, from time immemorial, and in consequence these Vedic texts were never used

> for any chronological purpose. The introduction of Western education, and with it the modern historical and critical methods, in our schools and colleges, have altered this state of things."

The "new" pandits

It is no wonder that Vishnushastri Chiplunkar, the promoter of "new ways", joined hands with Tilak in establishing in 1880 the New English School, and subsequently in 1885 the Fergusson College. These new Brahmins, i.e. Tilak, Chiplunkar, Apte, Agarkar, and Namjoshi, though proud of their Sanskritic heritage, did not want a turning back in the direction of the traditional Sanskrit education, away from the newly found Western education. In this orientation, the social conservatives and reformers of the period were all of the same opinion. On 24th October 1884, when the original founders of the New English School launched the Deccan Education Society, the Maharaja of Kolhapur was its President, Sir William Wedderburn was the Chairman of the Council, Sir R.G. Bhandarkar was the Vice-Chairman, and V.N. Mandlik and Wordsworth (the Principal of the Deccan College) were its trustees. K.T. Telang, M.G. Ranade, and Professor F.G. Selby (of the Deccan College) served as council-members. Most of the founders of the New English School were past students of the Deccan College. In his foundation speech at the inauguration of the Fergusson College in its current location in 1891, Sir James Fergusson, the Governor of the Bombay Presidency, observed that "far from there being any jealousy at the erection of a new college in the heart of Poona by the established institution of the Deccan College, faculty of the Deccan College hailed it as a child of their own, because it was commenced and carried on by old students of that college" (Sharma 1945:17). V.S. Apte, a graduate of the Deccan College, one of the founders of the New English School and the Deccan Education Society, and the first Principal of the Fergusson College, observed in 1883: "We have undertaken this work of popular education with the firmest conviction and belief that of all agents of human civilization Education is the only one that brings about material, moral, and religious regeneration of fallen countries and raises them up to the level of most advanced nations by slow and peaceful revolutions" (Sharma 1945:10). The self-confidence to open these new institutions and run them efficiently is not unrelated to the academic background of these young promoters. Again Apte said in 1883: "Fortunately, we may say, there would be no great difficulty as to an efficient staff of teachers; for three of us having had the honour of being appointed Fellows at the Deccan College, ... it would not be difficult for us to undertake to teach a P.E. Class after four years' additional experience of the teacher's duty" (Sharma 1945:10). While the founders of these new institutions were nationalists, they had no illusions about what brought about this educational transformation. Apte says: "... but we are fully certain that it (= establishment of more educational institutions) will come under the benign rule of the present rulers, who unlike the former conquerors of India that were only territorial conquerors, have won the hearts of the people by showering on them innumerable blessings *of which Education is the greatest*" (Sharma 1945:11). Speaking on the Indian Universities Act, G.K. Gokhale declared on 18th December 1903:

> "Let not Government imagine that unless the education imparted by Colleges is the highest which is at the present day possible, it is likely to prove useless and even pernicious; and secondly let not the achievements of our graduates in the intellectual field be accepted as the sole, or even the most important, test to determine the utility of this education. I think, my Lord,—and this is a matter of deep conviction with me—that *in the present circumstances of India, all Western Education is valuable and useful.* If it is the highest under the circumstances is possible, so much the better. But even if it is not the highest, it must not on that account be rejected. I believe, the life of the people, whether in the political or social or industrial or intellectual field, is an organic whole, and no striking progress in any particular field is to be looked for unless there be room for the free movement of the energies of the people in all fields. To my mind, the greatest work of Western education in the present state of India is not so much the encouragement of learning as the liberation of the Indian mind from the thraldom of old-world ideas, and the assimilation of all that is highest and best in the life and thought and character of the West. *For this purpose not only the highest but all Western education is useful*" (Sharma 1945:18).

The literary contributions of the faculty members of the Fergusson College in those early days are a remarkable demonstration of the emergence of modernity in the field of Indian Education, of which Sanskrit education was only a small part (Sharma 1945:61 ff).

This "liberation of the Indian mind from the thraldom of old-world ideas" was something that was shared by individuals, who were, otherwise, on opposite sides of many other issues. It is important to note that while Sir R.G. Bhandarkar and Tilak were often on opposite sides on the question of social reform and political methods, they were not far apart in their modern approach to the study of Sanskrit texts and Indian antiquity. In his reminiscences about Tilak, Professor S.K. Belvalkar (Bapat 1925:61-74) cites several instances of Bhandarkar approving Tilak's conclusions on certain issues, and Tilak himself expressing his satisfaction about Bhandarkar's approval of his ideas.

Ramakrishna Gopal Bhandarkar

A senior contemporary of Tilak, Ramakrishna Gopal Bhandarkar (1837-1925), played a crucial role in the transition of education in Maharashtra to modernity. He was born in a Sārasvata Brahmin family in Malwan on the Konkan coast. After completing his early education in an English-language school at Ratnāgiri, he matriculated from the Elphinstone High School in Bombay in 1854, and was awarded B.A. in 1858. With the award of a Dakṣiṇā fellowship he joined the Poona College and received his M.A. degree in Sanskrit in 1863. From 1868 to 1882 he was appointed Professor of Sanskrit. After Professor Kielhorn retired from Deccan College in Pune, Bhandarkar was appointed in his place in 1882, where he taught until he retired in 1893. Bhandarkar was the first fully modern Indian professor, who did not come from a Pandit background, and acquired Sanskrit through institutions like the Deccan College. In the diagram of *guru-śiṣya* lineages, K.V. Abhyankar (1954:101) records Kielhorn to be the disciple of Anantashastri Pendharkar, and Bhandarkar as the disciple of Kielhorn. In his presidential address at the First All-India Oriental Conference held at Pune in 1919, Bhandarkar refers to two classes of learned men: "(i) There are the Pandits of the old school who have spent long years in studying, in the traditional way, the authoritative Sanskrit texts of different branches of Sanskrit learning such as Vyākaraṇa and Nyāya. Their studies, exclusively confined to particular branches, are, no doubt, deep and sound, but they are lacking in historical, comparative, and critical outlook. (ii) Then there are those scholars who have been studying the literature of the country and the inscriptions and antiquities scattered in different provinces, by the application of the historical, comparative, and the critical method" (Bhandarkar 1933: Vol. I, p. 316). Bhandarkar obviously belonged to the second category.[27]

Bhandarkar's explicit departure from the traditional Sanskritic modes of thought in the direction of the contemporary critical scholarship from Germany may be seen in his suggestions for research on the Vedas (1933: Vol. I, p. 398):

> "The text of the Ṛgveda, there is reason to suppose, is not quite the same as it was originally. Some Sūktas and Ṛks are found in the other

27 In his own time, Bhandarkar was a controversial figure. His reformist social and religious ideas earned him both admirers and detractors. He was accused of being an opportunist and a collaborationist. For a critique of Bhandarkar, in comparison with V.K. Rajwade, see Shejwalkar 1977:376. The fact that Bhandarkar came from the Sārasvata Brahmin background also contributed to some of this negative feeling. Most of the other prominent Marathi Brahmins who were active in this period were Konkanastha Brahmins, and there was strong caste-based tension. The other Brahmins in Maharashtra (i.e. Konkanastha, Deśastha, and Karhade Brahmins) looked down upon the Sārasvata Brahmins. The open animosity between the different Brahmin groups is seen, for instance, in the debate over the caste of Bhaṭṭojī Dīkṣita in the book Bhaṭṭojidīkṣitajñātiviveka by V.A. Bambardekar, 1939, Bombay.

Vedas, and there the readings in some cases are different. What the original readings were will have to be determined, if at all possible, by comparing the variation and taking a good many other facts into consideration. The way has been shown by Oldenberg, and it is quite open to any of us to follow it."

Bhandarkar in some ways went much further than his European mentor, Professor Kielhorn, in modernizing the teaching of Sanskrit for the newly emerging schools and colleges. In 1870, Kielhorn's A Grammar of the Sanskrit Language was published "at the request and under the patronage of Mr. J.B. Peile, the Director of Public Instruction in this Presidency" and "is intended principally for Indian students. It contains as much of the Sanskrit accidence as is necessary for the ordinary B.A. examination. Those who look higher, I refer to the Siddhānta-Kaumudī and other indigenous works on grammar, without a careful study of which a scholarlike knowledge of the Sanskrit language appears to me unattainable (Preface, p. vii)." However, while Kielhorn produced an excellent reference grammar, it was not very useful for teaching Sanskrit. The first successful modern teaching grammar books for Sanskrit in India were produced by Bhandarkar, i.e. his First Book of Sanskrit and Second Book of Sanskrit.

In the Preface to the First Edition of his First Book of Sanskrit dated March 1864, Bhandarkar narrates the then current situation of Sanskrit education and the need for a new method of teaching Sanskrit:

"The study of Sanskrit has but recently risen in the estimation of the educated natives of this Presidency and of our educational authorities. The old Sanskrit College of Poona owed its existence and continuance rather to a spirit of conciliation and toleration in our rulers than to their conviction of the utility of Sanskrit as a branch of general education. The modern critical and progressive spirit was not brought to bear upon it. The old Śāstris were allowed to carry all things in their own way. After about thirty years since its establishment, the authorities began to exercise active interference, until at length the College was abolished and a new system inaugurated. ... This newly-awakened and more enlightened zeal in favour of Sanskrit cannot last, or produce extensive results, unless books are prepared to facilitate the general study of that language. ... Sanskrit would be considerably more easy than it is, if there were men educated in our English Colleges to teach it, and if books specially adapted for beginners were available."

Bhandarkar's books were meant to meet this need.

From all accounts, as teaching tools, Bhandarkar's books were enormously popular and successful. They were in fact so popular that they were quickly translated into Marathi to meet the needs of those modern students who went to Marathi schools. Vinayak Narayan Shastri, who was a Sanskrit teacher at the General Assembly's Institution in Bombay, translated Bhandarkar's First Book of Sanskrit into Marathi, and this Marathi version was directly supervised by Bhandarkar himself and was published by the Department of Public Instruction, Bombay. In the Sanskrit Preface to the second edition of this Marathi translation published in 1878, Vinayak Narayan Shastri says that there were no appropriate books to teach Sanskrit in Marathi schools and this need is now fulfilled by his translation of Bhandarkar's books. It is important to note that a Shastri was persuaded to make available Bhandarkar's modern method of teaching Sanskrit in Marathi schools.

V. S. Apte

V. S. Apte (1858-92), who was a student of Kielhorn at the Deccan College and is widely known for his Practical Sanskrit-English Dictionary, also produced an equally important modern tool for teaching Sanskrit at the newly emerging educational institutions in Pune, i.e. his The Student's Guide to Sanskrit Composition. In his Preface to the second edition which appeared in 1885, Apte remarks: "The rapid sale of a large edition in less than three years shows that the book, in some measure, supplied a felt want." Bhandarkar was a major promoter of Apte's modernist work, and Apte explicitly acknowledges his assistance: "I must not omit to tender my most sincere thanks to Dr. R.G. Bhandarkar, who was kind enough to spare time to go over the greater portion of the book with me, and to make several important suggestions which have been mostly acted upon; and secondly, to Mr. Lee Warner, Acting Director of Public Instruction who, at the recommendation of Dr. Bhandarkar, was pleased to sanction the work for use in High Schools." In 1891, V.S. Apte published the first edition of his Kusumamālā, which as the English title explains, was "a collection of choice extracts from standard Sanskrit writers in prose and verse, No. II, designed for students preparing for the matriculation examination, with explanatory notes." The use of English as the medium of instruction to teach Sanskrit had become well established by this time. In his Preface to the First Edition, Apte says: "Difficult words and expressions have been explained in the notes, but mere words have not been given, as Sanskrit-English Dictionaries are now accessible to even the poorest student. ... Thus the book is intended to supply the want of a Sanskrit reading book hitherto felt by senior students in High Schools." By 1901, this book underwent three editions, and by 1929, the twentieth edition had been published. In the Preface to the Third Edition, M.S. Apte joyfully refers to "the rapid sale of the first two editions". V.S. Apte was Professor of Sanskrit and the first Principal of the Fergusson College.

Other "new" graduates of institutions like the Deccan College also tried to extend the new teaching materials produced by R.G. Bhandarkar. One such instance is that of Sakharam Ramchandra Kirloskar, B.A. He describes himself as "Assistant Master, Elphinstone High School, Sometime Dakshina Fellow, Deccan College". In 1876, Kirloskar published a book titled " 'Gadyapadyāvalī', or Readings in Sanskrit: Prose & Verse, being a series of extracts from various Sanskrit works", with annotations. The book is dedicated "to F. Kielhorn Esq, Ph.D., Professor of Oriental Languages, Deccan College, as a token of sincere gratitude, for his many kindnesses". The Preface explains the purpose of the book: "These Extracts are intended to serve as a Reading Book for advanced Sanskrit students. They will be found especially adapted to the wants of those who have mastered, more or less thoroughly, Professor Bhandarkar's First Book and Second Book of Sanskrit." Bhandarkar's modernist project was quickly gaining followers, who were pushing it forward with added enthusiasm.

We should also note other contemporaries of R.G. Bhandarkar,[28] namely Shankar Pandurang Pandit, Mahadeo Moreshwar Kunte, K.T. Telang, and V.N. Mandalik. S.P. Pandit published a magnificent edition of the Śaunakīya Atharvaveda[29] with Sāyaṇa's Bhāṣya in four volumes (1895-98), and M.M. Kunte published in 1880 a prize-winning book: Vicissitudes of Aryan Civilization in India. Telang's English translation of the Bhagavadgītā,[30] the Sanatsujātīya, and the Anugītā appeared in the Sacred Books of the East (Vol. VIII) in 1900, and Mandlik published the voluminous edition of the Manusmṛti with eight commentaries in three volumes in 1886 (Bombay, Ganpat Krishnaji's Press). It were these scholars, including Tilak, who made a name as modern Sanskrit scholars, and came to be recognized as such by the contemporary European scholars.

---

28 For a general survey of the literary contributions of Indian graduates of this generation, see: Ranade 1915:311-312.

29 The excellence of Pandit's edition was deeply admired by W.D. Whitney who used it while producing his English translation of the Śaunakīya-Atharvaveda. Pandit's modernity and departure from the tradition may be illustrated by his description of his encounter with a traditional reciter of the Atharvaveda: "He was more shocked that the several mss. of that Veda ... exhibited numerous varieties of reading, and still more horrified when he found that the text he knew by heart and which was as it had been improved by Gaṇeś Bhaṭ Dādā was the worse for improvements" (Atharvaveda, VVRI edition, Vol. I, p. xvii).

30 In his Introduction (p. 5) to his translation of the Bhagavadgītā (Sacred Books of the East, Vol. VIII), Telang questions Wheeler's argument that the Mahābhārata represents an attempt to Brahmanize the history of the great war, but has his own doubts: "While, however, I am not prepared to admit the cogency of Mr. Wheeler's arguments, I am not, on the other hand, to be understood as holding that the Gītā must be accepted as a genuine part of the original Mahābhārata. I own that my feeling on the subject is something akin to that of the great historian of Greece regarding the Homeric question, a feeling of painful diffidence regarding the soundness of any conclusion whatever. While it is impossible not to feel serious doubts about the critical condition of the Mahābhārata generally; while, indeed, we may be almost certain that the work has been tampered with from time to time; it is difficult to come to a satisfactory conclusion regarding any particular given section of it." Also see Shejwalkar 1977:333 ff.

These "new" scholars also worked to promote vernacular education, and for the spread of the ideas contained in Sanskrit and English works through their vernacular translations. The government-sponsored Dakṣiṇā Prize Committee was a significant tool in this effort. For instance, the Jānakīpariṇayanāṭaka of Rāmabhadra Dīkṣita was translated into Marathi by Ganesh Shastri Lele and published in 1865 under the auspices of the Dakṣiṇā Prize Committee, with a second edition in 1866. The secretary of the Dakṣiṇā Prize Committee during the year 1865 was Krishna Shastri Chiplunkar, while the secretary during the year 1866 was Shankar Pandurang Pandit, the editor of the Śaunakīya-Atharvaveda, who was himself involved in a project of the translation of the Vedas into Marathi under the title Vedārthayatna. This was a new use of the old Dakṣiṇā funds.

Referring to this generation of newly emerging Indian scholars, R.N. Dandekar (1978:7-8) makes some valuable comments:

> "Since about 1870, Indian scholars, who had been trained in the newly started universities and who had thereby become acquainted with the methodology and results of western scholarship, began seriously to cultivate Indological studies in their own country. ... But they seem to have started with a kind of inferiority complex. On the one hand, they felt rather inordinately proud and jubilant at the new theory that the Indians belonged to the same stock as the Europeans, and, on the other, they were always on the defensive against the patronizing and mildly contemptuous attitude of the European scholars ..., and, therefore, in order to counteract that attitude, indulged in self-glorification by making exaggerated claims about their ancient heritage. ... But the most significant result of these developments was that the Indians no longer remained a passive object, like guineapigs in a scientist's laboratory, to be dissected and studied by European scholars."

One can detect this phenomenon in M.M. Kunte's 1880 book The Vicissitudes of Aryan Civilization in India. In his Preface (p. x), Kunte pleads: "Though I may have failed to establish my conclusions, I may safely believe that on that account the service to the cause of Indian history cannot be undone. As yet, Indians themselves have not undertaken seriously the investigation of important historical problems connected with their own country. But they have a stand-point of their own—a stand-point fixed by their antecedents, and the traditions of their country, a stand-point supported by overwhelming evidence, and a stand-point, which at once encourages and gratifies patriotism." Kunte's nationalist agenda is explicitly stated at the end of his Introduction (p. xxv): "Our motto is—There is a glorious future before the Āryas in India, now that their activities, dormant for centuries and threatening to become petrified, are likely to be revived and quickened by the ennobling and elevating many-sided civilization which the Western Āryas have developed, and which is brought to bear upon them." In appealing to the "Western Āryas", Kunte was essentially appropriating the discourse of the British Indologists of his times.[31]

Vaman Shastri Islampurkar

There was some tension between the promoters of the traditional teaching of Sanskrit and the modern teachers of Sanskrit typified by R.G. Bhandarkar. The modern teachers did not believe that the pandits had any critical sense, and the traditionalists did not see any depth in the knowledge of the modernists. This tension is best expressed by Vaman Shastri Islampurkar in the Preface to his 1889 edition and Marathi translation of Kālidāsa's Meghadūta. Islāmpurkar says (pp. 2-7):

> "Anyone who wishes to have a full understanding of Marathi must study at least some Sanskrit. ... It is obvious that the understanding of Sanskrit can only be acquired through the language with which one is most familiar. Before the spread of English in India, people residing in different regions used to gain knowledge of Sanskrit through the local regional languages. However, these days, due to the extensive spread of English, most students try to acquire the knowledge of Sanskrit through English. This is not the only difference. The teaching methods have changed completely. In the old ways, first the student had to memorize the paradigms, the Samāsacakra, and the Amarakośa, and then they taught him the Raghuvaṃśa, or some other poem. Once the student has good understanding of Sanskrit words and their meanings, then they used to teach him the Siddhāntakaumudī. This allowed a student proper entrance into Sanskrit. After that they used to teach him, according to his desire, logic, grammar, philosophy, or some other śāstra. ... These days an entirely new teaching system has come into vogue. Having adopted the English language of the foreigners, people are now studying Sanskrit through that medium, which is totally incongruous with it. In small and large (modern) schools, Sanskrit has been given a secondary place. There-

---

31 For a detailed discussion of the conceptions of the British orientalists, see: Trautmann 1997, and especially p. 5 for the Sanskrit inscription on the Clarendon Building:
śāleyaṃ prācyaśāstrāṇāṃ jñānottejanatatparaiḥ /
paropakāribhiḥ sadbhiḥ sthāpitāryopayoginī //1//
...
īśānukampayā nityam āryavidyā mahīyatām /
āryāvartāṅglabhūmyoś ca mitho maitrī vivardhatām //2//
"This building, dedicated to Eastern sciences, was founded for the use of the Aryas (Indians and Englishmen) by excellent and benevolent men desirous of encouraging knowledge. ... By the favour of God may the learning and literature of India be ever held in honour; and may the mutual friendship of India and England constantly increase!"

> fore, no one feels the need to study it beyond merely memorizing statements like '*vad*, to speak' which is sufficient to pass the examinations. Because of this strange (westernized) educational system, all knowledge has become bookish. Many degree-holders who have graduated from (these modern) universities are very proud of their having passed (the examinations) in Sanskrit. However, those who have not done any special study cannot read even one verse. Many people have seen such cases. But, now look at a person who has studied Sanskrit in the old ways. Even after many dozens of years after leaving the study of Sanskrit, such a person will not make errors in reading or writing. It is not the fault of the (modern) degree-holders that they lack the proper understanding of Sanskrit. It is the fault of the modern educational system."

In spite of such criticisms of the new ways of studying and teaching Sanskrit, Vāman Shastri Islampurkar finally ended up in Bombay, and he started working there under Dr. John Wilson. After he published his Marathi translation and annotations for the Meghadūta, he received favorable reviews from Professor Kielhorn and Professor R.G. Bhandarkar. Islampurkar proudly includes these reviews in the footnotes to his Preface (pp. 6-7) to the second edition. Islampurkar's own annotations go in the modernist direction in trying to simplify the complexities of the Sanskrit text of the Meghadūta for its Marathi readers.[32] In his letter sent to Vishnushastri Pandit, a friend of Islampurkar, Kielhorn says [my English rendition of Islampurkar's Marathi version of Kielhorn's note]:

> "I have carefully read the first issue of the *Kāvyārthadīpikā* composed by your friend, Mr. Vaman Shastri Islampurkar. I am pleased to say that this book is extremely useful for those who wish to learn Sanskrit through the medium of Marathi. The commentary is very accessible, and there is nothing left for students to exercise their brains! I wonder if they will become too lazy. Yet the author's efforts are praiseworthy. I hope the people will make use of this book and make your friend's efforts fruitful."

While Bhandarkar and others mentioned above represented one end of the spectrum of the emerging new Sanskrit scholarship, the traditional Sanskrit scholarship continued to flourish in Pune, though indeed under somewhat changing circumstances. The trend toward modern education including Sanskrit created a feeling among the people that the traditional

---

32 We may note that in 1886, Islampurkar published the first five cantos of the Kumārasambhava with Marathi annotation as part of his Kāvyārthadīpikā series (Bombay: S.N. Chitale & Associates). Before beginning the text, Islampurkar adds a section titled *Paribhāṣā* 'terminology', where he explains different Sanskrit tenses etc. in Marathi, but cites their English names as well.

Sanskrit education will not survive unless some special efforts were made.[33] Many prominent people in Pune came together in 1875 to establish the Vedaśāstrottejaka Sabhā ("Society for the Encouragement of the Study of the Vedas and Śāstras").[34] The initial document of sponsorship for this institution had 150 signatures including those of Mahadeo Govind Ranade and Mahadeo Moreshwar Kunte. Many of these supporters were themselves not traditional Sanskrit scholars, but were graduates of the western-style institutions like the Deccan College. These new Brahmins[35] worked hand in hand with scholars of the old school such as Ram Dikshit Apte, Narayan Shastri Godbole, and Janardan Bhataji Abhyankar.[36] Reformist members like Ranade and Kunte wanted to emphasize a more modernist approach in the functioning of this institution, though compared to other institutions, this institution remained relatively conservative. The Vedaśāstrottejaka Sabhā has continued to function in Pune to this date. Some modernist dimensions have entered in its examinations. For example, I myself remember having to present a speech in Sanskrit on the history of the Sanskrit literature. While the requirement reflected a more modernist tendency, the speech had to be in Sanskrit to fit the rules of the institution. The numbers of students examined and granted degrees in the subjects of Vedas and Śāstras by the Vedaśāstrottejaka Sabhā totaled 2195 during the period 1875-1939 showing the continuing demand for traditional Sanskrit education, besides the rising tide of western education in Pune.

The fear that the traditional ways of studying Sanskrit were dying[37] and that more efforts were needed to preserve what can be preserved becomes

---

33 Pandit Bhimacharya Jhalkikar, the author of the famous Nyāyakośa, says in the Preface to the second edition (dated July 1893): "The knowledge of Sanskrit is, comparatively speaking, dying out in India before the advance of English. A work written, as this is, wholly in Sanskrit is not so much respected and cared for as if the explanations had been put in English. Even our own countrymen do not appreciate works written in Sanskrit until praise of them comes out of the west. I hope my book will seem praiseworthy to foreign scholars like Professors Bühler, Max Müller, Weber and Kielhorn, but still more do I hope that my labours will prove to be of service to those, if they be only a few, whether Hindu or European, who are fellow-students with me of these old philosophies" (Nyāyakośa, 1928 edition, p. 16). The Preface to Vedaśāstradīpikā contains a strong statement of fear that the Sanskritic traditions are dying.

34 Vedaśāstradīpikā, Preface.

35 For the emergence of "new" Brahmins in the 19th century Maharashtra, see: Karve 1963, and Kumar 1968a and 1968b. For broader social and intellectual developments, see: Dobbin 1972, Seal 1971, and Lederle 1976.

36 The same mixture of traditionally trained and western trained individuals is seen among the secretaries of the Vedaśāstrottejaka Sabhā during the period from 1875 to 1938. This list is contained in the Preface to diamond jubilee volume Vedaśāstradīpikā published in Pune in 1941, p. 29. In this list of 20 names, there are many Shastris, but there are more individuals with B.A. and M.A. degrees, besides several Professors.

37 A similar fear for Marathi, due to the rising prominence of English, is expressed by Dadoba Pandurang in his Preface (dated 24 July, 1879) to the seventh edition of his

manifest in efforts to preserve the available manuscripts. Gopal Raghunath Nandargikar, who was a Sanskrit tutor at the New English School in Pune, wrote in the Preface (p. 30) to his 1894 edition of Kālidāsa's Meghadūta:

> "For the large number of MSS, which were placed at my disposal, I am very highly indebted to Dr. R.G. Bhandarkar. ... Owing to this supremely eminent scholar's efforts, most valuable MSS. are being collected at the Deccan College library and it is to be hoped that the Indian Government will not, for several years to come, abandon the important work of buying up the Sanskrit manuscripts hidden away in private libraries and being therefore out of reach for outsiders; although our learned citizen Rava Saheb M.C. Apte has established a valuable institution (= Anandashram in Pune) for the custody and preservation of MSS., still Government efforts are equally necessary for this important work. ... The old Śāstris who may be deemed living encyclopedias of ancient scholarship are fast disappearing from the scene, and their industry on this point is long at an end. It behoves us, therefore, to take the charge and to preserve and collect the repositories of our national lore from decay and obscurity."

The fear that the old traditions of Sanskrit learning are fast disappearing prompted the pandits and professors alike to work toward creating institutions for the purpose of preservation of these traditions, and both sought the assistance of the British-Indian authorities, the Indian princes, and the larger community in this task.

The European scholars working in India echoed the same feelings and joined the same efforts for preservation of a disappearing tradition. After expressing his indebtedness to his pandit-colleagues (some of whom were also his teachers), Kielhorn says in his 1874 Preface to his translation of the Paribhāṣenduśekhara (pp. xxiv-xxv):

> "It is sad to see the number of great Śāstris, distinguished no less for their humility and modesty than for their learning and intelligence, diminish year after year, and to feel that with them there is dying away more and more of that traditional learning which we can so ill dispense with in the interpretation of the enigmatic works of Hindu antiquity, but it appears to me all the more to be the duty of both Native and European Sanskrit scholars to save as much as can still be saved, and to fix in writing what in less than half a century will otherwise be irreparably lost."

In his Preface (p. 3) to his 1888 edition of the Mahānārāyaṇa-Upaniṣad, Colonel Jacob states his case in eloquent words:

---

path-breaking book A Grammar of the Marathi Language, 8th edition, Bombay, 1885, p. 7: "Since the past twentyfive years, people have placed a greater emphasis on learning English, and there is a growing disinterest concerning the mother-tongue (= Marathi)."

> "I am indebted therefore to the State for all the materials at my disposal, and my best thanks are due to the custodians of these valuable collections for the ready access to them which has been given to me. It is to be hoped that the Indian Government will not, for many a long year, abandon the important work of buying up the Sanskrit manuscripts hidden away in private libraries. ... The old Śāstrīs,— those living encyclopedias of learning—are fast disappearing from the scene, an inevitable result of our rule: let us, however, do what we can to preserve and utilize the *silent* witnesses to the literary activity of this great country in the remote past."

There is an uncanny similarity in the statements of Nandargikar, Kielhorn and Colonel Jacob, and it is this commonality of interests and aims which allowed the great manuscript collections at the Deccan College (and later at the Bhandarkar Oriental Research Institute) to be built with support from all the interested parties, pandits and professors, natives and Europeans.

The pandits were working hand-in-hand with western-trained Indians and western scholars through out the nineteenth century, and there was an incredibly intense interaction on all sides. The evidence for this comes from various sources. For instance, the Bālakāṇḍa of the Rāmāyaṇa was published in Pune in 1862 "for the Education Department of the Bombay Presidency". Martin Haug, who supervised this publication, says in his *Notice*: "This edition of the *Bālakāṇḍa* is only a reprint from Schlegel's work; but corrected and revised by the Pandits of the Poona College. It is mainly intended for the students of the Poona College and other institutions, who are desirous of preparing for one of the Sanskrit Examinations at which the first book of Rāmāyaṇa is a standard author" (13 August 1862). The pandits were correcting and revising a European edition of a Sanskrit text under the supervision of a European in Pune. In 1889, Peter Peterson, who was Elphinstone Professor of Sanskrit at Bombay, published his edition of Bāṇa's Kādambarī. It was published by the Department of Public Instruction in Bombay (*Bombay Sanskrit Series*, No. XXIV). Peterson dedicated this edition to R.G. Bhandarkar: "Offered as a tribute of respect and of cordial friendship to Ramakrishna Gopal Bhandarkar." Who is using these editions published by a European in Bombay? The books published by the Department of Public Instruction were meant for the use of the students in Bombay Presidency. My personal copy of this book was originally owned by one Mr. D.T. Bhave, a Brahmin student at the Fergusson College, Pune. In his own handwriting, the cover-page reads: "Bhave D.T. bought and got bound this book on the 25th Dec. 1889. Student in the Fergusson College, Poona. This book belongs to D.T. Bhave, B.A., & handed over to his friend Mr. V.R. Sane (another Brahmin name)." H.M. Bhadkamkar (B.A.) prepared a "Translation into English of the Aitareya-Upanishad with Śaṅkarāchārya's Bhāshya" which was awarded in 1893 the

Sujna Gokulji Zala Vedanta Prize, and this work was published "for the University of Bombay" in 1899. Bhadkamkar dedicates his book "to Ramakrishna Gopal Bhandarkar, M.A., Ph.D., C.I.E., Hon. M.R.A.S., &c., &c., Late Vice-Chancellor of the University of Bombay and Late Professor of Oriental Languages in the Deccan College, Poona, as a token of deep respect and gratitude, this humble attempt is dedicated by his old pupil." Colonel G.A. Jacob of the Bombay Staff Corps published his edition of the Mahānārāyaṇopaniṣad in 1888 under the auspices of the Department of Public Instruction, Bombay (Bombay Sanskrit Series, No. XXXV). Colonel Jacob, in his Preface (p. 3) to his book acknowledges "with pleasure the assistance which I received on points of grammar, from Chintāmaṇi Śāstrī Warūḍkar, the Pandit of the Deccan College" (Poona, November 21, 1887).

Finally, I would like to refer to the cooperation between Vāsudev Shastri Abhyankar and his professor disciples like Professor C.R. Devadhar. The 1922 edition of the Nyāyasāra of Bhāsarvajña (Pune: The Oriental Book Supplying Agency) was prepared by Vāsudev Shastri Abhyankar and C.R. Devadhar working together. The title-page reads: "Critically Edited with notes including translation by Mahāmahopādhyāya Paṇḍita Vāsudeva Shāstri Abhyankar and Professor C.R. Devadhar, M.A., Fergusson College, Poona". In the Preface (p. ii) to this book, C.R. Devadhar says: "But above all, to my Guru, Mahāmahopādhyāya Vāsudeva Shāstri Abhyankar, I owe a debt which it would be extremely ungrateful not to acknowledge. To him I owe the explanation of many technical subtleties, many difficult points which unaided were formidable indeed. In fact all the merit that the book may have is due to him". There was cross-fertilization in all directions.

Peter Peterson

As a specific example of this collaboration between European professors in India and their Indian successors, I would like to discuss Peter Peterson's Hymns from the Ṛgveda. Peterson was Professor of Sanskrit at the Elphinstone College in Bombay. The first edition of his book was published in the Bombay Sanskrit Series (No. XXXVI) in 1888 under the auspices of the Department of Public Instruction. Peterson's Preface to the First Edition begins with this statement:

> "The Hymns from the Ṛgveda in this volume are those appointed to be read by candidates for the degree of B.A. in the University of Bombay; and the book is little more than an attempt to furnish students here with the material without which anything like a full study, or commencement of study, of the Ṛgveda is hardly now practicable. I hope it may be accepted as a text-book in other Universities, in India or elsewhere, where Sanskrit is studied. But my primary object has been to fulfil a pledge, given I do not like to think how long ago, when

> I induced the University of Bombay to lead the way in making some knowledge at least of the Ṛgveda part of the ordinary qualification for a degree in Sanskrit."

Through his book, Peterson was motivating the study of the Ṛgveda by his Indian students in the direction of western scholarship of the day. Expressing his indebtedness to other scholars, Peterson says (Preface to the First Edition): "The obligations my book is under to Max Müller, the St. Petersburg Dictionary, Muir's Sanskrit Texts, Geldner and Kaegi's Siebenzig Lieder, Grassmann's Dictionary and Translation, Ludwig's Translation, are, I hope, apparent everywhere on the surface. I have given throughout references to Whitney's Sanskrit Grammar, a book which must be useful to every student of the Ṛgveda." The second edition of Hymns from the Ṛgveda was published by Peterson himself in 1897. The third edition of Hymns from the Ṛgveda was published in 1905 by S.R. Bhandarkar (M.A., Professor of Sanskrit, Elphinstone College, Bombay). Bhandarkar now carried forward the project of keeping up with the latest western research on the Ṛgveda. In his Preface to the Third Edition, Bhandarkar says: "The original notes have, however, been supplemented by a few new ones. These have been drawn from Pischel and Geldner's Vedische Studien (3 vols.), Vedic Hymns (Parts i and ii) in the Sacred Books of the East, Muir's Sanskrit Texts (5 vols.), Whitney's Grammar, Lanman's Noun-inflection in the Veda, and other works." In 1917, the fourth edition of Hymns from the Ṛgveda was published by A.B. Dhruva (Professor of Sanskrit, Gujarat College, Ahmedabad). The book had continued to be used as a text-book prescribed for the students at the University of Bombay. Referring to his new additions, Dhruva says in the Preface to the Fourth Edition: "The new matter thus added comprises references to standard works on points of grammar, accent, metre, philology and mythology. ... The subject of Vedic mythology is brought more prominently before the student; while the introduction of Indo-Iranian philology is an entirely new feature of the present edition. ... With a view to helping the student to a systematic study of the work apart from the Notes, I have added to the old brief list a longer classified list of principal books in English bearing upon the subject." The fourth edition was reprinted by R.D. Karmarkar (Professor of Sanskrit, S.P. College, Pune) in 1937, and by H.D. Velankar (Professor of Sanskrit, University of Bombay) in 1959. The edition in 1959 was "printed and published by Dr. R.N. Dandekar, M.A., Ph.D." at the Bhandarkar Oriental Research Institute in Pune. With Professor R.N. Dandekar, we enter the modern phase of Sanskrit studies in Pune. The successive editions and reprints of Peterson's Hymns from the Ṛgveda are a good illustration of collaboration between European and Indian professors in the introduction of modernity in Sanskrit studies in the region of Maharashtra.

The cooperation between European and Indian professors and traditional pandits can be illustrated with another example. Previously I have discussed the misgivings of Vaman Shastri Islampurkar about the value of modern ways of teaching Sanskrit initiated under the westernized system of education in Maharashtra. These misgivings were expressed by Islampurkar in 1889 in the Introduction to the 2nd edition of his Marathi translation of the Meghadūta. Islampurkar eventually went to Bombay and started working with John Wilson, and gradually was fully integrated into the modernist project. This may be seen from the fact that a number of works edited by him subsequently appeared in the Bombay Sanskrit Series published by the Department of Public Instruction. Among them are his editions of the Parāśaradharmasaṃhitā with the commentary of Sāyaṇa-Mādhavācārya (Bombay Sanskrit Series, Vols. XLVII, XLVIII, LIX, LXIV, and LXVII) and his edition of the Navasāhasāṅkacarita (Bombay Sanskrit Series, Vol. LIII). In fact, the names of the editors of the various volumes of this series is a virtual demonstration of this cooperation. The title page of Vol. III, Part II of the Parāśaradharmasaṃhitā (Bombay Sanskrit Series, No. LXXIV, 1919) reads: "Edited with various readings, critical notes, indexes, &c. by Pandit Vāman Śāstri Islāmpurkar and R.G. Bhadkamkar, M.A., Acting Professor of Sanskrit, Elphinstone College, Bombay." Bhadkamkar was a student of R.G. Bhandarkar. Among the European editors of volumes in the Bombay Sanskrit Series we find the names of G. Bühler, F. Kielhorn, Pischel, A.A. Führer, Peter Peterson, and G.A. Jacob. Among the Indian names, we have a mixture of pandits and professors: S.P. Pandit (M.A.), Justice K.T. Telang (M.A.), R.G. Bhandarkar (M.A., Ph.D.), Professor A.V. Kathawate, Pandit Durgaprasad, N.M. Dvivedi, Mahāmahopādhyāya Rajaram Shastri Bodas, Vaman Shastri Islampurkar, N.B. Godbole, Y.V. Athalye, K.P. Trivedi, H.H. Dhruva, and Mahāmahopādhyāya Vasudev Shastri Abhyankar. Many volumes show joint editorial work by European and Indian scholars, as well as cooperation between Indian pandits and professors.

Vāsudev Shastri Abhyankar

The last important figure I would like to discuss is Mahāmahopādhyāya Vāsudev Shastri Abhyankar (1863-1942).[38] He was born in Satara in a family of learned Sanskrit pandits. He lost his father when he was three years old, and his grandfather, the famous grammarian of the day, Bhāskaraśāstrī Abhyankar (1783-1871), died when Vāsudev Shastri was only eight years old. The responsibility of training Vāsudev Shastri was taken up by Rāmaśāstri Godbole, who was a disciple of Bhāṣkaraśāstri Abhyankar. Bhāskara-

38 For the details of Vasudev Shastri Abhyankar's life and work, see: K.V. Abhyankar 1954:44-55.

śāstri's teacher was Nīlakaṇṭha-śāstrī Thatte (1760-1834), who was trained by Vaidya- nātha Pāyaguṇḍe, a direct disciple of Nāgeśabhaṭṭa (1650-1730). Without ever going to an outside school, Vasudev Shastri studied at home the Sanskrit shastras along with arithmetic, history, geography and Marathi. In twelve years, he finished the study of Sanskrit grammar including the entire Mahābhāṣya, and he simultaneously achieved firm understanding of other shastras such as Nyāya, Alaṃkāra, Mīmāṃsā, Vedānta, and Dharmaśāstra. He passed all the three levels of the examinations in Vyākaraṇa offered by the Vedaśāstrottejaka Sabhā in Pune at once, and wrote Sanskrit commentaries on the Paribhāṣenduśekhara and Laghuśabdenduśekhara before he was twenty. In 1890, Vasudev Shastri left Satara for Pune, where he started teaching in the Sanskrit Pāṭhaśālā,[39] and was soon appointed as a Śāstrī in the Fergusson College at the behest of R.G. Bhandarkar. He continued to teach at both the institutions, mornings at the Pāṭhaśālā and afternoons at the Fergusson College. He taught at the Fergusson College from 1892 to 1929, and continued teaching students at home after his retirement. The British government of India granted him the title of Mahāmahopādhyāya in the year 1921.

While Vasudev Shastri was thus at the peak of his excellence in traditional Sanskrit scholarship, he was brought into close contact with western-educated scholars in Pune. His great supporter in Pune was Professor R.G. Bhandarkar, who offered him Shastri positions in the Elphinstone College and the Deccan College, but he remained committed to teaching at the Fergusson College. He developed closed raport with R.G. Bhandarkar, with whom he had many sessions to discuss the Mahābhāṣya. Many people who were professors at different colleges in Pune also came to study with Vasudev Shastri, e.g. Professor Chandorkar, Professor Panse, Professor Belvalkar, Professor Gune, and Professor V.G. Paranjpe.

It was this close contact with traditions of western-style education in Pune which also transformed Vasudev Shastri himself to a certain extent. This transformation is reflected in the formats of some of his publications, such as his monumental Marathi translations of the Mahābhāṣya (1938-54) and Brahmasūtraśāṅkarabhāṣya (1911). The translation of the Mahābhāṣya is complete with hundreds of footnotes, and the partial introduction (Prastāvanā) that he wrote also shows a more modernistic presentation, though he is nowhere questioning the basic premises of the tradition. The same can be said about his Marathi translation of the Brahmasūtraśāṅkarabhāṣya. Here he provides a tabulated comparison of the different interpretations given by

39 This Sanskrit Pāṭhaśālā was established in 1885 in Pune in Nagarkar Wada with the support of many Shastris and also of many western-educated persons like M.G. Ranade, R.G. Bhandarkar and others. This Pāṭhaśālā is also a continuing institution in Pune to this day, and I myself studied at this institution for several years under Narayan Shastri Dikshit.

different schools of Vedānta, a clearly modernist presentation. His edition of Madhusūdanasarasvatī's Siddhāntabindu (BORI, Pune 1928) also illustrates the same pattern. Here he adds his own Sanskrit commentary to the original text, and this commentary would fit the general traditional style. However, he records textual variants on every page, indicating a modernist approach. His general introduction, though in exquisite Sanskrit, is particularly modernist in that he is discussing dates of authors and comparing their views, tracing the doctrinal evolution of the Advaita tradition from Gauḍapāda through Śaṅkara to his disciples. The Sanskrit vocabulary of his Introduction (p. 20) is in some ways indicative of this modernity. He uses the newly coined Sanskrit terms *mānasaśāstra*, *jñānaśāstra*, and *devatāśāstra* to refer to disciplines of psychology, epistemology, and theology, and says that Indian philosophers were principally interested in *adhyātmaśāstra* 'science of knowledge relating to self', and only occasionally paid attention to psychology, epistemology, and theology. Hence they wrote independent works only in *adhyātmaśāstra*, and not in the other *śāstras* mentioned above.[40] While discussing the dates of Sanskrit authors, even while writing in Sanskrit, Vasudev Shastri makes use of the Christian era, rather than the older Śaka or Vikrama eras.[41] We see the same kind of modernity in the Sanskrit Introductions by a number of Sanskrit pandits during this period. One may mention the Sanskrit Introduction by Vamanacharya Jhalkikar to his edition of Mammaṭa's Kāvyaprakāśa, with Jhalkikar's own Sanskrit commentary Bālabodhinī published in 1900 (as part of the Bombay Sanskrit Series, but outside the main series). Jhalkikar discusses the dates of the different commentaries on the Kāvyaprakāśa, and compares their interpretations. At the end of his Introduction, he says that since the subject of the Kāvyaprakāśa is a difficult one, wherever there was doubt, he consulted R.G. Bhandarkar, his older brother Bhimacharya Jhalkikar (the author of the famous Nyāyakośa), and other scholars. The inclusion of R.G. Bhandarkar among those consulted by Vamanacharya Jhalkikar shows the circulation of ideas between pandits and professors. Appropriating Bhandarkar to the category of pandits, Jhalkikar refers to him as Rāmakṛṣṇapaṇḍita, though he does not fail to refer to his title 'C.I.E'. The Sanskrit Introduction by

40 *mānasaśāstrajñānaśāstradevatāśāstrādiṣu viṣayeṣu svatantragranthanirmāṇe bhāratīyānām ācāryāṇām pravṛttiḥ kādācitkī samupalabdhā yato duḥkhātmakaprapañcasvarūpayāthātmyajñānenākhiladuḥkhamokṣaṃ lipsavaḥ sarve 'pi purātanā munayo 'dhyātmaśāstrasyādhyayane tasminn eva ca svatantragranthaviracane svabhāvataḥ pravṛttā babhūvuḥ* / Introduction to Siddhāntabindu, p. 20, (Vasudev Shastri Abhyankar 1928). Also note Abhyankar's use of the term *bhāratīya* in the sense of 'Indian'. This is the modern sense of this term.

41 ... *khristīyasaptadaśaśatakasyottarārdhe* ...in the latter half of the 17th century of the Christian era", Introduction to Siddhāntabindu, p.25. (Vasudev Shastri Abhyankar 1928)

Pandit Durgaprasad and Kashinath Pandurang Parab to their 1888 edition of Jagannātha's Rasagaṅgādhara (Kāvyamālā Series, No. 12, Bombay) is another example. While discussing the location of Śṛṅgaverapura, where Nāgeśabhaṭṭa received patronage from the local king, the editors refer to H.T. Colebrooke's Miscellaneous Essays and provide a Sanskrit rendering of his opinion (p. 7).

Conclusion

I would like to conclude this discussion with a consideration of the limits of modernity among these various individuals who are situated variously on the spectrum from traditional Pandit to modern Professor. With all the presentational modernity in Vasudev Shastri Abhyankar's works, one needs to observe that he never transgressed the notion of traditional authority (*prāmāṇya*). Within the tradition of grammar, this would be the ranked authority of the first three grammarian-sages (*uttarottaram munitrayasya prāmāṇyam*). On the other hand, individuals like B.G. Tilak and R.G. Bhandarkar were willing to go beyond the norms of traditional authority and place their foremost emphasis on the critical and historical methodology, which was openly inherited from western education. Their conclusions could go contrary to the traditional doctrines, and yet they would forge ahead with their new directions of research with faith in the critical methods. This duality has continued to exist into our own times in India. Among my own teachers, Vāmanaśāstrī Bhagavat was not willing to go beyond the limits set by the traditional rule of authority (*trimuniprāmāṇya*). On the other hand, someone like Professor S.D. Joshi began as a traditional pandit, but in the course of his life got transformed into a professor, in such a way that he finds it acceptable, or rather necessary, to disagree with the conclusions reached by Patañjali.[42] This is an on-going tension between different traditions of Sanskrit education in modern India, and the beginning of this tension goes back to the coming of the colonial rule.

---

42 I remember an occasion in Pune on March 13, 1966, when there was a gathering of traditional Pandits (*Paṇḍitasabhā*) organized to mark the hundredth anniversary of Vāsudev Shastri Abhyankar's birth. My teacher Vāmanaśāstrī Bhāgavat had trained me to take part in a debate on some topic in Sanskrit grammar. As an award, I received a copy of Vāsudev Shastri's Marathi translation of Śaṅkara's Brahmasūtrabhāṣya, signed by five chief pandits. Professor S.D. Joshi was in the audience at this gathering and wanted to raise some issues. I remember that Ramachandra Sastry, the Pandit presiding over the gathering, explained its ground-rules, the most important of which was the full acceptance of Patañjali's authority and the rule of *uttarottaraṃ munīnām prāmāṇyam*.

REFERENCES

Abhyankar, K.V. 1954. (In Marathi). *Prastāvanā Khaṇḍa* ("Introductory Volume"), containing an Introduction to Vasudev Shastri Abhyankar's six volume Marathi translation of Patañjali's Mahābhāṣya, including the Prastāvanā ("Introduction") by Vasudev Shastri Abhyankar. Pune: Deccan Education Society, Fergusson College.

Abhyankar, Vasudev Shastri (ed.). 1928. *Siddhāntabindu* of Madhusūdana Sarasvatī, edited with an Original Commentary and Introduction by Vasudev Shastri Abhyankar. *Government Oriental Series - Class A, No. II.* Pune: Bhandarkar Oriental Research Institute.

———. 1911. *Marathi Translation of the Brahmasūtraśāṃkarabhāṣya*, in 3 volumes. Baroda: Gaikwar Government.

———. with C.R. Devadhar. 1922. eds. *Nyāyasāra* of Bhāsarvajña with the *Nyāyasārapadapañcikā* of Vāsudeva of Kashmir. Pune: The Oriental Book Supplying Agency.

Aprabuddha (= V.K. Palekar). 1926. (In Marathi). *Brahmarṣi śrī. aṇṇāsāheb paṭavardhan* ("Biography of Annasaheb Patwardhan"). Pune: Diwakar Yashwant Phatak.

Apte, Vaman Shivaram. 1885. *The Student's Guide to Sanskrit Composition, being a treatise on Sanskrit syntax for the use of schools and colleges.* 8th edition in 1921. Bombay: The Standard Publishing Company.

———. 1891, 1929. *Kusumamālā or a Collection of Choice Extracts from Standard Sanskrit Writers in Prose and Verse.* No. II. 20th edition (revised) by M.S. Apte, in 1929. Bombay: B.M. Apte for Apte Brothers.

Bapat, S.B. (ed.). 1925. (In Marathi). *Lokamānya ṭiḷak yāṃcyā āṭhaṇī va ākhyāyikā* ("Reminiscences about Lokamānya Ṭiḷak"). Vol. II. Pune: Sadashiv Vinayak Bapat.

Bedekar, V.M. 1976. "Research Methodology" (of R.G. Bhandarkar), in: Dandekar 1976, 183-191.

Bhadkamkar, H.M. 1899. *Translation into English of the Aitareya-Upanishad, with Śankarācārya's Bhāshya.* Bombay: The University of Bombay.

Bhandarkar, R.G. 1864. *First Book of Sanskrit.* 34th edition in 1966. Bombay: Karnatak Publishing House.

———. 1868. *Second Book of Sanskrit.* 16th edition. 1921. Bombay: Radhabai Atmaram Sagoon.

———. 1887. *Report for the Search for Sanskrit Manuscripts in the Bombay Presidency during the year 1883-84.* Bombay: Government Central Press.

———. 1933. *Collected Works.* In three volumes. Edited by N.B. Utgikar. *Government Oriental Series.* Pune: Bhandarkar Oriental Research Institute.

Bhate, Saroja. 1996. "Position of Sanskrit in Public Education and Scientific Research in Modern India", in: Houben (ed.), *Ideology & Status of Sanskrit: Contributions to the History of the Sanskrit Language*, pp. 383-400. Leiden: E.J. Brill.

Chiplunkar, Krishnashastri. 1893, reprinted in 1971. (In Marathi). *Marāṭhī Vyākaraṇāvar Nibandh* ("Essays on Marathi Grammar"). First edition published by Ramachandra Bhikaji Joshi. Second edition, 1971. Pune: Continental Prakashan.

Chiplunkar, Vishnushastri. 1891. (In Marathi). *Saṃskṛtakavipaṃcaka* ("Five Sanskrit Poets"). 2nd edition. Bombay: Janardan Mahadev Gurjar, at Nirnaya

Sagara Press.

———. 1926. (In Marathi). *Nibandhamālā* (Collected Essays by Vishnushastri Chiplunkar"). 3rd Edition. Edited by V.V. Sathe. Pune: Chitrashala Press.

Choksey, R.D. 1976. *Twilight of the Maratha Raj, 1818*. Pune: R.D. Choksey.

Dandekar, R.N. (ed.). 1972. *Sanskrit and Maharashtra: A Symposium. Publications of the Centre of Advanced Study in Sanskrit*, Class E, No. 1. Pune: University of Pune.

———. (ed.). 1976. *Ramakrishna Gopal Bhandarkar as an Indologist*. Pune: Bhandarkar Oriental Research Society.

———. 1978. *Recent Trends in Indology*. Pune: Bhandarkar Oriental Research Institute.

Deshpande, Madhav M. 1991. *Preface to Pāṇinian Studies, Professor S.D. Joshi Felicitation Volume*. Edited by Madhav M. Deshpande and Saroja Bhate. Ann Arbor: Center for South and Southeast Asian Studies, University of Michigan.

Dobbin, Christine. 1972. *Urban Leadership in Western India: Politics and Communities in Bombay City 1840-1885*. London: Oxford University Press.

Duff, James Grant. 1826, reprinted in 1990. *History of the Mahrattas*. Vols. I, II, and III. Originally published in 1826 in London: Longman, Rees, Orme, Brown, & Green. Reprinted in 1990, Delhi: Low Price Publications.

Gadre, Narayan Krishna. 1903. (In Marathi). *Kai. Pro. Śrīdhar Gaṇeś Jinsīvāle yāṃce troṭak caritra* ("A Brief Biography of the Late Prof. Shridhar Ganesh Jinsiwale"). Bombay: Mahadeo Keshav Kale, Editor, Shri Sarasvati Mandir.

Gordon, Stewart. 1993. *The Marathas, 1600-1818. The New Cambridge History of India*. Cambridge: Cambridge University Press.

Inamdar, N.R. 1983. *Political Thought and Leadership of Lokmanya Tilak*. Delhi: Concept Publishing Company.

Islampurkar, Vaman Shastri. 1886. (In Marathi). *Kumārasambhava* (5 cantos), *with a Marathi commentary titled Kāvyārthadīpikā*. Bombay: S.N. Chitale & Associates.

———. 1889. (In Marathi). *Meghadūta of Kālidāsa, with a Marathi commentary titled Kāvyārthadīpikā*. Bombay: Karnatak Press.

Jacob, G.A. Colonel. 1888. (ed.) *The Mahānārāyaṇa-Upanishad of the Atharva-Veda, with the Dīpikā of Nārāyaṇa. Bombay Sanskrit Series*, No. XXXV. Bombay: The Department of Public Instruction.

Jhalkikar, Bhimacharya. 1874. *Nyāyakośa*. 2nd edition revised and re-edited by Vasudev Shastri Abhyankar. *Bombay Sanskrit and Prakrit Series*, No. XLIX. 1928. Pune: Bhandarkar Oriental Research Institute.

Jhalkikar, Vamanacharya. 1900. *Kāvyaprakāśa of Mammaṭa, with the Bālabodhinī of Vāmanācārya Jhaḷkīkar*. Bombay: Department of Public Instruction. 7th edition by R.D. Karmarkar, 1965. Pune: Bhandarkar Oriental Research Institute.

Jinsiwale, Shridhar Ganesh. 1882. Personal Diaries for the year 1882. (The manuscript in possession of Madhav Deshpande).

Jog, R.S. (ed.) 1965. (In Marathi). *Marāṭhī vāṅmayācā itihās (i.sa. 1800-1874)*, Vol. 4. ("History of the Marathi Literature, A.D. 1800-1874"). Pune: Maharashtra Sahitya Parishad.

Karve, D.D. (Translator). 1963. *The New Brahmans: Five Maharashtrian Families*. Selected and translated by Karve with editorial assistance of Ellen E.

McDonald. Berkeley and Los Angeles: University of California Press.

Kelkar, Narsimha Cintaman. 1915. (In Marathi). *Keḷkarkṛta lekhasaṃgraha* ("Collected Essays by N.C. Kelkar"). Pune: Chitrashala Press.

Kielhorn, Franz. 1870. *A Grammar of the Sanskrit Language*. Bombay: Government Central Book Depot.

Kirloskar, Sakharam Ramchandra. 1876. *Gadyapadyāvalī or Readings in Sanskrit, Prose & Verse*. Bombay: Nirnaya Sagara Press.

Kumar, Ravinder. 1968a. "The New Brahmans of Maharashtra", in: D.A. Low (ed.), *Soundings in Modern South Asian History*, pp. 95-130. Berkeley and Los Angeles: University of California Press.

———. 1968b. *Western India in the Nineteenth Century: A Study in the Social History of Maharashtra*. London: Routledge & Kegan Paul.

Kunte, Mahadeo Moreshwar. 1880. *The Vicissitudes of Aryan Civilization in India*. Bombay: Oriental Printing Press.

Lederle, M.R. 1976. *Philosophical Trends in Modern Maharashtra*. Bombay: Popular Prakashan.

Lele, Ganesh Shastri. 1866. *Jānakīpariṇayanāṭaka* by Rāmabhadra Dīkṣita, with a Marathi translation. 2nd edition. Bombay: Dakṣiṇā Prize Committee.

Mote, H.V. (ed.). 1972. (In Marathi). *Viśrabdha Śāradā* ("Confidential Letters"), Vol. I, Covering the period of 1817-1947. Bombay: H.V. Mote Prakashan.

Nandargikar, Gopal Raghunath. 1894. (ed.). *The Meghadūta of Kālidāsa, with the commentary of Mallinātha*. Bombay: Messrs. Gopal Narayen & Co.

Pandurang, Dadoba. 1865. (In Marathi). *The Kekāvalī or 'Cries of the Peacock', of Moropant*, edited with a copious and continuous commentary, annotations, and illustrations. Bombay: Ganpat Krishnaji's Press.

———. 1885. (In Marathi). *A Grammar of the Marathi Language*. 8th edition. Bombay: Mazagaon Printing Press. [1st edition in 1836].

Paribhāṣenduśekhara of Nāgeśabhaṭṭa. Vol. I. Sanskrit text edited by K.V. Abhyankar, 1962. Vol. II. English Translation by Franz Kielhorn, with an Introduction. Second Edition, 1960. Pune: Bhandarkar Oriental Research Institute.

Peterson, Peter. 1888. (ed.) *Hymns from the Ṛgveda*. Bombay Sanskrit Series. 2nd reprint of the 4th edition by H.D. Velankar in 1959. Pune: Bhandarkar Oriental Research Institute

———. 1889. (ed.) *Kādambarī by Bāṇa & his son*. Vol. I. Sanskrit Text. *Bombay Sanskrit Series*, No. XXIV. Bombay: The Department of Public Instruction.

Pinge, S.M. 1960. (In Marathi). *Yuropiyanāṃcā marāṭhīcā abhyās va sevā* ("The Study of Marathi by Europeans and their Contributions"). Aurangabad: S.M. Pinge.

Potdar, D.V. 1922. (In Marathi). *Marāṭhī gadyācā iṅgrajī avtār athvā iṅgrajī amlātīl marāṭhī gadya vāṅmayācā nibandhamālepūrvīcā itihās, i. sa. 1810-1874* ("The Appearance of Anglicized Marathi Prose, or The History of the Marathi Prose Literature during the Early British Rule before the publication of *Nibandhamālā*, A.D. 1810-1874"). Pune: A.P. Bapat & Brothers, Booksellers and Publishers.

Puranik, S.S. 1992. (In Marathi). *Viṣṇuśāstrī*. ("Life and Contribution of Vishnushastri Chiplunkar"). Pune: Raviraj Prakashan.

Rajwade, Shankar Ramchandra. 1980. (In Marathi). *Āhitāgni Rājvāḍe: Ātmavṛtta* ("Autobiography of Āhitāgni Rajwade"). Pune: Shrividya Prakashan.

Rāmāyaṇa (Bālakāṇḍa). 1862. Edited by pandits of the Poona College, and supervised by Martin Haug. Pune: The Educational Department of the Bombay Presidency.

Ranade, M.G. 1900. *Rise of the Maratha Power*. Originally published in 1900 by Punalekar & Co., Bombay. Reprinted in 1966. Nasik: Publications Division, Government of India.

———. 1915. *Miscellaneous Writings of the late Hon'ble Mr. Justice M.G. Ranade*. Pune: Mrs. Ramabai Ranade.

Rasagaṅgādhara of Jagannātha Paṇḍita, with the commentary of Nāgeśabhaṭṭa. Edited by Paṇḍit Durgaprasad and Kashinath Pandurang Parab. 1888. *Kavya mālā* 12. Bombay: Nirnaya Sagara Press.

Seal, Anil. 1971. *The Emergence of Indian Nationalism: Competition and Collaboration in the Later Nineteenth Century*. Cambridge: Cambridge University Press.

Sharma, R.S. 1945. *Fergusson College Through Sixty Years*. Bombay: Karnatak Publishing House.

Shejwalkar, Tryambak Shankar. 1977. (In Marathi). *Nivaḍak Lekhasaṃgraha* ("Selected Articles"). Edited by H.V. Mote. Bombay: H.V. Mote.

Telang, Kashinath Tryambak. 1900. *The Bhagavadgītā, with The Sanatsujātīya and The Anugītā*, translated into English. *Sacred Books of the East*, Vol. VIII. American Edition. New York: Charles Scribner's Sons.

Tilak, B.G. 1903. *The Arctic Home in the Vedas*. Pune: The Manager, Kesari.

———. 1915. (In Marathi). *Gītārahasya athavā karmayogaśāstra* ("The Secret of the Bhagavadgītā, or the Science of Karmayoga"). First Reprint. Pune: Kesari Office.

———. 1925. *Vedic Chronology and Vedanga Jyotisha* (containing also Chaldean and Indian Vedas and other miscellaneous essays). Pune: Tilak Bros, Gaikwar Wada.

Trautmann, Thomas R. 1997. *Aryans and British India*. Berkeley and Los Angeles: University of California Press.

Vedaśāstradīpikā, Hīraka-mahotsava-smāraka-grantha. (In Marathi: "Exposition of the Vedas and Śāstras: Diamond Jubilee Felicitation Volume"). Pune: Vedaśāstrottejaka Sabhā. 1941.

Vijapurkar, Vishnu Govind. 1963. (In Marathi). *Pro. Vijāpūrkar yāṃce lekh* "(Collected) Articles by Professor Vijapurkar". Edited by M.G. Deshpande. Pune: Continental Prakashan.

Viśvaguṇādarśacampū by Veṅkaṭādhvarin. Edited by B.G. Yogi. Revised by M.G. Bakre. 1923. Bombay: Nirnaya Sagara Press.

Walimbe, R.S. 1974. (in Marathi). "pune śaharātīl śikṣaṇ: ekoṇisāve śatak" ("Education in the Pune City: 19th Century"), in: *Puṇe Vidyāpīṭha Raupya Mahotsava Smaraṇikā*, pp. 9-20. Pune: University of Pune.

MONIKA HORSTMANN

A Pandit among the Modernists and a Modernist among the Pandits

In 1930, a twenty-three year old Sāhitya-Śāstrī and Śāstrācārya in Jyotiṣa who had graduated from the Saṃskṛt Mahāvidyālay of Banaras Hindu University set out for Śāntiniketan. Here, at what was to emerge as the Viśvabhāratī University, he had been appointed, on recommendation of Madan Mohan Mālvīya, by Rabindranath Tagore as a Hindi teacher and in-charge of all chores relating to his trade of a *jyotiṣī*. In Banaras he had lived in abject conditions of poverty and, unable to pay even the admittance fees, could not go for advanced studies. In 1950, he returned to Banaras Hindu University (BHU), as Professor and Head of the Hindi Department. In the intervening two decades he had changed the face of scholarship in the field of medieval and modern Hindi and the very paradigm of Hindi literary history and criticism. Back in Banaras, he was soon accused of being a detractor of the hallowed *ācārya*-tradition of Hindi. He retreated from the battlefield of Banaras in 1960 to become Professor and Head of the Hindi Department of Chandigarh University. In 1967, he was once again for a brief spell Rector of the BHU. He died in 1979. Departing from being a pandit, he worked out a vision for modern India in the twentieth century. Being a committed modernist, he was bound to become embroiled in the battles of the Hindi *ācāryas* who were engaged in construing a tradition of Hindi literature which to him seemed illusory and inappropriate for modernity. He was and remained a pandit among modernists and the quintessential modernist among the latter-day pandits of modernity. His name was Hazārīprasād Dvivedī.[1]

In Dvivedī, the tension between pandit and modernist was creative and sparked off in a plurality of personae which he created in his fictional writ-

1 For the personal and professional hostility of which Dvivedī became the target in Banaras, cp. Siṃh 1982:22-42 (ch. 2, "Brāhmaṇ samāj meṁ achūt"). A documented study of Dvivedī's life remains a desideratum. Let it be added that as late as 1997 Dvivedī became the target in the Dalit discourse in which he was castigated as a *brāhmaṇvādī*. In the process, Dharmvīr (1997) strongly opposed his treatment of Kabīr. He took issue with Dvivedī's attempt to present Kabīr as someone who did not go against the grain of Hindu orthodoxy. He accused Dvivedī of accepting Kabīr as a respectable representative of the tradition of Hindi literature only by virtue of his being the brahmin Rāmānand's disciple, a discipleship much disputed but taken by Dvivedī as a fact. The major argument put forth by Dharmvīr, namely, that Dvivedī sought to establish *one* continuous stream of Indian literary tradition which would naturally also encompass Kabīr, whom the author now claimed to be exclusive Dalit property and thus non-Hindu, points to a problem in Dvivedī's concept, although I feel that Dharmvīr's excessively polemical stance did much to diminish his point.

ings but also enacted in life. He spoke from behind the mask of these personae (Siṃh 1982). These multiple personae found literary expression in his first pseudonym, Vyomkeśśāstrī. Actually he had used this first when, as a young *jyotiṣī*, he dissented with his guru's ideas but wanted to publicise his own findings without jeopardizing his loyalty to him. This dissimulation ran him into a comical nightmare, for in recognition of his achievements the All-India Jyotiṣa Conference invited him to Indore to present a paper at the very conference where his guru would be in the audience. What else could he do but decline the invitation?[2] It was also Vyomkeśśāstrī who "edited" Bāṇabhaṭṭa's alleged autobiography, this being Dvivedī's first novel, historical on the face of it, but in fact a book of man coming of his own and braving timeless challenges (*Bāṇbhaṭṭ kī ātmakathā*, 1947). One aspect of the novel is that it is a masterpiece of reflexive reception of Bāṇa's original works and, if it does not require, it is certainly best enjoyed by readers with an interest in Sanskrit literature. Dvivedī is also Anāmdās, the alleged author of Anāmdās kā pothā (1976), Dvivedī's fourth and last novel and a modern humanist utopia. The theme of this novel is the image of man, man as he will be able to cope with the demands of present-day India while he will, at the same time, remain true to his quest for ultimate liberation. This is also the overarching theme of Dvivedī's life. The book is based on a persona and plot in the Chāndogya-Upaniṣad. Its introduction is an exuberant play of names, misnomers and dissimulation. Dvivedī plays with his own name Hazārīprasād, which has proved many ties disconcerting to the orthodoxy, with his identity, with the identity of Anāmdās and the very idea of an identity vested in a name. He pokes fun at his own ilk, the *jyotiṣīs*. Wondering about the method by which names come to figure in horoscopes and may entail great discomfort, he says:[3]

> "On the basis of exactly this strange method marriages are brought about. One's caste is established by it, one's birth origin is deter-

---

2 "Vyomkeśśāstrī urph Hajārīprasād Dvivedī", first published in Ālok-parv, place and date of first publication not verified, 9.114-17. The edition of Dvivedīs collected works (Dvivedī 1998) is missing in accuracy as for the references to its sources. Cp. also Siṃh 1982:109-18 (ch.8, "Vyomkeśśāstrī urph Hajārīprasād Dvivedī")

3 In the following, Dvivedī is much more radical than for example, P.V. Kane in his History of Dharmaśastra where he writes:

> "The question arises then how far religious matters, such as Upanayana and marriage, should be regulated by astrological considerations. ...in respect of religious ceremonies like Upanayana and marriage the author would advise, as a first step towards getting rid of oppressive and meaningless astrological conditions, that people should revert to the simple rules of the gṛhyasūtras and Manu. ... In these times one may at most follow the astrological rules provided by the sūtras and Manu. Though the author has pointed out great flaws in the whole structure of Indian astrology, he does not think that it is his duty as a mere historian of Dharmaśāstra to advise people how far they should accept or discard astrology in general." (Kane 1974,V.1:639-40)

All translations from Dvivedī's writings are my own.

mined by it, the subgroup of the lunar mansion is determined by it, the *kuṇḍalī* is added to it by this method—and thereby the match is fixed. A friend of mine was the pride of a famous brahmin family. But on account of this horrendous arithmetic his son had emerged as being of the *śūdra-varṇa*. So he could only marry a brahmin girl who, by this astrological arithmetic, would belong to the *śūdra-varṇa*. Many a father came to offer him their daughters to be married to that boy. Whatever girl seemed suitable to him turned out either to be a brahmin or a *kṣatriya* or a *vaiśya*. He simply could not arrange the marriage and was in great trouble. In the end, a *jyotiṣī* recited to him the *vivāha-vṛndāvana-śloka* and thus put an end to his trouble, for *maitrī yadā syāt śubhado vivāhaḥ* (A marriage will be auspicious in proportion to the friendliness that prevails), 'If there is friendliness in a family, you need not worry about anything else'. 'Friendliness' he did encounter, indeed. Somehow he was relieved of his calamity. To him, Anāmdās's words seemed to carry weight.

Many primitive tribes try to conceal their names. Primitive tribes believe that the name and the bearer of that name are identical. If their name becomes known, they fear that an enemy may be able to use it against them in a spell. 'Let Devadatta die!', by this phrase Devadatta does not really die, but this is what people are about to claim these days. Far back in the primitive period they thought that if you only uttered the word 'Devadatta' with concentration, it would not just be the word 'Devadatta', but the object of that word, the *padārth*, that would die, that is, Devadatta himself. If you make an image of someone and stab a knife into the image's chest, the knife will pierce the image's object—a live man. Now people will argue that all this is irrelevant, but also now, in abuses and curses a rest of this has survived! And also astrology is operated on the basis of this old system. No belief vanishes entirely from the world. It changes in form, but, in fact, it lives on. If it did not, how could people, who call themselves 'progressive' and are conceited about this, burn effigies of their opponents and shout at these "To death with him!". Primitive mentality stays alive! And it will continue to flourish!

Anāmdās was not aware that the world does not ask *what* is being said; it asks who says something. 'Who', that is, what name. There are prominent critics who will first look at the name and only then write their review. An examiner will weigh the supervisor's name and only then allow a candidate to cross the Vaitaraṇī of academic honours. A 'name' is fraught with many tasks. There may be a book that needs to be read; then, if it is good or if I have found it passable, I will have to say that Mr. Nameless writes well although nobody knows him. Then the publisher will put on a show. He may, in fact, approve of it but will ask you to have a reputed person write a foreword to it. It's a great mess. All the world looks for a name. Books on *dharma* are full of the greatness of the name. It's all a sham, honest only is Mahātmā Anāmdās." (2. 306-307)

Dvivedī had planned to write a continuation of Anāmdās kā pothā. Of this only a fragment was completed. To this I will return later, for it contains the sum total of a life of great achievement and failure.

In the following, I will point to incidents that show the way in which Dvivedī grappled with the tensions between traditional erudition and modernity. I have already mentioned the embarrassing episode of Pt. Vyomkeśśāstrī's failed appearance before the *jyotiṣīs* at Indore. Of course, this did not temper his taste for writing on his *jyotiṣa* trade and attend specific conferences. One such conference, obviously at Banaras, spurred an essay on modernity as a challenge to Indian culture.[4] The major issue of that meeting seemed to be an entrenched debate on the solar day on which the *śuklapakṣā ekādaśī* of Vaiśākha would fall in such and such a year. Was it Thursday or Friday? To Dvivedī the entire event seemed weird, it resembled a village council meeting rather than a conference of scholars, and the distinguished pandits behaved like village astrologers churned up from the local hinterland; in view of this he "took the pledge that from the beginning of the conference to its very last he would not give vent to a single independent idea of his own" (9.454). One of the pandits was quick to point out to him the cause of all that confusion: "Bhāī, coercion may work elsewhere, but with the *śāstra*, coercion will not work!"

This remark Dvivedī takes as his point of departure and allows to pass before his inner eye the olden days, a period rather of independent thought when there was relatively little narrow-mindedness in the name of tradition. He sees Bhāskara boldly state: "Here in this type of mathematics, the only authority can be reasoning; here no *āgama* will hold authority." But how is it today? He is worried to see the pandits tenaciously turning the pages of the Nirṇayasindhu and the Dharmasindhu and scanning the words of famous and not so famous ancient authorities. Was India doomed to this? While these pandits scooped up obscure texts, another civilization had self-assertively conquered India, mounted with both the sword and the great promise of immortality which irresistibly attracted those who were exposed to it. Were *nibandhas* and commentaries the armor in which to face this? Could there be no fresh beginning? All that pandit culture, did it not exhaust itself in alarmingly sharp quibbles which aimed at keeping all and discarding nothing of the old?[5] A tradition of incessant *nanus* by which

4 "Paṇḍitoṁ kī pañcāyat"; place and date of first publication not verified, 9.454-60.

5 This is a *leitmotiv* of Dvivedī's criticism of late medieval Indian culture and its belated present-day custodians and it is reminiscent of what P.V.Kane, a devout modernist of the Maharashtrian brand, for whom see also note 4, wrote in 1962. (Kane 1977,V.2:1623)

> "Intellectuals were mostly engaged at least from the 11th century onwards in composing works of thousands of pages on such topics as Vrata, Dāna, Śrāddha (as the very learned minister Hemādri did) or in mental gymnastics about logic, Vedānta, Poetics and similar subjects and appear to have

something new that cropped up in the *pūrvapakṣa* in the *uttarapakṣa* was twisted to give support to tradition? And what about western modernity? Have Indians truly realised the enormous options of western thinking? No, India keeps dragging its feet, it is afraid of confronting challenges. And the conference in which Dvivedī finds himself presently is a manifestation of this cultural bewilderment, a bewilderment that has become more acute due to a growing awareness of the irreconcilable discrepancies between the traditional modes of *jyotiṣa* calculation and the results yielded by modern science. In the face of this, Dvivedī feels that it is futile to desperately try to reconcile those discrepancies or force a decree or a consolidated calendar upon them instead of looking for the founding principles of Indian civilization. It is in these that will be found the ever renewed vitality of India's ancient culture. He sees India as lost in a strange limbo between old ways that are doomed to be abandoned and a new way not yet found. It will not do to adopt some alien device, India will have to find a way of its own. And so far, "Let them be, those various opinions, those various points-of-view, the mind of the Indian people will choose the best out of these for itself. Seen in this way, this conference is rather important. It is the endeavour of straying people to find their way, and this is certainly for the good" (9.460).

Dvivedī conceived of man as deeply rooted in his own cultural history. Modernity is nourished on tradition, *paramparā*.[6] "Tradition helps man to fully comprehend himself. There can be no modernity without tradition. Tradition is the basis of modernity, it prevents it from becoming a dry and sapless intellectual pastime, it makes its projects meaningful, it guards it from unrestrained and erratic folly. Both are not in conflict with each other, they complete each other" (9.363). Although he did not point a finger to how precisely Indians would identify the traditional guidelines (and also this makes him an utopian), to him tradition was not the *śāstric* heritage alone, but the ever intertwined written and oral traditions of his country.

In 1948, Dvivedī published a series of essays entitled Aśok ke phūl, the name being taken from the title of one of these. That one is expressive of Dvivedī's cultural vision and his idea that in the mind of the pandit traditional learning will not clash with modern culture unless tradition hinders him to move with the flux of development.

> "The form of society that we see before us today is a form brought about by endless appropriation and rejection. The pure culture of this country and its pure race exist only *ex post facto*. It is all mixed, all is alloyed. Unalloyed is only man's indomitable will to live. It is like the boundless indestructible stream of the Ganges that is pure in spite

---

bestowed little thought on finding means of meeting the onslaught of foreigners or the remedies of removing their own weaknesses and defects."

6 "Paramparā aur ādhuniktā", place and date of first publication not verified. 9.358-63.

> of digesting all. The deluded conceit at one's civilization and culture makes for obstacles. Sophistication in righteous manners after a little while will run against the current, and all of it is eventually carried away by that indomitable stream. Hail, Mahākāl, so often you have broken the pride of the God of Delusion, so often you have started a revolt in the prison of King Righteousness and swallowed the poison of pitiless King Death, you have crushed the creator's haughteous conceit at his own omnipotence. ... Who knows how much of what I may consider infinitely valuable and praise and hoarse my throat to propagate will last, and how much will be washed away! ... What today we hold dear as a most valuable culture, will that last? ... All will change, all will be transformed ... all will be renewed...
>
> What has changed is [not the Aśok flower, but] man's mentality. If it achieved progress without changing, it perhaps would not change. And had it not changed as the vicissitudes of industrialisation set in—with its machine-wheels rattling away—and had science just overrun it, it would have been disastrous. We would have been crushed. How good that our mentality has undergone a change. Of course, it cannot be said that it has fully changed. But it keeps changing. He who looks [at the Aśok flower that is bound to wither] with an old mind, will be saddened. He considers himself a pandit [who prides himself of his farsightedness]. Also pandit-dom is a burden, the weightier it is, the faster it will drown you. If it becomes a part of life, it becomes light, it will not remain a burden. And at that stage it also does not sadden you. Why should it? The Aśok flower [over the long period of Indian civilization] has not withered a bit. See how it sways wantonly! Kālīdās could inhale its fragrance—in his own way. I, too, can inhale it, in my own way. There is no point in feeling sad" (9.24-25).

Modernity as the actual moment in the flux of an ever-changing tradition. Belief in a self-regulating appropriation of tradition induced by the exigencies of modern life. Modernity as an option for freedom and human dignity for all. These are some of the ulitmately utopian concepts lying behind Dvivedī's words. His approach is utopian also because he is himself convinced of the necessity and beneficence of change but does not make an effort to point out how the traditional-minded resentful of change might be induced to become reconciled with, and adapted to, that change. As a pandit, Dvivedī is the care-taker of a tradition on which, as a modernist, he wishes to rest his plea for change of that very same tradition.

This being so, Dvivedī ran squarely into the *ācāryas* of Hindi who saw themselves as defenders of a tradition in fact only established in this century. With Hindi writers, critics and literary historians, the title *ācārya* is used in the broad sense of one who has gained an authoritative position, say, by his creative oeuvre or as propounder of a particular theory. The most famous of these *ācāryas* is certainly Rāmcandra Śukla. Irrespective of the factual or missing attribution of that designation to the powerful authorities whom Dvivedī confronted, I use the term *ācārya* for them because of the authoritative thrust with which they put forth their ideas. In the narrower technical sense of the term, Dvivedī was the only *ācārya* amongst them, albeit one of *jyotiṣa*! Dvivedī's alleged iconoclasm was found in his vindication of the folk and popular religious and literary heritage as integral to the mainstream of Indian literature. This passionate vindication has reasons of its own (and will not be explained here) that were, in fact, not too remote from those that guided his opponents. Both camps looked for the continuity of a tradition. Suffice it to say that to Dvivedī Indian literature represented an uninterrupted stream that ran from the ancient period through the early twentieth century. Unlike them, however, he thought that by the first decades of the twentieth century a break with that tradition had occurred. The *ācāryas*, in their own various ways, had sought to vindicate an unbroken tradition of classical Indian literature and in that project used the *rasa* theory as a salvaging device. They tenaciously tried to force the *rasa* concept down the throat of modern poets and their audience. In the hands of R. C. Śukla, the *rasa* theory had already undergone a significant re-interpretation in taking on a societal dimension. For him, *rasa* was an aesthetical experience that would not be possible unless the unspeakable suffering of the world had been conquered (Gaeffke 1967: 95). In fact, literature and its *rasa* had to fulfil the purpose of pointing to, and healing, society's evils. Śukla had taken this turn much under the influence of Ernst Haeckel, whose Hindi translator and commentator he was. From Śukla's belief in science and progress ensued his belief that literature must advance progress. Hence, his attempt to make aesthetics an instrument of social reform. Also seminal for the remarkably powerful renewed appropriation of the *rasa* theory was the emergence of I.A. Richards's "New Criticism" (NC) and of the theory of literature propounded by Benedetto Croce (Russo 1991). Both theories largely dissociated poetry from social and political reality. Of this recent development Śukla was well aware. Reacting to the NC, the influential critic Nagendra established the *rasa* theory anew and claimed that it was viable for all Hindi literature, except for the so-called "New Poetry" (*nayī kavitā*, NK) which focused on the present moment and was distinctly intellectual. The NK did not pretend to capture an impersonal or metaphysical reality. From this, Nagendra concluded that the NK, entrapped in intellectualism and dissociated from the world of *rasa*, had become "Non-Poetry", *akavitā*, and to the new poets he addressed the adhortation to rather mend their ways and strive for the transcendental dimension of poetry in which was to be found its *brahmānanda*, its sublime aesthetic enjoyment (Nagendra 1964: especially 330-63).

As for chiefly Marxist criticism, it reacted on Nagendra's *tour de force* in a sarcastical yet also remarkably *ācārya*-like fashion. It took Nagendra by his word and set out to defeat his theory from the inside of it, arguing that Nagendra had overlooked salient aspects of the ancient theory especially as it appeared in the sublimely enriched *dhvani* theory. The fight proliferated and eventually looked strikingly like a twisted *śāstrārtha* rather than a modern debate. I think, that *śāstrārtha* was put to rest for good after 1968 when Nāmvar Siṃh had published his "New Models of Poetry" (*Kavitā ke naye pratimān*). Dvivedī was non-alligned in this *śāstrārtha*, for he had opted out of such a debate as early as 1940 when he published his early major work Hindī sāhitya kī bhūmikā ("An Introduction to Hindi Literature"). Here he had argued that Hindi literature in the twentieth century had undergone an irrevertable change. The old system of poetry as much as the relationship between patron, poet and *rasik* had broken down, whereas new issues and values had come to prevail. Transcendental values and sublime *rasa* had been superseded by the paradigm of the individual and humanity. Modern Hindi literature had lost the *rasa* principle and its aesthetic values. That loss, he deplored, had led to the supersession of Indian literary values by realism which also led to the estrangement from all non-concrete reality. The new western literary modes, eagerly adopted and imitated by Indians, enabled them to successfully describe momentary facts and emotions, whereas their capacity to describe the eternal had slipped away from them. India's literary art had lost its most valuable aesthetic asset, *rasa*, and, consequently, a lot of literature relishing in the detestful had cropped up of late. However deplorable this be, he ends in an optimistic turn by quoting Rabindranath Tagore,

> "History has proved that the sandalwood-scented breeze from a distant country is able to produce in another country a festival of flowers in the bowers of its literature. From wheresoever it come or of whatever kind it be, life awakens by the blow of life, for a long time this has held genuinely true for the human mind."[7]

Against all mental reservations, he argues as a radical modernist and wishes his readers to look ahead to seek empowerment by new ideas which will help them build contemporary India.

Although many of his greatest achievements and honours in public life lay still ahead of him, Dvivedī never fully recovered from the disillusionment with the academia that he had suffered at the BHU. A sense of sorrow and failure, always present in his work and in stark contrast with the exuberance that was in him, too, grew more prominent. What was the sum of his life? A hint to this can be found in the five and a half page long fragment of

---

7 1.143. Dvivedī mentions the author of this passage by *kavi*. This must refer to Tagore whom he mentions earlier in the same paragraph.

the second volume of Anāmdās kā pothā that he drafted shortly before his death. It is a satire on academia and self-aggrandisement.

> "Sometimes people ask you difficult questions. Once a gentleman came to see me, a well-educated youth. He was engaged in a research project at some university. The topic of his research was 'Common people's philosophy of life'. In his shoulder-bag he had a questionnaire in many printed copies. One of this he kindly handed to me. Earlier he had already doled it out to villagers. First it seemed to me that he must be quite in trouble. But then I realized that he really was not. He told me that his only trouble was to analyse and categorize his collection of what people had told him. He had not worked out a special argument nor did he want to. His university would by quite content if he only collected facts in a reliable way and if his analysis was carried out critically and thoughtfully. The result of this was a concern neither of his nor of his university's. He was just an industrious traveller who tried to proceed unbiased. He did not know about man and did not want to know about him" (2.480).

Whereas this young chap is in no trouble, Anāmdās definitely is. What is that "philosophy of life"? He has gathered some idea about life, he has also heard the word "philosophy", but what is that term all about? Anāmdās is desperate for *pramāṇas* to come to grip with that problem. He seeks resort to, and *darśan* from, a sadhu reputed as a great *mahātmā*, for a problem of such dimensions requires a *sadguru* to solve. It turns out that holy man distinguishes himself by an unusual wealth of foul words and curses that in his tantrums he hurls at his sheepish devotees. As the *darśan* comes to a close and the crowd dissipates, Anāmdās can access the saint who is surprised that a widely recognised scholar should have chanced into that crowd of fools. In the ensuing conversation the saint quite unexpectedly confides to him: "Honestly, I am no sadhu at all, although I may not be totally lecherous and vile." Anāmdās is taken aback. The *mahātmā* goes on, "For long I have been waiting for some straightforward pandit like you... Paṇḍitjī Mahārāj, I am weary and distraught. Now that you have come, do me a favour and do not leave hurriedly." At Anāmdās' polite phrase, "Well, if I can help you...", the unhappy sadhu retorts passionately: "Mahārāj, who can help another? You can never tell, it remains a secret. All our strategies and plans remain a play of words. Look at that crowd who think that I can help them. Their stupidness infuriates me, but those few disconnected words of mine still seem to be of use to them. If I don't produce them, they are not content.... I have construed for myself some sort of philosophy of life, you know...". Anāmdās is spell-bound. A philosophy of life? The fragment ends with the *bābā*'s reply:

> "You have come in search of a philosophy of life? Strange thing. But I told you right in the beginning that we cannot help one another, and yet we have to come forth to help. No one knows why this should be

> so. Well, let me finish what I have to say. Maybe I can help you in the same way that I help those pitiable fools. And who knows, Mahārāj, if you will not in some way be of help to me" (2.484).

That light hope and the light burden of *pāṇḍitya*, the sum of a pandit's life —no mean achievement, indeed.

REFERENCES

(Reference to H.P. Dvivedī's collected works [Dvivedī 1998] is made by volume and page.)

Dvivedī, Hazārīprasād. 1998. *Hajārīprasād Dvivedī granthāvalī*, ed. by Mukund Dvivedī. 11 vols. 2nd ed. (1st ed. 1981). New Delhi.

Eagleton, Terry. 1994. *Einführung in Literaturtheorie*. 3rd. ed. (tr. of *Literary theory*. Oxford. 1983). Stuttgart and Weimar.

Gaeffke, Peter. 1967. "Strömungen der Hindiliteratur im Lichte der einheimischen Literaturkritik", *Wiener Zeitschrift für die Kunde Süd- und Südostasiens* XI: 86-108.

Kane, Pandurang Vaman. 1930-42. *History of Dharmaśāstra*. 5 vols. in 9 pts. 2nd ed. 1968-77. (vol.V.1: 1974; vol.V.2: 1977) Pune.

Nagendra. 1964. *Ras-siddhānt*. Delhi.

Russo, John Paul. 1991. "Antihistoricism in Benedetto Croce and I. A. Richards", in: David Perkins (ed.), *Theoretical issues in literary history*. Cambridge, Mass., 268-99.

Siṃh, Nāmvar. 1968. *Kavitā ke naye pratimān*. Repr. of the 4th ed. 1990. Delhi 1995.

———1982. *Dūsrī paramparā kī khoj*. 2nd ed. 1989. New Delhi.

Tripāṭhī, Viśvanāth. 1982. *Hindī ālocnā*. 1992. Repr. of the 2nd. ed. (1st ed. 1970). New Delhi and Patna.

IV

Transmission and Scholarship

JOHANNES BRONKHORST

Traditional and Modern Sanskrit Scholarship: How Do They Relate to Each Other?

Indologists are lucky. Unlike most other scholars who study the intellectual history of a major culture, their object of study does not exclusively consist of old texts. In India there is a living tradition of indigenous scholarship, which continues, in a more or less unbroken succession, the subjects that interest the modern scholar. It is no coincidence that the early European explorers of Sanskrit literature worked with Indian pandits, and that many modern scholars, too, draw considerable advantage from working with them. I am personally proud to have worked with several outstanding pandits in Poona, and there can be no doubt that this has been a major privilege.

Those who have worked with traditional pandits—and I repeat that I count myself among them—know that there is little hope that they will ever be able to compete with these pandits in their areas of specialisation, whether it be grammar, poetics, or one of the schools of Indian philosophy. Few modern scholars, and practically no modern western scholars, have been exposed to the various traditional disciplines of India at such a young age and in such an intensive fashion as the traditional pandit. This is a disadvantage which few modern scholars will ever completely overcome.

We arrive, then, at the following picture. The scholar of, say, early Greek thought has to reconstruct the object of his study with the help of surviving old texts, and with nothing else. There is no one around to help him (except other modern scholars who are in the same situation as he is), so that he is condemned to try to reach results on his own. The scholar of early Indian thought, on the other hand, finds that thought, those same branches of knowledge and enquiry, alive and well in modern India, and that at a level of competence which he cannot dream of attaining. This gives rise to some important questions, but perhaps not the ones that are most often asked. The question is not "What is the place of traditional Sanskrit scholarship in the study of Indian thought?", but rather: "What is the place of modern scholarship in the study of Indian thought?" or even better: "Is there place for modern scholarship in the study of Indian thought?" Is there anything modern scholarship can contribute to this field of study? Are modern scholars not doomed to be at best pale copies of the traditional scholars whom they cannot but try to imitate, normally with limited success?

It seems that some modern Sanskrit scholars do indeed think that imitating traditional scholars should be their aspiration. Others disagree, and point out that traditional and modern Sanskrit scholars do not normally study the same subject-matter. Modern Sanskrit scholars—with the exception of some very few who study living traditional scholars and their ideas in their own right—concentrate on the past: on a particular period in the past, or on the development of certain ideas through a certain length of time. Traditional Sanskrit scholars, on the other hand, embody the present state of the tradition to which they belong.

This may be true, but it does not change the fact that both modern and traditional Sanskrit scholars study by and large the same texts. Moreover, if it is true, as is often maintained, that the traditional scholars are linked to the authors of the texts they study through an unbroken tradition, their interpretation of those texts will be more reliable than that by modern scholars, because it can make use of elements to which the modern scholar has no access, except by consulting the traditional scholar. Once again the question imposes itself whether anything is left for modern scholars to do beyond trying to become traditional scholars themselves.

Modern scholars may have reservations with regard to the unbroken tradition sometimes invoked by traditional scholars. In this they can draw inspiration from Dharmakīrti, the famous Buddhist philosopher who was confronted with the same argument from the side of the Mīmāṃsakas. The latter claimed that not only the Veda, but also its explanation (i.e. the interpretation offered by the Mīmāṃsakas) was not made by human or other living beings (*apauruṣeya*), because it had been handed down by an unbroken tradition (*saṃpradāyāvicchedāt*).[1] Dharmakīrti is not impressed and points out that cases are known where traditions have been changed for various reasons. That is to say, the modern scholar's sceptical attitude is not new, and the history of Indian thought itself provides examples of such an attitude.

I will discuss some concrete examples where it can be maintained that modern Sanskrit scholarship has its mite to contribute. These examples have been taken from my own recent research. They are just examples meant to illustrate a possible justification of modern Sanskrit scholarship besides traditional Sanskrit scholarship. I will begin with a general question: the question whether and to what extent it is possible to understand Indian philosophy.

How can Indian philosophy be understood

This question may look surprising at first. At closer inspection, however, I assume that all of us have sometimes wondered how this or that thinker, or this or that school of thought, could have adhered to their sometimes quite extraordinary doctrines. We may doubt whether we really understand these doctrines, and what is more, we may wonder whether the thinkers

1 Dharmakīrti, Pramāṇavārttikasvavṛtti, ed. Pandeya p. 350 l. 4: *vedavad vyākhyānam apy anādy apauruṣeyaṃ saṃpradāyāvicchedād āgataṃ tato 'rthasiddhiḥ.*

themselves understood them. The Sāṃkhya philosophy, to take an example, proclaims the existence of twenty-five factors (which it calls *tattvas*) which somehow evolve out of each other so as to create the phenomenal world. Did individual Sāṃkhya thinkers know why exactly these twenty-five factors had to be accepted, and not any others? Did they perhaps accept these factors simply because they had been sanctioned by their particular tradition, and because early exposure lent them a degree of plausibility which they are unlikely to acquire for those who do not become acquainted with them until later in life? If this is the case, how much understanding can we, modern scholars, ever hope to attain? Are we condemned to merely record what the Indian thinkers thought, perhaps adding a historical dimension by investigating how some of these ideas succeed more or less similar earlier ones? Or a social one by pointing out that this or that position serves the interests of this or that particular philosopher and those of his group? Such investigations, which put Indian philosophy in its historical and social contexts, are certainly possible and extremely important. Historical continuities have been studied and more will no doubt be discovered. The link between at least certain philosophical doctrines and the social reality of those who accepted them deserves more attention than it has received so far.[2] But is this as far as we can go? If so, our understanding of Indian philosophy will not be very different from that of Indian mythology: a number of just-so stories which we can study in their historical and social contexts.

Advocates of Indian philosophy will no doubt object that there is much more to Indian philosophy than just this. They will point out that some of the discussions and analyses resemble, sometimes anticipate, certain discussions and analyses found in Western philosophy. Such advocates often have a tendency to take these discussions and analyses out of their original context and concentrate, say, on the development of logic in the Indian schools. There can be no doubt that logic underwent a remarkable development in India, and this still draws far too little attention outside a limited group of experts. But this logic was used—and this is too easily overlooked—to defend the basic doctrinal positions of the schools concerned. These doctrinal positions themselves are often somehow taken for granted, or even played down, by modern investigators. If we wish to give these positions their due, we are back with our original question: To what extent can we understand the thought of an Indian philosopher, not merely those aspects of it which we choose (and which we remove from their original context) because they remind us of issues in Western philosophy?

---

2 A recently completed study by Vincent Eltschinger (2000) concentrates on Brahmanic efforts—strongly criticized by Buddhist thinkers—to reify caste.

I will argue that a deeper understanding, one that goes beyond mere historical and sociological analyses, is possible in the case of at least part of Indian philosophy. This is due to a factor which only too rarely draws the attention of modern scholars. I am speaking of the presence of a tradition of rational enquiry. I use this expression to refer to a tradition which came to establish itself in India—or at least in the main philosophical schools—and which obliged thinkers to listen to the criticism of often unfriendly critics, even where it concerned their most sacred convictions, such as those supposedly based on revelation, tradition or inspiration. Confrontations between thinkers so radically opposed to each other were no doubt facilitated by the debates organised from time to time by kings, about which we have some first-hand information from the writings of Chinese pilgrims visiting India in the middle centuries of the first millennium. Little is known about the reasons why, and the date at which, this tradition of critical debate came to establish itself in India. Its effects are however visible in the efforts made by Indian thinkers to systematise their positions, to make them coherent and immune against criticism.

These reflections allow us to identify a particularly important factor in the development of Indian philosophy. Under pressure from competitors, the Indian thinkers of the early classical period were forced to do more than just preserve the teachings they had received; they had to improve and refine them—perhaps in order to avoid becoming the laughing stock of those they might have to confront at a royal court or on some other occasion. In doing so, they created systems of philosophy that might deviate considerably from the pre-systematic teachings which they had inherited.

The history of Indian philosophy, seen in this way, becomes the story of the search for coherence and immunity against criticism, starting normally—but not always, it seems—from some form of traditional teaching. This traditional teaching is usually of a non-philosophical nature. Buddhist philosophy in its various manifestations, for example, based itself ultimately on the teaching of the Buddha, which concerned the escape from suffering and rebirth and had no philosophical pretensions whatsoever. Several centuries separate the Buddha from the beginning of Buddhist systematic philosophy, centuries during which well-meaning monks had ordered and organised the original teaching in various ways. Buddhist systematic philosophy, when it finally arose, was based upon, and continued, these attempts at ordering and organising. It tries to introduce coherence and draws conclusions. In this way Buddhist philosophy arises out of the attempt to introduce order and coherence in the received teachings. Other schools of philosophy proceed similarly.

The extent to which different schools are willing to yield to criticism varies, at least in theory. A thinker like Bhartṛhari represents one extreme.

Bhartṛhari was both grammarian and philosopher. In the grammatical tradition he represents a change of attitude which Madhav Deshpande (1998:20) does not hesitate to characterise as a paradigm-shift. Unlike his main predecessors who lived a number of centuries earlier, with Bhartṛhari "an entirely new tone has set in. There is a strong feeling that the current times are decadent, and that there are no truly authoritative persons around. Grammarians in this decadent period must look back to the golden age of the great ancient grammarians and seek authority in their statements." In philosophy, too, the value of tradition cannot be overestimated. Here Bhartṛhari observes: "Without tradition, logic cannot establish virtue (*dharma*); even the knowledge of seers derives from tradition."[3] And again: "He who bases himself on tradition ... is not hindered by logical arguments."[4]

The author of the Mokṣopāya—a text of unknown date which became the kernel of a larger work, the Yogavāsiṣṭha—may illustrate the opposite extreme. We find here the following statement:[5] "Even [if it is] of human origin, a treatise has to be accepted if it teaches with arguments. [If it is] different, on the other hand, it is to be discarded even if revealed by a seer. Only logic (*nyāya*) is to be adhered to. Even [if it comes] from a child, an argued statement has to be accepted. [Every statement that is] different is to be discarded, even if it has been uttered by [the creator god] Brahmā."

It is hard to deny that Indian philosophies tended to gradually become more and more fossilised with the passing of time. To some extent many of them may have been rather rigid right from the beginning. Buddhist philosophers, for example, were not ready to abandon the words of the Buddha, even though they found various ways to reinterpret them, or even to discover and accept so far unknown, i.e. new, sermons which they ascribed to him. Bhartṛhari's unwillingness to seriously consider anything that deviated from tradition has already been mentioned. Others did try to work independently of any particular tradition (with more or less success). I have the impression that Vaiśeṣika started off in this way. But Vaiśeṣika, too,

---

3 Bhartṛhari, Vākyapadīya, 1.30: *na cāgamād ṛte dharmas tarkeṇa vyavatiṣṭhate / ṛṣīṇām api yaj jānaṃ tad apy āgamapūrvakam //*

4 Bhartṛhari, Vākyapadīya, 1.41: *caitanyam iva yaś cāyam avicchedena vartate / āgamas tam upāsīno hetuvādair na bādhyate //*

5 Yogavāsiṣṭha 2.18.2-3 (as cited in Slaje 1994:167): *api pauruṣam, ādeyam śāstraṃ ced yuktibodhakam/ anyat tv, ārṣam api, tyājyam; bhāvyaṃ nyāyaikasevinā// yuktiyuktam upādeyaṃ vacanaṃ bālakād api/ anyat tṛṇam iva tyājyam, apy uktaṃ padmajanmanā//* Slaje translates: "Auch wenn es von einem Menschen stammt, muss man ein Lehrwerk akzeptieren, soferne es mit Argumenten lehrt. [Jedes] andere dagegen ist zu meiden, auch [wenn] es von den Ṛṣis stammt! Es ist nur die Methode (*nyāya*), der man anhängen darf. Sogar [wenn sie] von einem Kinde [kommt], ist eine argumentative Aussage akzeptabel. [Jede] andere [dagegen] verwerfe man wie [nutzloses] Gras, selbst wenn sie von Brahmā behauptet wurde!"

became a system whose doctrines were meant to be defended, not thoroughly revised.[6]

An ideal history of Indian philosophy—which should include the story of the search for coherence and immunity against criticism—will have to deal in detail with the ways in which various early teachings were transformed into coherent systems of thought. This is of necessity a somewhat technical endeavor, which I do not plan to undertake, at least not in this paper. I will however cite some observations by Ben-Ami Scharfstein which seem to me appropriate in the Indian situation (1998:522): "[The] progress [of every tradition of philosophy] depends ... on its necessary elaboration. This in turn depends on the answers given in the course of debate within the tradition itself and debate with external opponents, not to speak of the assimilation of useful fragments of other philosophies. If its historical continuity is unbroken, each philosophy is provided with successively better answers to its rivals and goes on building its structure higher, more firmly, and more elaborately. Given time, philosophical structures become fully elaborated, that is, worked out in the full detail that enriches and individualizes their culture. They then become summary expressions of these cultures, like the great Christian cathedrals, or the great Muslim mosques, or the great Hindu or Chinese temples or Buddhist stupas." But, "although it has progressed, [each philosophical school] appears no closer to victory over its rivals, which have also progressed" (p. 523). The history of Indian philosophy as I see it is the history of the elaboration of the different systems conditioned by the ongoing critical questioning by their rivals, and by the confrontation with other issues that threaten their internal coherence.

Shared convictions in Indian philosophy

In their search for coherence and immunity against criticism Indian philosophers were confronted with the question to what extent their doctrines were compatible with certain convictions shared by all, or practically all, of them. Such shared convictions existed. I mention two of them in particular. Practically all philosophers of classical India believed in the doctrine of *karma*, and in the close connection between language and reality. The reflective analysis of these two convictions exerted a profound influence on the doctrines of the various schools. Some of these doctrines can indeed be looked upon as the direct outcome of this intellectual challenge.

The doctrine of *karma* exerted its influence at different times, and in different ways. It determined to a considerable extent the way in which the Brahmanical philosophies (to be distinguished from the Buddhist and

6 A noteworthy exception is Raghunātha Śiromaṇi who, though in the tradition of Nyāya-Vaiśeṣika, demolishes a number of Vaiśeṣika categories; see Potter & Bhattacharyya 1992:529 f.

Jaina schools of thought) were initially formulated, and raised again new questions centuries later. Let us first consider the earlier period.

The doctrine of *karma*, it may here be recalled, states that the deeds of living beings lead to punishment or reward (depending on the nature of the deeds) in this life or in a next one. Those who accept this doctrine are most often depicted in the Indian situation as looking for ways to escape from the resulting cycle of rebirths. Some do so by trying to abstain from all activity whatsoever; they practise asceticism in ways that cannot be considered at present. Others are convinced that their innermost self is different from all that acts; knowing one's true inactive nature implies being separated from one's deeds and freed from the effects of those deeds. In other words, knowledge of the self equals, or leads to, liberation.

Most Brahmanical philosophies are based on this vision of a totally inactive self which somehow interacts with the rest of the world which is constituted of everything that moves or acts. This division into two fundamentally distinct realms—an inactive but conscious self (*puruṣa*) and an unconscious but active rest of the world (*pradhāna* / *mūlaprakṛti*)—is the basis of the Sāṃkhya philosophy. The other major Brahmanical ontology of early classical India, Vaiśeṣika, adopts basically the same division, be it in a more sophisticated garb. Most other Brahmanical philosophies stick to the same basic scheme, so that it is possible to maintain that most of them are, at their very basis, responses to the challenge posed by the doctrine of *karma*.

I do not wish to dwell for long on this early period, but rather leave the doctrine of *karma* for the time being aside and turn to the other shared conviction I mentioned: the belief in the correspondence between language and reality. This belief has roots both in Vedic religion and in certain developments inside Buddhism, but since this lecture concentrates on the attempts at systematisation in response to challenges rather than on the origin of the challenges, I will not explore this issue here (cp. Bronkhorst 1996).

Correspondence between language and reality means first of all that the objects in the phenomenal world correspond to the words of language. This may sound innocent enough, but was given quite amazing twists by certain thinkers. Many Buddhists, for example, had come to believe that the objects of our phenomenal world do not really exist. What are they then, and why do we tend to think they exist? The answer is: they are nothing but words, or if you like: notions imposed upon reality by the words of language. Most Brahmanical thinkers disagreed with the imputed unreality of the phenomenal world, but agreed that there is a close connection between words and things. Some of them went to the extent of analysing the use of words in order to arrive at a deeper understanding of objective reality.

All these developments, though important, cannot be dealt with in this paper. However, the belief in the correspondence between language and reality was, during the early centuries of the common era, extended from a mere belief in the correspondence between words and things to something more encompassing which includes the conviction that also *statements* correspond to the situations they describe, or more precisely: the words that make up a statement correspond to the "things" that constitute the situation described. Once again this conviction looks relatively harmless at first sight. After all, a statement like "John eats an apple" might be taken to describe a situation which is constituted by the three elements John, the apple, and the act of eating. Many, perhaps most, statements are such that they do not necessarily clash with this conviction, but some do. Take "John makes a vase". This statement describes a situation in which John and the act of making have their place, but the vase is not yet there. In other words, the words that make up the statement "John makes a vase" do not correspond to the "things" that constitute the situation described. The same difficulty arises whenever statements are made about making something or about coming into being. If we say "The vase comes into being" there is clearly nothing in the situation described corresponding to the word "vase".

I am sure that many people nowadays would conclude from statements like "John makes a vase" and "the vase comes into being" that apparently the words of a statement do *not* always correspond to the elements that make up the situation described. This would certainly be my reaction. Interestingly, to the best of my knowledge all Indian thinkers of the first five or more centuries of the common era did not draw this conclusion. I have studied the question in some detail and considered the writings of authors belonging to practically all currents of philosophy belonging to the three major religions of that period: Brahmanism, Buddhism and Jainism. The results of this investigation have appeared in a recently published monograph (Bronkhorst 1999). To my growing surprise I found that all these thinkers held on to this position and tried in various ways to resolve the difficulties it gave rise to. All of them believed that the words of a statement correspond to the elements that make up the situation described, also in the case of statements like "John makes a vase" and "the vase comes into being".

I will discuss below some of the solutions that were offered to the problems that arise in this manner. First however I wish to deal with a question that may cross your minds at this point. Why did the Indian thinkers of that period, all of them, hold on to a conviction that is so obviously in contradiction with everyday experience? Is this another example of intellectuals accepting a position whose absurdity is visible to a child? Is this one more case of philosophers gone haywire?

I am not at all inclined to draw any such conclusions, and I would like to draw attention to two factors which no doubt encouraged the thinkers of that time not to give up their position simply because it seemed to contradict everyday experience. For one thing, a number of thinkers, most notably the Buddhists, had already for other reasons come to the conclusion that the phenomenal world is not ultimately real. A contradiction between phenomenal reality and the conviction they cherished could not, therefore, endanger this conviction. Equally important is the presence in India at that time of a tradition of rational enquiry, which I mentioned earlier. Philosophers had become convinced that their reasons and arguments were entitled to being taken seriously, as seriously or even more so than tradition, revelation, and insight. We know that in ancient Greece some thinkers, the Eleatics, did not hesitate to reject perceived reality on the basis—not of tradition, revelation, or special insight—but of mere argument. The early Indian thinkers, too, proceeded on the basis of their newly acquired confidence in the power of human reason. Those of us who feel superior to them might do well to recall that our phenomenal reality, too, hides a plethora of entities that deviate widely from our experience—molecules, atoms, subatomic particles—the existence of which we willingly accept on the basis of reasons provided and experiments carried out by others.

What solutions did the Indian thinkers offer to the difficulties they thus encountered, and which we might be tempted to consider to be of their own making? What does the word "vase" refer to in the sentences "John makes a vase" and "the vase comes into being"? The literature concerned contains a variety of answers, as I said earlier. Here I will concentrate on only two of them.

Perhaps the simplest and in a way most obvious answer was adopted by the Sāṃkhya school of Brahmanical philosophy, mentioned above. We have various sources that contain information related to the early history of this school, even though the correct evaluation of this material by scholars has not so far been fully successful. In spite of this, most elements of its classical teachings figure in early works, such as the great epic of India, the Mahābhārata, and other texts.[7] One important element, however, is never mentioned in these earlier accounts, and must have been a rather recent innovation. I am speaking of *satkāryavāda*, the doctrine according to which the effect is present in its material cause. Very concretely this means that the situation described by the statement "John makes a vase", or "the vase comes into being", contains already a vase, be it that the vase at that moment is not yet visible.

Satkāryavāda becomes an essential part of classical Sāṃkhya philosophy, is taken over by some schools and vehemently combated by others.

7 For recent discussions of Sāṃkhya in the Mahābhārata, see Bisschop/Bakker 1999 and Brockington 1999.

The scholastic debates about this issue in later texts make one easily forget how profoundly strange this doctrine really is—not only for modern Western readers. They may have as a further effect that the doctrine becomes familiar, and that one stops being surprised by its extraordinary content. Familiarity is easily mistaken for understanding. A better understanding, I submit, can be obtained by becoming aware what specific problem the doctrine was meant to solve. In the case of *satkāryavāda*—I maintain—this problem was the direct consequence of certain ideas regarding the relationship between language and reality shared by all thinkers of that time.

The problem was shared by all thinkers, but they did not all propose the same solution. An altogether different solution was proposed by a particularly famous thinker, Nāgārjuna. In order to understand his solution we have to take into account that Nāgārjuna was a Buddhist. The Buddhists of his time, as I pointed out earlier, had come to believe that the phenomenal world does not really exist. This belief had not been part of the message taught by the historical Buddha. It was rather the result of subsequent elaborations and reinterpretations of the early teachings. Whatever the details of this development—with which we cannot deal at this moment—the Buddhists had come to *believe*, on the presumed authority of the Buddha, that the phenomenal world does not really exist; they could not prove this. This changed with Nāgārjuna. Nāgārjuna could prove what many Buddhists of his time were convinced of at any rate, viz., that the phenomenal world does not exist. It does not exist, because it cannot exist. And it cannot exist because it is self-contradictory.

The basic argument to prove this has already been sketched above. The statement "the vase comes into being" describes a situation which must contain a vase. It does not, however. The statement is therefore contradictory and nothing comes into being. I will cite one verse from Nāgārjuna's Mūlamadhyamakakārikā which deals with this particular problem. It states:[8] "If any unproduced entity is found anywhere it could be produced. Since that entity does not exist, what is produced?" In the case of our vase this means: if there is a vase at the time it is going to be produced, it can be produced. If there is no such vase, the subject of "the vase is produced" has nothing to refer to, and the statement is empty. This is true if we assume, as did apparently Nāgārjuna, that the terms of a statement have to refer to something that is there in the situation described.

Nāgārjuna proved, with this and similar arguments, what a number of Buddhists had already believed before and without him. He did however more. By introducing these rather nihilistic arguments into Buddhist philosophy he created his own school of philosophy which, known by the name

---

8 Nāgārjuna, Mūlamadhyamakakārikā 7.17: *yadi kaścid anutpanno bhāvaḥ saṃvidyate kvacit/ utpadyeta sa kiṃ tasmin bhāve utpadyate 'sati//.*

Madhyamaka or Mādhyamika, survived for a long time in India and to this day among Tibetan Buddhists.

My reflections so far have shown, I hope, that at least two crucially important doctrines held by different schools of Indian philosophy found their historical origin, not in meditative experience or supernatural revelation, but in the need to deal with difficulties arising from positions taken. The *satkāryavāda* of Sāṃkhya and the nihilism of Madhyamaka are both to be understood as responses to a conviction, shared by all thinkers of that time, concerning the relationship between language and reality which at first view would barely seem to justify such encompassing metaphysical conclusions.

Let me add a few more words about the doctrine of *karma*. We have already seen that this dogma profoundly influenced the fundamental shape of several Brahmanical schools of thought. We now turn to some later effects of this dogma on Indian thought.

I have already several times mentioned the tradition of rational enquiry without which the history of classical Indian philosophy cannot be correctly understood; I think this is a point that cannot be sufficiently emphasized. The classical Indian schools of thought could not afford to present a mere bunch of incoherent ideas. They had to deal with inconsistencies and other blemishes, and somehow iron them out. This critical, and therefore self-critical, approach could not but force them to confront the question as to how *karma* is supposed to work. If the deeds I carry out in this life bring about results in a next life, by what mechanism do they do so? The question became particularly difficult for those thinkers who were of the opinion that the deeds of living beings literally shape the future world. Texts like Vasubandhu's Abhidharmakośabhāṣya—one of the most important dogmatic texts of Indian Buddhism during the classical period—leave no doubt about it that the shape of the world is determined by the deeds that living beings have carried out in an earlier world period. How should we imagine this process to have taken place?

Time does not permit me to discuss the issue and the solutions offered in detail. It seems however likely that Praśastapāda introduced the notion of a creator God into Vaiśeṣika precisely in order to explain the mechanism of karmic retribution. And Vasubandhu, the Buddhist thinker who turned to idealism later in his life (if the legend about his life is to be believed) did so in order to make the link between deeds and their effects intelligible: both now found their place in the mental continuum of a person, and karmic efficacy was no more puzzling than the occurrence of a dream.

Both Praśastapāda and Vasubandhu took radical decisions which were to have consequences for the further development of Indian thought. They did so because they saw no other way to account for a dogma which they accepted as certain: the dogma of karmic retribution.

The case of satkāryavāda

After these examples of major doctrines that can be understood, or even *have* to be understood, as reactions to challenges which their authors had to face, I would like to consider one of these, the *satkāryavāda* of the Sāṃkhyas, somewhat more closely. This doctrine, even though originally an answer to a challenge, gradually became one more dogma characterising the Sāṃkhya school of thought. From a solution to a dilemma it became another truth one had to accept if one wanted to be a Sāṃkhya. The original problem is slowly forgotten and seems to gradually attract less attention in the philosophical literature.

Compare now our understanding of the doctrine of *satkāryavāda* with that of a Sāṃkhya thinker for whom this doctrine is no more than a simple dogma, who is no longer aware of the original problem which this doctrine was meant to solve. In such a case it can plausibly be argued that we understand this doctrine better than the Sāṃkhya thinker concerned, in the sense that we know—supposing that the explanation I have proposed is correct—something which this Sāṃkhya thinker does not know. We presumably know why this doctrine was introduced in the first place, while he doesn't. Some of his predecessors did, of course. The Sāṃkhya thinkers who introduced *satkāryavāda* knew why they did so, and so did some later Sāṃkhya thinkers, though perhaps less clearly.

Consider with this in mind the following criticism of the historical approach, exemplified in a passage formulated by Gerald James Larson almost twenty years ago (1980:305): "Quite apart from the merit or lack of merit of an historical interpretation, it appears that South Asians themselves seldom if ever used such an explanation. ... [B]y providing historical interpretations of South Asian thought and culture modern interpreters are more or less talking to themselves. There is nothing wrong with the latter enterprise, for at some stage in our work we as modern interpreters of South Asian culture must 'encompass' (in Dumont's sense) what South Asian culture represents in our experience. The crucial methodological issue, however, is that the 'encompassed' can never pass itself off as an adequate characterization of an indigenous interpretation. In other words, to put it directly, historical interpretation is *ours*, not *theirs*! In a South Asian environment, historical interpretation is *no* interpretation. It is a zero-category." This passage suggests that modern scholarship in an important way misses the point, and cannot claim to add anything to the understanding of Indian thought beyond an attempt to adjust it to our experience. If Larson is right, a traditional scholar cannot possibly learn anything from modern scholarship, except perhaps an understanding of how *we* think.

Let us stick to the example of *satkāryavāda*. Our historical interpretation maintains that this doctrine was introduced to answer a specific problem, which I have tried to identify. The modern Sāṃkhya-pandit supposedly is no longer aware of this problem. He knows *his* Sāṃkhya and is not looking for a historical understanding of its doctrines. Does this mean that our historical interpretation is only *ours*, not *theirs*, as Larson maintained? I hope you will agree with me that our historical interpretation, assuming it is correct, may not be that of the modern adherent of the Sāṃkhya system, but is nevertheless very much *theirs*, in the sense that those who introduced *satkāryavāda* did it for the reasons which our historical method has tried to rediscover. If, then, modern interpreters of Sāṃkhya are more or less talking to themselves, as Larson puts it, then for the simple reason that the creators of classical Sāṃkhya have been dead for a long time, and because today's Sāṃkhya-pandits are not interested to know why the doctrine of *satkāryavāda* was created in the first place. Let me add immediately that this example is hypothetical. I do not know whether today's Sāṃkhya-pandits are or are not interested in this question, and what is more, I am not sure there are nowadays traditional scholars in India who adhere to the Sāṃkhya tradition.[9] If there are, and if they share our interest in the question why the doctrine of *satkāryavāda* was created, they will join us in our research, and provide historical interpretations of South Asian thought just like *us*. Of course, Larson is right if he maintains that historical research will not help us much to understand a modern pandit who is not interested in the how and why of his received beliefs. But he is wrong if he thinks that historical research cannot answer questions that anyone, including a traditional pandit, may ask.

Conclusions

Let me, by way of conclusion, return to the question of the relationship between the modern academic study of Indian philosophy and the still living traditions of philosophy in present-day India. I know from experience that many traditional scholars—whose numbers, unfortunately, are dwindling—have a mastery over their particular fields which few scholars who have not already in their childhood had the advantage of a traditional training can hope to attain. I am therefore deeply convinced of the value of the Indian traditions, and of the importance to learn from them as long as this is still possible. But this does not mean that modern scholars should have as principal aim to become imitation pandits. In some ways modern scholars may never understand Indian philosophy as well as traditional scholars do. In other ways, they may understand it better. They may understand it better by bringing in the historical dimension, by taking into consideration the context

9 K.C. Dutt's *Who's Who of Sanskrit Scholars in India 1991* enumerates, to be sure, twenty-two names under the heading Sāṃkhya (p. 560-61). But they all have other areas of specialisation besides this one, and Dutt's book says nothing about the personal allegiance of the scholars mentioned.

in which the various schools of thought arose and survived, and by bringing to light the problems which the central doctrines of the philosophical schools were meant to solve. Traditional scholars are of course more than welcome to join and contribute to a better understanding of the thought of their spiritual and philosophical ancestors, and it is very rewarding to see that a number of them actually do so. There can and should in this way be no question of *us* against *them*.

REFERENCES

Bhartṛhari, *Vākyapadīya*, ed. W. Rau. Wiesbaden 1977.

Bisschop, Peter, and Bakker, Hans. 1999. "Mokṣadharma 187 and 239-241 reconsidered", *Asiatische Studien / Études Asiatiques* 53(3):461-474.

Brockington, John. 1999. "Epic Sāṃkhya: texts, teachers, terminology", *Asiatische Studien / Études Asiatiques* 53(3):475-492.

Bronkhorst, Johannes. 1996. "Sanskrit and reality: the Buddhist contribution", in: *Ideology and Status of Sanskrit: Contributions to the history of the Sanskrit language*, ed. Jan E.M. Houben. Leiden etc.: E.J. Brill, 109-135.

———. 1999. *Langage et réalité: sur un épisode de la pensée indienne*. Turnhout: Brepols Publishers.

Deshpande, Madhav M. 1998. "Evolution of the notion of authority (*prāmāṇya*) in the Pāṇinian tradition", *Histoire Épistémologie Langage* 20(1) ("Les grammaires indiennes") 5-28.

Dharmakīrti, *Pramāṇavārttika with svavṛtti*. Ed. Ram Chandra Pandeya. Delhi etc.: Motilal Banarsidass, 1989.

Dutt, K.C. 1994. *Who's Who of Sanskrit Scholars in India 1991*. New Delhi: Sahitya Akademi.

Eltschinger, Vincent. 2000. *Caste et philosophie bouddhique. Continuité de quelques arguments bouddhiques contre le traitement réaliste des dénominations sociales*. Wien: Arbeitskreis für Tibetische und Buddhistische Studien Universität Wien.

Larson, Gerald James. 1980. "Karma as a 'sociology of knowledge' or 'social psychology' of process/praxis", in: Wendy Doniger O'Flaherty (ed.), *Karma and Rebirth in Classical Indian Traditions*. Berkeley - Los Angeles - London: University of California Press, 303-316.

Nāgārjuna, *Mūlamadhyamakakārikā* ed. J.W. de Jong. The Adyar Library and Research Centre, Madras 1977.

Potter, Karl H., and Bhattacharyya, Sibajiban. 1992. *Encyclopedia of Indian Philosophies, volume VI. Indian Philosophical Analysis: Nyāya-Vaiśeṣika from Gaṅgeśa to Raghunātha Śiromaṇi*. Princeton, New Jersey: Princeton University Press.

Slaje, Walter. 1994. *Vom Mokṣopāya-Śāstra zum Yogavāsiṣṭha-Mahārāmāyaṇa. Philologische Untersuchungen zur Entwicklungs- und Überlieferungsgeschichte eines indischen Lehrwerks mit Anspruch auf Heilsrelevanz*. Wien: Österreichische Akademie der Wissenschaften.

HARRY FALK

The Galitas in the Ṛgveda Padapāṭha: On the Origins of the Saṃhitapāṭha and the Padapāṭha

Introduction

The Ṛgvedasaṃhitā (RV) and the *saṃhitās* of other Vedic schools can be recited in many different ways. For sacrificial purposes and daily rehearsal the *saṃhitapāṭha* (SP) is used, that means the continuous flow of words interlinked according to the rules of euphonic combination, *sandhi*.

The *padapāṭha* (PP), on the other hand, is additionally recited only by some teachers. It avoids *sandhi* and includes pauses between the words, uses repetitions and deviations which serve to clarify the nature of compounds and it presents word forms unchanged by, for example, metrical requirements. Its purpose is to support an understanding of the stanzas.

The *kramapāṭha* (KP), lastly, combines SP and PP, in that it proceeds in pairs of succeeding words, like a-b, b-c, c-d, d-e etc., where every word—but the first—occurs first in its pausa form, and the next time in *saṃhita* form.

These three forms of recitation are regarded as basic, *prakṛti*, whereas all other forms, like *jaṭa* and *ghana* etc., are seen as further developments, *vikṛti*.[1]

How old are these *prakṛti* forms? We have very few original works dealing with the technical side of them. The Ṛkprātiśākhya (ṚPrā) is the most elaborate work we have on *saṃhita* and *pada* recitations; it specifically mentions *krama* recitation and gives all its details. Furthermore we have the old Upalekhasūtra (UpS),[2] and the recent work of K.V. Abhyankar, the Vedapadapāṭhacarcā, published in 1974. Apart from mentioning Śākalya—the supposed author of the Ṛgveda PP—several times (Bronkhorst 1981:84 f.), the grammarian Pāṇini, who lived in the 4th century BC (Falk 1993:304, 1994a:327), teaches the designation *kramaka* (4.2,61) for someone who has learned the *krama*(*pāṭha*)[3] and

---

1 For more details and modern practices see Staal 1961:24 ff.; for an old account cf. *Alberuni's India, I*, ed. Edward C. Sachau, London 1910:62 (1914:128).

2 For editions etc. see Aithal 1991:155-159; I use the text as edited in Abhyankar 1974:41-82.

3 Cf. Bronkhorst 1985, who regards this *sūtra* as an interpolation and argues for a post-pāṇinian date of the *kramapāṭha*.

also gives at least one rule of *sandhi* pertaining solely to the KP (Kulkarni 1991/92).[4]

Other Vedic schools possess similar texts. The most elaborate of these are the Vājasaneyiprātiśākhya (VPrā) of Kātyāyana (Weber 1858) and the two Prātiśākhyas belonging to the Atharvaveda (Suryakanta 1939, Deshpande 1997). The Prātiśākhya of the Taittirīya school does not deal with our topic.

The middle Vedic texts have already stated that none of the three versions of recital is identical with what the Ṛṣis once pronounced. Because of the rigorous application of *sandhi* rules the metre of hundreds of verses got crippled. Why would someone change the flow of words obeying a pleasant metre to something out of metre? Our traditional explanation dates from the days of Benfey (e.g. 1874:227) and Oldenberg (e.g. 1888:370 ff.) who envisaged a group of redactors who collected and reshaped the hymns in a process called *orthoepic diaskeuasis*. Here, some *sandhi* rules were generally applied although they were originally of a rather limited or local validity. Since this process had been going on even while some parts of the RV were still not composed, some of the over-applied rules gained a general acceptance, leading, *inter alia*, to the strict vowel-*sandhi* rules of classical Sanskrit.[5] The motive behind the *diaskeuasis* has been seen by modern scholars as lying in the wish of the Vedic scholars to preserve the text as unchanged as possible—although it seems somewhat contradictory to assume that changes are necessary to prevent changes.

The development as seen by the scholars of the 19th century can be presented as in table 1.

The solution I will propose at the end of this paper is the result of a different approach which tries to elucidate the nature of the omitted passages called, indiscriminately, *samaya, saṃkrama, galita* or *galanta* in some of the works cited above.

The galitas

When Max Müller published the first complete RV from 1849 until 1874 he supplied the reader with the version of the SP juxtaposed to the PP. His sort of arrangement was copied later by the editors of the Poona and the Hoshiarpur editions in the 20th century. Max Müller changed the picture

---

4 I do not agree with Kulkarni that the rule *aplutavad upasthite* must have its origins in a different work. Her proposal **nopasthite* would be in conflict with 6.1,125 *plutapragṛhyā aci nityam*, by implying that also *pragṛhya* forms should undergo *sandhi* when in *upasthita* position.

5 In popular vernaculars initial *a-* could be combined or not, cf. Dhammapada 11: *sāre cāsāradassino* and 12: *asāraṃ ca asārato*. Similar license can be found in the RV for the *praśliṣṭa sandhi* as well as for the *abhinihita sandhi*, which seems to have started with the *a-* of words beginning in *ava-*; cf. Pāṇ. 6.1,115.

Table 1

Sūkta... ... ...

orthoepic diaskeuasis:
assembling in maṇḍalas and application of sandhi-rules

↓

SP

→ PP (= analysis of SP, by Śālakya)

↓

KP (combination of SP and PP, by Bābhravya)

→ ṚPrā (mediation between SP and PP)

↓

Jaṭapāṭha, Ghanapāṭha etc.

of the PP considerably in that he provided a PP to every word of the SP, disregarding a particular feature of all of his PP-manuscripts: on almost every manuscript page a circle inside two *daṇḍa*s replaces some part of the text. The passages omitted as well as the graphical sign is called *galita* or *galanta* in present times. The passages omitted involve usually three or more words; in rare cases one circle replaces more than a complete stanza.

These *galita*s have an old history. They are known to the ṚPrā by the name of *samaya*; the VPrā calls the process *saṃkrama*; as *samaya* they occur also in the UpS. In the 16th century one Lakṣmīdharasūri of Candrapura composed the Galitapradīpa (GalPra) of the RV, which speaks of *samaya* and *galita* indiscriminately. These terms were originally coined for a portion of the text completely omitted, as was already noted by Weber (1858:289 f.). But the treatment of parallel passages was different in different schools of the PP, as we learn from an old saying transmitted in the commentary to the VPrā 4;173 (Weber 1858:278):

> *punaruktāni lupyante padānīty āha śākalyaḥ,*
> *alopa iti gārgasya kāṇvasyārthavaśād iti,*
> "'Repeated words are to be omitted', says Śākalya.
> 'No omission!' according to Gārga Kāṇva,
> 'out of need for meaning[ful sentences]'."

The definition of a galita

In his Vedapadapāṭhacarcā, K.V. Abhyankar defines a *samaya* like this: "*Samaya* or conventional omission is the non-recital of three or more words in the Padapāṭha after they have occurred thrice in the same order as a group in the Saṁhitā recital" (p. 28).[6] Although Abhyankar is talking about the RV PP or KP, his definition is copied from the VPrā, *adhyāya* 4: *tripadādyāvartamāne saṃkramaḥ.166.* and *trir āvṛtte.173.* In the GalPra skipping is prescribed for *pāda*s and *ardharc*s occurring for the fourth time in a *varga*,[7] or for any other series of three words.[8] A look at the *galitas* of the present PP manuscripts shows that these definitions are not correct, because the triple repetition is not at all necessary in RV PP. With regard to the omission it has to be stated that the ṚPrā nowhere gives details about the *galitas* in the PP. It always connects them with the KP. ṚPrā 10.3,12 (608) is crucial in this regards and needs to be cited in full:

> *dṛṣṭakramatvāt samayānt sandadhyāt sarvaśaḥ krame,*
> *padena ca padābhyāṃ ca prāg avasyed atītya ca*
> "Because their *krama* fashion is (already) known, *samaya*s should be united on all sides in one *krama*,
> first (uniting them) with one word, then ending (the *krama*) with two words after passing over (the *galita* portion)."

The same rule is again found in ṚPrā 11.2,12 no. 636, as *atho padābhyāṃ samayaṃ padena ca krameṣv avasyed atigamya saṃdadhyāt*, "moreover, inside the *krama* portions, one should unite the *samaya* with two words and one word, pass over (the *samaya*) and end (the *krama*)." The diction is rather ambiguous; the translation follows the traditional interpretation, where the "one word" and the "two words" are taken as the first word of the *galita* and the two words after the *galita*. This way a sequence of 10 words with *galita* on words 5 to 7 would go like this, with hyphens indicating *sandhi* and dashes indicating pausa form:

```
SP:  a - b - c - d - f - g - h - i - j - k
PP:  a / b / c / d //    o    // i / j / k /
KP:  a - b /
         b - c /
             c - d /
                 d - f /
                     f - g - h - i - j /
                                     j - k /
```

6 64. *trayāṇāṃ tryadhikānāṃ vā padānāṃ saṃhitāpāṭhe tryadhikavāram āvartane padapāṭhe teṣām agrahaṇaṃ samayaḥ.*

7 GaḷPra 1,4 *trir ādigata ekasmin varge'rdharco'ṅghrir eva vā, galet...*

8 GalPra 1,5 *galet... caturādigataṃ varge yac caikasmin padatrayam.*

This way the "one word" is f, i.e. the first word of the *galita* portion, and the "two words" are i-j, joined to the *galita* in *saṃhita*-fashion.[9] The absolutives *atītya* and *atigamya* in the given rules seem to speak of the *galita* as being "passed over" in *saṃhita* style, although not using the word. It might seem tempting to interpret the "passing over" as simply omitting the *galita*, just as in *pada* recitation, but the "combination" (*sandadhyāt*) clearly refers to the *samaya*, and not to the two parts before and after it. That means, the *galita* portion is not omitted, but inserted into the *krama* text.

Before I go into details I would like to refer to an exchange of ideas I had with Pandit K.P. Aithal seven years ago in the wake of my review of his Vedalakṣaṇa. In the review I had pointed out that contrary to a passage in his preface (p. 8) there are two printed editions of the RV PP (*kṛṣṇācārya* 1902, Josyer 1947), and Pandit Aithal replied in a private communication that he knew these editions and found them very defective. After having worked with both editions for a while I realized that the younger one from Mysore shares some strange mistakes with the older one, and that the Mysore text is most likely nothing but a resetting of the Bombay edition. So I took the Bombay edition to the Staatsbibliothek at Berlin and compared it with 5 manuscripts, all written in Nāgarī letters, most of them part of the Chambers collection and thus not very recent.[10] There are some occasional anomalies in one or the other of these copies, but on the whole it became clear that the Bombay edition is a pretty faithful representation of the North Indian mss tradition.

A cursory glance at the *galitas* as found in this tradition makes it very difficult to see a logic behind the selection. First, contrary to what Abhyankar said, a passage need not be repeated thrice to be skipped. One precursor is absolutely sufficient. I guess this rule is so often repeated because it helps to do away with the question why there are so many repetitions not marked as *galitas*.[11] In fact, even after occurring more than 3 times a passage need not be recognized.

That means, there can be a *galita* after just one precursor, and there may not be a *galita* when many precursors are there.

What then is the use of these *galitas*? The chaotic mixture forbids the idea that the text was subject to a deliberate abbreviation. If shortening the PP was intended many more passages could have been eliminated. And since the omitted passages are not simply omitted, but replaced by the re-

---

9 Occasionally, the mss of the PP add one or more words of the *galita* portion to the *circle* in *daṇḍas*; ms Chambers 60 once reads the complete *galita tvaṃ no agne* inside *galita* marks; ms Ms.or.oct. 699 ends 2.41,5 with *asate iti /7/ tā samrājā //o// sacete*, where "/7/", probably indicates the length of the *galita* portion; *tā saṃrājā* is the begin of the *galita* portion and *sacete* denotes the first word of 2.41,6c.

10 Ms.or.oct. 699 a-b; Chambers 60/61, 63, 73-76 (Weber 1853:4 f.).

11 Chapter 3 of the GalPra contains nothing but non-recognized parallels.

spective SP, a significant cut in the volume of the text is not apparent. Instead, with all these omissions and non-omissions to be kept in mind, the amount of knowledge necessary to deal with *galita*s surpasses the amount necessary to simply going on reciting all of the available *pada*s. The fact that the ṚPrā (11.3,12 no. 608) argues on the basis of "the *kramapāṭha* form, which has already been perceived" (*dṛṣṭakramatvāt*), cannot be regarded as convincing.

Therefore it has been stated repeatedly that the *galita*s are only found in instances where identical passages also share an identical meaning (Jog 1969, 1976; Aithal 1991:8 f. with further literature). But this is not true, as C.G. Kashikar (1947) has observed: there are cases with identical meaning not omitted, and there are cases with different meanings marked as *galita*s.

In 1994 I reported about a first attempt to solve the question with the help of the computer. I cut the 4th *maṇḍala* into all possible sequences of three successive words and compared them with the *galita*s. The result was simple: most *galita*s reacted to sequences found at the beginning of a stanza. This I explained provisionally as an attempt to distinguish a *pratīka* from any succession of the same words someplace else.

For this paper it was planned to go through all of the Ṛgvedic *galita*s, but finally only the first four *maṇḍala*s could be thoroughly checked. The result is not at variance with my first surmise. The *galita*s will be classified in three sections, those within one *sūkta*, then those in the same *maṇḍala*, and finally those reacting to passages in previous *maṇḍala*s. This division did occasionally reveal some apparently significant differences. Generally, the parallels provide two sets of answers, one from passages marked as *galita*s, and one from those unmarked. It seems more important to observe the second batch, because it is easier for a redactor to add *galita*s, even if he violates the rules observed of his predecessors, than to eliminate existing *galita*s. That means, *galita*s non-observed should have been non-observed right from the start, whereas observed *galita*s can be original or later additions.

That there are stages in the composition of the RV-Padapāṭha has been observed more than once (Jha 1976, 1992:68ff). The ṚPrā tells us that its own complicated rules dealing with ungrammatical words like *ā́raik* in the KP are not observed by some teachers who simply go through the RV in *krama*s of two words every time (10.2,11ab, no. 636). This way of teaching looks more like the original one, and the present *krama* rules appear like *paṇḍita* elaborations. The ṚPrā 11.6,33 (no. 676) reports that the *kramaśāstra* is the work of Bābhrava, but also that other teachers had their own, imperfect way of reciting in *krama* fashion.[12] The Mahābhārata[13] adds

12 *yathopadiṣṭaṃ kramaśāstram āditaḥ punaḥ pṛthaktair vividhair na sādhuvat, iti pra bābhravya uvāca ca kramaṃ kramapravaktā prathamaṃ śaśaṃsa ca.*

13 Mbh 12,330: *pāñcālena kramaḥ prāptas tasmād bhūtāt sanātanāt, bābhravya-gotraḥ*

the information that he belonged to the Pāñcāla clan and that his personal name was Gālava,[14] belonging to the *bābhravya* gotra.[15] By his *gotra* name he is also mentioned in several lists of Ṛgvedic teachers, usually in close succession to Śākalya, creator of the PP (ĀśGS 3.4,5; ŚGS 4.10,3; 6.1,1). Bābhravya can thus be regarded as the author of the final *kramaśāstra*, but he certainly was not the first to use this technique. So we should always be aware of the possibility that even the KP follows rules which date from rather different stages in its development.[16]

For understanding the evidence we must be aware of several rules, each one expressed in some of the texts:

1) The basis for the *kramapāṭha* is the *ardharc*. So, a-b is in many respects equivalent to *pādas* c-d, because the end of b does not merge with the beginning of c (ṚPrā 11.3,11 no. 607; UpS 1,16).

2) The end of each *ardharc* is wrapped in a process called *parigraha* or *veṣṭana*, which implies the addition of *iti* and the repetition of the last word. This way the end of *pāda* a or c is very much different from the end of *pādas* b and d (ṚPrā 11.2,8 no. 598).

3) Words consisting of only a vowel, like *ā*, *u* or *ī*, are not regarded as full words. When they occur first, they are put together with the following word in groups of three (ṚPrā 11.1,2 no. 615), in the following fashion: 1-2/2-*ā*-3/*ā*-3/3-4/. That means that *pratīkas* which start as 1-2-*ā*-3 will never produce a *galita* in a stanza starting with 1-2-*ā*-4.

The result can be surveyed in the sequel where all possible connections are listed—without trying to be exhaustive. For abbreviations a dot is used to indicate at least one word, a hyphen represents the whole *pāda*, a slash marks a final *pāda* c or other (e.g. "c-/" represents a closing *pāda* c). This way "a." means "occurring at the beginning of *pāda* a"; ".a" stands for "occurring at the end of *pāda* a"; ".a." would be "in the middle of *pāda* a".

The examples list cases from the first four *maṇḍalas* and some occasional material from *maṇḍalas* 5 to 10. Wherever I found exceptions to the rules

---

sa babhau prathamaḥ krama-pāragaḥ.37. nārāyanād varam labdhvā prāpya yogam anuttamam, kramam pranīya śikṣām ca pranayitvāsa gālavaḥ.38.

14 Vyāḍi and Gālava are ascribed a particular form of *sandhi* with *ya-* and *va-śrutis* (e.g. *dadhi-y-atra*) in Puruṣottamadeva's Bhāṣāvṛtti on Pāṇ. 6.1,77. Bronkhorst (1981:84 f.) dealing with this passage shows that only Vyāḍi is mentioned in the ṚPrā. If Gālava is the author of the *kramaśāstra*, he is at least mentioned by this designation several times.

15 Pāñcāla Bābhravya is also an old authority on *kāmaśāstra*, see Kāmasūtra 1.1,10.

16 An old system of *galita* could be the basis for RV 1.166,15, where only the first three words *eṣá va stómo* are omitted, although the whole stanza is identical with 1.165,15. The difference touches only the *pratīka*! A similar inconsistency is met with in RV 1.191,10-11, where the third (out of six) *pādas* read *sáḥ, cit, nú, ná, marāti* in 10, introduced in 11 by *so:iti* (*galita* for the rest), probably because 12 reads *tā́ḥ*, (*galita* for *cit, nú, ná*) *maranti*.

these exceptions are attached immediately, accompanied by an attempt to explain them—if possible. When a rule is sufficiently documented further examples have been neglected:

Rule 1: *Galita* for full stanza
b) in the same *maṇḍala*
1.176,6 < 1.175,6
2.2,23 < 2.1,16
2.14,12 < 2.13,13
2.15,10; 2.16,9; 2.17,9; 2.18,9; 2.19,9; 2.20,9 < 2.11,21
4.14,5 < 4.13,5;
4.44,7 < 4.43,7
c) in a previous *maṇḍala*
4.4,13 < 1.147,3
4.32,16 < 3.52,3
[Exception: no *galita*
10.90,16 < 1.164,50: long distance]

Rule 2: *Galita* for *ardharc*
a) in the same *sūkta*
1.29,2-7(c-d-e-) < 1(c-d-e-)
2.22,2(f-g-*l*) < 1(g-h-*l*)
4.42,2(c-d-) < 1(c-d-)
4.48,2,3,4(c-d-) < 1(c-d-)
8.102,5(c-*l*) < 4(c-*l*) [misunderstood by GalPra 1,7 who regards this final *pāda* of a *gāyatrī* as a rare case of "two words" repeated in the whole of the RV]
b) in the same *maṇḍala*
1.5,4(c-*l*) < 1.4,10(c-*l*)
1.13,10(c-*l*) < 1.7,10(c-*l*)
3.31,18(c-d-) < 3.1,19a-b-
3.59,4(c-d-) < 3.1,21(c-d-)
c) in a previous *maṇḍala*
4.8,2(c-*l*) < 1.1,2(c-*l*)
4.55,7(a-b-) < 1.106,7(a-b-)
7.66,19(c-*l*) < 3.62,18(c-*l*)

Rule 3: *Galita* from and for *pratīka*
[a.<a.]
a) in the same *sūkta*

evā́ hy àsya	1.8,10(a.) < 8(a.)
devó ná yáḥ	1.73,3(a.) < 2(a.)
tám u tvā	1.78,3+4(a.) < 2(a.), 6.16,15(a.) < 14(a.); 6.45,11(a.) < 10(a.)
yā́ te dhā́māni	1.91,19(a.) < 4(a.)
utá na īṃ	1.186,7(a.)+8(a.) < 6(a.)

ádhvaryavo yáḥ śatám	2.14,7(a.) < 6(a.)
tád ín nv asya	3.38,8(a.) < 7(a.)
trír ā́ diváḥ	3.56,7(a.) < 6(a.)
ā́ na índro	4.20,2(a.) < 1(a.)
ā́ yātv índro	4.21,3(a.) < 1(a.)
tā́ tū́ te	4.22,6(a.) < 5(a. SP *ta*)
utá smāsya	4.38,9(a.) < 8(a.)
índrā yuvám varuṇā	4.41,5(a.) < 4(a.)
[Exception: no *galita* because of enclitic?	
vā́yav índraś ca	1.2,6(a.) < 5(a.)
trír no aśvinā	1.34,7(a.) < 6(a.)]
b) in the same *maṇḍala*	
yuváṃ narā stuvaté	1.117,7(a.) < 116,7(a.)
śatám meṣā́n vṛkyè	1.117,17(a.) < 116,16(a.)
sāsmā aram	2.18,2(a.) < 17,6(a.)
asmā́kam átra pitáras	4.42,8(a.) < 1,13(a. = SP *pitáro)*
yác cid dhí	4.32,13(a.) < 12,4(a.)
ráthaṃ yé cakrúḥ	4.36,2(a.) < 33,8(a.)
[Exception: no *galita* because of enclitic?	
tád vāṃ narā	1.183,8(a.) < 117,6(a.)
ní tvā dadhe	3.27,10(a.) < 23,4(a.)
tám u tvā	6.45,10(a.) < 16,14+15(a.) too many cases: *gal.* only inside *sūkta*
tám u tvā nūnám	8.90,6(a.) < 24.26(a.) to avoid confusion with the many *tám u tvā*-cases?
c) in a previous *maṇḍala*	
etāni vām aśvinā	2.39,8(a.) < 1.117,25(a.)
ā́ tū́ na indra	3.41,1(a.), 4.32,1(a.), 8.81,1(a.) < (1.10,11(a.),
ūrdhvá ū ṣú ṇo	4.6,1(a.) < 1.36,13(a.)
práty agnír uṣáso	4.14,1(a.) < 3.5,1(a. SP *uṣásaś*)
tvám mahā́ṁ indra	4.17,1(a.) < 1.63,1(a.)
abhí tvā gótamā girā́	4.32,9(a.) < 1.78,1(a.)
anaśvó jātó anabhīśúr	4,36,1(a.) < 1.152,5(a.)
sá suṣṭúbhā sá	4.50,5(a.) < 1.62,4(a.)
[Exception: no *galita* because of enclitic?	
síndhur ná kṣódaḥ	2.25,3(a.) < 1.66,10(a.)
vā́yav índraś ca	4.47,3(a.) < 1.2,5+6(a.)
tám u tvā	6.16,14(a.) < 1.78,2-4(a.) too many cases: *gal.* only inside *sūkta*
tám u tvā	9.17,7(a.) < 6.16,14 (a.) too many cases: *gal.* only inside *sūkta*
yā́ te dhā́māni	10.81,5(a.) < 1.91,4+19(a.): long distance]

Rule 4: *Galita* for begin of *pāda* c [c.<a.][c.<c.] [c.<d.]

a) in the same *sūkta*

vidúṣ ṭe tásya 1.11,7(c.) < 6(d.)

yuṣmā́kam astu táviṣī 1.39,4(c.) < 2(c.)

rátho ha vām 3.58,9(c.) < 8(c.)

[Exception: no *galita*:

ṛṅór ákṣaṃ ná 1.30,15(c.) < 14(c.)]

b) in the same *maṇḍala*

yó dhṛṣṇúnā śávasā 1.56,4c. < 54,2(c.)

devó no átra savitā́ 1.124,1c. < 123,3(c.)

ā́d asya té 1.141,8(c.) < 140,5(a.)

ádha yád eṣāṃ 1.186,9(c.) < 167,2(c.)

[Exception: no *galita*:

asmā́kam bráhma pṛtanāsu 1.157,2(c.) < 152,7(c.)

prá yád váyo ná 2.31,1(c.) < 19,2(c.)]

c) in a previous *maṇḍala*

[Exception: no *galita*:

yā́ te dhā́māni 8.21,4(c.) < 1.91,44+19(a.)]

Rule 5: *Galita* from and for initial *pāda* [a-<a-] [c-<a-] [c-<c-]

b) in the same *maṇḍala*

ágne devā́ṁ ihā́ vaha 1.15,4(a-) < 12,3(a-)

áminatī daíviyāni vratā́ni 1.124,2(a-) < 92,12,(c-)

eṣā́ divó duhitā́ praty adarśi 1.124,3(a-) < 113,7(a-)

arvāváto na ā́ gahi 3.40,8(a-) < 37,11(a-)

índra sómāḥ sutā́ imé 3.42,5(a-) < 40,4(a-)

ūrdhvám bhānúṃ savitā́ devó aśred 4.14,2(a-) < 13,2(a-)

c) in a previous *maṇḍala*

imā́ u ṣú śrudhī gíraḥ 2.6,1(c-) < 1.26,5 (c-)

sá dhārayad pṛthivī́m papráthac ca 2.15,2(c-) < 1.103,2(a-)

puraḥsadaḥ śarmasado na vīrā 3.55,21(c-) < 1.73,3(c-)

áhann áhim pariśáyānam árṇaḥ 4.19,2(c-) < 3.32,11(a-)

etā́ te agna ucáthāni vedhó 4.2,20(a-) < 1.73,10(a-)

ā́prā dyā́vāpṛthivī́ antárikṣaṃ 4.14,2(c-) < 1.115,1(c-)

hótāram agním mánuṣo ní ṣedur 5.3,4(c-) < 4.6,11(c-)

áhann áhim pariśáyānam árṇaḥ 4.19,2(c-) < 3.32,11(a-)

táṃ vāṃ ráthaṃ vayám adyā́ huvema 4.44,1(a-) < 1.180,10(a-)

Rule 6: *Galita* from and for initial *pāda* extending into final *pāda* [c-d.]

a) in the same *sūkta*

yátrā ráthasya bṛható nidhā́naṃ / vimócanaṃ vājíno 3.53,6(c-d.) < 5(c-d.)

Rule 7: *Galita* from and for final *pāda* [c-/<d-] [d-<b-] [d-<d-]

a) in the same *sūkta*

víśvaṃ sám atríṇaṃ daha	1.36,20(d-) < 14(b-)
pātáṃ sómam ṛtāvṛdhā	1.47,5(d-) < 3(b-)
uṣā ajīgar bhuvanāni viśvā	1.113,5+6(d-) < 4(d-)
utó téṣām abhígūrtir na invatu	1.162,12(d-) < 6(d-)
sárvā tā́ te ápi devéṣv astu	1.162,9(d-)+14(d-) < 8(d-)
prā́vo vā́jeṣu vājínam	1.176,5(d-) < 4,8(c-/)
dyā́vā rákṣatam pṛthivī no ábhvāt	1.185,3-8(d-) < 2(d-)
vā́tāpe pī́vaíd bhava	1.187,9+10(c-/) < 8(c-/)
yás tā́kṛṇoḥ prathamáṃ sā́si ukthiyàḥ	2.13,3+4(d-) < 2(d-)
sómasya tā́ máda índraś cakāra	2.15,3-9(d-) < 2(d-)
yáṃ-yaṃ yújaṃ kṛṇuté bráhmaṇas pátiḥ	2.25,2-5(d-) < 1(d-)
svàr ṇá śukráṃ tanvánta ā́ rájaḥ	4.45,6(b-) < 2(d-)
[Exceptions: no *galita*:	
tāni dhármāṇi prathamā́ny āsan	1.164,50(b-) < 43(d-)
asmín yajñá úpa hvaye	1.13,7(b-) < 3(b-)]
ráthe dasrā hiraṇyáye	1.139,4(e-/) < 3(g-/)

b) in the same *maṇḍala*

bṛhád vadema vidáthe suvī́rāḥ	2.11,21(d-) < 2.13(d-)
prajānán vidvā́ṁ úpa yāhi sómam	3.35,4(d-) < 29,16(d-)
índrehá táta ā́ gahi	3.40;9(c-/) < 37,11(d-)
tváṃ vṛtā́ṁ ariṇā indra síndhūn	4.42,7(d-) < 19,5(d-)
[Exceptions: no *galita*:	
úpedáṃ sávanaṃ sutám	1.21,4(b-) < 16,5(b-)
trír ā́ divó vidáthe pátyamānaḥ	3.56,5(d-) < 3.54,11(b-)
várco dhā yajñávāhase	3.24,1(d-) < 3.8,3(d-)

c) in a previous *maṇḍala*

ní rīraman yájamānāso anyé	2.18,3(d-) < 3.35,5(b-)
pātáṃ sómam ṛtāvṛdhā	8.87,5(d-) < 1.47,3(b-),5(d-)
[Exceptions: no *galita*:	
vrajáṃ gómantam uśíjo ví vavruḥ	4.16,6(d-) < 1,15(d-)
vṛtráṃ jaghanvā́ṁ asṛjad ví síndhūn	4.19,8(b-) < 18,7(d-)]

Rule 8: No *galita* from initial *pāda* for final *pāda* [b-<a-] [b-<c-]

a) in the same *sūkta*

[exception:	
ágne devā́ṁ ihā́ vaha	1.12,10(b-) < 3(a-)

b) in the same *maṇḍala*

ágne dūtó viśā́m asi	1.44,9(b-) < 1.36,5(a-)
índrasya kárma súkṛtā purū́ṇi	3.34,6(b-) < 32,8(a-)
píbataṃ dāśúṣo gṛhé	4.49,6(b-) < 46,6(c-/)
[Exception	
jāyéva pátya uśatī́ suvā́sāḥ	4.3,2(b-) < 1.124,7(c-)

praminatī́ manuṣyā̀ yugā́ni 1.124,2(b-) < 92,11(c-): the whole stanza is a composition of four *galita*-portions!]

Rule 9: No *galita* from final *pāda* for initial *pāda* [a-<c-/] [c-<d-]

b) in the same *maṇḍala*

agnír bhuvad rayipátī rayīṇā́m 1.72,1(c-) < 60,4(d-)
yáḥ śáṃsantaṃ yáḥ śaśamānám ūtī́ 2.20,3(a-) < 12,14(b-)
índra píba vŕ̥ṣadhūtasya vŕ̥ṣṇa(ḥ) 3.43,7(a-) < 36,2(d-)
yáḥ śáṃsantaṃ yáḥ śaśamānám ūtī́ 2.20,3(c-) < 2.12,14,(b-)
ūrvī́ gabhīré rájasī suméke 4.56,3(c-) < 42,3(b-)

c) in a previous *maṇḍala*

píbā tv àsyá girvaṇaḥ 8.1,26(a-) < 3.51,10(c-/)
píbā tv àsyá súṣutasya cā́ro 7.29,1(c-) < 3.50,2(d-)
pātáṃ sómam r̥tāvr̥dhā 3.62,18(c-/) < 1.47,3(b-),5(d-)

[Exception, *galita*

1. *tā́ samrā́jā ghr̥tā́sutī* 2.41,6(a-) < 1.136,1(d-); note that one ms shows the begin of this line together with the *galita*-sign (cf. fn. 9).
ādityā́ dā́nunas pátī 2.41,6(b-) also comes from the same *sūkta*, 1.136,3(e-)?
ā́ tvā viśantv índavaḥ 8.92,22(a-) < 1.15,1(b-)
jánmañjanman níhito jātávedāḥ 3.1,21(a-) < 20(d-): the parallels follow each other immediately]

Rule 10: No *galita* for begin of final *pāda* [d.<b.] [d.<c.] [d.<d.]

0) in the same stanza

yát saṃvátsam r̥bhávo 4.33,4(b.) < (a.)

a) in the same *sūkta*

yá ít tád vidús 1.164,39(d.) < 23(d.)
brávaḥ kád agne 4.3,7(d.) < 6(d.)
ghr̥tásya dhā́rā abhí 4.58,9(d.) < 5(c.)

[Exception: *galita* in

mámac caná tvā 4.18,8(b.) < (a.): same stanza
trír ā́ divó vidáthe 3.56,8(d.) < 5(d.): there are some more cases of *t.a.d.* in this same *sūkta*
ágne tváṃ ródasī naḥ 3.15,6(b.) < 5(d.)
tvāyā́ havíś cakr̥mā 1.101,9(b.) < 8(d.)
sárvā tā́ te 1.162,17(d.) < 14(d.): line 14d is itself marked *galita*]

b) in the same *maṇḍala*

diváś ca gmáś ca 1.37,6(b.) < 25,20(b.); 10.49,2(b.) < 22,6(d.)
yó gā́ udā́jaḍ 2.14,3(b.) < 12,3(b.)
ráthā áśvāśa uṣáso 4.45,2(b.) < 14,4(b.)
tán no mahā́n 4.53,1(d.) < 22,1(b.)

c) in a previous *maṇḍala*	
asmā́kam sú maghavan bodhi	4.22,10(d.) < 3.31,14(d.), 1.25,20(b.)
divás ca gmás ca	5.38,3(d.), 10.22,6(d.), 49,2(b.) < 1.37,6(b.)
devó ná yáḥ	9.97,48(d.) < 1.73,2+3(a.)

Rule 11: No *galita* for same end [.a<.b] [.a<.d] [.b<.b] [.b<.c] [.b<.d] [.c<.c] [.c<.d] [.c<.g] [.d<.d]

0) in the same stanza	
mádāya práti dhat píbadhyai	4.27,5(.e) < (.d)
a) in the same *sūkta*	
sám iṣā́ rabhemahi	1.53,5(.a.) < 4(.d)
bhū́ri te vásu	1.81,6(.d) < 2(.e)
vācáḥ paramáṃ vyòma	1.164,35(.d) < 34(.d)
narā́ṃ ná śáṃsair	1.173,10(.a) < 9(.b)
anyásya pīpáyanta vā́jair	1.181,6(.c) < 5(.c)
bhāratā sómam asmai	2.14,7(.d) < 6(.d)
dūrā́d ánasā ráthena	3.33,10(.b) < 9(.b)
víśvāni kā́vyāni vidvā́n	3.1,18(.d) < 17(.b)
agne médaso ghṛtásya	3.21,4(.b) < 1(.c)
víśvā adhithā indra kṛṣṭī́ḥ	4.17,7(.b) < 6(.d)
váruṇam me manīṣā́ḥ	4.41,9(.a) < 8(.d)
divo duhitaro vibhātī́r	4.51,10+11(.a) < 1(.c)
b) in the same *maṇḍala*	
devā́ṁ ihā́ vaha	1.14,12(.c) < 1.12,3(.a), 10(.b)
prá ririce mahitváṃ	1.61,9(.a) < 59,5(.b)
no avitā́ bhava	1.91,9(.c/) < 81,8(.e/)
átyaṃ ná vājínam	1.135,5(.c) < 129,2(.g)
pāyúbhiḥ pāhi śagmaíḥ	1.143,8(.b) < 130,10(.b)
maghávāno vayáṃ ca	1.141,13(.c) < 136,7(.d)
nítya ā́ śaye	1.141,2(.a) < 140,7(.b)
punānā́ḥ kavíbhiḥ pavítrair	3.31,16(.c) < 1,5(.b)
vṛ́ṣṇe sávanā kṛtémā́	3.30,2(.c) < 1,20(.c)
cid agne mahinā́ pṛthivyā́ḥ	3.7,10(.c) < 6,2(.c)
yáḥ pṛthivī́ṃ dyā́m utémā́ṃ	3.34,8(.c) < 32,8(.c)
sákhibhiḥ sutáṃ naḥ	3.51,8(.b) < 47,3(.b)
asyā́ uṣáso vyùṣṭau	4.23,5(.a) < 1,5(.b)
budhné rájaso asyá yónau	4.1,17(.d) < 1,11(.b)
śarádaś ca pūrvī́ḥ	4.18,4(.b) < 16,19(.d)
asyā́ uṣáso vyùṣṭau	4.23,5(.b) < 1,5(.b)
púraṃdhir ajahād árātīr	4.27,2(.c) < 26,7(.c)
mā́m uṣásaḥ sūdayantv	4.40,1(.b) < 39,1(.c)
c) in a previous *maṇḍala*	
sú maghavan bodhi godā́ḥ	4.22,10(.d) < 3.30,21(.d)
mahī́ ródasī ā́ viveśa	10.80,2(.b) < 3.61,7(.b)
maghávāno vayáṃ ca	7.78,5(.b) < 1.136,7(.d)+141,13(.c)

no avitā́ bhava	7.96,5(.c/) < 1.81,8(.e/)+91,9(.c/)
bhū́ri te vásu	8.32,8(.c/) < 1.81,2(.e)+6(.d)

[Exceptions: *galita* is frequent

1. when end functions as refrain in one *sūkta*, like

sá janāsa índraḥ	2.12,3-14(.d) < 2(.d)
2. *uśíjaḥ śáṃsam āyóḥ*	5.3,4(.d) < 4.6,11(.d): preceeding *pāda* is identical [5.3.4c=4.6,11c]
3. *hitámitro ná rā́jā*	3.55,21 (.b) < 1.73.3 (.b):the b-*pādas* start *upakṣéti* (1.73,3) and *úpa kṣeti* (3.55,21)
4. Inexplicable is:	
no dámyebhir ánīkaiḥ	3.54,1(.c) < 3.1,15(.d): this violates first against the general rule regarding ends, and then also against the different treatment of initial and final *pādas*]

Rule 12: No *galita* for same end even when followed by full final *pāda* [.a/b-] [.c/d-]

a) in the same *sūkta*

amṛ́tānām / manāmahe cā́ru devásya nā́ma	1.24,2(.a/b-) < 1(.a/b-) (This case is mentioned in Müller ṚPrā p. CCXX, without an explanation]
no mahyā́ áditaye púnar dāt / pitáraṃ ca dṛśéyam mātáraṃ ca	1.24.2(.c/d-) < 1(.c/d-)

b) in the same *maṇḍala*

ságaṇo marúdbhiḥ / sómam piba vṛtrahā́ śūra vidvā́n	3.52,7(.c/d-) < 47,2(.a/b-)

Rule 13: No *galita* from or for parallels within a *pāda* [.a.] [.b.] [.c.] [.d.]

a) in the same *sūkta*

ā́ yātam úpa	1.2,6(b.) < 5(.c.)
svávṛṣṭim máde asya	1.52,14(.c.) < 5(.a.)
hí tvā pūṣann	11.138,4(.f.) < 2(.a.)
cid dhí ṣmāśvinā́v	1.180,8(.a.) < 7(.c.)
ín nú śūra	2.11,17(.a.) < 3(.a.)
nú ta indra	2.11,7(.a.) < 6(.a.)
tváṃ no agne	4.1,5(.a.) < 4(a.)
vo vājā ṛbhavo	4.36,3(.a.) < 2(.d.)
no vājā ṛbhukṣaṇaḥ	4.37,8(.a.) < 7(.a.)

b) in the same *maṇḍala*

sám íṣo didīhy	3.54,22(.a) < 3,7(.b.)
chocíṣā sahasas putra	3.18,4(.a.) < 14,4(.c.)
sú maghavan bodhi	3.31,14(.d.) < 30,21(.d.)
ín nv èvá samanā́	4.51,9(.a.) < 5,7(.a.)

[Exceptions:

prathamoṣā vi	1.124,2(.d.) < 113,15(.d.): already *pādas* a to c are *galitas* from various sources]

Rule 14: No *galita* when parallels cross *pāda*-line [.a/b.] [.c/d.]

a) in the same *sūkta*	
jāmír jánānām / ágne	1.75,4(.a/b.) < 3(.a/b.)
níkhātam / úd ūpathur	1.117,12(.c/d.) < 5(.c/d.)
śavaso napātaḥ / saúdhanvanā	4.35,8(.c/d.) < 1(.a/b.)
b) in the same *maṇḍala*	
práti praváta āśáyānam / áhiṃ vájreṇa	4.19,3(.c/d.) < 17,7(.c/d.)
[Exception, *galita*:	
óṣadhīr utā́po / rayíṃ	3.55,22(.a/b.) < 51,5(.c/d.)]

Rule 15: No *galita* when one-vowel-word involved, even in *pratīka*

b) in the same *maṇḍala*	
ā́ ródasī apṛṇad	2.22,2(c.) < 15,2(b.)
diváś cid ā́	3.39,2(a.) < 6,7(a.)
imā́ u te	3.57,4(c.) < 38,2(c.)
idám u tyát	4.51,1(a.) < 5,9(a. SP *tyán*)
c) in a previous *maṇḍala*	
ā́ ródasī apṛṇad	3.2,7(a.) < 2.22,2(c.), 2.15,2(b.)
ā́ yātam úpa	7.74,3(a.) < 1.93,11(c.) [1.2,5(.c.), 1.2,6(b.)]

These listings show that identical stanzas and verses produce *galitas*. This is what was to be expected. When it comes to the beginnings of *pādas* we see a great difference between the beginnings of initial *pādas* (a. and c.), where *galitas* are the norm, and the beginnings of final *pādas* (b. and d.), where *galitas* seem to be forbidden.

For whole *pādas* the rules are: initial *pādas* are relevant for initial *pādas*, and final *pādas* are relevant for final *pādas*. But cross-references are avoided, although there are exceptions: the closer, the more likely.

Parallels covering the ends of *pādas* are not recognized for *galitas*, except in the case of refrains at the end of final *pādas*. Also irrelevant are sequences inside *pādas* and sequences crossing *pāda* divisions.

That means, whole *pādas* in the same position are recognized, *pāda* beginnings are only recognized for the beginnings of the *ardharc*, not for the final *pāda*. Most numerous are the beginnings of *pāda* a, the *pratīka* of the stanza, i.e. the three or more initial words by which a particular stanza is referred to in other contexts.

It also seems as if longer *galitas* block shorter parallels: the words *tváṃ tám indra párvataṃ* start 1.55,3, and are marked as *galita* in 1.57,6(a.); the shorter *pratīka* '*tváṃ tám indra*' in the same *maṇḍala* 1.131,7(a.) is not marked, as in the further *maṇḍala* 5.35,5(a.). There are many such cases; another one is *evā́m no agne samídhā vṛdhānó revát pāvaka śrávase ví bhāhi* of 1.95,11(ab), omitted as *galita* in 1.96,9 (ab), thus blocking the short *pratīka 'evā́m no agne'* in 2.2,9(a.) and in 7.43,5(a.). The four words *tvám na indra rāyā́m* start 1.129,9(a.) and are *galita* in 1.129,10(a.); the three-word *pratīka 'tvám na indra'* in 2.20,2(a.), 7.31,3(a.) and 8.70,10(a.) is not marked, only 8.70,12(a.) reacts again to the same beginning two stanzas earlier.

These rules are partly consistent and partly full of exceptions. This may be due to our misunderstanding or to a complicated history of the PP. Certainly, further research is necessary, but it should already be clear that care has been taken to distinguish the beginning of a half-line from the beginning of final *pādas*. Why so?

The answer I would like to propose starts from our knowledge about the process of teaching Vedic texts. We know from several Gṛhyasūtras that the Sāvitrī at least was taught first quarter by quarter, then in half-stanzas and finally in total, e.g. Āpastambagṛhya 4.11,8-10: *anvārabhyaāha sāvitrīṃ bho anubrūhiti. tasmā anvāha tat savitur iti. paccho 'rdharcaśas tatas sarvam*, "(The novice) touches (the teacher) and says '*bho*, repeat the sāvitrī stanza'. He repeats '*tat savitur*'. (Thus they proceed) *pāda*-wise, (then) the half-stanza, then the whole (stanza)." This rule is found in almost every Gṛhyasūtra. A comparable rule is known from the Suśrutasaṃhitā where teaching proceeds either in *pādas*, half-stanzas or full stanzas depending on the capacity of the pupil (SS 1.3,54: *śiśyāya yathāśakti gurur upadiśet padaṃ pādaṃ ślokaṃ vā*). After that the taught portions are to be combined one by one (*te ca padapādaślokā bhūyaḥ krameṇānusaṃdheyāḥ, evaṃ ekaikaśo ghaṭayet*). Unfortunately, the process referred to by *krameṇa* is not described in full.[17]

The Baudhāyanadharmasūtra 2.10(17),14[18] adds that in addition the Sāvitrī should be recited *samastayā* and *vyastayā*. This singular expression may be explained with the help of ṚPrā 15.3,12ab, where a similar combination of *sam-as* and *vyava-so* is found. This line prescribes that stanzas consisting of only two *pādas* are to be combined in recitation to one single unit, with no *veṣṭanam* after the middle, while other stanzas consisting of the usual 3 or more *pādas*, are kept separate: *samasyantaś ca dvipadāv ardharcau*[19] *vyavasyanta itarāś carcayeyuḥ*. So, *sam-as* seems to be used for *sandhi* within a stanza in both cases, whereas *vi-as* and *vi-ava-so* seem to refer to the separation of words or parts of the stanza: UpS 1,17 says *nāvasyet*

17 The Carakasaṃhitā 3.8,7 is still less explicit: *...vāgbhiḥ sūtram anukrāman punaḥ punar āvartayed...*

18 BDhS 2.10(17),14 (...) *paccho'rdharcaśas tatas samastayā ca vyastayā ca.*

19 Müller's mss read *dvipadādardharcau* and *dvipadārdharcau*; he emends to *dvipadādyardharcau*.

for cases of *ūṃ* or *īṃ*, i.e. it uses *ava-so* for the termination of each two-word *krama* unit. So, with some reserve, *samastayā* and *v̂yastayā* in BDhS 2.10(17),14 can be interpreted as hinting at a sort of SP and PP used for the Sāvitrī.

How old this rule is we do not know. Some more information of how teaching proceeded is found at the end of the ṚPrā in 15.1,1 ff. (nos. 828ff.). The teacher, "when asked proceeds according to his *krama*" (835: *pracodito 'bhikramate yathāsya kramaḥ*). After he has pronounced the unit of two or more successive words a pupil repeats the first word (837: *abhikrānte dvaipade vādhike vā pūrvaṃ padaṃ prathamaḥ prāha śiṣyaḥ*). The two words or more can be explained on the basis of the KP, where two is the unit, unless a one-vowel-word or a typical *saṃhita* form (like *āraik* instead of *araik*) is included. The progression in two words is again treated in 841: "the teacher speaks one initial word, in case of a compound, and two words, if no compound" (*guruḥ śiṣyasya padam āha mukhyaṃ samāsaś ced asamāso yadi dve*). After having completed a full *praśna* this way all the students together repeat it together for themselves (15.2,9ab, no. 842). Having done so they repeat it in a sort of PP, if Müller's explanation is correct: "Darauf mögen alle Schüler ohne Unterbrechung repetieren, und zwar durchweg mit dem ebenen Hochton, wobei selbständige Wörter nicht contrahiert, Compositionsglieder leise getrennt werden" (*tata ūrdhvaṃ saṃtataṃ saṃvṛtena pravigraheṇa mṛdvavagraheṇa, sarvodāttena carcayeyuḥ sarva imāny upasthāpayantaḥ padāni*). There are some difficult terms involved, but it is clear, nonetheless, that a different form of recitation is added.

The *sūktas* were divided into *praśnas*, each *praśna* normally consisting of 3 stanzas (850: *praśnas tṛcaḥ*). Sixty *praśnas* make an *adhyāya* (858: *te ṣaṣṭir adhyāya(ḥ)*), or 180 stanzas. Having learned an *adhyāya* the pupils are dismissed to their respective duties (848: *evaṃ sarve praśnaśo 'dhyāyam uktvopasaṃgṛhyātisṛṣṭā yathārthaṃ*).

The *galitas* would occasionally diminish the daily repertoire considerably, if they were simply skipped. There is a rule in ṚPrā 15.3,14, but the manuscripts are not unanimous. No. 853 reads *samayās tu gaṇyā parāvarārdhyā(ḥ)* as also *tv agaṇyā*, "the *samayas*, be they small or large,[20] are (not) to be counted [as part of the daily pensum]". The end of the chapter has an interesting statement, which unfortunately is not easy to understand. It says, that according to some teachers the recitation of a certain text is advised to follow the *saṃhitā* way of recitation (15.3,16ab, no. 860: *athaike prāhur anusaṃhitaṃ tatpārāyaṇe pravacanaṃ praśastam*). Combining the evidence it seems safe to say that the ṚPrā describes throughout a procedure of teaching which comes very close to the KP: the text progresses in units

---

20 Cf. the discussion on *parāvarārdhya* by Müller, p. CCXCIX.

of two words. The last line in this chapter seems to react to that by saying that some teachers prefer the SP.

Conclusion

We have seen that the *pratīkas* receive particular attention in the system of *galitas*. The *galitas* could be used for the PP, but are treated in the ṚPrā as an integral part of the KP. We have also seen that the old way of teaching is more or less identical with the progression of the KP. This leads me to assume the existence of two sorts of *kramapāṭhas*, one originally nothing more but a teaching technique, providing the basis for the SP and PP, and secondly the KP of Bābhravya, continuing on the one hand the old teaching technique and in addition combining the fully developed SP and PP, using the *galitas* to distinguish *pratīkas*.

Why put such an emphasis on *pratīkas*? Given the predilection for oral teaching in Vedic circles *pratīkas* may have been used in examinations. Until a few decades ago a brahmin student would have been questioned by his teacher who uttered the beginning of a stanza of a work and asked the student to continue the recitation. As long as there are no *galitas* a *pratīka* could have been ambiguous and the student might have continued in a stanza different from the one intended. This presupposes that such examinations followed the *krama* style, because in SP all identical *pratīkas* sound alike. Only if the KP is required would a proposed beginning of "1-2-3" lead to the correct place where the *pratīka* is divided into "1-2/2-3" etc. Once the student is proficient in reciting in Bābhravya's *krama* style he really knows everything about the proper *saṃhita* recitation and also everything about irregularly formed words and irregular *sandhis* on the basis of Śākalya's analysis. Thus the *galita* system looks like an integral part of Bābhravya's *kramapāṭha*.

The arising of our SP and PP from teaching in *krama* fashion could go back to a sort of didactic game, i.e. adding to the recitation of the stanzas in the metrically correct form also a combination of all *saṃhita* forms in a row or a continuous flow of all the *avasāna* forms. In course of time out of these two side-lines the *saṃhita* recital must have been regarded as the most genuine shape of the poems being closest to the original wording, because it preserves all morphological irregularities. Needless to say that the rigorous application of *sandhi* rules produced new mistakes, not to speak of the extensive destruction of the metre.

The *pada* reciters, on the other hand, seem to have developed into a school of their own, not receiving later additions like the six stanzas RV 7.59,12, 10.20,1, 10.121,10, 10.190,1-3 (cf. Bronkhorst 1981:87), which are without counterpart in the PP. The *pada* recital received a new dimension through the additions, introduced by Śākalya like compound separation via *avagraha*, indication of some dual-forms by appending *iti*, or substitution of poetical forms by regular ones, like *āraik* and *araik*. Needless to say, this process too was not possible without some inconsistencies or even mistakes, as e.g. the non-separation of some doubly accented *devatādvandvas* (Insler 1998:289).

This way the enlarged SP and the refashioned PP drifted apart, getting reunited again in recitation practice by the KP of Bābhravya. This rescue party was somewhat later joined by the author of the ṚPrā, who still knew about very different ways of reciting the KP or about alternatively teaching not in *krama* but strictly in *saṃhita* fashion.

The processes described can be surveyed in table 2.

Table 2

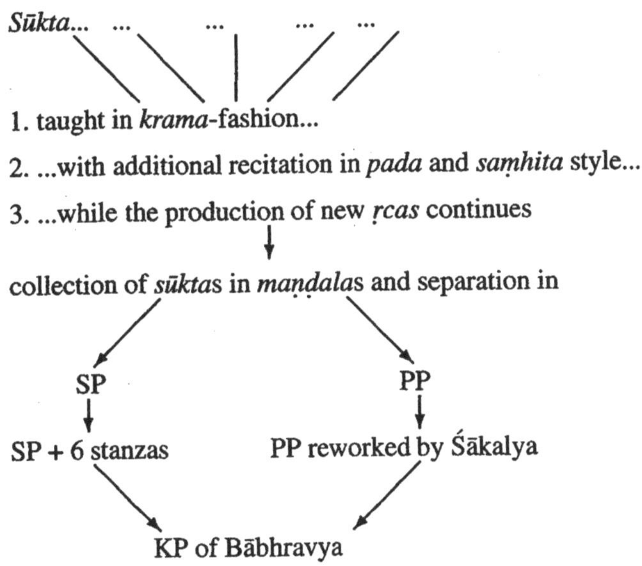

Applying the theory

The peculiar rules of the KP may shed some light on one of the strangest parts of the SP: there are some shortenings mostly at the end of *triṣṭubh* verses, where forms like *ūtī́* or *nṝ́n* occur which stand in place of the instr.sg. *ūtyā́* or dat.sg. *ūtaye*, or gen.pl. *nṝṇām*. Ickler (1976) has checked all occurrences and hinted at the fact that a closing syllable was deliberately dropped, thus changing the metre from *jagatī* to *triṣṭubh*. When seen in the framework of KP rules it seems possible that *ūtī́* once was *ūtiyā́* and *nṝ́n* stands for an originally pronounced *nṛṇā́ṃ*:

We know that the nasalized one-syllable word *āṃ* was rigidly avoided at the end of a *krama*. Whenever it appears it is packed into a *krama* of three words, like *abhrá ā́ṁ apáḥ / apo vṛṇānā́m* etc (RV 5.48,1). At the end of a verse a nasalized *-ā* is equivalent to an unnasalized, since at the end every simple vowel is changed to an *anunāsika*, as says ṚPrā 64: *aṣṭāv ādyān avasāne 'apragṛhyān ācāryā āhur anunāsikānt svarān*, "the first 8 vowels (*a,ā,ṛ,ṝ,i,ī,u,ū*) in pausa position are defined as *anunāsika* vowels by the teachers, if not *pragṛhya*". The same idea may have served Pāṇini for his rule 6.1,126 (*saṃhitāyām*) *āṅo 'nunāsikaś chandasi*, "the prefix *ā* becomes *anunāsika* in the veda". We know from ṚPrā 11.1,2ab (no. 615, *apṛktam ekākṣaram adviyoni yat tad ānunāsikyabhayād atīyate*) that a word consisting of just one vowel, not being a diphthong, is passed over in the KP "because of fear of the state of *anunāsika*", a state it would inevitably assume in any final position, and be it only at the end of a two-word *krama*. The passing over is also mentioned in ṚPrā 592 (*ekavarṇam ...atītyaitāny avasyanti*) and 622 (*saha-iti ca_īm; ā-iti rakta-saṃhitaṃ*), "nasalized *īṃ* and *āṃ* are passed over". All this "passing over" does not mean that the vowels are omitted from recitation, they are only put into brackets so that they cannot appear in pausa position. Now what to do with a verse-final *ā*? First, it needs to be nasalized, if it was not already. But then it cannot be put into brackets, since there is no word following it.

From the Atharvavedic side we are told that there are two sorts of nasalizations: if a stanza is recited in units of *ardharcs*, then the last vowel of the final *pāda* and any following consonant are dropped and replaced by the *praṇava*, i.e. *-oṃ* (Vaitānasūtra 21,4a: *ardharcaśasya ṛgantaṃ praṇavenopasaṃtanoti svarādim apanīya*). If a stanza is recited in units of *pādas*, then every line end and the end of the recitation receive only an additional nasal, *m* (4b: *pacchaḥśasye 'rdharcāntaṃ śastrāntaṃ makārāntenaiva*). For stanzas ending in *ūtyā́* or *nṛṇā́ṃ* the last rule would lead to *ūtyāṃ*, whereas the first case would lead to *ūtyoṃ* and *nṛṇoṃ*. A replaced final vowel (and consonant) might well have led to the wrong impression that the *oṃ* was simply added, so that *nṛṇā́ṃ* > *nṛṇoṃ* led to an analysis of *nṝ́n* and *oṃ*, and spoken *ūtyāṃ* changed to *ūtyoṃ* became analyzed as *ūtī* plus *oṃ*. But this mistake is only possible as long as the stanzas are transmitted in a modified form.

We do not yet know everything about the process which led to our ṛgvedic *pāṭhas*. There are so many irregularities and inconsistencies that we must reckon with everything. It would indeed be a solution to the problem of the shortened forms like *ūtī́* and *nṝ́n*, if we could assume that originally they were nothing but an instr.sg. *ūtyā́*, nasalized *ūtyā́ṃ*, and an original gen.pl. *nṛṇā́ṃ*, mistaken to consist of two words each, leading to the elimination of the assumed *apṛkta* word *ā́ṃ*, out of the same dislike which led to three-word *kramas* with an *ā́m* in their middle. With the elimination of *-ā́ṃ*, the verse could then be terminated by the *veṣṭana* "*ūtī́ty ūtī́* ", or "*nṝ́nnity nṝ́n*", producing new forms like inst.sg. *ūtī́*, being later also used for other cases, and a gen.pl. *nṝ́n*, also used then for other cases (Ickler 1976:71). Their basic form *ūtyā́* and *nṛṇā́ṃ* would perfectly fit most of their locations at the end of present *triṣṭubh* lines, which were originally perfect *jagatī* lines

(Ickler 1976:71 and 74). One such case is RV 5.7,10c *ā́d agne ápṛṇato 'trìḥ sāsáhyād dásyūn iṣáḥ sāsáhyān nṝ́n*, were the last *pāda* should sound like *iṣáḥ sāsáhiān nṛṇā́ṃ*. Ickler is perfectly right in proposing: "Liegt es bei diesem Befund nicht nahe, das Problem der verstümmelten Form *nṝ́n* mit dem metrischen der Katalexis in Beziehung zu setzen?" The key to the two deficiencies could be in a nasalized ending *ā́ṁ*, skipped by some teachers for reasons only vaguely discernible for us, but certainly during the process of transmitting the *ṛṣis*' words in the *krama* technique and out of "fear" for the nasalized *apṛkta* syllable *ā́ṃ*.

It goes without saying that the use of *ūtī́* or *nṝ́n* in other cases than inst.sg. and gen.pl. can only be explained on the supposition that the shortening took place while the production of *ṛca*s still went on: the shortened forms were misunderstood and taught as blanco forms fit for all cases.

REFERENCES

Aithal, K. Parameswara. 1991. *Veda-Lakṣaṇa. Vedic ancillary literature—a descriptive bibliography*. Stuttgart: Franz Steiner Verlag.

Benfey, Theodor. 1874. "Die Quantitätsverschiedenheiten in den Samhitâ- und Pada-Texten der Veden". *Abhandlungen der königlichen Gesellschaft der Wissenschaften zu Göttingen* 19; Göttingen, 223-264.

Bronkhorst, Johannes. 1981. "The orthoepic diaskeuasis of the Ṛgveda and the date of Pāṇini". *Indo-Iranian Journal* 23: 83-95.

———. 1985. "Pāṇini and the Kramapāṭha of the Ṛgveda". *Annals of the Bhandarkar Oriental Research Institute* 66: 185-191.

Deshpande, Madhav M. (ed.). 1997. *Śaunakīya Caturadhyāyikā. A Prātiśākhya of the Śaunakīya Atharvaveda critically edited, translated and annotated.* Cambridge: Harvard University Press.

Falk, Harry. 1993. *Schrift im alten Indien*. Tübingen: Gunter Narr.

———. 1994a. "Von Götterfiguren und menschlichen Göttern", in: N. Balbir and J. Bautze (eds.), *Festschrift Klaus Bruhn*, Reinbek: Verlag Inge Wezler, 313-331.

———. 1994b. Review of Aithal 1991, *Zeitschrift der Deutschen Morgenländischen Gesellschaft* 144: 413-415.

Ickler, Ingeborg. 1976. "Zum Problem der 'Kürzungen' in der Ṛgveda-Saṃhitā". *Studien zur Indologie und Iranistik* 1: 65-112.

Insler, Stanley. 1998. "*mitrā́mváruṇā* or *mitrā́ váruṇā*", in: Jay Jasanoff, H. Craig Melchert and Lisi Olivier (eds.), *Mír Curad, Studies in Honor of Calvert Watkins*. Innsbruck: 285-290.

Jha, Vashishta Narayan. 1976. "Stages in the composition of the Ṛgveda-Padapāṭha", *Bulletin of the Deccan College Research Institute* 35: 47-50.

———, 1992. *A linguistic analysis of the Ṛgveda-Padapāṭha*. Delhi.

Jog, K.P. 1969. "On the Galitas in the Padapāṭha as a means of Ṛgvedic interpretation", in: *Indian Antiquary* (3rd series) 3: 56-82.

———. 1971. "On the *Galitapradīpa* of Lakṣmīdharasūri", *Journal of the Gan-*

ganath Jha Kendriya Sanskrit Vidyāpīṭh 27: 275-287.
———. 1976. "Mādhava's Ṛgveda-vyākhyā and the system of Galitas", *Sambodhi* 5: 21-28.
Josyer. G.R. = *Gomaṭhaṃ Rāmānuja Jyautiṣika* (ed.). 1947. *ṛgvedasaṃhitāpada-pāṭhaḥ*. Mysore: Coronation Press.
Kashikar, C.G. 1947. "Repetition in the Ṛgvedapadapāṭha", *Annals of the Bhandarkar Oriental Research Institute* 28: 301-305.
———. 1951. "The problem of the gaḷantas in the Ṛgveda-padapāṭha", *Proceedings of the All India Oriental Conference* 13 (Nagpur 1946), II: 39-46.
Kṛṣṇācārya, Kī.Ār. (ed.) and Tukārāma Jāvāji (publ.), 1902. (*śaka* 1824) *Ṛksaṃhitā-padapāṭhaḥ [padāni]*. Bombay: Nirnayasagar Press.
Kulkarni, Nirmala. 1991/92. "On aplutavad upasthite (P. 6.1.129)", *Journal of the Oriental Institute, Baroda* 41:17-26.
Lakṣmīdharasūri. 1970 (*saṃvat* 2016). *galitapradīpaḥ (laghugranthararatnaprabhāvali, 13). sampādakaḥ śrīkṛṣṇavāmanadevaśāstrī*. Varanasi.
Müller, Max (ed.). 1869. *Rig-Veda-Pratisakhya. Das älteste Lehrbuch der vedischen Phonetik. Sanskrittext mit Übersetzung und Anmerkungen*. Leipzig.
Oldenberg, Hermann. 1888. *Metrische und textgeschichtliche Prolegomena zu einer kritischen Rigveda-Ausgabe*. Berlin (repr. Wiesbaden 1982).
Staal, J. Frits. 1961. *Nambudiri Veda Recitation*. s'Gravenhage
Suryakanta (ed.). 1939. *Atharvavedaprātiśākhya*. Lahore (repr. Delhi 1968).
Weber, Albrecht. 1853. *Die Handschriften-Verzeichnisse der königlichen Bibliothek zu Berlin, I: Verzeichnis der Sanskrit-Handschriften I*. Berlin.
———. 1858. "Das Vâjasaneyi-Prâtiçâkhyam", *Indische Studien* 4: 65-160, 177-331.

GAYA CARAN TRIPATHI

संस्कृतपाण्डुलिपीनां संरक्षणे पण्डितानामवदानम्

संहितोपनिषद्ब्राह्मणे, वासिष्ठे धर्मशास्त्रे, निरुक्तादौ च पद्यमेकमुपलभ्यते यत्र विद्या ब्राह्मणमागत्य प्रार्थयति यद् अहं तव निधिः, अतस्त्वया रक्षणीयास्मि-

विद्या ह वै ब्राह्मणमाजगाम
गोपाय मा, शेवधिष्टेहमस्मि॥

वस्तुतः वैदिककालादेव पारम्परिकज्ञानसरणेः रक्षकत्वेन, तद्व्याख्यातृत्वेन च ब्राह्मणानां पण्डितानां वा महती भूमिका भारतीयसंस्कृतौ विद्यते, इति सुविज्ञातमेव सर्वेषाम्। ग्रन्थरचनया, ग्रन्थानां कण्ठस्थीकरणेन, तद्व्याख्यान-भूतटीकाभाष्यादिनिर्माणेन, विद्वद्गोष्ठीषु शास्त्रचिन्तनेन, अथ च भूर्जपत्र-ताडपत्रादिषु लेखनद्वारा ग्रन्थानां संरक्षणेन, पण्डितैः भौतिकसुखान्यनादृत्य भारते अविच्छिन्नतया प्रवहमाणायाः ज्ञानधारायाः सततं संरक्षणं कृतम्। महता त्यागेन, तपस्ययैव चैतत् शक्यमासीत्। व्रतबन्धनानन्तरम् अष्टमवर्षादारभ्य चतुर्विंशतितमवर्षपर्यन्तं, एवं षोडशवर्षाणि यावत्, सर्वाणि भौतिकसुखानि परित्यज्य भूयोभिः कष्टैर्विद्यामर्जयित्वा, तदनन्तरं गार्हस्थ्यमङ्गीकृत्य जिज्ञासुभ्यो विद्यार्थिभ्यः आजीवनं निःशुल्कं विद्यां ददानाः, अवकाशे ग्रन्थनिर्माणं- ग्रन्थलेखनादिकं च कुर्वाणास्ते असौविध्यम् असौकर्यं चापि सोढ्वा विद्यायाः संरक्षणे तदभिवर्धने च सर्वदैव कृतप्रयासाः बभूवुः। श्रीमद्भिः ऽआक्सेल् मिषाइल्-ऽ महोदयैरायोजितायामस्यां गोष्ठ्याम् एतादृशां पण्डितानामवदानम् इह समुपस्थितानां विदुषां भाषणैः स्पष्टतरं भविष्यतीत्यत्र नाधिकमुच्यते। अस्यामपि शताब्द्यां महापण्डितेन ऽराहुल् - सांकृत्यायनेनऽ अवर्णनीयानि महान्ति कष्टानि सोढ्वा, भिक्षुकरूपेण तिब्बतदेशस्य चतुर्वारं यात्रां कृत्वा, योनेकेषां भारते लुप्तानां ऽप्रमाणवार्त्तिकऽ – ऽयोगाचारभूमिशास्त्रम्ऽ इत्यादीनां दुर्लभानां संस्कृतग्रन्थानामुद्धारः कृतः स पण्डितानां परम्परागतप्राचीनविद्यासंरक्षणप्रयासेद्यापि सर्वेषां कृते निदर्शनभूतः॥

केचन सर्वशास्त्रनिष्णाताः संस्कृतपण्डिताः संस्कृतपाण्डुलिपीनां विशालं संग्रहं कृत्वा स्वकीयं विपुलं पुस्तकालयमपि निर्मान्ति स्म, यस्य उदाहरणं सप्तदशशताब्द्यां विद्यमानानां ऽसर्वविद्यानिधानऽ - इत्युपाधिविभूषितानां

वाराणसेयानां श्रीकवीन्द्राचार्यसरस्वतीमहाभागानां पुस्तकसंग्रहस्य दीर्घया सूच्या प्राप्यते यस्यां परःसहस्रं ग्रन्थाः सन्ति। सूच्येषा गंगानाथझा-महोदयेन वटोदरनगरात् (Baroda) प्रकाशिता। अद्यत्वेपि उत्कलेषु, आन्ध्रेषु, कर्णाटकेषु, केरलेषु – अन्यत्र चापि – बहूनां पण्डितानां गृहेषु पाण्डुलिपीनां विशालाः संग्रहा विद्यन्ते। ते इदानीं प्रायः एतानि पुस्तकानि नैव वाचयन्ति किंतु पितॄणां, पूर्वजानां वा संपत्तिरेषा इति मत्वा तानि महत्या श्रद्धया संरक्षन्ति पूजयन्ति च। विक्रयणे चाप्येतेषां ते भृशं मन्दोत्साहाः। यदि नाम केचिदत्र संदिह्युः यत् पाण्डुलिपिलेखकास्तु प्रायः कायस्थजातीया आसन् अतः पाण्डुलिपिसंरक्षणस्य श्रेयस्तेर्हन्ति तदास्माभिरुच्यते यद् ग्रन्थानां रचनाकाराः, तेषां प्रथमलेखकाः, पाण्डुलिपीनां शोधकाः, तासां पाठकाः, तासां संरक्षणकर्तारश्च पण्डिता एवासन्, न तु कायस्थाः। पण्डितानां सदनेष्वेव पाण्डुलिपयोद्य सुरक्षितास्तिष्ठन्ति, न तु कायस्थानां गृहेषु। अतः नास्ति तेषां तद्रक्षणे किमपि कर्तृत्वम्॥

॥ पाण्डुलिपीनां प्राचीनता॥

प्रकृतमनुसरन्तः प्रथमं तावद् विचारयामः- कियती प्राचीना खलु भारतीया ग्रन्थलेखनपरम्परा? वैदिककाले सर्वमेव मौखिकमासीत् श्रुति- शब्द-वाच्यत्वाद् सर्ववेदानाम्, ऽलेखनकलायाः लिपेर्वा ज्ञानं नासीत् तत्कालिकानां जनानाम्ऽ इति बहूनां विपश्चितां, विशेषतः पाश्चात्त्यानां, मतमिदम्। किंतु चिन्त्यमेतत्। एतत्तु विद्वद्भिर्विचारणीयं यद् विभिन्नगोत्रीयैः ऋषिभी रचितानि, अथ च विविधपरिवारेषु यज्ञार्थं देवानामावाहनाय उपयुज्यमानानि, सूक्तानि संकलय्य महर्षिणा वेदव्यासेन, केनचिदन्येन वा ऋग्वेदसंहिताया रचना कृता। ऽसंहिताऽ इतिशब्दस्य समाहारः संकलनं वेत्यर्थः। अत्र विचार्यं भवति- केन प्रकारेण बहुभ्यः ऋषिपरिवारेभ्यः सूक्तानि आनीतानि? किं सर्वतस्तानि कण्ठस्थीकृत्यैव कश्चिदानीतवान्? नैतत् श्रद्धास्पदं प्रतिभाति। संग्रथितायामेकदा संहितायां तस्याः मौलिकं स्वरूपं, मण्डलेषु विभाजनं, सूक्तानां संख्या, तेषामानुपूर्वी चेत्यादि केन प्रकारेण स्थिरं, सुरक्षितं च स्थातुं शक्यते यदि तेषां भौतिकं, चक्षुर्ग्राह्यं, प्रत्यक्षं स्वरूपं नैव स्यात्? वैदिकसंस्कृतेः समकालिक्यां पूर्ववर्तिन्यां वा सैन्धव-सरस्वतीसंस्कृतौ लेखनकला सुविज्ञाता आसीत्। भारतीया वणिजः एशिया-महाद्वीपस्य मेसोपोटामियादि देशेषु सुमेरादिजनैः सह वाणिज्यं कुर्वते स्म इति ऐतिह्यविदः सम्यक्तया विदन्ति। तत्र लेखनकला भृशमुन्नता आसीत्। किं भारते निवसताम् आर्याणां मनसि लेखनद्वारा वैदिकसंहितानां स्वरूपसंरक्षणस्य विचारोपि नोदैत्, इति न श्रद्धास्पदम्। वर्ततां नाम गुरुशिष्यात्मिका मौखिकी परम्परा, कण्ठस्थीकरणपरम्परा, श्रुतीनां शुद्धतया

संरक्षणार्थम्। किंतु प्रथमतया तु तासां स्थिरीकरणं लेखनेन आवश्यकमासीत् इत्यस्माकमभिमतम्। शतपथब्राह्मणादीनां विपुलकायानां ग्रन्थानां निर्माणमथ च तेषां मौलिकस्य स्वरूपस्य स्थिरीकरणं प्रथमतया तेषां लेखनेन विना नैव संभवति। आदौ तावत् तेषां लिखितं रूपं, तेषां चक्षुर्ग्राह्यत्वम् अपेक्ष्यते॥

पाणिनेः समयेपि प्राचीनानां भारतीयानां लेखनस्य लिपेर्वा ज्ञानं नासीद्-इत्यपि केचिद्विद्वांसोभिप्रयन्ति। तर्ककर्कशधिया समीक्षणेन किंतु एतदपि मतं समीचीनं नैव प्रतिभाति। गभीरायाः संस्कृतभाषायाः किमपि संपूर्णं व्याकरणं रचयितुं विपुलं सामग्रीसंकलनं, सामग्र्याः सविवेकं विश्लेषणं, क्रमबद्धरूपेण च विवेचनं, सूत्रनिर्माणप्रक्रियायां च यत्र-तत्र सुत्राणां संशोधनं, विस्तृतीकरणं-संक्षिप्तीकरणं वा अपेक्ष्यते। तेषामानुपूर्वी अपि एकदा प्रथमवारं लिखितरूपं विना नैव स्थिरीभवितुं शक्नोति। अपरञ्च इदमप्यवधेयं यत् पाणिनिः अष्टाध्याय्याम् ऽअधिकृत्य कृते ग्रन्थेऽ (4. 3. 87), इति च ऽकृते ग्रन्थेऽ (4. 3. 116) इति च सूत्रद्वयनिर्माणेन तत्समये ग्रन्थानामस्तित्वं निर्भ्रान्ततया प्रमाणयति। ग्रथिधातोर्निष्पन्नस्य ऽग्रन्थऽ-शब्दस्य आशयो लिखितं पुस्तकमेव भवितुमर्हति, नान्यत् किमपि। ग्रथनं नाम सूत्रेण केषाञ्चिद्वस्तूनां परस्परं संघटनं निबन्धनं वा। ऽपुष्पाणि [मालारूपेण] ग्रथ्नातिऽ, ऽपत्राणि संग्रथ्नातिऽ इत्यादयो भाषायां प्रयोगाः भवन्ति। वैदिकोयं धातुः तैत्तिरीयकाठकसंहितादिषु अस्मिन्नेवार्थे प्रयुक्तो दृश्यते। ग्रथनं नाम पुस्तकरचनाकर्म। ऽवाल्मीकिरादौ च ससर्ज काव्यं जग्रन्थ यत्र च्यवनो महर्षिःऽ इति बुद्धचरिते (1. 48) अश्वघोषवचनम्। ऽअधिकृत्यऽ इत्यस्य अर्थो भवति कमपि विषयमवलम्ब्य, अतः ऽअधिकृत्य कृते ग्रन्थेऽ ऽकृते ग्रन्थेऽ इति सूत्रयोः तात्पर्यं कमपि एकं निश्चितं विषयमवलम्ब्य कृतेन, लिखितरूपेण चोपलब्धेन पुस्तकेन चैव भवितुं शक्नोति। एवमेव ऽस्वरितेनाधिकारःऽ (1. 3. 11) इति सूत्रेण स्वरितप्रकाशकेन केनचिच्चिह्नेन अंकनस्य, अथ च ऽदिवाविभा...लिपिलिबिबलिभक्ति...अरुःषुऽ (3. 2. 21) इत्यादि सूत्रे लेखनवाचिलिपिशब्दस्योल्लेखः स्पष्टतया पाणिनिना कृतः। अतः पाणिनिसमये लेखनकलायाः, ग्रन्थानां पाण्डुलिपीनां च अस्तित्वं निर्भ्रान्ततया प्रमाणितं भवति॥

पाणिनेरनन्तरं संकलितेषु, किंतु आंशिकरूपेण पाणिनेरपि प्राग्वर्तिषु, बौद्धजातकेष्वपि राजशासनपत्राणाम्, ऋणपत्रादीनां, धर्मनियमानां, व्यक्तिगतपत्राणां चोल्लेखेन लेखनकलाया तत्समयेस्तित्वं सिद्ध्यति इत्येष विषयो नाधिकं प्रपञ्च्यते॥

॥ लेखनाधारा: ॥

यवनाधिपतेः अलेक्साण्डरस्य सेनया सह भारतमागतेन तत्सेनान्या ऽनेआर्खोस्ऽ इत्यनेन उल्लिखितं यद् भारतीया कार्पासं कुट्टयित्वा तेन कर्गदपत्राणि निर्मान्ति, ग्रन्थांश्च तदुपरि लिखन्ति। ऽआउरेल् स्टाइन्ऽ -महाभागेन मध्य-एशियाभागे प्राप्तेषु ग्रन्थेषु कतिचन एतयैव विद्यया निर्भितस्य कर्गदस्योपरि एव लिखिताः सन्ति। राजस्थानस्य मेदपाटक्षेत्रे प्राचीनेभ्यो वस्त्रखण्डेभ्यः किञ्चित्कालात् प्राक् आधुनिके युगेपि एतादृशं कर्गदं निर्मीयते स्म इति गौरीशंकर ओझा स्वकीये ऽप्राचीन भारतीय लिपिमालाऽख्यग्रन्थे सूचयति। अनेन नेआर्खोस्- महोदयस्य कथनं प्रतीतियोग्यं प्रतिभाति। सामान्यतस्तु मध्ययुगे कार्पासनिर्मितं पटं गोधूमचूर्णनिर्मितश्लेषेण, शालिमण्डादिभिश्च छिद्रपूरणपुरस्सरं दृढीकृत्य, क्वथितचिञ्चाबीजकल्कलेपनेन समतलं मसृणं च विधाय क्षौद्रमिश्रितखटिकादिलेपनेन श्वैत्यमानीय, शंखादिसंघट्टनेन चिक्कणं च कृत्वा लेखाधाररूपेण प्रयुञ्जते स्म जनाः इति बहुषु ग्रन्थागारेषु सुरक्षिताभिर्मातृकाभिर्ज्ञायते। एतादृशानि पुस्तकानि प्रायः कुण्डलीरूपेण (Scrolls) वलितानि भवन्ति। जैनमतावलम्बिभिः एतादृशी लेखनसामग्री लेखनाधाररूपेण पर्युषणपर्वानन्तरं लिखितानां ऽक्षमापणऽ -पत्राणां कृते, अथ च साधूनामामन्त्रणार्थं प्रहितानां विज्ञप्तिपत्राणां कृतेद्यत्वेपि प्रयुज्यते। उत्कलेषु पटोपरि शोभनानि चित्राण्यपि निर्मीयन्ते यानि तु पुरी-भुवनेश्वरादिस्थानेषु सर्वत्र क्रेतुं शक्यन्ते॥

भारतीयानां प्राचीनतमौ ग्रन्थाधारौ भूर्जपत्रं तालपत्रं च स्तः। तत्रापि ऽग्रन्थऽ शब्दस्य व्युत्पत्तिलभ्यार्थस्यानुशीलनेन कदाचित् तालपत्रस्यैव प्राचीनतरत्वं सिद्ध्यति यतः स्थूलत्वात् मुख्यतः तालपत्राण्येव छिद्राण्यासाद्य सूत्रेण संग्रथ्यन्ते। भूर्जपत्राणि तु उपरि अधस्ताच्च निहितेन काष्ठफलकद्वयेन सुरक्षितानि भवन्ति। अतिसूक्ष्मतया सहजभंगुरतया च भूर्जत्वचस्तस्यां छिद्रकरणं, सूत्रेण संग्रथनं च प्रायशः पत्राणां विनाशायोपकल्पते। भूर्जपत्रं तालपत्रं चातिरिच्य ऽयोगिनीतन्त्रेऽ ग्रन्थाधाररूपेण तेजपत्रस्य अगुरुत्वचश्चाप्युल्लेखो विद्यते-

> भूर्जे वा तेजपत्रे वा ताले वा ताडिपत्रके।
> अगुरुत्वचापि देवेशि पुस्तकं कारयेत् प्रिये॥

इत्यस्मिन् श्लोके। किंतु तेजपत्रेषु अगुरुत्वचि वा लिखितानि पुस्तकानि अद्यत्वे नैव दृष्टिगोचरीभवन्ति॥

भूर्जवृक्षस्तु हिमालये प्राप्यते। शर्मण्यभाषायाम् स बिर्के (Birke) -

इतिशब्दवाच्यः। भारोपीयभाषासु अस्य उपलब्धेर्ज्ञायते यद् आर्याणां परिचयोनेन वृक्षेण अतिप्राचीनः। कालिदासः स्वकीये कुमारसंभवे (1. 9) अस्य वृक्षस्य त्वचः उल्लेखं पत्रादिलेखनार्थम् आधारसामग्रीरूपेण करोति। हिमालये बाहुल्येन वर्तमानाः भूर्जत्वचो विद्याधरसुन्दरीणाम् अनङ्गलेखनार्थं प्रयुज्यमानाः सत्यः सार्थकत्वम् उपयोगित्वं च भजन्ते-

न्यस्ताक्षरा धातुरसेन यत्र भूर्जत्वचः कुञ्जरबिन्दुशोणाः।
व्रजन्ति विद्याधरसुन्दरीणामनङ्गलेखक्रिययोपयोगम्॥

भूर्जवृक्षाणाम् आन्तरिकी तन्वी त्वक् तीक्ष्णेण क्षुरेण लूना, काष्ठफलकानां मध्ये आस्तृता सती ऋजुतां प्रापिता, अथ च छायायां शुष्का, लेखनार्थमुपयुज्यते स्म। भूर्जपत्रेषु लिखितं प्राचीनतमं पुस्तकं ऽस्टाइन्ऽ महोदयैः खोतानतः प्राप्तं खरोष्ठीलिपिनिबद्धं पालीभाषात्मकं ऽधम्मपदंऽ, यत्तु द्वितीयशताब्दीकं (तृतीयशताब्दीकं वा) विद्वद्भिराकलितं वर्तते। काश्मीरेषु नेपालदेशे च मध्ययुगे भूर्जपत्रेषु विलिखितानि बहूनि पुस्तकानि अद्यत्वेप्युपलभ्यन्ते। भूर्जपत्रेषु केवलं श्यामवर्णया रक्तवर्णया वा मस्या लेखितुं शक्यते॥

ताडपत्रं तु तालवृक्षस्य पत्रम्। तस्य श्रीताल-खरताल इति प्रकारद्वयं भवति। श्रीतालः मसृणश्चिक्कणो नम्यः आयतश्च। खर-तालस्तु किञ्चित् स्थूलः, सारल्येन भंगुरश्च। अस्य पत्राणि क्षुद्राणि। प्राचीने भारते तालपत्रोपरि प्रायः मस्या लिखन्ति स्म पण्डिताः। शर्मण्यदेशीयविद्वद्भिः मध्य-एशियास्थ-तुरफानतः आसादितं, प्रो. ल्यूडर्स्-महोदयैश्च प्रकाशितम् अश्वघोषविरचितं शारद्वतीपुत्रप्रकरणाख्यं नाटकं ताडपत्रेषु मस्या एव लिखितम्। लिपिशास्त्रज्ञैरस्याः पाण्डुलिपेः कालनिर्धारणम् ईशवीयद्वितीयशताब्द्यां कृतम्। कठिनतरे खरताले लौहलेखन्या अक्षराणि उट्टंक्यन्ते, तदनन्तरं तैलमिश्रितकज्जलेन, यदि वा शिम्बालतायाः पत्राणां रसेन तत्तालपत्रम् उपलिप्यते येन कज्जलं रसो वा अक्षररेखासु प्रविशति, तत्रैव च संतिष्ठते। पत्रोपरि वर्तमानम् अवशिष्टं कज्जलादिकं कार्पासेन चैलेन वा अपमृज्यते। उत्कलेषु दक्षिणावर्तगतेषु अन्येषु च प्रदेशेषु एषा एव प्रणाली पाण्डुलिपिनिर्माणस्य।

कर्गदपत्रेषु वर्तमानः प्राचीनतमः पाण्डुलिपिसंग्रहो मध्य-एशिया-स्थिताद् ऽयारकन्द्ऽ – नगराद् महापण्डितेन वेबरेण आसादितो यस्य कालनिर्धारणं ऽह्योर्नलेऽ महोदयेन पञ्चमशताब्द्यामकारि। अत्र विद्यमानानां पाण्डुलिपीनां मध्ये काश्चन चैलखण्डकार्पासादिनिर्मिते कर्गदपत्रे लिखिताः सन्ति इति तज्ज्ञाः वदन्ति। दशमशताब्दीतः एकादशशताब्दीतो वा कर्गदस्य व्यापकः प्रयोग उत्तरभारते दृश्यते, यद्यपि दक्षिणभारते ताडपत्रस्यैव प्राचुर्यम्। कर्गदोपरि लेखनार्थं प्राचीनकाले या मसी निर्मीयते स्म सा अतीव

स्थायिनी। निमज्जितेष्वपि जले पाण्डुलिपिपत्रेषु, लिखितं विवर्णं, दुष्पाठ्यं वा नैव भवति। एषा मसी तु अक्षोटादीनां (walnut) कठोराणि शल्यकानि दग्ध्वा तत्समुत्थितेन अंगारेण, कज्जलं, कीकरवृक्षनिर्यासादिकं च विमिश्र्य निर्मीयते स्म। अस्माकं पितृचरणा अपि अस्मद्बाल्यकाले एतादृशीं मसीं निर्मान्ति स्म, इत्यस्माकं स्मृतिपथे वर्तते॥

॥ पाण्डुलिपीनां संरक्षणम्॥

कर्गदानां ताडपत्राणां च संरक्षणं भारतीयायां जलवायुपरिस्थित्याम् अतीव दुष्करम्। कर्गदपाण्डुलिपीनां सदैव वम्रीभ्यः (उपदीकाभ्यः, white ants) भयं भवति। प्रायः वर्षाकाले ताः लक्षलक्षसंख्याकाः गृहेषु भूमितलाद् आविर्भूय कर्गदपत्राणि भक्षयित्वा तानि सर्वाणि मृत्तिकारूपेण परिणामयन्ति। अतः कर्गदपाण्डुलिपीनां सुरक्षा वर्षर्तौ अवश्यं करणीया भवति। भारते पण्डिताः स्वकीयानि हस्तलिखितानि पुस्तकानि प्रायः रक्तवर्णरञ्जितेन पटेनावेष्ट्य धारयन्ति, भूमौ च तानि नैव निक्षिपन्ति। पटं तु वम्र्यो नैव तादृशेन सारल्येन अभिपतन्ति। भाद्रपदमासे यदा सूर्यस्त्वकास्ति तदा पण्डिताः सर्वाणि वेष्टनानि उद्घाट्य, हस्तलेखानां च पत्राणि शिथिलीकृत्य तेषामार्द्रतापसारणार्थं तानि ऽभाद्रवरौद्रेऽ रविकिरणैः शोषयन्ति। सायं च पत्राणां मध्ये यत्र तत्र निम्बपत्राणि निधाय पुस्तकं पुनरपि दृढं बध्नन्ति॥

तालपत्राणां भयं तु मुख्यतः क्षुद्रकीटेभ्यो भवति ये पत्राणां मध्ये प्रविश्य च तत्र दीर्घकालम् उषित्वा अण्डान्यादधति। एते कीटविशेषाः नैरन्तर्येण संवर्धितपरिवाराः शनैः शनैः पत्राणि खादन्तस्तेषु छिद्राणि च कुर्वन्तः कालेन सर्वमपि पुस्तकं विनाशयन्ति। एतेषामपसारणार्थं मारणार्थं वा पत्राणि सम्यक्तया संमार्ज्य, धूल्यादिकं चापसार्य निम्बबीजतैलं लेपयन्ति पण्डिताः। केचिद् हरिद्रादिविविधौषधिमिश्रितं सर्षपतैलमपि कार्पासेन आरोपयन्ति पत्रेषु। तदपि कृमिनाशकम्। कर्पूरसारो, यवानिकासारश्चापि (Thymol) कृमीन् विनाशयतः। ताडपत्रीयकोषाणां संरक्षणार्थमद्यत्वे दाक्षिणात्येषु निम्बुकशष्पतैलं (citronella) प्रयुज्यते यस्य तीव्रो गन्धः कीटान् उद्वेज्यति॥

विश्वस्मिञ्जगति मूषका एतादृशानां वस्तूनां जातशत्रवः। ते वेष्टनान्तर्गतानि पुस्तकानि प्रायो नैव कर्तयन्ति किंतु इतस्ततो गृहकोणेषु विकीर्णानि, बहुकालम् उपेक्षितानि पुस्तकानि अवश्यमेव कदाचिन् मूषकाणां भोजनं भवन्ति, अत एवैषा प्राचीना उक्तिः:-

स्थलाद् रक्ष, जलाद् रक्ष, रक्ष मां श्लथबन्धनात्।
आखुभ्यः परहस्तेभ्य, एवं वदति पुस्तकम्॥

पुस्तकानां भूमौ निधानेन भूमिगता आर्द्रता तान्युपसर्पति येन

उपदीकादीनामन्येषां च कीटानां तत्राक्रमणं भवति, मूषकादीनामपि तानि सारल्येन भक्ष्यं भवन्ति। श्लथबन्धनिवारणं कीटादिभ्यो रक्षणार्थम्। दृढतया बद्धे पुस्तके पत्राणां मध्ये कृमयो नैव प्रवेष्टुं शक्नुवन्ति। स्वकीयस्य पुस्तकस्य परहस्तेषु प्रदाने महान्तं संकोचमनुभवन्ति पण्डिताः। परहस्तगतं पुस्तकं महता आयासेन, वारं वारं याचनानन्तरमेव पुनः प्राप्यते, पुनरायातस्यापि प्रायः तस्य पत्राणि भ्रष्टानि भवन्ति इति तेषामनुभवः, अत एवोक्तिः-

लेखनी पुस्तकं दाराः परहस्तं गता यदि।
कष्टाच्चेत् पुनरायान्ति नष्टा, भ्रष्टा, विमर्दिताः॥

हस्तलिखितपुस्तकानां संरक्षणार्थं केचिदतीव उपयोगिनो निर्देशाः प्रदत्ताः केनचित्पण्डितेनास्मिन् पद्ये-

संभूष्यं सदपत्यवत्, परकराद् रक्ष्यं च सुक्षेत्रवत्
संशोध्यं व्रणिताङ्गवत् प्रतिदिनं, वीक्ष्यं च सन्मित्रवत्।
बन्ध्यं वध्यवदश्लथं दृढगुणैः, स्मर्यं हरेर्नामवत्
नैवं सीदति पुस्तकं बहुतिथं ह्येतद् गुरूणां वचः॥

स्निग्धपुत्रवत् पुस्तकं वाससा परिधापनीयम्, स्वकीयप्रियभार्यावत् परकरेभ्यो रक्षणीयम्, व्रणवत् धूल्यादिकमपसार्य संशोधनीयम्, मित्रवत् प्रतिदिनमुद्घाट्य स्निग्धेन चक्षुषा वीक्षणीयम्, दृढैः सूत्रैः अश्लथं- निविडं- बन्धनीयम्, अथ च कुत्र किंरूपेण तत् तिष्ठति इति सदैव स्मृतिपथे धारणीयम्, तस्योपेक्षणं नैव कार्यम्। यद्येवं क्रियते तदा पुस्तकं बहुकालं यावत् विनाशं नैव उपयाति, इति तत्संरक्षणकृते व्यावहारिकाः निर्देशाः कस्यचित् पाण्डुलिपिसंरक्षणविशेषज्ञस्य॥

॥ पुस्तकलेखनं लेखकाश्च॥

ग्रन्थलेखकः कीदृशः स्यादित्यस्मिन् विषयेपि तन्त्रग्रन्थेषु, पुराणेषु, चाणक्यनीतौ च निर्देशाः प्राप्यन्ते। चाणक्यनीतिः लेखकानां गुणान् एवं प्रकाशयति-

सकृदुक्तगृहीतार्थो लघुहस्तः स्फुटाक्षरः।
सर्वशास्त्रसमालोकी प्रकृष्टो ग्रन्थलेखकः॥

एकवारमेव श्रुत्वा यो हि उक्तं गृह्णाति, धारयति च, स सकृदुक्तगृहीतार्थः। ऽलघुहस्तःऽ इति शब्देन शीघ्रं, जवेन वा लेखनकलाकौशलं व्यज्यते। जवेन लिख्यमानानामपि अक्षराणामाकारस्य आकृतेश्च व्यत्यासो मा भूत् इत्येवाशयः। ऽसर्वशास्त्रसमालोकीऽ इति शब्देन सर्वेषां शास्त्राणां यत्किञ्चित्

ज्ञानं प्रत्येकं लेखकस्य कृतेपेक्ष्यते येन स पारिभाषिकशब्दान् शुद्धतया लिखेत्। राजशेखरकृतायां ऽकाव्यमीमांसायाम्ऽ अपि दशमेध्याये प्रायः अस्यैवाभिप्रायस्यानुवादो दृश्यते-

> ऽसर्वभाषाकुशलः शीघ्रवाक्, चार्वक्षरः, इंगिताकारवेदी,
> नानालिपिज्ञो लाक्षणिकश्च लेखकः स्यात्ऽ

मत्स्यपुराणस्य 189 तमेध्याये लेखकस्य योग्यता इत्थं वर्णिता-

> सर्वदेशाक्षराभिज्ञः सर्वशास्त्रविशारदः।
> बह्वर्थवक्ता चाल्पेन लेखकः स्यान्नृपोत्तम॥
> शीर्षोपेतान् सुसम्पूर्णान् शुभान् श्रेणिगतान् समान्।
> अक्षरान् वै लिखेद् यस्तु लेखकः स वरः स्मृतः॥

लेखकस्य बहुज्ञतात्रापि प्रशंसिता। विविधदेशेषु प्रयुज्यमानानां लिपीनां ज्ञानं, सर्वशास्त्रावलोकित्वं, मिताक्षरैर्बह्वर्थप्रकाशनसामर्थ्यम् अथ च सुलेखलेखनक्षमत्वं तस्मादपदेक्ष्यते। अक्षराणि सर्वाभीरेखाभिः समन्वितानि, समानाकृतीनि, एकश्रेणिगतानि भवितुमर्हन्ति। एवं लेखनीयं यथा द्वयोर्वर्णयोरन्तरा भूयान् अवकाशो न स्यात्। अत्र कस्यचित् (दाक्षिणात्यस्य सहृदयसमालोचकस्येदं प्राचीनं पद्यं स्मृतिपथमवतरति-

> अक्षराणि समानानि वर्तुलानि घनानि च।
> परस्परसुलग्नानि तरुणीकुचकुम्भवत्॥

पुस्तकस्य आकारप्रकारः, दैर्घ्यादिकं, मानं च कीदृशं भवेदित्यस्मिन् विषयेपि निर्देशाः प्राप्यन्ते प्रायशस्तन्त्रग्रन्थेषु। ऽयोगिनीतन्त्र-ऽ कारस्य मतानुसारं पुस्तकस्य दैर्घ्यं मुष्टिमानाद् आरभ्य बाहुपर्यन्तं भवितुं शक्नोति- षडङ्गुलं (मुष्टिः), अष्टाङ्गुलं, दशाङ्गुलं, द्वादशाङ्गुलम्, अष्टादशाङ्गुलं, हस्तमात्रं (चतुर्विंशत्यङ्गुलं), यदि वा बाहुमात्रं (षट्त्रिंशदङ्गुलम्) इति पुस्तकस्य मानानि। कुत्र, कियन्ति वा पुस्तकपत्रेषु छिद्राणि क्रियेरन् इत्यस्यापि विवेको विद्यते-

> हस्तमात्रं मुष्टिमात्रमाबाहु द्वादशाङ्गुलम्।
> दशाङ्गुलं तथाष्टौ च, ततो हीनं न कारयेत्॥
> वेधद्वयं मुष्टिहस्ते बाहुमात्रे त्रिरन्ध्रकम्।
> समभागे महेशानि हस्तादौ रूपरन्ध्रकम्॥
> अष्टाङ्गुलं परित्यज्य मध्ये वेधं तु कारयेत्।

प्रादेशादौ भवेद् रन्ध्रं द्व्यङ्गुले वा समाचरेत्॥

ऽहयशीर्षपाञ्चरात्रस्यऽ तृतीये संकर्षणकाण्डे, एकत्रिंशत्तमेध्याये पुस्तकानां प्रतिष्ठाविधिर्वर्ण्यते। कस्यापि महत्त्वावहस्य ग्रन्थस्य लेखनात् प्राक् वाग्देव्याः सरस्वत्याः पूजा कार्या। स्वस्तिवाचनपुण्याहवाचनानन्तरं लेखकः प्राङ्मुखमुपविश्य रजतपात्रे मसीं स्थापयित्वा स्वर्णलेखन्या प्रथमान् पञ्चश्लोकान् लिखेत्। अक्षराणि स्निग्धानि, नातिकृशानि, नातिस्थूलानि, ह्रस्वदीर्घादिमात्रासंयुतानि, संपूर्णावयवानि, यथास्थानं बिन्दुविसर्गदण्डादियुक्तानि, शुद्धानि च भवितुमर्हन्ति। उत्तरभारते प्रणीतत्वाद् हयशीर्षसंहिता नागराक्षरैः शारदाक्षरैर्वा ग्रन्थस्य लेखनं वरं मनुते-

ततः पुण्याहघोषेण प्रारभेल्लेखनं बुधः।
प्राङ्मुखः पद्मिनीं ध्यायन्नालिखेच्छ्लोकपञ्चकम्॥
रौप्यपात्रे मषीं स्थाप्य लेखन्या हेमया शुचिः।
काश्मीरैर्नागरैर्वर्णैः समशीर्षैः समांशकैः॥
स्निग्धैर्नातिकृशैः स्थूलैर्ह्रस्वदीर्घादिलक्षितैः।
संपूर्णावयवैर्मात्राबिन्दुसंयोगलक्षितैः।
लेखयेल्लेखको धीमान् शब्दशास्त्रविशारदः॥

॥ पाठसंशोधनम्॥

स्वयं लेखकेन वा पुस्तकस्य लेखनानन्तरं पण्डिताः तत्पुस्तकम् अतिसावधानतया निरीक्षन्ते स्म, तत्र वर्तमानाः लेखनत्रुटीर्निरस्य भ्रष्टं पाठं च संशोधयन्ति स्म। योंशः अधिकः अशुद्धो वा, तं हरतालेन आच्छाद्य, तदुपरि शुद्धं पाठं लिखन्ति स्म। कुत्रचिद् अवशिष्टं च्युतं वा पाठं ते ऽकाकपदऽ (v)- चिह्नाङ्कनपूर्वकं, पङ्क्तिसंख्यामुल्लिख्य तस्यैव पत्रस्य उपरि अधस्ताद् वा योजयन्ति स्म। कस्यापि ग्रन्थस्य सामीक्षिकसंपादनपूर्वकं मौलिकशुद्धपाठनिर्धारणस्य य आधुनिको विधिः तस्यापि किञ्चित् परिज्ञानं प्राचीनानां पण्डितानामासीत् इत्यत्र नास्ति कापि संशीतिः। भाष्यटीकादिनिर्माणसमये ते आलोच्यग्रन्थस्य यथाशक्ति अधिकाधिकाः मातृकाः संगृह्य, शुद्धं च पाठं सम्यक्तया विविच्य तत्पश्चादेव स्वकीयां टीकां विरचयन्ति स्म॥

कालिदासस्य यशस्वी टीकाकारो मल्लिनाथः कालिदासकृतीष्टीकयन्ननेकशः पाठविवेचनं करोति, पाठस्य शुद्ध्यशुद्धिविषये च स्वाभिमतं प्रकाशयति। स्थालीपुलाकन्यायेन केवलम् एकमेवोदाहरणामत्र प्रस्तूयते। मेघदूतस्य द्वितीये श्लोके ऽआषाढस्य प्रथमदिवसे मेघमाश्लिष्टसानुम्ऽ इति तृतीयश्चरणः। अत्र ऽप्रथमऽ इत्यस्य स्थाने ऽप्रशमऽ इत्यपि पाठोनेकासु मातृकासु

अवलोक्यते। केचिट्टीकाकाराः अमुमेव पाठं साधुं मन्यन्ते, किंतु ऽप्रशमदिवसेऽ (अर्थात् पूर्णिमादिवसे आषाढमासस्य) इति पाठो मल्लिनाथस्य नोभीष्टः। संजीवनीटीकायां स्वकीयम् अभिमतं पक्षं च सविस्तरं पोषयन् स लिखति- ऽकेचिद् ऽआषाढस्य प्रथमदिवसेऽ इत्यत्र ऽप्रत्यासन्ने नभसिऽ इति वक्ष्यमाणनभोमासप्रत्यासत्त्यर्थं ऽप्रशमदिवसेऽ इति पाठं कल्पयन्ति, तदसंगतम्, प्रथमातिरेके कारणाभावात्, प्रथमदिवसातिक्रमेण मेघदर्शनकल्पनायां प्रमाणाभावेन तदसम्भवात्ऽ इत्यादि॥

महाभारतस्य ख्यातनामा टीकाकारो नीलकण्ठः उल्लिखति यत् महाभारतस्य शुद्धपाठनिर्धारणे तेन महत् काठिन्यमनुभूतम्। अतः तेन विभिन्नेभ्यो देशेभ्यो विविधासु लिपिषु लिखिताः बह्व्यः मातृकाः आनीताः, सर्वास्ताः सम्यगालोचिताश्च । समालोचनानन्तरं स्वविवेकपूर्वकं तेन शुद्धः प्रकृष्टश्च पाठोङ्गीकृतः। गुरवोपि तेन पाठनिर्धारणविषये पृष्टाः, प्राचीनाः टीकाश्चापि दृष्टाः। एवं शुद्धतमं पाठं विनिश्चित्य तेन तदनन्तरमेव टीका विहिता-

बहून् समाहृत्य च भिन्नदेश्यान्
कोषान् विनिश्चित्य च पाठमग्र्यम्।
प्राचां गुरूणामनुसृत्य वाचं
प्रतन्यते भारतभावदीपः॥

आनन्दतीर्थोऽपि (1238-1317 ई.) स्वकीये ऽमहाभारततात्पर्यनिर्णयेऽ पाठाविलत्वं प्रति स्वकीयमुद्गारमेवं प्रकटयति-

क्वचिद् ग्रन्थान् प्रक्षिपन्ति, क्वचिदन्तरितान्यपि।
कुर्युः क्वचिच्च व्यत्यासं प्रमादात् केचिदन्यथा॥

येन स्पष्टं प्रतिभाति यत् पाठाविलत्वं अर्थात् पाठप्रक्षेपम् (अधिकं, ग्रन्थकर्त्रा नैव रचितं पाठं), पाठभ्रंशं, पाठवैपरीत्यादिकं प्रति जागरूकाः प्राचीनाः पण्डिताः परिशील्यमानग्रन्थस्य शुद्धं मौलिकं च पाठं निर्धारयितुं सततं सचेष्टा आसन्। एतादृश्यस्त्रुटयः तु प्रमादाद् अपि भवितुं शक्नुवन्ति, दुराशयेनापीति ते जानन्ति स्म॥

अस्मत्सविधे महेश्वरविरचितस्य ऽशब्दभेदप्रकाशऽ इत्याख्यस्य कोशग्रन्थस्यैका वाराणसीतः समानीता मातृका विद्यते। एषा मातृका द्वे प्राचीनतरे मातृके अवलोक्य तयोः पाठं च परस्परं तुलयित्वा केनचित् पण्डितेन निर्मिता यतः प्रायः प्रत्येकं पृष्ठस्य प्रान्तभागे उपरि अधस्ताद् वा पाण्डुलिपिलेखकस्य एवंविधा टिप्पणी वर्तते- ऽद्वितीयमातृकायां तु ... पाठःऽ। एवं यदि कश्चिद् अंशः पाठे त्रुटितः (Lacuna) स्यात्तदा त्रुटिस्थाने

ऽकाकपदंऽ दत्त्वा त्रुटितांशं प्रान्तभागे संयोज्य, तल्लेखनानन्तरं लेखकः त्रु. इति संकेतं प्रददाति।

संस्कृतग्रन्थलेखकाः स्वकीयानाम् अन्यमनस्कत्वात् प्रमादाद् वा संजातानां त्रुटीनां कृते पाठकानां सविधे सर्वदैव क्षमाशीला आसन्। क्षमां याचमानास्ते पुस्तकस्यान्ते लिखन्ति-

> यदतिहृदयवेगाल्लेखनीभ्रान्तिभावा-
> न्नयनचलनसंगाच्छ्रोत्रशब्दावलम्बात्।
> लिखितमपकृतं यन्मामकीनात् प्रमादात्
> करकृतमपराधं क्षन्तुमर्हन्ति सन्तः॥

ग्रन्थः शोधयित्वा पठनीयः, लिपिकाराय दोषो न दातव्यः, अयमेव सज्जनानां स्वभावो यत् क्वचित् स्खलने जाते दुर्जना हसन्ति किंतु सज्जनाः त्वरितमागत्य पतन्तं समालम्बन्ते, पुनरपि चैनमुत्थापयन्ति-

> गच्छतः स्खलनं क्वापि भवत्येव प्रमादतः।
> हसन्ति दुर्जनास्तत्र समादधति सज्जनाः॥

कष्टेन लिखितस्य ग्रन्थस्य स्वकीयपुत्रवत् सस्नेहं पालनं संरक्षणं च विधेयमित्यपि ग्रन्थलेखकेन प्रार्थ्यते-

> भग्नपृष्ठकटिग्रीवं तुल्यदृष्टि ह्यधोमुखम्।
> कष्टेन लिखितं ग्रन्थं पुत्रवत् परिपालयेत्॥

पर्यन्ते ग्रन्थशोधकानां पाठकानां च कृते प्रायः आशीर्वचनमपि प्राप्यते संस्कृत-पाण्डुलिपिषु। सर्वेषां तद्ग्रन्थसंबन्धिनाम् आयुष्यमारोग्यं चिरञ्जीवितां च कामयमानो विद्वान् लेखको विरमति। वयमपि अस्मच्छ्रोतॄणां मङ्गलं कामयमानाः अनेनैव पारम्परिकेण पद्येन विरमामः-

> शोधकाः पाठकाश्चैव चिरं जीवन्तु पण्डिताः।
> चिरं जीवन्तु विद्वांसो ये पठन्तीह पुस्तकम्॥

इति शुभम्।

ALBRECHT WEZLER

Some Remarks on Nirukta 1.20

sākṣātkṛtadharmāṇa ṛṣayo, etc.

1. All beginnings are difficult ("Aller Anfang ist schwer"),[1] but not in my case, for I do not have taken recourse to Gaṇeśa, the Vighneśa par excellence. What I want to discuss is not, of course, just the initial expression *sākṣātkṛtadharmāṇa ṛṣayo* of Nirukta (Nir.) 1.20, but the passage as a whole. It reads thus:

> *sākṣātkṛtadharmāṇa ṛṣayo babhūvus te 'varebhyo 'sākṣātkṛtadharmabhya upadeśena mantrān saṃprādur upadeśāya glāyanto 'vare bilmagrahaṇāyemaṃ granthaṃ samāmnāsiṣur vedaṃ ca vedāṅgāni ca / (bilmaṃ bhilmaṃ bhāsanam iti vā) /.*

The last sentence was put into brackets by Roth (1852:39) in order to indicate that in his view it is, like other similar explanatory phrases in the Nir.,[2] a later addition to the text.[3]

---

1 Is this an idiomatic expression or a proverbial saying? Mackensen (1973:19, No. 122) refers to the Latin *omne principium grave*, Röhrich (1992) does not list it.

2 Cf. e.g. p. 36 of Roth's edition.

3 In his "Erläuterungen" (p. 14) Roth refers to the "Einleitung" p. XIII where indeed his paraphrase and interpretation of this passage is found. In the note itself Roth states: "The words put within brackets one will not ascribe to Y., if one does not want to regard him as a fatuous pedant who explains his own words" ("Die in Klammern stehenden Worte wird man J. nicht zuschreiben dürfen, wenn man ihn nicht für einen abgeschmackten Pedanten halten will, der seine eigenen Worte erklärt"). Indeed, it would be strange to give a *nirvacana*-explanation of an expression used by one-self, and above all an alternative one. If the explanation is nevertheless considered as an authentic part of the text, only two conclusions would be possible, viz., firstly, that the passage as such is not the words of Yāska himself, but the quotation of a legend, an *arthavāda* or, secondly, as was indirectly proposed by Dhadphale (1982), that Yāska wants to exemplify his method here, too. Roth, in the note referred to just now, also points out that Durga found these —bracketed— words already in the text of the Nirukta as received by him ("Indessen hat D. dieselben vorgefunden)". The reception of this passage of the Nirukta in general (see §§ 3.4 and 10 below) should, of course, be examined in this regard. The quotation found in the Yuktidīpikā (231.22-252.2) is noteworthy in that the *iti* is placed after (*vedāṅgāni*) *ca* and that the explanation (*bilmaṃ bhāsanaṃ samyakpratibhāsāya viśiṣṭaḥ saṃketa uktaḥ*) is not absolutely identical and, what is even more important, is not also followed by an *iti* (or an *itīti* which one would rather expect); see, however below § 10: Further (?) evidence for the knowledge of a pre-Durga commentary on the Nir. on the part of the author of the YD (cf. Bronkhorst 1985)? —The Vṛtti on Vākyapadīya, Brahmakāṇḍa 5, however, fully agrees with the text of Nir. 1.20 (except for *'parebhyo*, and *'pare*, in the place of *'varebhyo*, and *'vare*, on which see below n. 19).

Since my student days in Tübingen the problems posed by this Nir. passage have been on my mind, and I have been able to collect some material on it, i.e. quotations, references etc., although I should frankly state that I never really started a search for such material, not to mention a systematic one, if this is at all possible in our discipline, and that what I am presenting now is not by any means the result of systematic work carried out over years, but rather a rough and partly incomplete sketch only. Let me bring these biographical indiscretions to an end by just adding that in 1984 it was pointed out to me by R. P. Das that Gajanan Balkrishna Palsule had announced a paper on "The Nirukta 1.20: *sākṣātkṛtadharmāṇa ṛṣayo* etc., with Special Reference to *Bilmagrahaṇa*" which he intended to, but eventually did not read out at the "VIth World Sanskrit Conference" in Philadelphia. Palsule was kind enough to respond to a letter which I sent him, but what he wrote was that he himself had not found a solution to the problem, and he wondered whether perhaps I had an idea. Well, I think I have, but for various reasons —one of them being the fact that ideas, too, sometimes have to ripen first, and that this process is beyond the individual's conscious control—I could not set it forth on an earlier occasion. But this "Colloquium" and the highly impressive *pāṇḍitya* of Dr. Parameswara Aithal—the fruits of which later he most generously gave also to me—presents an excellent and worthy opportunity for doing away with the remaining self-critical shyness, and for having trust in the benevolence and clemency of the audience.

2. The passage under discussion follows, in the so-called Naigamakāṇḍa,[4] upon the commentary on Ṛgveda (RV) 10.71.5[5] , but it does not really form part of it. In my view, it is rather to be connected with the statement at the very end of Nir. 1.17: *athāpi jñānapraśaṃsā bhavaty ajñānanindā ca*, "(m)oreover, there is praise of knowledge and censure of ignorance" (Sarup 1967:18), viz. in the verses immediately afterwards quoted from Saṃhitopaniṣad Brāhmaṇa 3. Since the quotation and explanation of RV 10.71.5 is similarly introduced by a transitional remark at the end of Nir. 1.19, viz. ... *ity arthajñapraśaṃsā / tasyottarā bhūyase nirvacanāya /*, "this is the praise of one who understands the meaning. The stanza following this explains it still more (explicitly)" (Sarup 1967:19), and since at the beginning of 1.19, i.e. of the commentary on RV 10 71.4,[6] the first half of this

4 The various editors of the Nir. do not, however, agree as regards the designations of this *kāṇḍa* (on the basis of (the) mss.?). According e.g. to Bhadkamkar (1985:146 ff.) the passage forms part of the Naighaṇṭukakāṇḍa, and the Naigamaṃ kāṇḍam starts at IV.1 only (347 ff.).

5 *utá tvam sakhyé sthirápītam āhur*
naínaṃ hinvanti ápi vā́jineṣu /
ádhenvā carati māyáyaiṣá
vā́caṃ śuśruvā́m̐ aphalā́m apuṣpā́m // Cf. Nir. 1.8.

6 *utá tvaḥ páśyan ná dadarśa vā́cam*
utá tvaḥ śṛṇván ná śṛṇoty enām /

ṛc[7] is said to deal with the *avidvān*, though this refers first of all to the verse quoted immediately afterwards, I am of the opinion that the passage at issue, i.e. Nir. 1.20, has to do, i.e. also deals with the praise of those who know the meaning—of course of the Veda—[8] and the censure of those who do not, and that it only indirectly, if at all, answers the question as to the origin(s) of the *nirukta-śāstra* and the other *vedāṅgas*, but it is not directly meant to do so. That is to say, I disagree with the commentators of the Nirukta, all of whom regard the passage as introducing a new topic, viz. that of "the origin/transmission of the Nirukta the aim of which has just been taught" (*evam uktaprayojanasya niruktasya*[9] *pareṇa* [by the [immediately] following [section/part]" *āgamaḥ* [10] *kathyate*[11]), to quote Skandasvāmin-Maheśvara, a topic which, as Durga says, is an answer to the question "where has this śāstra of the Nirukta, which is the most important [of them],[12] and the other *aṅgas* come from" (*kutaḥ punar idam āyātaṃ niruktaśāstraṃ pradhānam itarāṇi cāṅgānīti*[13]).[14] It is not, of course, that I refuse to show respect to these commentators; on the contrary, I am fully, even painfully aware of the superiority of their scholarly erudition[15] and their knowledge of Sans-

---

utó tvasmai tànvam ví sasre
jāyéva pátya uśatī́ suvā́sāḥ //

7 Note that Sarup's (1967:19) rendering of part of the explanation of this *ṛc*, viz. of (*jñānaṃ prakāśanam arthasyāhānayā vācā*) *upamottamayā vācā* by "(the manifestation of meaning is described by this speech,) i.e. the third verse", is not correct. He should have said "(... by this speech,) i.e. the speech (i.e. that part of RV 10.71.4) which aims at an *upamā*".

8 Cf. e.g. the passage from the explanation of RV 10.171.4 quoted in n. 6.

9 On the appellative meaning of *nírukta*, and *ánirukta* in the Veda see Renou-Silburn 1954.

10 Note the meaning *āgama* has here, viz. "the coming here, i.e. origin/appearance in this world", and note that Durga (see next quotation) uses the verb *ā-yā* to express the same idea. For a different meaning see below n. 58.

11 Quoted from Sarup 1982:113.

12 It is not at all surprising that commentators on the Nirukta voice the opinion that this particular Vedāṅga is the most important of all—just like Pāṇinīyas declare grammar to be the most significant (cf. e.g. Mahābhāṣya I 1.19 f., or the verse (*mukhaṃ vyākaraṇaṃ* etc.) quoted by Haradatta at the end of his commentary on the third *ārambhaśloka* of the Kāśikā). Regarding the high(est) rank of the Nir. see especially the beginning of Durga's Ṛjvarthā Niruktavṛtti (Bhadkamkar 1985:27 f.)—As against the view of the commentators it has to be pointed out that in the Nir. passage itself it is the *veda* and the *vedāṅgas* (in general) which are spoken of; that one of the latter, i.e. the Nirukta, is ascribed a higher rank could only be supported by a rather complex argument. There is, similarly, no direct and clear statement about the origin of the Nirukta!

13 Quoted from Bhadkamkar 1985:146,13.

14 Devarāja Yajvan's commentary covers only the Nighaṇṭus.

15 And according to their self-understanding it is this erudition, "the fact of being trained by [the study of the sciences] of Nirukta[-śāstra] Grammar etc. which have a formative effect on the mind" (*niruktavyākaraṇasaṃskāreṇāsaṃskṛtatvāj jñātum asamarthatvat*,

krit, and they are, no doubt, not just very intelligent indeed, but also of a remarkable pensiveness. But they, too, were children of their times, and had their prejudices, or perhaps it is better to say that they shared certain views prevalent during their period and were, as stated by Halbfass (1988:328) with regard to Durga, heavily influenced by Mīmāṃsā.[16] In short, I respect them as earlier philological predecessors whose interpretation should always be carefully studied and taken into account, but whom one should not follow blindly, even if they agree with each other, and do not offer, or report, as Skandasvāmin-Maheśvara does in this case, alternative interpretations.[17] Such uncritical dependence would, in my view, be a betrayal of what they themselves did, and evidently regarded as their duty, viz. to form for themselves an independent opinion with regard to the problems posed by the Nirukta, i.e. to carry out a *parīkṣaṇa*. And let me add, firstly, that the two views, that of the commentators and my own, are not incompatible,[18] and, secondly, that I would equally be able to defend the central point I am going to make if the commentators' view about the purport of the passage should eventually prove to be preferable to mine.

Yet, significantly enough, the passage under discussion here does not dwell on the dichotomy as such of the *vedārthajñas* and those ignorant of the meaning of the Veda, but offers an explanation for it which is quite clearly of a historical nature in that the *sākṣātkṛtadharmāṇa ṛṣayaḥ* are contrasted with the *asākṣātkṛtadharman*s who are at the same time characterized as *avara* (*'varebhyo, 'vare*);[19] for this latter expression cannot but be used here in its temporal meaning of "posterior, later, younger" as was already recognized by Roth (1832:XIII) and, as far as I can see, never explicitly disputed, although the original meaning of this expression, "below", should not be

said with reference to Kautsa and similar people by Skandasvāmin-Maheśvara (Sarup 1982:102)).

16 Cf. n. 17.

17 Cf. Sarup 1982:125 (*ye tu sṛṣṭpralayan necchanti ta etaṃ grantham evaṃ vyācakṣate*).

18 The difference is mainly one of stress; I myself want to bring into relief the internal connection of Nir. 1.20 with some of the passages preceding it, and thus ultimately the importance of the Nirukta for the understanding of the *vedārtha*, while the commentators are primarily concerned with what is new in Nir. 1.20, i.e. that it is a statement about the origin of this *śāstra*.

19 As stated already above (n. 3; cf. also below § 10) the reading attested by Bhartṛhari, or the Vṛttikāra (on their identity see Aklujkar 1972 and 1993, but also Houben 1999), is *(a)parebhyo* and *(a)pare* (rendered as "others" by Aklujkar forthcoming:22), and this is confirmed, so to say, by the Yuktidīpikā. *apara* is not semantically clearer than *avara*, and both words also mean "low, inferior" (cf. e.g. Gautama-Dharma-Sūtra 6.11 and 14 (= 2.5).27). The secondarily attested reading, not found in mss. of the Nir. itself, is hence most probably due to a scribal mistake (made possible by the similarity of the *akṣaras* for *va* and *pa* in a number of Indian scripts).

lost sight of in this connection.[20] The choice among and distribution of the tenses (*babhūvus* versus *samprādur* and *samāmnāsiṣur*), however, seem to be based on the distinction between the functions of stating a fact[21] or denoting a state, on the one hand, and reporting or describing an event/a series of events, on the other ("there have been/there have existed (the) *ṛṣis* who ...". versus "they delivered ... wholly over ..." and "they handed down from memory ...").[22] To say it in other words, the passage at issue explains the origination of the dichotomy between the *sākṣātkṛtadharmāṇa ṛṣayaḥ* and those called *asākṣātkṛtadharmans* by putting it into a temporal sequence, but this does not imply, and certainly does not mean (because this could clearly contradict an easily observable fact) that the two classes of people, Brahmins,[23] cannot and do not exist side by side at a given later period of time. This later existence side by side is, so we are told by Yāska, the result of, i.e. is only made possible by, a historical development which led to the emergence of people "ignorant of the meaning [of the Veda]". This is the kernel, or rather part of the kernel of the passage, and in this statement one has apparently to recognize its primary importance in terms of a history of Indian ideas,[24] and for this reason it was taken note of quite early in India

20 What I want to draw attention to is, of course, the particular conception of the past and organization of collective, cultural memory according to which the ancestors etc., are "above" or "before", and the later generation "below" or "behind", (for which cf. e.g. Śatapatha Brāhmaṇa 1.1.2.7)—although this perception of time is not by any means specific for India (yet nevertheless obviously it went unnoticed by Assman/Hölscher 1988 as also by Assman 1999 (who refers, however, to the "kommunikativen, in der Regel drei Generationen verbindenden Gedächtnis" [13])). I hope to fill this gap with an article still under preparation.—"Inferior" (e.g. Falk 1990 and 1993) is in my view not acceptable, especially because the distinction of superiority and inferiority, in a particular regard, is most clearly expressed by *sākṣāt-* and *asākṣātkṛtadharman*. Besides, the assumption that *avara* is meant to express a temporal posteriority is confirmed by the parallels presented below (cf. p. 6 ff.).

21 Cf. Renou 1961:458 ff. (§ 337).

22 Or is this an instance of stating a narrative in the perfect and continuing it in the aorist (on which see Renou 1961:459 (§ 337))? The possibility that the aorist refers to not so distant a past, something witnessed by the speaker, should perhaps also be taken into account; as for this latter possibility, or rather the problem of the various past tenses in Vedic prose etc., see Witzel 1987: especially p. 392 ff. and notes 31, 32, 36, 40 and 41. To the secondary literature referred to by Witzel one should add Von Hinüber 1982/83 and 1986 (with further references) as well as Tichy 1997.—Or, finally, does the perfect refer to the remote past and the past tense to the recent past?

23 The special duty of the Brahmins, as viewed by themselves, is particularly clearly, albeit mythologically, expressed by Manu 2.114. In connection with the immediately preceding verses it shows, however, that this strictly exclusivistic attitude may well (also) be responsible for the disappearance of Vedic schools and their textual traditions.

24 Oetke (1999:84) rightly distinguishes different meanings of "idea"—as I did myself a little earlier (elsewhere). Nevertheless, i.e. after such a necessary semantical clarification, the term "history of ideas" may be, and should be, adhered to.

herself and in Indological research.[25]

What needs some justification, as the discussion of the "Colloqium" has shown, is the assumption made by me, though, as by many earlier interpreters of Nir. 1.20, that two, and not three, "generations", i.e. temporally separated[26] groups of people, are referred to here,—in addition to that of Yāska himself. External evidence, I think, strongly, supports this interpretation, although it is found in a different strand of the Indian tradition, albeit roughly contemporaneous, viz. certain Dharmasūtras. Most of this evidence was already presented by Kane (1973:889), but done so in the context of his attempt to determine the "meaning of *yuga*", and as negative evidence since the latter expression is significantly absent in the passages drawn upon by him. The most telling passage, however, is not even mentioned by Kane; it is Baudhāyana-Dharma-Sūtra 2.9.16.9:

saptāvarān sapta pūrvān
ṣaḍ anyān ātmasaptamān /
satputram adhigacchānaḥ /
tārayaty enaso bhayāt //

"(h)e who obtains a virtuous son saves from the fear of sin seven in the descending line and seven in the ascending line, (viz.) six others (in each), himself being the seventh" (Bühler 1882:272).[27]

The meaning *avara* has in this verse is absolutely clear, especially because of the opposition in which it stands to *pūrva* "the earlier, the preceding (ones)". The same opposition is attested in GautDhS. 1.1.4 (cf. also the parallel in Āpastamba-Dharma-Sūtra 2.6.13.9),[28] and it can even be traced back further to the level of the Śrautasūtras.[29] Equally clear, though lacking this opposition, is ĀpDhS 1.2. 5.4:[30] *tasmād ṛṣayo 'vareṣu na jāyante niyamātikramāt*, "(o)n account of that (transgression of the rules of studentship) no Rishis are born amongst the men of later ages" (Bühler

25 Cf. Muir 1868-1872:III 210 f.

26 The length of period separating the two groups from each other cannot even be roughly estimated; similarly it is not clear at all whether each group by itself comprises just one generation or more than one, and whether it forms a unified whole or not. The prevalent idea is evidently that of the temporal distance combined with a significant qualitative difference.

27 Olivelle (1999:203) does not differ in substance.

28 It reads thus (Pandey 1966:2): *avareṣām asmadādīnāṃ durbalatvāt / tathā ca śrūyate ... /*. Rocher's (1976) critique of the earlier, "traditional" interpretation of the first *sūtras* of Gautama is inappropriate, as I shall show elsewhere (in a refutation of his article). It is also not accepted by Olivelle (1999).

29 Cf., e.g. Lāṭyāyana-Śrauta-Sūtra 1.3.19 (= Drāhyāyaṇa-Śrauta-Sūtra 1.3.21) *athāvareṣāṃ yathājyesthaṃ strīpumsāṃ ye jīveyuḥ* where *avare* is explained by Agnisvāmin to mean *putrapautraprapautrāḥ*, or Āśvalāyana-Śrauta-Sūtra 2.19.22 and 5.20.6.

30 I thank Madhav Deshpande for drawing my attention to this passage during the discussion of my paper.

1879:19).[31] At first sight this statement could be taken to confirm the assumption made above (p. 5) that the *asākṣātkṛtadharmāṇo 'vare*, of Nir. 1.20, are not classed with the *ṛṣis*. But our text continues (ĀpDhS 1.2.5.5-6): *śrutarṣayas tu bhavanti kecit karmaphalaśeṣeṇa punaḥsaṃbhave // yathā śvetaketuḥ //*, "(b)ut some in their new birth, on account of a residue of the merit acquired by their actions (in former lives), become (similar to) Rishis by their knowledge (of the Veda), (l)ike Śvetaketu" (Bühler 1879:19). That is to say, the contention that "no Rishis are born amongst the men of later ages" has to be qualified: There were no *ṛṣis* in the proper sense of the word, i.e.—according to the commentator Haradatta—"persons who see the mantras" (*mantradṛśaḥ*), but only people comparable to those *ṛṣis* of olden times, viz. Brahmins who were able "to learn all four Vedas within a short period of time" (*alpena yatnena/kālena caturo vedān gṛhṇanti/jagrāha*). These latter are therefore called *śrutarṣis*, "*ṛṣis* because of their learning [of the Veda]", and Bühler is evidently right in saying that they are "similar to *ṛṣis*",[32] even though the similarity does not consist in what, according to Yāska, constitutes *ṛṣitva* in the proper, and primary sense of the word. It is not known whether the expression *śrutarṣi*, whose first occurrence may well be this passage from the ĀpDhS,—while the *bahuvrīhi* compound *śrutarṣa* is clearly older[33] —originated in the spoken language of the Brahmins and was coined as a polite, or perhaps overpolite, flattering term for very learned members of this class of people.

In any case, ĀpDhS 1.2.5.5 f. deserves full attention in the context of the present essay, for more than one reason, viz. firstly, because the—obviously remarkable—intellectual quality referred to by *śrutarṣi* is, here too,[34] explained, though this time in terms of the theory of *karman* and rebirth, and, secondly, because the expression *śrutarṣi* is met with also in one of the Nirukta commentaries; for, Durga explains (Bhadkamkar 1985:147,27 f.) *avarakālīnebhyaḥ śaktihīnebhyaḥ śrutarṣibhyaḥ /*, "i.e. to [people] of later times who were deprived of [this] power/capacity [and] were *ṛṣis* [only] on account of their learning", and he adds (Bhadkamkar 1985:147.3 f.): *teṣāṃ hi śrutvā tataḥ paścād ṛṣitvam upajāyate na yathā pūrveṣāṃ sākṣātkṛtadharmaṇāṃ śravaṇam antareṇaiva /*, "for their *ṛṣi*-hood arises [only] after hearing (i.e. learning) [the Veda], i.e. some time after this (i.e. the period of studentship), not like that of the earlier ones, by whom the *dharma* is directly perceived, without any hearing (i.e. learning) whatsoever." The

31 Olivelle's (1999:12) translation does not deviate, although it is clearly much better (for a modern reader).

32 Olivelle (1999:12), however, seems to be of different opinion.

33 Cf. Śatapathabrāhmanṇa, Mādhyandina Rec. 2.4.4.5, and Kāṇva Rec. 1.3.4.3, as well as Taittirīya Saṃhitā 3.10.9.11 and Jaiminīya-Ārṣeya-Brāhmaṇa 1.4 (in the latter case, however, *śrautarṣa*).

34 Cf., however, below n. 51.

concept of the *śrutarṣi*[35] cannot be examined further here, but it should at least be noted that the possibility, admitted by Bhartṛhari (see below n. 58), that there may be people who are/become *ṛṣis* "because of the *āgama*", is if not just a circumlocution of the concept of *śrutarṣi*, in any case related to it and that the threefold division of the *ṛṣis* as reported by Haldar (see below n. 51) is most probably derived from the much older dichotomy by extending the scheme so as to include the authors of the Epics and Purāṇas too. Last but not least, what deserves the scholar's attention is the fact, highly significant for and typical of traditional Indian culture as a whole, that in spite of the later and clearly prevalent ideas of the *apauruṣeyatva*, on the one hand, and the divine origin of the Veda, on the other, it was not forgotten that the *ṛṣis* on their part were human beings, although of a particularly high order, beyond the capacity of all those born later, who belonged to a different age.

Finally, and thirdly, what the *sūtras* from the ĀpDhS quoted just now show us, and thus confirm once more, is the appropriateness of the interpretation of Nir. 1.20 as referring to two, not (as was also maintained by Sköld (1926:7 following Belvalkar 1915:6)) three, "generations", and in this probative function lies their greatest importance. Along with the other Dharmasūtra material drawn upon by Kane and myself, they ultimately cause one to realize that the distinction between the *sākṣātkṛtadharmāṇa ṛṣayaḥ* and the *asākṣātkṛtadharmāṇo 'vare*, and thus between the *pūrve* and the *avare*, is nothing but an archetypical, most probably not specifically Indian, pattern of culturally organizing the contrast between "those of olden times", the ancestors of a hoary past, and later generations, perhaps also including one's own, in any case ancestors of a more recent past. What is characteristic of this pattern of dividing the past, and hence also one's cultural memory, is not so much the indeterminability of the temporal distance between the two groups, but the very fact that the distance is viewed—or should I say felt?—to be quantitatively indetermined, or that it is conceived of as a "grey area". Another characteristic element of this conception of the past is the idea of a drastic qualitative difference between the two groups (which significantly enough are thought of as groups), the awareness, or rather projection, of a loss, a decline[36] in the historical process: In the past everything was not just better, but almost unbelievably better, more perfect, happier etc. We are, of course, immediately reminded of the ideas about the *kṛta*- and other (previous) *yugas*,[37] but also of the modern Indian transfiguration of, especially, Vedic India—which I shall deal with elsewhere and which can evidently not be reduced only to European influence, viz., as my friend Srinivasa A.

---

35 Cf. also Ludwig 1878:23.

36 Aiyangar's (1941:182) "decadence", though he finds it "expressed in Āpastamba (II, 6,13,7-9) and Gautama (I,3-4)", is clearly a misnomer.

37 Aklujkar (forthcoming:6) speaks of the age of the *ṛṣis* of Nir. 1.20 as "absolutely corruption free first age".

Srinivasan keeps suggesting,[38] by the famous German intellectual Herder (1744-1803).

I do not, of course, want to dispute that in India there is also a three-generation pattern; but this latter is clearly different in that it refers to three succeeding generations (grandfather, father, son (oneself)) and is hence less mythical than the *pūrve-avare*-archetype, and of a more private, individual character.[39]

3. By way of clarification I stated earlier that I do not want to focus on the expression *sākṣātkṛtadharmāṇa (ṛṣayo)*, but I also don't want entirely to avoid addressing the problems involved. Still, what I certainly should like to evade is entering again[40] into a discussion about this expression as it is used by Pakṣilasvāmin in his Nyāyabhāṣya,[41] despite the fact that the Naiyāyika most probably silently refers to the Niruktakāra and that the passage at issue here has no doubt to be studied in the context of the origin(s) and development of the conception of the *āpta*, a person whose statements are a reliable means of valid cognition, a conception so important for the history of Indian philosophy and religion.[42]

Now, it would seem that at least the meaning of the prior member *sākṣātkṛta* is clear; but this is evidently not the case as can be seen from just a few examples: Kane (1973:889)[43] renders the compound by "the (ancient) sages had an intuitive perception of *dharma*";[44] and Falk (1990:109; cf. also Falk 1993:241) by "persons who had direct insight into *dharma*",[45] while Halbfass (1988:328) reports that "the Vedic 'seers' (*ṛṣi*) are described as having attained a direct experience of *dharma*", and Kahrs (1998:28) lets the *ṛṣis* have "direct access to Dharma (ritual and social duty)"; the interpretation, too, is controversial, for Ramanathan (1993:66) writes: "In other

---

38 By oral communication.

39 I shall deal with the three generation-pattern in an article (still to be finished) on the Skt. expression *tripuruṣānūka*.

40 Cf. Wezler, 1982.

41 It reads thus (part of the commentary on NS 2.1.68 (*mantrāyurveda* ...) (Nyaya-Tarkatirtha/Tarkatirtha 1936:566:1 f.)): *āptāḥ khalu sākṣātkṛtadharmāṇaḥ idaṃ hātavyam idam asya hānihetur idam asyādhigantavyam idam asyādhigamahetuḥ iti bhūtāny anukampante* / ...

42 Cf. e.g. Wezler 1982 and, now also, Franco 1997, referring among others to the important article of Seyfort Ruegg 1994.

43 The context in which Kane deals with Nir. 1.20 is, as already stated (cf. p. 6), that of the "meaning of *yuga*".

44 "and they imparted the Vedic mantras by instruction to later (sages) who had no intuitive perception of dharma".

45 "turned into poets ("seers"). They handed down their verses by way of teaching to those who were inferior, i.e. who had no direct insight into *dharma*. These inferior persons were tired of teaching and arranged this opus, i.e. the Veda and its ancillary literature in order to grasp (or: it with) a *bilma*". Note that Falk quotes and himself rejects the translation of Oliver 1979.

words it is possible to get a correct picture of dharma only when we study and understand Nature in all its entirety which is very difficult for a normal human being. The Vedic seers alone had this capacity and therefore they were called "*sākṣātkṛtadharmāṇaḥ*" and their interpretation of *dharma* becomes automatically authoritative." One is tempted to react by saying "I know what you are getting at". For, does not Durga, as also noted by Halbfass (1988:328), expressedly state that the expression *sākṣātkṛtadharmāṇaḥ* is used "*aupacārikyā vṛttyā*", "by the figurative mode of expression", and does he not also give the reason by adding: *na hi dharmasya darśanam asty* [,] *atyantāpūrvo hi dharmaḥ*?[46] Yes, there is no denying this fact; but on the other hand, what has to be noted is that, firstly, Durga gives himself away, so to say, in that he refers to Yāska's—famous—*nirvacana* explanation of *ṛṣi*, viz. *ṛṣir darśanāt*"[47] [the word] *ṛṣi* is derived from [the root] *dṛś* ['to see']", and, secondly, that this is precisely what has to be questioned, viz. whether Yāska indeed started from the assumption that no human (or should I say: living?) being is able to "see", to "perceive" the *dharma*. What Durga quite evidently takes for granted is the absolute, unrestricted correctness of the view well-known first of all from Mīmāṃsā and Dharmaśāstra texts,[48] that what is called *dharma* in these strands of the Indian tradition is by its very nature beyond perception (*atīndriya*.)

What if Yāska was of a different opinion, i.e. admitted the possibility that certain beings of former times,[49] of the hoary past, were able to have

---

46 Quoted from Bhadkamkar 1985:146.18 f.

47 *iti vakṣyati* (Bhadkamkar 1988:146.17); the reference is to Nir. 2.11, where Durga adds the explanation *paśyati hy asau sūkṣmān arthān* (Bhadkamkar 1985:199.12 f.), while, on Nir. 1.20 (Bhadkamkar 1985:146,16 f.) he goes more into detail by stating: *ṛṣanty* [=] *amuṣmāt karmaṇaḥ evam arthavatā mantreṇa saṃyuktād amunā prakāreṇaivaṃlakṣaṇaḥ phalapariṇāmo bhavatīti paśyanti te ṛṣayaḥ / ('ṛṣir darśanāt' iti vakṣyati) /*, "they spear (with their eyes, i.e. they see) / they see (?), i.e. those, who [recognize] that from the ritual action X, connected with a mantra having such [and such] a meaning, in the manner Y a fruition-of-result of this and that character arises, are *ṛṣis*". Cf. also the phrase (*ity*) *ṛṣer dṛṣṭārthasya prītir bhavaty ākhyānasaṃyuktā* at Nir. 10.10 and 46. See also Sköld (1926:223). This explanation of *ṛṣi* is, quite expectedly, almost regularly referred to by commentators etc.; see e.g. Medhātithi on Manu 2.254. In passing only I should like to refer to Nyāyabhāṣya on NS 2.1.68 (I 568. 3 f.) *draṣṭṛpravaktṛsāmānyāc cānumānam / ya evāptā vedārthānāṃ draṣṭāraḥ pravaktāraś ca ta evāyurvedaprabhṛtīnām ity āyurvedaprāmāṇyavad vedaprāmāṇyam anumātavyam iti /*. As for earlier *nirvacana*-explanations of *ṛṣi*, cf. Deeg (1995:328) (also for *ṛṣ*).

48 Cf. Halbfass 1988:325f., and, e.g., Wezler 1999 a and b.

49 The author of the Vṛtti on Vākyapadīya 1.5 (see below § 10) calls a story, which he narrates before quoting Nir. 1.20, a *purākalpa*, "an old legend", a term taught at NS 2.1.62 [with which cf. ĀpŚS 24.1.33!] as one of the classes subsumed under the category of *arthavāda* [cf. also Vṛṣabhadeva on VP 1.5] (which in its turn is, according to Maitrāyaṇī-Saṃhitā 6.7.26, a *vidhiśeṣa*, "something subordinate to an injunction") and explained by Pakṣilasvāmin Vātsyāyana (Nyāyabhāṣya 530.6) to be

this perception, and that the *asākṣātkṛtadharmans* were inferior to them precisely in this regard? After all, there is clear evidence, albeit from later texts, that particularly outstanding, "holy" men really "perceive (the) *dharma*", "all the elements of the *dharma*". Thus we read in the Carakasaṃhitā (sūtrasth. 25.3):

> *purā pratyakṣadharmāṇaṃ bhagavantaṃ punarvasuṃ /*
> *sametānāṃ maharṣīṇāṃ prādur āsīd iyaṃ kathā //,*

that "long ago the following discussion[50] arose for (i.e. among) the *maharṣis* who had gathered around[51] the venerable Punarvasu to/by whom the *dharma* was perceptible/ perceived"; and in the Vanaparvan (Mbh. [Poona] 3.181.12 ff.)[52] certain Brahmins of old (*brahmabhūtā narāḥ ... purāṇāḥ*) who at their own will freely moved between heaven and earth, and met, i.e. associated with the gods etc., are finally characterized as:

> *draṣṭāro devasaṅghānāṃ ṛṣīṇāṃ ca mahātmanām /*
> *pratyakṣā[53] sarvadharmāṇām dāntā vigatamatsarāḥ //.*

---

an *aitīhyasamācarito vidhiḥ*, "a [statement (vāda)] about an injunction, i.e. a ritual procedure, practised in accordance with tradition". This story is similar to Nir. 1.20 (the transition to which is formed by the expression *āha khalv api*, paraphrased by Vṛṣabhadeva by *āgamāntaram apy āha*; (cf. also below § 10) so that the latter passage may well be classed as a *purākalpa*, too. This use of the word *purākalpa* is quite evidently a metonymy—as is also shown by the Vṛtti on VP 1.147 (235.1) which refers to, in fact resumes, the locative *purākalpe* found almost at the very beginning of the Vṛtti on the preceding *kārikā* (253.7) and explained by Vṛṣabhadeva to mean *pūrvasminn ādisargakāle*. Now, the meaning *purākalpa* has here and in similar contexts is precisely the problem we are confronted with. Joshi and Roodbergen (1986:87 n. 315) render it by "in olden days", just like Iyer (1965:135), and expressly state (1986:68 n. 254), albeit with reference to *purākalpe* in Mahābhāṣya (ed. Kielhorn) I. 5.6, that "(t)his refers to historic times, not to a mythological age, as Nāgeśa interprets it".

50 Cf. Cakrapāṇidatta's explanation (117.4) of *kathā* (of Carakasaṃhitā, Sūtrasthāna 25.3) by *tattvajijñāsārtham anyonyapṛcchā*.

51 The variant reading for the second half of this verse, viz. *maharṣaya upasīnāḥ prāduścakrur imāṃ kathām*, reported in the NSP-edition, is most probably an attempt to improve upon the construction of the original (less easily grasped) with the accusative being governed by the past participle (*punarvasuṃ sametānāṃ maharṣīnāṃ prādurāsīd ...kathā*). In this connection it should be mentioned that Śrī Gurupada Śarma Hāldār (Haldar 1955:64) in his Vṛddhatrayī (a book "not for sale", but "written, published and distributed free for advancement of the cause of historical researches on the Hindu Medical Science", to which my attention was drawn many years ago by R. P. Das) distinguishes three types of *ṛṣitva*, viz. a *mukhya*, consisting in *mantradraṣṭratva*, an *ātideśika*, because of *mantrakartṛtvatulyatā* like that of the authors of the Kalpasūtras and Brāhmaṇas, and, finally, a *tārtīyīka*, "a tertiary", caused by *bahujñatva*, *bahumānatva* and *pūganīyatva*, e.g. of the authors of the Vedāṅgas, the two Epics, the Purāṇas etc.

52 For the reference to this passage I am indebted to Kane 1973: 889 n. 1743.

53 Note that it is here the subject of cognition that is characterized as *pratyakṣa*. The idea of the "supernatural" cognitive capacity/capacities of the Vedic *ṛṣis* does not only form

And it is of no importance for the problem at issue, i.e. the meaning of *sākṣātkṛtadharmāṇaḥ*, that this Epic passage is evidently a constituent part of the description of the *kṛtayuga*, the "Golden Age" of Indian mythology:[54] The ideas connected with the Vedic *ṛṣis* found, not unexpectedly, entrance into the four-*yuga*-doctrine and were conveniently amalgamated with it.

The passage of the Nirukta seems to be the first occurrence in a literary work of a compound formed from *sākṣāt*[55] and the root *kṛ*, or a derivative of it, to judge from the Large Petrograd Dictionary and Viśvabandhu. But since Pāṇini teaches this connection (1.4.74), there cannot be any doubt that the compound represents a real element of the *bhāṣā* of his days. The substitution of *pratyakṣa* for *sākṣātkṛta* in later texts—among which Patañjali's Mahābhāṣya[56] ranks first, not only for chronological reasons, and which directly or indirectly refer to the Nirukta and therefore show us how the expression *sākṣātkṛtadharman* was received by post-Yāska intellectuals—most clearly supports the view that *sākṣāt-kṛ*, literally meaning "to see [something] with one's own eyes", was used, most probably right from the beginning of its appearance, to denote "the direct and complete perception of an object".[57]

---

the root, or one of the roots, of the better known and more intensively studied concept of *yogipratyakṣa*, but is found, lives on, so to say, in the idea of the 'third eye' (see e.g. Ruben 1929:622), in the expression *divyacakṣus*; of the Buddhists and Hindus (*ārṣaṃ cakṣus* (cf. e.g. VP 1.38, on which s. also Aklujkar forthcoming:16), the *divyadṛś*, *-darśin* (on which see also Moghe 1997:150), *divyajñāna* (cf. Pūrṇasarasvatiī in his Vidyullatā or Meghadūta 1), *jñānanayana* (cf. e.g. Kṣemendra, Caturvargasaṃgraha 12), *jñānacakṣus* (see e.g. Manu 2.8, and Medhātithi's Bhāṣya on this verse) etc. Note also that omniscience is transferred from persons to the Veda, and that this quality of the Veda plays quite some role within its transfiguration in modern Hinduism. Cf. e.g. Saundaryalaharī of Shri Shankarabhagavatpadacharya with Commentaries (in Sanskrit ...). Editor A. Kuppuswami, Delhi, Nag Publishers, 1991, Introduction (p. VII): "Such a knowledge", viz. of God, soul and matter, "is beyond the view of human physical senses and could be had only from the omniscient Veda, the repository of the transcendental wisdom which revealed itself to the pure saintly souls who meditated deep and long to discover the truth."

54 For the *kṛtayuga* cf. Mette 1973, the authors listed in Von Stietencron (1992:1895) and Grafenhorst 1997 all of whom could not, of course, exhaust the subject.

55 *sākṣāt* alone is attested since the Atharvaveda and Taittirīya Saṃhitā.

56 Viz. (ed. Kielhorn) I 11.12 f.: *evaṃ hi śrūyate / yarvāṇas tarvāṇo nāmarṣayo babhūvuḥ pratyakṣadharmāṇaḥ parāpaṛajñā viditaveditavyā adhigatayāthātathyāḥ / ....*

57 Note that *sākṣātkāra* is used later, e.g. Nirālambanopaniṣad, as synonym of *anubhava* and *jñāna*. Typical of the state of Indological research there is no, at least no comprehensive, study of the ideas concerning the manner of cognition of the *mantras*—or related to the *ṛṣi* (cf. n. 270) or the means of "supernatural" cognition in general (cf. also n. 53). The use of the root *paś*, and semantically related roots/verbs, in order to denote—not by the well-known metaphor ("seeing" → "perceiving" → "cognizing"), but by ascribing to persons a corresponding "supernatural", in any case extraordinary, unique capacity—the (visual?) perception of objects, which are imperceptible to "normal" human beings, would first of all deserve a comprehensive study. See, however,

I agree with the commentators of the Nirukta, at least in principle, and hence don't dispute the linguistic fact that the meaning of the prior member of the compound *sākṣātkṛtadharman* is not entirely separable from that of the posterior. Therefore the problem of the meaning of *dharma(n)* has to be addressed next. Although Joshi-Roodbergen (1986:156 n. 632) state, albeit with reference to Mahābhāṣya (ed. Kielhorn) I 11.12, that "(i)t is not clear what *dharma* means here. It could mean 'what is right' or 'a constituent element of reality', like the *tattvas* of Sāṃkhya, just to mention a few possible interpretations", I think it is possible to practically exclude the second alternative, viz. that *dharma* is used here in the meaning it typically has in Vaiśeṣika and allied literature. In contradistinction to Joshi-Roodbergen, I do not find Bhartṛhari's explanation of *pratyakṣadharmāṇaḥ* of the Bhāṣya (Mahābhāṣyadīpikā 31.25) to be "not clear", for even if the text as constituted by Abhyankar and Limaye (1970:38.7)[58] were not correct, the fact that Bhartṛhari uses the plural without any specification, i.e. explains: *dharmā ye parokṣā lokasya te pratyākṣās teṣām*, would be indication enough that what he refers to are "the elements of the *dharma*",[59] i.e. that *dharma* which is identified by Vṛṣabhadeva[60] as *abhyudayaniḥ-*

Aklujkar forthcoming:22. This idea seems to be connected with the *ṛṣi*, and *kavi*, already at the time of the Ṛgveda (cf. e.g. Findly 1989:24 or Elizarenkova 1995:20); but its later development has, of course, equally to be taken into account (cf. e.g. ŚB 1.7.2.23, Taitt.B. 2.3.7), also as regards the difference between *mantra* and *brāhmaṇa* (*mantro dṛṣṭaḥ, brāhmaṇaṃ proktam* as quoted by Ludwig 1878:23). Of particular interest is, in my view, also the history of the reception of the "mantra- (cf. Aklujkar forthcoming 5 and n. 31 (p. 12)) or *sāman-* (cf. Pāṇ. 4.2.7!) seeing *ṛṣi*", especially in Indian Poetry and in the Alaṃkāraśāstra (cf. e.g. Kāvyālaṃkāravṛtti 3.2.7 (Capeller 1875:32; see also 1.3.17 (p. 9)) or Ruben (1929:624, 626)). I leave it to my Buddhological colleagues to examine the question whether Pāli *saṃkhātadhamma* (on the phonetic aspect see Von Hinüber 1994:224 f.) is also to be taken as related to the Vedic idea; see in any case also Aramaki (forthcoming).

58 ***pratyakṣadharmāṇaḥ*** */ dharmā ye parokṣā lokasya te* ***pratyakṣās*** *teṣām / parāparajñāḥ / yuktāyuktajñāḥ / syuś ca tāvad āgamāt pratyakṣadharmāṇo na tu yuktāyuktajñāḥ / ... //*

59 On the plural, see Wezler (1999b:96fn.19) Note in this connection also the contrast between the collective-singular *sūtram*, in Mahābhāṣya I 39.11 (*pramāṇabhūta ācāryo ... sūtraṃ praṇayati sma ...*), and the plural *sūtrāṇi*, in Mahābhāṣya I 12.10 (*na cedānīṃ ācāryāḥ sūtrāṇi kṛtvā nivartayanti*), which is quite evidently called for because several individual *sūtras* are aimed at. Cf. also Weber's (1881:189) remarkable observation regarding certain plural forms in the Meghadūta. Indian commentators use to explain this use by quoting the dictum *vyaktyapekṣaṃ bahutvam* (cf. e.g. Medhātithi on M. 2.84).

60 Is he inspired by VaiśeṣikaS. 1.1.2 or does he rather follow an old general tradition, attested also e.g. in first section of the Vṛtti on VP 1.5?—Bhartṛhari expectedly starts from the assumption that each of the predicates in the Mahābhāṣya passage (quoted in n. 56) has its own specific purpose. Thus *parāparajñāḥ* is explained by him to mean *yuktāyuktajñāḥ*, which, I think, should not be rendered, as Bronkhorst does (1987:95), by "those who know what is proper and what is not", but rather "who know

śreyasasādhana. And the reading *lokadharmā* suggested by Bronkhorst (1987:31; cf. 95) for *ślokadharmā* of the ms.[61] can also not mean "the characteristics of the world": *loka* is not "world" in this, philosophical sense; and his proposal suffers also from the disadvantage that Bhartṛhari would use, in the same phrase, the word *loka* two times and with two different meanings. In my view, the reconstruction proposed by Abhyankar/Limaye (1970:38.7) is to be preferred, if the clarification is added to it that some kind of *aberratio oculi* must be responsible for the repetition of *loka*—which in its turn led to (the unintelligible) *śloka*.[62]

Besides, and more importantly what should be taken into account with regard to the semantic problem posed by *dharma(n)* is the evidence of Pāṇini: In all cases[63] where he teaches the formation of derivations of *dharma* it is never any other meaning than "[traditional] norm/'law'/[normatively correct] behaviour and [its subtle] result"[64] that is referred to, if I am not mistaken. This observation is confirmed by Horsch's (1967) study into the early history of the word *dharma(n)*, in which he notes (1967:52) that BĀU 1.4.14[65] "gives expression to the sociological-juridical aspect of our concept according to which the primaeval *brahman* after the four castes created a still better phenomenon, [viz.] the law".[66]

Yet, as is well known, there are no research tools available to Indologists which would allow them to decide with regard to the semantic history of a word that it was used in a particular meaning only up to the period X and that

---

what is true/correct [because of a corresponding *yukti*] and what is false/incorrect". And, so Bhartṛhari continues, "it is possible that/there may be [people who] are *pratyakṣadharmans* because of the tradition [consisting in the sacred texts of the Veda], but they [certainly] do not know what is true and what is false". If I am not mistaken, this shows that the *ṛṣis*, referred to by Patañjali, are in Bhartṛhari's view said to "have direct perception of the *dharma*" for a different reason, i.e. not because of the/an *āgama* serving as means of cognition.

61 Viz. folio 25r line 8.

62 Kaiyaṭa (I 76 a 20 f.) is of no help unless one accepts the emendation *yogāt* (to be construed with the preceding word). Attempts to explain the extraordinary cognitive capacity of the *ṛṣis*, and similar persons, by ascribing it to the power of *tapas*, *yoga*, *karman* etc., are, quite expectedly, not rare, nay almost common in the later texts; cf. nos. 53 and 57 above.

63 Viz. 4.4.41; 4.2.46; 4.4.7; 4.4.91 f.; 5.2.132; 5.4.124 and 6.2.65.

64 "Religion", proposed by Rajavade (1993:289), is of course not acceptable, as already stated by Hacker (1965).

65 Which reads thus: *sa naiva vyabhavat / tac chreyorūpam atyasṛjata dharmam / tad etat kṣatrasya kṣatraṃ yad dharmaḥ / tasmād dharmāt paraṃ nāsti / atho abalīyān balīyāṁsam āśaṁsate dharmeṇa / yathā rājñaivam / vai sa dharmaḥ satyaṃ vai tat / tasmāt satyaṃ vadantam āhur dharmaṃ vadatīti / dharmaṃ vā vadantaṁ satyaṃ vadatīti / etad dhy evaitad ubhayaṃ bhavati) //.*

66 "Den soziologisch-rechtlichen Aspekt unseres Begriffes bringt Bṛhad-Āraṇyaka-Upaniṣad 1.4.14 zum Ausdruck, wonach das unanfängliche *brahman* nach den vier Kasten noch eine bessere Form, das Gesetz, geschaffen hat."

its earliest meaning was sublated by a later one etc.; and in India we have to do not just with very learned authors, but with authors of whom many possessed an extremely solid education in Vedic texts and are hence able, if not even likely, at any time to refer to an older, "obsolete" meaning of a word. This is, of course, particularly true of all those scholars who study a *śāstra* directly connected with the Veda. Therefore it is recommendable, to say the least, to take into account the possibility that Yāska, or whoever formulated the passage in question, thought of (an) older meaning(s) of *dharman*, too; this has likewise been suggested by Horsch (1967:52), who registers that "in the Upaniṣads mythic-cosmological ideas still linger on".[67] The second stage in the semantic development of *dharman* distinguished by Horsch, and significantly "accompanied by the replacement of the *nomen actionis dhárman* by the abstract noun *dhármaḥ*" (1967:61),[68] should hence not be excluded in the attempt to come to terms with the expression *sākṣātkṛtadharmāṇa (ṛṣayo)* of the Nirukta. This second stage is described by Horsch (1967:60 f.) as follows: "At an early point of time *dhárman* detaches itself as an independent power of numinous nature from the mythical function of 'supporting' certain gods, and thus becomes a universal principle of 'hold'/'upholding', stability and duration of the cosmos. This explains the semantical development from the concrete, mythic idea to the abstract notion 'law'."[69]

Returning to the translation and interpretation of *sākṣātkṛtadharmāṇa (ṛṣayo)*, it has to be stated that the direct perception of this universal "law", this order of the world, of all its inhabitants, but especially men,[70] was made the object of (a) perception by the *ṛṣis*—a perception which could even have been merely an interior one, or one accompanied by a similar interior one.

As for the first sentence (*sākṣātkṛtadharmāṇa ṛṣayo babhūvus*), if *ṛṣayo* alone is the subject, thus calling for the rendering: "The seers were [men] by whom (the) *dharma* was directly and wholly perceived", one of the im-

---

67 "In den Upaniṣaden klingen mythische kosmologische Vorstellungen nach, ..."

68 "(Diese Sinnverschiebung und -erweiterung) ... ist begleitet von der Umformung des Nomen actionis *dhárman* in das Abstraktum *dhármaḥ* (das zuerst im Atharvaveda auftritt)."

69 "Früh löst sich *dhárman* als selbständige Macht numinoser Natur von der mythischen Funktion des Stützens bestimmter Götter und wird damit zu einem universalen Prinzip von Halt, Festigkeit und Dauer des Kosmos. Dies erklärt die semantische Entwicklung von der konkreten, mythischen Vorstellung zum abstrakten Begriff Gesetz." Regarding the semantical development of *dhárman* / *dhárma* cf. also Halbfass (1988:310-333), taking up Horsch's study, yet continuing and elaborating it. Lariviere (1997:98 n.6: "... the notion that the parameters of *dharmic* behaviour changes over time is an old one, see, for example, Nirukta 1.20 and Gautamadharmasūtra 1.3-5") apparently assumes that *dharma* has the meaning well known from the Dharmaśāstra.

70 Following the example set by Hacker (e.g. 1965) I take over, however, the Sanskrit word itself.

plications will be that the *avare* are not classed along with (the) *ṛṣis*, or, if *babhūvuḥ* is to be taken as a finite verb and *sākṣātkṛtadharmāṇa* consequently as an attribute of *ṛṣayo* (and not as predicate)[71] so that the sentence would have to be rendered "There were *ṛṣis* who ...," the implication that the *avare* are possibly also "seers" cannot entirely be precluded (because of the absence of a definite article in Sanskrit). Word order seems to point in the direction of the first alternative; extra-textual considerations, viz. the antiquity, and persistence, of the idea of a very special gift, a peculiar, not normal, cognitive capacity of the Vedic *ṛṣis*[72] speak in favour of the assumption that the *avare* do not themselves form part of the group of *ṛṣis*, i.e. that the presence and absence of the capacity of the *sākṣātkāra* of *dharma*, respectively, defines each group, i.e. constitutes the *ṛṣitva* in the first case, and the lack of this status, in the second. There is, however, as we shall see a little later, some evidence for the contrary assumption, viz. that the *avare* were regarded as *ṛṣis*, too, albeit of markedly inferior quality.

4. The question to be dealt with next is that of the relation in which *mantrān*, "the object of genuine Veda revelation" (Aklujkar forthcoming:11 and n. 27), stands to *dharma* as object of the direct perception of the seers. One of the commentators[73] voices the opinion that *mantra* includes *brāhmaṇa*, too; but I don't find this interpretation immediately convincing,[74] especially in view of the famous Kautsa controversy[75] which quite clearly refers to *mantras* only, and which discussion is not far removed from the subject-matter of our passage. Regarding the relation between *dharma* and the *mantras* of the Vedic Saṃhitās, several possibilities have to be taken into account, if we start from the assumption, strongly suggested by the text, that the *mantras* were not just arbitrarily delivered over by the *ṛṣis* to the *avare*,

---

71 The interpretation preferred by Falk 1996—and pointed out to me in the discussion as the more natural one—, viz. to take *sākṣātkṛtadharmāṇa* as subject, is in my view the least probable one: It is true that *bahuvrīhi* compounds, as all adjectives, may be nominalized; but this possibility is practically confined (cf. Renou (1961:120, § 95D) to well-known names, i.e. cases where the *anyapadārtha* (of Pāṇ. 2.2.24) can be left out because the compound has developed into another of its names. In the case given what would be strange in addition, if Falk would be right, were the exchange of the syntactical functions (predicate and subject, respectively) of the substantive (*ṛṣayo*) and the adjective (*sākṣātkṛtadharmāṇa*).

72 The views held by the Indians about *ṛṣis*, and their development and changes, still remain to be studied comprehensively. They cannot be addressed here; see also nos. 53 and 57 above.

73 Viz. Skandasvāmin-Maheśvara; cf. Sarup (1982:114 l. 15): *mantragrahaṇaṃ cātra brāhmaṇānāṃ pradarśanārtham, mantrān brāhmaṇānīti saṃprāduḥ /.*

74 Although there are undoubtedly cases where *mantras* and *brāhmaṇas* are not only taken together, as forming one whole, but also referred to by one single term; cf. Aithal 1996:4, and Aklujkar forthcoming.

75 Nir. 2.25; cf. also, quite recently, Bronkhorst 1992:402. Kautsa anticipated, as it were, Staal 1989, on which see among others Michaels 1998:252 f. and 1999.

but were handed over because these later-born Brahmins were no longer able to perceive the *dharma* for themselves, delivered over by seers who still had this capacity and **wanted to instruct them about** (the) ***dharma***. These possibilities are:

1. the *mantras* of the *dharma* are directly perceived by the seers,
2. the *mantras* "contain" the *dharma*
3. they "contain" part of the *dharma*
4. some of the *mantras* "contain" the *dharma* etc.

I don't want to sorely try your patience—and follow the example of my admired friend Claus Oetke—and hence leave it to you to complete my enumeration and thereby to imagine all the logical and factual possibilities of analysing the meanings of the opaque expression "contain", deliberately yet cautiously used by me.

5. The question of the relation between *dharma* and the *mantras* cannot, however, be disconnected from that of the meaning of *upadeśena* and, so I should like to add, the syntactical role of *upadeśena*. (Finally I come to the point I want to make!) Regarding the meaning of this expression the discussion has nowadays to set out from Cardona's (1972) article about "Pāṇini's use of the term *upadeśa*..."[76] although the very special, technical meaning the expression has in the Aṣṭādhyāyī cannot be transferred to the Nirukta. But this much is clear: What is referred to is a particular oral instruction which is not identical with the teaching of Pāṇini's Sūtra as such: It is closely related to it, it forms an integral part of grammatical instruction, but is not coextensive with it.[77]

When perusing the translations etc., of the Nirukta, I have always found it hard to believe that what Yāska wants to tell us here is that the *ṛṣis* delivered over the *mantras* "by oral instruction to later generations" (Sarup 1967:20).[78] For, by what else could they have passed on the *mantras*?[79] Was there any other means known to the Indians in Vedic times for passing on knowledge in general, let alone knowledge of the Veda, to the next generation? Was the use of script already known to Yāska,[80] and, if so,

76 Cf. also Cardona (1976:163 ff.)

77 Durga (Bhadkamkar 1985:147.4 f.) glosses *upadeśena* by *śiṣyopādhyāyikayā vṛttyā* which is also the explanation given by Skandasvāmin-Maheśvara (Sarup 1952:114.13).

78 Kane 1973:889 "by instruction", Falk 1993:241 "by way of teaching", Kahrs 1998a:28 "through [this initial] instruction".

79 And does not *saṃ-pra-$\sqrt{}$dā* by itself already imply orality? Cf. e.g. ŚB 1.5.2.7.

80 On the problem of the first use of writing in India see Falk 1992 in general, and with regard to Nir. 1.20 p. 242 f. Janert 1955/56, published 1995 should rather be passed over in silence: To all appearances he was not aware of (the) other meaning(s) the word *grantha* has. Even if there were clear evidence that the script was known at that early point in time in India, taking the expression *grantha* at Nir. 1.20 to refer a written text, a "manuscript", could not but be styled a *kliṣṭaṃ vyākhyānam*.

was it also used for the transmission of Vedic texts so widely, and as a matter-of-course, that Yāska deemed it necessary to clarify that he refers to a different, much earlier period of time when orality alone was at the *ṛṣis*' disposal? And what about the third sentence, i.e. the statement that the *avare* were *upadeśāya glāyanto*? Are we really to believe Sarup (1967:20) that this means "declining (in power of) oral communication"? In my view, and I should like to refer in this regard to the Dhātupāṭha where the meaning of the root *glai* is determined by *gātravināme* (*harṣakṣaye ca*), what is said is that "the *avare* as they became tired of/disinclined to oral instruction (i.e. discontinued it)"... . And quite evidently this cannot mean that they did not any longer hand down the *mantras*, or, if this word is indeed used symbolically (*pars pro toto*)[81] to include other elements of Vedic literature, too, the sacred Vedic texts, for it is stated in the passage itself that this is precisely what they did (*...imaṃ granthaṃ samāmnāsiṣur*[82] *vedaṃ ca vedāṅgāni ca*)!

For this, and the aforementioned reasons, I should like to propose to take *upadeśena* as a comitative instrumental. The existence of this function of the instrumental is attested beyond doubt already for Vedic Sanskrit (cf. Delbrück 1888:123-126),[83] and if Pāṇini should indeed be of a different opinion, i.e. recognize this function only if the caseform is accompanied by *saha* (cf. P 2.3.19),[84] this could not be given much weight in view of the facts of the object language itself.

Now, if and since "oral instruction" accompanied the delivering over of the *mantras* by the "seers", it becomes perfectly understandable that the *avare* are said to have become disinclined to continue it: They thought it enough to pass on the *mantras*, or the sacred Vedic texts, formulated and ready, and did not care, for whichever reason, to additionally explain them; for, that is what in my view is referred to, at least above all, by the "oral instruction" given by the "seers" in addition to teaching "the *mantras*" as such, an "explanation" of the *mantras*—which also could well cover (all) the

---

81 See above p. 17; in contradistinction to the Nirukta commentator, however, what I take into account here is the possibility of a particular type of synecdoche. The fact that in the immediately following sentence it is the *veda* which is spoken of does not render any assistance, at least not as long as the relation in which it stands to *mantra* has been clarified.

82 On *sam-ā-√mnā* cf. also Aklujkar (forthcoming).

83 Cf. also Speyer (1896:10 (§ 32)).

84 Which reads as follows: *sahayukte 'pradhāne*; note that Cardona 1997:164 renders this *sūtra* by "an ending of the third triplet (*tṛtīyā*) is introduced after a nominal stem that refers to an indirect participant (*apradhāne*) and is syntactically connected **or connectible**" (the emphasis is mine) "with *saha* 'with' (*sahayukte*)". Note also that the Kāśikā, at the very end of its commentary on 2.3.19, adds (according to Haradatta, however, this is only read in some ms.(s) (*kvacit*')): *vināpi sahaśabdena bhavati, 'vṛddho yūnā ...'* [Pān. 1.2.65] *iti nipātanāt*—not intending an exhaustive enumeration of all such examples found in the Aṣṭādhyāyī.

realm of (the) *dharma*—an instruction meant to ensure a comprehensive and deep **understanding** of the words of the *mantras*, i.e. of the *vedārtha*. For the sake of clarity, it should be added that by "oral instruction" (*upadeśa*) what is referred to is not the method of teaching the wording of the *mantras* to students (which is already implied by *sam-pra-dā*), or, a commentary or anything similar which forms a fixed, formulated text by itself. Nor do I think that the Brāhmaṇa-texts, or rather the individual "exegetical" *brāhmaṇa* sections—which could after all be regarded as some, albeit a very peculiar, type of commentary,[85] —, are meant, not so much because this would contradict my refutation of Skandasvāmin-Maheśvara's interpretation of *mantrān* in Nir. 1.20,[86] but rather because the Brāhmaṇa-texts have indeed been handed down so that the statement *upadeśāya glāyanto* would become contrafactive, or could at best be taken to attest to the idea that from a particular point in time onwards *brāhmaṇas* were not composed any longer, or that the *brāhmaṇas* do not suffice for a full understanding of the *mantras*. In my view what is meant by *upadeśa* is "a method of teaching students" (*śiṣyopādhyāyikā vṛtti*),[87] to borrow Durga's expression, which aims at a correct and full understanding of the wording of a *mantra*, the syntax and the semantics at least of some of the expressions used, and, above all, of the meaning of the *mantra* at a whole.. In short, I basically agree with Durga and Skandasvāmin-Maheśvara (who are later than the former)[88] who explain that the *sākṣātkṛtadharmāṇa ṛṣayo* delivered the *mantras* "with regard to the wording as also to the meaning" (*granthato 'rthataś ca*).[89] That the *avare* failed to continue the sacred tradition in this regard is tantamount to the contention, i.e. awareness, or feeling, of an **important loss** in this sacred tradition. But it does not imply that there are no means at all that would enable a student to find out the "meaning of the Veda"; it is however of an essentially different nature: not an "oral instruction" which can be traced back to the *sākṣātkṛtadharmāṇa ṛṣayo* themselves, the most trustworthy and authoritative source of knowledge, but ancillary texts only, the *Vedāṅgas*, compiled by human beings, as is well known, and—like part of the Vedalakṣana-literature—[90] forming the outcome of the attempt to systematically open avenues leading to an understanding of the *vedārtha*, undertaken by men who are actually aware of the lack of a corresponding tradition and try their very best to make good for it.

---

85 Cf. e.g. ŚB 1.1.1.2; see Wezler 2000.
86 See above p. 17 and n. 73.
87 On *vṛtti* see Thieme (1958:23 ff. (= 739 ff.)).
88 Sarup 1982:4.
89 Quoted from Bhadkamkar 1985:147.5. This syntagma is, as is well-known, not rare at all.
90 On which cf., of course, Aithal 1991.

In fact the loss which Yāska, or his generation, or the generations preceding him, were aware of is an almost unavoidable concomitant of history. What I am aiming at is not the fact that it is knowledge and texts which are passed on, and hardly ever texts along with their correct interpretation, i.e. along with information about what their authors wanted to say,[91] but the—equally trivial—truth that languages change in the course of time. Vedic Sanskrit was no exception to this rule, although the changes which occurred had practically no effect on the phonology, but clearly one on the morphology and particularly on the vocabulary. (Historical) linguists[92] put categories at our disposal which allow for the description of the disappearance of old words and the appearance of new ones, the various changes of meaning, and they even reflect on the causes of these changes. But I don't know whether they have also given some thought to the—perhaps—most important consequence of this type of changes of a language, viz. that texts written in an earlier period gradually become more and difficult to understand and finally almost totally unintelligible to later generations of the "same" linguistic community, that words occurring in them are "no longer used" (*aprayukta*; cf. Mahābhāṣya (ed. Kielhorn) I 9.6 ff.), and that it is the awareness of this "alienation" which then possibly provokes philological attempts to gain knowledge about the "dead" language. If descriptions, and an analysis, of this linguistic process should exist, it would directly be applicable to the situation in which Yāska saw himself vis-à-vis the Vedic *mantras*; yet, and this is even more important, the modern linguists, or semanticists, would have to admit that a central element of their theory (if it would be called a theory by them) was already recognized by Yāska, viz. the transition from a text still understandable, albeit with some difficulty, to an almost unintelligible text, calling for methods for its decipherment.

In any case, there cannot be any doubt that this is what happened in Vedic India, especially with regard to the oldest of the Samhitās, the Ṛgveda,[93] although there is evidence from much earlier sources that verses of the RV were not any longer properly understood. And in this connection it has to be remembered (although one has to distinguish between not any longer fully understanding a text and the awareness of this lack of understanding) that Yāska's work has a long prehistory—which has been studied with particu-

91 Cf. Wezler 1982/83:164 f.

92 See e.g. Beekes 1995:82-89 or Ullman 1973:243-296.

93 The reason one often finds given for this development, viz. that transmitters' endeavours were first of all directed towards an accurate preservation of the wording of the text(s) and that they fell prey to a mechanical learning which involved a growing negligence of the contents (on which see e.g. Dhadphale 1952:94 f., but also Staal 1989: 51), is, I think, alluringly plausible, i.e. in my view—simplistic.

larly impressive thoroughness by Kahrs (1980 (cf. 1996), 1983 and 1984)[94] and Deeg (1995), the knowledge of which, however, may certainly still be increased—[95] not to mention the reception of the Nirukta,[96] or rather the later history of the *nirvacana* tradition.[97]

Being (significantly) based on certain lists of words,[98] the Nighaṇṭus, "this same *āmnāya*" as it is called by Yāska himself (Nir. 1.1), the Nirukta ultimately wants to contribute to an understanding of the Veda, especially the RV, by "demonstrating a method of explanation",[99] as was stated with particular emphasis by Dhadphale (1982), who adds that it wants "to restore or achieve this meaning" by "the method of *nirvacana* analysis" "outlined

---

94 A classical example—at least for me it is classical because it was pointed out to me by my guru Thieme in one of his courses—is ŚB 11.5.1.1-17 (selected by Böhtlingk for his Sanskrit-Chrestomathie) with its quotations from "*Purūravas* and *Urvaśī*", i.e. RV 10.95.

95 See Kahrs 1995, also as regards his own earlier work on the Nirukta.

96 Particularly successful was Yāska's division of the parts of speech into four categories which has been taken over even by Pali grammarians (cf. Pind 1997:27).

97 What I have in mind here are passages like MS 2.4.8, (*mándā vā́śā jyótiṣmátīr ámasvasīr ity etā́ni vā́ apā́ṃ nāmadhéyāni*, "... are names of water (i.e. are used to refer to water?)"), or Aitareya-Brāhmaṇa 1.13 *yajño vai sutarmā nauḥ, vāk vai sutarmā nauḥ, kṛṣṇājinaṃ vai sutarmā nauḥ*, to which attention is drawn by Dhadphale (1982:100) and which he finds "very important from the point of view of giving us an idea of how Vedic *nighaṇṭus* must have gradually developed by noting the Vedic metaphorical terms". Indeed, this latter passage may have been responsible for the inclusion of *nauḥ* under the "names of speech" (*vāṅnāmāni*), of Nigh. 1.11, as rightly suggested by Dhadphale, and the MS-passage certainly is an early predecessor of the "lists of words" as found in the Nighaṇṭu, even if the individual words (*mándā* etc.) do not appear in it. But there is more to be noted here, viz. Durga's statement (Bhadkamkar 1985:29.13 ff.) that "this (i.e. this complex whole consisting of five *adhyāyas* (i.e. the Nighaṇṭu)), this collection of *sūtras* ... has been handed down for a [proper] understanding of the meaning of the *mantras*, after having collected/compiled it piece by piece repeatedly from the Vedic hymns" (*sa (= ...eṣā gavādyā devapatnyantā pañcādhyāyī sūtrasaṃgrahaḥ) ca punar iyaṃ ... mantrāvabodhāya chandobhyaḥ samāhṛtya samāhṛtya samāmnātā)*—which goes back to, and partially repeats verbatim, the famous phrase from Nir. 1.2 *chandobhyaḥ samāhṛtya samāhṛtya samāmnātāḥ*; it is hence ultimately Yāska himself who claims the Vedic origin of the Nighaṇṭus, and this claim has indeed not only to be taken seriously, but seems also to be in principle justified, although especially the MS-passage quoted just now shows that there are earlier testimonies of this "compilatory" activity, this culling of words from certain Vedic texts, and not only the taking over of earlier such lists into the Nighaṇṭu. Cf. on the whole problem, of course, Sköld 1926. On the reception of the Nirukta, see now also Kahrs 1998b.

98 "Devarāja Yajvan in the introduction to his commentary on the Nirukta" rightly states "that Yāska has 'incidently' (*prasaṅgāt*) discussed only 350 of the total 1765 words from the Ngs." (Dhadphale 1982:97 n. 11).

99 For the time being, Indology can only dream of having its own Curtius (1948), and hence also a history of the "Wirkung" of the Nirukta, and the particular *śāstric* tradition it represents, in classical and medieval Indian literature.

and put into practice in the Nirukta".[100] Western Vedology does not, at least not since R. v. Roth, distinguish itself by deep respect for the indigenous interpretation of, i.e. commentaries on Vedic texts; it has developed its own philological and other methods, in increasing number, and produced also quite some literature on the problems of methodology. I do not want to examine whether, or to what extent, this feeling of superiority, of being able to understand the Veda better than the Indians themselves, is justified, and, if so, why—and how the Indians can be made to agree; yet, even if this self-assessment were entirely justified, it should not, as it in fact does, lead to ignoring, at least neglecting, the vast material available from all kinds of texts and from almost all periods continuously, most clearly testifying to the persistence, in India herself, of the claim of being able to understand passages from/parts of Vedic texts[101] quoted or drawn upon by an author.[102] And Yāska's Nirukta has quite evidently contributed to the emergence and continuity of this self-confidence. The existence of this tradition within traditional Indian culture has by all means to be recognized, and the tradition itself to be studied in detail, and as compared to this primary task the question of the justification of the claim is clearly of secondary importance only.

6. The (if one keeps to the sequence of words) next expression, of Nir. 1.20, at which a good look should be taken, viz. *bilmagrahaṇāya*, is so problematic that its examination has to be postponed, if not given up completely. I agree with Falk (1990:109) that "(t)he word *bilma* is of uncertain meaning"; he is of the opinion that "most probably it denotes a helmet", or, still more cautiously "a protective weapon" ("Schutzwaffe"), as Rau (1957:101) proposes, i.e. that "the term *bilma* is too rarely attested in Vedic literature to allow a definite conclusion". In other words, the reader finds himself, as only too often[103] in Vedic literature, in the unpleasant situation of having first to understand a sentence/passage as such before being able to venture a guess about the meaning of an expression or a comparison forming part of it but meant to illustrate the main proposition, or to clarify it by a concretization. The communicative function of the expression is entirely hollowed out, the process reversed.

7. The two immediately following words, the direct object of the predicate *samāmnāsiṣur*, viz. *imaṃ granthaṃ* is taken by most of the modern interpreters, in accordance with the explanation of the indigenous commentators, to refer to the "lists [of words]", i.e. the Nighaṇṭus (composed by the

---

100 Quoted from Kahrs 1998a:28. Note that Durga (Bhadkamkar 37.11 f.) regards the Nighaṇṭus alone to give the clue for understanding the *mantras* (... *ity ata ucyate ta eva jñāpakā bhavantīti*).

101 Cf. Kahrs, l.c.

102 Cf. also Wezler 1999a:151n.18; a paper dealing with the so-called "Vedic Mathematics" is under preparation.

103 Cf. e.g. Wezler 1982/83.

avare, as stated by Sköld (1926:7)), in commenting on which Yāska unfolds the *niruktaśāstra*.[104] Indeed, *grantha* cannot but have the—well-known and frequently attested—meaning of "text"/"piece of text"/"utterance in form of a fixed sentence, or rather series of sentences"; and the deictic function of the pronoun *ayam*, described by Delbrück (1988:209 f.) as referring to that "what is regarded as near by the speaker",—an observation improved upon by Klein (1978:38) who states "that the basic function" of it "is to refer to something nearby[105] which has not yet been mentioned"—has also to be given its due, since the definitions quoted, although concerning *ayam* in Vedic/ Ṛgvedic Sanskrit, hold good for this pronoun's use in the classical language, too, as is confirmed by Speyer (1896:40 = § 131). Yet, if *ayam* refers not only to something physically, or temporally near(by), but also to what is mentally in the foreground, so to say, then the possibility that *imaṃ granthaṃ* anticipates, and is explained by, *vedaṃ ca vedāṅgāni ca*, cannot a limine be precluded,[106] the fact that the two groups of words are separated by the finite verb not speaking against such a syntactical relation. The verb used here by Yāska, viz. *sam-ā-√-mnā*, however, furnishes us with a strong argument in favour of the first alternative; for it is precisely this compound verb that is used by him also at the very beginning of the Nir. (1.1), and with palpable emphasis at that, in that he states—perhaps also referring to the fictitious moment when the "recitation of the Nighaṇṭus" is completed—: *samāmnāyaḥ samāmnātaḥ, sa vyākhyātavyaḥ*, "[this] traditional list of words has been handed down [to us]; it has to be explained [here by me]". In the immediately following sentence Yāska even uses the pronoun *ayam*, too: *tam imaṃ samāmnāyaṃ nighaṇṭava ity ācakṣate*, "this same list of words (literally: the list mentioned just now and being in the foreground of [my/the reader's] mind) is called *nighaṇṭus*".

Now, if, or rather in so far as the expression *grantha* refers to the "list of words", the relation in which these *nighaṇṭus* stand in the view of the author of Nir. 1.20 to the *upadeśa*, formerly accompanying the instruction of the *mantras* themselves, can best be defined by the German word "Ersatz", in the sense of something replaced for something else, but of clearly inferior quality than the original: the *nighaṇṭus* are an aid to the understanding to

---

104 It should also be noted that Sāyaṇa, in the introduction to his commentary in the Ṛgveda (in a passage quoted by Bronkhorst 1993:402 because Sāyaṇa refers to the Nighaṇṭu as "Nirukta") uses the expression *grantha* with reference to the Nighaṇṭu (*...tasmin granthe padārthāvabodhāya parāpekṣa na vidyate / etāvanti pṛthivīnāmāni etāvanti hiraṇyanāmāni ity evaṃ tatra tatra vispaṣṭam abhihitatvāt*).

105 It seems to me that Delbrück's description is to be preferred in that it includes mental proximity, too.

106 It should, however, be noted that there are scholars like e.g. Rajavade (1940: Notes 290), who "express the view that *vedaṃ ca vedāṅgāni ca* is an interpolation" (quoted from Kahrs 1998:28 n. 38 who himself adds: "I would not be surprised if he is right".)

the *vedārtha*, but they certainly do not come up to the *ṛṣis' upadeśa* of old! But they are what alone was handed down by the "later ones" who, most unfortunately and for unknown reasons,[107] "became averse to delivering on this instruction", too, and we —Yāska intimates—have to make the best of it. And this is precisely what he does, with a view to demonstrating the usefulness of the *nighaṇṭus* and his method, in commentating on them and thereby expounding the *niruktaśāstra*.

8. This latter *śāstra* forms, as is well known, one of the six "ancillary sciences of the Veda", and thus is subsumed under the term *vedāṅgāni (ca)* of the final phrase (*vedaṃ ca vedāṅgāni ca*) which is evidently asyndetically[108] added after the predicate: the author's intention, to all appearances, is to give a correct, though brief description of the work done by the "later ones", viz. the transmission of the *veda* and the *vedāṅgas*, the difference in gender probably being caused by the wish to express the idea of a homogeneous unitary whole, in the case of the former, and the systematic, thematic and methodical diversity, in the case of the latter. The concept of *veda* comprises that of the *mantras*, but is, no doubt, wider, although the question as to exactly what else is included remains open. That other elements of the (oral) transmission are not mentioned here does not necessarily mean that Yāska did not know of any others. It is quite possible that he deliberately confines himself to the Veda alone, and what is important for the understanding of it, i.e. the *Nighaṇṭus* and the six *vedāṅgas*.

9. No matter whether the explanation *bilmaṃ bhilmaṃ bhāsanaṃ vā*, concluding the passage under discussion, forms an original part of it or not,[109] the problems we are confronted with are really intricate: it is not the fact that an alternative interpretation, i.e. *nirvacana*, is offered which is puzzling, but the unpleasant circumstance that one of the explicans is itself a word not known. But, and this is even more important to remember, what I called an "explanation" is, as was shown with particular clarity by Kahrs (1983), an answer to the question why a particular linguistic sign is used to denote/to refer to an object X, and it thus de facto presupposes a knowledge of its lexicographical meaning. It is hence practically impossible to arrive at a clear idea what the author, be it correctly or wrongly, took *bilma* to mean.

---

107 Conspicuously no reason is mentioned in the Nir. passage. Is the idea of *glāna* the product of pure fantasy, or is it a projection of later experience(s)—of the lack of enthusiasm of feelings or reluctance, or real aversion to having to memorize more and more (for which see Mahābhāṣya (ed. Kielhorn) I 5.5 ff.)?

108 A least this is, in my view, a more probable assumption than that the *ca* after *vedaṃ* connects the latter expression with *imaṃ grantham*, and accordingly the second *ca*, after *vedāṅgam*, this word with *vedaṃ*. Sköld (1926:7) voices the opinion that "(t)he last four words" of the passage "look a little out of place, but may be taken as summing up the preceding statements".

109 See above n. 3.

And, as I stated above, the number of occurrences of *bilma*, and *bilmin*, is so small that its lexical meaning cannot be determined with the necessary certainty. "Helmet" is apparently not generally accepted, as becomes obvious from Mayrhofer (1996/II: 226) who sticks to "Span" ("shaving") of the Larger Petrograd Dictionary. Even though I myself am also not able to offer more than mere guesswork, I may be allowed to add some more possibilities to those already proposed by others.[110]

bilmagrahaṇāya could mean

- "in order to grasp [at least] (the) shavings [since/if the log is not available any longer]"; or
- "in order to grasp [the meaning of the Veda] by shavings [from the Veda itself]"[111] or
- "in order to grasp a protection (i.e. something that protects the transmission of the Veda from a further loss)", or
- "in order to grasp the helmet/the armament (i.e. at least the external cover)", or
- "in order to grasp/take hold of the/a helmet [when it is impossible to grasp the hair]", or[112]
- in order to grasp/take hold of the [outer, hard] shell [which covers the soft kernel]."[113]

Perhaps a decision can be taken between these proposals in the future if more occurrences of the word *bilma-* should come to light; for, is it not strange that Yāska should himself use a word which seems to be a *hapax*?

10. Space and time being limited it is not possible to enter into a discussion of the reception of Nir. 1.20,[114] the most important examples of which have already been mentioned in earlier parts of this essay. Still, a few remarks are in order. As stated above (p. 14), it is rather doubtful whether Mahābhāṣya (ed. Kielhorn) I 11.11 ff. can be regarded as a case of reference to the Nir. passage at issue; perhaps it should better be regarded as just an occurrence, in a relatively old text, of the expression *pratyakṣadharman*.

The situation is entirely different when we come to the Vṛtti on Vākyapadīya I: the author quite evidently quoted the Nirukta even though the quotation itself is introduced by a formulaic *āha khalv api*, and even though Vṛṣabhadeva confines himself to a—non-committal—*āgamāntaram apy āha* ... (Iyer 1966:25.7). Besides, this quotation has in view of the context, i.e.

---

110 Viz. the Larger Petrograd Dictionary or Falk 1990.

111 Cf. that is how the commentators explain *samāhṛtya*.

112 Cf. Hara 1986; cf. also Aklujkar (forthcoming).

113 This proposal is based on the assumption that *bilma-* means "nut-shell", and is in fact derived from the root *bhid*, and was secondarily, and metonymically, used to denote a "helmet".

114 Not to mention that of the Nirukta as a whole—which would be tantamount to writing the Indological equivalent to Curtius (Cf. n. 98 above).

the narrower of the Vṛtti on this *kārikā* as well as the wider of the Vṛtti on the Brahmakāṇḍa as a whole,[115] to be classed as the most significant one in terms of a history of Indian ideas. At least I do not know another one of equal intellectual importance. In view of the textcritical problems pertaining to the VP, and to the Vṛtti, I think it is useful to quote this part of the Vṛtti on 1.5 in full from Aklujkar's new critical edition —the publication of which many Indologists look forward to with both impatience and no little anticipation—, with his kind permission, of course; the text as constituted by him reads as follows.[116]

> *anukāra iti / 'yāṃ sūkṣmāṃ nityām atīndriyāṃ vācam ṛṣayaḥ sākṣātkṛtadharmāṇo mantradṛśaḥ paśyanti tām asākṣātkṛtadharmabhyaḥ parebhyaḥ pravedayiṣyamāṇā bilmaṃ samāmananti, snapnavṛttam iva dṛṣṭaśrutānubhūtam ācikhyāsanta' [ ] ity eṣa purākalpaḥ / āha khalv api / 'sākṣātkṛtadharmāṇa ṛṣayo babhūvuḥ / te 'parebhya upadeśena mantrān saṃprāduḥ / upadeśāya glāyanto 'pare bilmagrahaṇāyemaṃ granthaṃ samāmnāsiṣur vedaṃ ca vedāṅgāni ca / bilmaṃ bhilmaṃ bhāsanam iti veti [Yāska 1.20] /.*

The use of *bilma* in the first, unidentified quotation, the "*purākalpa*",[117] cannot be considered to form another, new occurrence, although the relation between the two quotations in terms of relative chronology as also of the ideas expressed, respectively, still remain to be clarified (if at all possible).

What should be noticed next is the quotation in the Yuktidīpikā, viz. on Sāṃkhyakārikā 51 abc, in which the eight *siddhis*, "perfections", are enumerated. As for the first three of them, viz. *ūha*, "contemplation/reflection", *śabda*, "communication" and *adhyayana* "studying", it is stated that "these three are the means of acquiring knowledge (establishing truth) and gaining success by which living beings up to [God] Brahmā reach an intended object/a goal aimed at [in terms of cognition etc.]" (*ta ete trayaḥ sādhanopāyā yair ā brāhmaṇaḥ prāṇino 'bhipretam arthaṃ prāpnuvanti* (Wezler/Motegi 1998:251.21)). The transition to the quotation from the Nirukta is formed by *āha ca*; "and it is said"—, and the passage is quite evidently quoted in order to give a particularly significant example for the operation of the second and third of the *siddhis*: The *sākṣātkṛtadharmāṇa ṛṣayo* communicate what they cognized/perceived to "the later ones", and these in their turn learn and study this knowledge. The quotation itself does not deviate from the wording as repeated just now by me, except for the variant

115 As for the reception of the Nirukta itself cf. p. 22 and n. 96 above.

116 In addition to the Vṛtti on 1.5 cf. also the Vṛtti on 1.137.

117 On which cf. Aklujkar (forthcoming:Appendix I passage 1 b)). The expression *purākalpa* is met with also at Manu 9.227, Auśanasasmṛti (The Smriti Sandarbha III, 1565) 3.50, Yama (as quoted in Dharmakośa III (Saṃskāra) 3027) and Bṛhadyogiyājñavalkyasmṛti (ed. by Swāmī Kuvalayānanda and Pt. Raghunāthashāstri Kokaje, Pune 1951).

'parebhyo, and accordingly also *'pare* mentioned already above,[118] and except for the fact that it ends with *vedāṅgāni ca*. The *nirvacana* explanation found in Nir. 1.20 itself, and quoted verbatim also by Bhartṛhari, is not really quoted[119] in the Yuktidīpikā, too, but it clearly forms the foundation of the statement added to the quotation, viz. (Wezler/Motegi 1998:252.1 f.): *bilmaṃ bhāsanaṃ samyakpratibhāsāya viśiṣṭaḥ saṃketa ucyate*, "*bilma* [means] 'shining', [that is to say] what is denoted/expressed [by it] is a particular concise explanation[120] leading to a/the correct appearance-to-the-mind (i.e. correct understanding) [of the text explained in this way]". Yet, it is very unlikely indeed that this interpretation of *bilma* is more than a—intelligent—guess, made on the basis of Nir. 1.20 alone, and perhaps a commentary on it.[121]

Another instance worth noticing where Nir. 1.20 is—not quoted[122] but—clearly referred to is Medhātithi's Bhāṣya on Manusmṛti 2.12. In explaining the final *pāda* of this verse (*sākṣād dharmasya lakṣaṇam*) Medh. states (Dave 1972: 185. 23 f.) that "*etat*", i.e. the four "authorities" enumerated in the preceding quarters, viz. *veda, smṛti, sādācāra* and "*svasya ca priyam ātmanaḥ*", "are the characteristic feature (of *dharma*), [i.e.] that which lets one recognize (the *dharma*), but not [the means of cognition consisting in] perception, as it has been stated by others (i.e. Yāska) [with reference to quite different people in the passage which starts with '*ṛṣis*] by whom *dharma* was directly experienced' " (*etat sākṣād dharmasya lakṣaṇaṃ nimittaṃ jñāpakaṃ, na punaḥ pratyakṣam / yathānyair uktaṃ 'sākṣātkṛtadharmāṇa' iti*).[123]

When talking about the reception of Nir. 1.20, it may, finally, be pointed out that no clear line can be drawn between quotations or references in old(er) texts and in (more) modern ones: the language of the author quoting or referring to the passage may even still be Sanskrit;[124] in any case, the history of its reception extends, practically, till the present day.[125]

---

118 Viz. n. 19.

119 Cf. above n. 3.

120 If the text is, however, corrupt here, viz. *bhilmaṃ*, and a—second —*iti* left out by mistake, the situation would, of course, be different.

121 Cf. Monier-Williams s.v. *saṃketa*.

122 As it is in fact by Helarāja on VP 3.1.46, viz. as support for the proposition *santi sarvajñāḥ*.

123 *bilma* is taken to mean *upāya* by Skandasvāmin-Maheśvara (Sarup 1982:115.2; cf. 116.3).

124 See, e.g., Shastri 1959:62 n. 4.

125 Cf. e.g. Shastri 1959:62, in a note on the famous dictum, found in Kaiyata's Pradīpa on Pāṇ. 1.1.29 (NSP-edition: I 339 b 4) and in the Siddhāntakaumudī on Pāṇ. 1.1.29 *yathottaraṃ munīnāṃ prāmāṇyam*, "the authoritativeness of the [three] *munis* (i.e. Pāṇini, Kātyāyana and Patañjali) corresponds to [their] order of succession", on which cf. also Subrahmanyam 1999:13.

11. The question whether or to which extent the picture drawn by Yāska of the early phase, the first millenium at least, of the transmission of Vedic literature, is historically correct, I cannot examine here. What I instead wanted to say in conclusion is that this is how I understand the passage in the Nir., and that my interpretation has rather far-reaching consequences for our understanding of the views Indians had about the most sacred part of their literary heritage, and about the possibility of **regaining** the—lost—*vedārtha*. Yet what is of primary importance is not to check the historical correctness, let alone to carry out a narrow-minded or arrogant critique of these ideas, but to see them within their own historical and cultural and intellectual context, and to achieve a deeper understanding of them than I have been able to do here.

Ceterum censeo terram Tibetanam
in veterem dignitatem ac libertatem
esse vindicandam,
sericos istos tyrannos imperio potestateque
esse depellendos atque adducendos
in iudicium constitutum
consensu et auctoritate iuris gentium.

ACKNOWLEDGEMENT: My thanks are, again, due to Anne MacDonald who corrected my English with great patience and admirable competence and understanding. I should like to state that Aklujkar (forthcoming) became accessible to me only during a later phase of the composition of the present article, and in view of the fact that it is not yet published, it seemed to me advisable just to refer to it here and there but not to enter into a discussion of Aklujkar's opinions where, and if at all, they differ from my own. A detailed discussion has to be postponed, and should perhaps better be undertaken by a third party.

REFERENCES

Abhyankar and Limaye. 1970. *Mahābhāṣyadīpikā of Bhartṛhari.* Critically edited by Professor K. V. Abhyankar and Ācārya P. V. Limaye (Bhandarkar Oriental Research Institute, Post-graduate and Research Department Series No. 8), Poona.

Aithal, K. Paramesvara. 1991. *Veda-Lakṣaṇa. Vedic Ancillary Literature. A Descriptive Bibliography* (Beiträge zur Südasienforschung, Südasien Institut, Universität Heidelberg, Stuttgart: Franz Steiner Verlag.

———. 1996. "Pāṇini's Aṣṭādhyāyī and Vedic Ritual Literature", in: *Nānāvidhaikatā. Festschrift für Hermann Berger.* Hrsg. von Dieter B. Kapp, Wiesbaden: Otto Harrasowitz, 1-7.

Aiyangar, K. V. Rangaswami. 1941. *Rājadharma*, Adyar.

Aklujkar, Ashok. 1972. "The authorship of the Vākyapadīya-vṛtti", *Wiener Zeitschrift für die Kunde Südasiens* 16, 181-198.

———. 1993. "Once again on the authorship of the Trikāṇḍī-Vṛtti", in: *Asiatische Studien XLVII 1. 1993—Proceedings of the First International Conference on*

Bhartṛhari, University of Poona, January 6-8, 1992. ed. by Saroja Bhate and Johannes Bronkhorst, Berlin: Peter Lang.

———. (forthcoming), "The Manner of Veda Revelation according to Bhartṛ-Hari" (print-out of 22 pages, with two appendices, viz. "Appendix I: Textual etc. Notes on the Relevant TK Passages" (18 pp.) and "Appendix II: Comments on Halbfass' presentation of B's concept of the Veda" (10 pp.).

Aramaki, Noritoshi (forthcoming), "The Jaina and Early Buddhist *saṃkhyā*- and the Epic *sāṃkhya*" (to be published in the Jaini Felicitation Volume).

Assmann, Aleida. 1999. *Erinnerungsräume. Formen und Wirkungen des kulturellen Gedächtnisses*, München: C. H. Beck.

Assmann/Hölscher. 1988. *Kultur und Gedächtnis*. Hrsg. von Jan Assmann und Tonio Hölscher, Frankfurt a. M.: Suhrkamp.

Beekes, Robert S. P. 1995. *Comparative Indo-European Linguistics. An Introduction.* Amsterdam/Philadelphia: John Benjamins Publishing Company.

Belvalkar, Shripad Krishna. 1915. *An Account of the Different Existing Systems of Sanskrit Grammar being the Vishwanath Narayan Mandlik Gold Medal Prize-Essay for 1909*, Poona.

Bhadkamkar, R. G. 1985. *The Nirukta of Yāska* (with Nighaṇṭu) edited with Durga's Commentary by H. M. Bhadkamkar, assisted by R. G. Bhadkamkar, (Bombay Sanskrit and Prakrit Series, No. LXXIII), Bombay 1918

Böhtlingk, Otto. 1909. *Böhtlingk's Sanskrit-Chrestomathie.* Dritte verbesserte und vermehrte Auflage, hrsg. von Richard Garbe, Leipzig: H. Haessel.

Bronkhorst, Johannes. 1985. "A possible quotation from the Niruktavārttika known to Durga in the Yuktidīpikā", in: *Proceedings of the Vth World Sanskrit Conference*, New Delhi: Rashtriya Sanskrit Sansthan, 90-100.

———. 1987. *Mahābhāṣyadīpikā* of Bhartṛhari. Fascicule IV: *Āhnika I*, critically edited by Johannes Bronkhorst (Bhandarkar Oriental Research Institute, Post-Graduate and Research Department Series No. 28), Poona: Bhandarkar Oriental Research Institute

———. 1993."Buddhist Hybrid Sanskrit: the original language", in: K. M. Mishra (ed.), *Aspects of Buddhist Sanskrit* (Proceedings of the International Symposium on the Languages of Sanskrit Buddhist Texts, Oct. 1-5, 1991). Sarnath: Central Institute of Higher Tibetan Studies, 396-414.

Bühler, Georg. 1879 and 1882. *Sacred Laws of the Āryas as taught in the Schools of Āpastamba, Gautama, Vāsistha, and Baudhayana* transl. by Georg Bühler, 2 Pts. (SBE II and XIV), Oxford (repr. Delhi 1965, etc.).

———. 1982-94. *Āpastambīyadharmasūtram. Aphorisms of the Sacred Law of the Hindus by Apastamba* edited with Extracts from the Commentary, by George Bühler, Sec. Edition, Revised Bombay (The Department of Public Instruction Bombay, Bombay Skt. Series No. XLIV) Bombay, Part I 1892, Part II 1894.

Burnell, A. C. 1876. *The Ārsheyabrāhmaṇa* (Being the Fourth Brāhmaṇa of the Sāma Veda. The Sanskrit Text edited together with the Extracts from the Commentary of Sāyaṇa etc. and Introduction, and Index of Words by A. C. Burnell, Mangalore: Basel Mission Press.

Cappeller, Carl. 1870. *Śrīvāmanaviracitā Kāvyālaṃkāravṛttiḥ. Vāmana's Lehrbuch der Poetik*, zum ersten Mal herausgegeben. Jena: H. Dufft.

Cardona, George. 1972. "Pāṇini's use of the term *upadeśa* and the *ekānta* and *anekānta* views regarding *anubandhas*", *First International Sanskrit Confer-*

ence, Summaries of Papers ... (New Delhi).
———. 1976. *Pāṇini. A Survey of Research* (Trends in Linguistics. State of the Art Reports 6), The Hague-Paris: Mouton.
———. 1997. *Pāṇini: His Work and its Traditions. Vol. 1: Background and Introduction.* Second Edition Revised and Enlarged, Delhi (first ed. 1988).
Curtius, Ernst Robert. 1948. *Europäische Literatur und lateinisches Mittelalter.* Bern-München: Francke, (4. Aufl. 1963).
Dave, Jayantakrishna Harikrishna. 1972. *Manu-Smṛti.* With nine commentaries by Medhātithi, Sarvajñanārāyaṇa, Kullūka, Rāghavānanda, Nandana, Rāmacandra, Maṇirāma, Govindarāja and Bhāruci, Vol. I (Adhyāyas 1-2). Ed. by Jayantakrishna Harikrishna Dave, Bombay, Bharatiya Vidya Bhavan.
Deeg, Max. 1995. *Die altindischen Etymologie nach dem Verständnis Yāska's und seiner Vorgänger. Eine Untersuchung über ihre Praktiken, ihre literarischen Verbreitung und ihr Verhältnis zur dichterischen Gestaltung und Sprachmagie* (Würzburger Studien zur Sprache und Kultur). Dettelbach: J. H. Röll.
Delbrück, Bertold. 1888. *Altindische Syntax* (Syntaktische Forschungen, V). Halle an der Saale (Nachdruck: Darmstadt 1968, Wissenschaftliche Buchgesellschaft).
Dhadphale, M. G. 1982. "Nirukta: Its precise purpose", in: *Golden Jubilee Volume* ed. by T. N. Dharmadhikari, = Poona, Vaidika Saṃśodhana Mandala, 94-101.
Duerr, Hans Peter. 1978. *Traumzeit.* Frankfurt: Syndikat.
Elizarenkova, Tatyana J. 1995. *Language and Style of the Vedic Ṛṣis.* Edited with an Introduction by Wendy Doniger. Albany: State University of New York Press.
Falk, Harry. 1996. "Goodies for India—Literary, Orality, and Vedic Culture", in: W. Raible (Hrsg.): *Erscheinungsformen kultureller Prozesse* (Script Oralia, 13). Tübingen: Gunter Narr Verlag, 103-120.
———. 1993. *Schrift im alten Indien. Ein Forschungsbericht mit Anmerkungen.* Tübingen: Gunter Narr Verlag.
Findly, Ellison Banks. 1989. "*Mántra kaviśastá*: Speech as Performative in the Ṛgveda", in: H. P. Alper, *Mantra.* Albany: The State University of New York Press, 15-47.
Franco, Eli. 1997. *Dharmakīrti on Comparison and Rebirth.* (Wiener Studien zur Tibetologie und Buddhismuskunde, Heft 38), Wien. Arbeitskreis für Tibetische und Buddhistische Studien Universität Wien, 1992 (especially p. 29 f. along with notes 38 ff.).
Grafenhorst, Rainer. 1997. *Das Kosmographische System der Purāṇas. Zur Funktion und Struktur indischer Kosmographie.* Reinbek: Dr. I. Wezler Verlag für Orientalistische Fachpublikationen.
Hacker, Paul. 1965. "Dharma im Hinduismus", *Zeitschrift für Religions- und Missionswissenschaft* 49, 93-106 = *Kleine Schriften.* hrsg. von L. Schmithausen, Wiesbaden 1978, 496-509.
Halbfass, Wilhelm. 1988. *India and Europe. An Essay in Understanding.* Albany: State University of New York Press.
Hāldar, Vṛddhatrayī. 1955. *Kalīghaṭṭasthitaśrīśrīkālikāmahādevīsevābhṛtkulodbhave - Śrīgurupadaśarmmahāladāsapranītā. Kālikātānagaryyām ... em. e. bī. el.-upādhinā Śrībhāratīvikāśaśarmmahāladāreṇa prakāśitā* / 1362 vaṅgābdāḥ [= 1955 n. Chr.].

Hara, Minoru. 1986. "The Holding on the Hair (*keśa-grahaṇa*)", *Acta Orientalia* 47, 67-92.

von Hinüber, Oskar. 1982/83. "On the Perfect in Pali", 30-32 = *Selected Papers on Pāli Studies*. Oxford: The Pali Text Society, 1994, 173-176.

———. 1986. *Das ältere Mittelindisch im Überblick.* (Österreichische Akademie der Wissenschaften. Philosophisch-historische Klasse, Sitzungsberichte, 467. Band, Veröffentlichungen der Kommission für Sprachen und Kulturen Südasiens. Heft 20), Wien: Verlag der Österreichischen Akademie der Wissenschaften.

———. 1994. *Selected Papers on Pāli Studies*, Oxford: The Pali Text Society.

Horsch, Paul. 1967. "Vom Schöpfungsmythos zum Weltgesetz", *Asiatische Studien* XXI, 31-61.

Houben, Jan E. 1999. "On Syntactic and Stylistic Evidence regarding the Authorship of the Vākyapadīya-Vṛtti (Bhartṛhari's Vākyapadīya and the Ancient Vṛtti 3)", *Wiener Zeitschrift für die Kunde Südasiens* XLIII, 167-197.

Janert, Klaus Ludwig. 1955/56. *Von der Art und den Mitteln der indischen Textweitergabe. Bericht über mündliche und schriftliche Tradierungsmethoden sowie die Schreibmaterialien in Indien.* Jahresarbeit zur Diplomprüfung für den Höhe- ren Dienst an Wissenschaftlichen Bibliotheken. Köln (Ms.) = Bibliographie mit den Berichten über die mündliche und schriftliche Textweitergabe sowie die Schreibmaterialien in Indien (Berichtszeit bis 1955), Bonn: VGH Wissenschaftsverlag.

Joshi, S. D. and J. A. F. Roodbergen. 1986. *Patañjali's Vyākaraṇa-Mahābhāṣya. Paspaśāhnika.* Introduction, Text, Translation and Notes by S. D. Joshi and J. A. F. Roodbergen (Publications of the Centre of Advanced Study in Sanskrit, Class C, No. 15). Pune: University of Poona.

Kahrs, Eivind G. 1980. *Bidrag til interpretasjonen av Nirukta*, University of Oslo (Diss.), cf. Kahrs 1996.

———. 1983. "Yāska's use of *kasmāt*", *Indo-Iranian Journal* 25, 231-237.

———. 1984. "Yāska's Nirukta: the quest for a new interpretation", *IT* 12, 139-154.

———. 1996. *Substitution and change: foundations of traditional Indian hermeneutics*. University of Oslo (Diss.).

———. 1998a. *Indian Semantic Analysis. The Nirvacana Tradition* (University of Cambridge Oriental Publications: 55). Cambridge.

———. 1998b. "L'interpretation et la tradition indienne du *Nirukta*", in: *Histoire, Epistemologie, Langaga* XX, Fasc.1, *Les Grammaires Indiennes*, 63-75.

Kane, Pandurang Vaman. 1973. *History of Dharmaśāstra* (Ancient and Mediaeval Religious and Civil Law), Vol. III. 2nd Ed., Poona: Bhandarkar Oriental Research Institute.

Kielhorn, F. 1962. *The Vyākaraṇa-Mahābhāṣya of Patañjali.* Ed. by F. Kielhorn. Third Edition by K. V. Abhyankar, Vol. I, Pune: Bhandarkar Oriental Research Institute.

Klein, Jared S. 1978. *The Particle* u *in the Rigveda. A Synchronic and Diachronic Study*. Göttingen: Vandenhoeck and Ruprecht.

Lariviere, Richard W. 1997. "Dharmaśāstra, Custom, 'Real Law' and 'Apogryphal' Smṛtis" in: *Recht, Staat und Verwaltung im klassischen Indien (Schriften des Historischen Kollegs Kolloqium 30)* hrsg. von B. Kölver unter Mitarbeit von

E. Müller-Luckner. München: R. Oldenbourg, 97-110.

Ludwig, Alfred. 1878. *Der Rigveda oder die heiligen Hymnen der Brâhmana*. 3. Bd.: *Die Mantraliteratur und das alte Indien*. Prag: F. Tempsky.

Mackensen, Lutz. 1973. *Zitate, Redensarten, Sprichwörter*. Brugg-Stuttgart-Salzburg: Fackelverlag.

Mahābhāṣyadīpikā of Bhartṛahi (sic!), (Bhandarkar Oriental Research Institute, Post-Graduate and Research Department Series). Poona: Bhandarkar Oriental Research Institute, 1980 (facsimile edition of the only extant ms.).

Mayrhofer, Manfred. 1996. *Etymologisches Wörterbuch des Altindischen* 2nd vol., Heidelberg: C. Winter.

Mette, Adelheid. 1973. *Indische Kulturstiftungsberichte und ihr Verhältnis zur Zeitalterssage* (Abh. der Akademie Mainz, Geistes- und Sozialwiss. Kl. 1973 Nr. 1). Wiesbaden.

Michaels, Axel. 1998. *Der Hinduismus. Geschichte und Gegenwart*. München: C. H. Beck.

———. 1999. "'Le rituel pour le rituel' oder wie sinnlos sind Rituale", in: *Rituale heute: Theorien—Kontroversen—Entwürfe*, hrsg. von Corinna Caduff und Joanna Pfaff-Czarnecka. Berlin: Reimer, 23-47.

Moghe, S. G. (Ed.). 1997. *Prof. Kane's Contribution to Dharmaśāstra Literature*. Compiled and edited by S. G. Moghe. Delhi: D. K. Printworld.

Muir, J. 1868-1872. *Original Sanskrit Texts, on the Origin and History of the People of India, their Religion and Institutions*, collected, translated and illustrated by J. Muir. 5 Vols. London: Trübner.

Oetke, Claus. 1999. *Zur Akademischen Krise in der Indologie und den Möglichkeiten ihrer Überwindung*. Reinbek: Dr. I. Wezler Verlag für Orientalistische Fachpublikationen.

Olivelle, Patrick. 1999. *Dharmasūtras. The Law Codes of Ancient India*. A New Translation by Patrick Olivelle (Oxford World's Classics). New York.

Oliver, Curtis F. 1979. "Some Aspects of Literacy in Ancient India", *The Quarterly Newsletter of the Laboratory of Comparative Human Cognition* 1, 57-62.

Pandey, Umesh Chandra. 1960. *The Gautama-Dharma-Sūtra with the Mitākṣarā Sanskrit Commentary of Haradātta*. edited with the Hindi Commentary and Introduction by Dr. Umesh Chandra Pandey (Kashi Sanskrit Series). Varanasi, 1966.

Pind, O. H. 1997. "Pāli Grammar and Grammarians from Buddhaghosa to Vajirabuddhi: A Survey", *Buddhist Studies* 26 (1977), 23-88.

Rajavade. 1940. (see next entry)

Rajavade, V. K. 1993. *Yāska's Nirukta*. Volume I: *Introduction. Full Texts of Nighaṇṭu and Nirukta. Cursory Examination of Nighaṇṭu. Notes on chapters I-III of Nirukta. 25 Indexes*. Ed. by V. K. Rajavade, 2nd Ed., Poona 1985, Bhandarkar Oriental Research Institute (First ed.: Poona 1940, B.O.R.I [Government Oriental Series - Class A, No. 7].

Ramaṇathan, A. S. 1993. *What is Veda?* (The Logic of Vedic Thought—1). Jaipur: Rajasthan Patrika Limited.

Rau, Wilhelm. 1950. *Staat und Gesellschaft im alten Indien nach den Brāhmaṇa-Texten dargestellt*. Wiesbaden: O. Harrassowitz, 1957.

Renou, Louis. 1961. *Grammaire Sanscrite*. Tomes I et II réunis. Paris: Adrien-Maison-neuve.

Renou Louis and Liliane Silburn. 1954. "*Nírukta* and *Ánirukta* in Vedic", in: *Sarūpa-Bhāratī or The Homage of Indology Being the Dr. Lashman Sarup Memorial Volume*, ed. by Jagannath Agrawal and Bhim Dev Shastri. Hoshiarpur: Vishveshvaranand Institute Publications, 68-79.

Rocher, Ludo. 1976. "The Introduction of the Gautamadharmasūtra", *Adyar Library Bulletin* XXXIX, 90-100.

Röhrich, Lutz. 1992. *Das große Lexikon der sprichwörtlichen Redensarten*. 2 Vols. Freiburg.

Roth, Rudolph. 1852. *Jāska's Nirukta sammt den Nighaṇṭavas* herausgegeben und erläutert von Rudolph Roth. Göttingen: Verlag der Dieterichschen Buchhandlung.

Ruben, Walter. 1929. "Die Theorien der Inder über das dichterische Schaffen", *Orientalistische Literaturzeitung* XXXII 8/9, 618-630.

Sāmasrami, Satyavrata. 1885. *The Nirukta with Commentaries* ed. by Paṇḍit Satyavrata Sāmasrami (sic!) (Bibliotheca Indica, New Series). Calcutta.

Śarman. 1941. *The Charakasaṃhitā by Agniveśa*, Revised by Charaka and Dṛidhabala with the Āyurveda-Dīpikā Commentary of Chakrapāṇidatta, ed. by Vaidya Jādavaji Trikamji Achārya (= Ācāryopāhva Trivikramātmaja Yādavaśarman). Third Ed. Bombay: Nirṇaya Sāgar Press.

Sarup, Laksman. 1967. *The Nighaṇṭu and the Nirukta, The Oldest Indian Treatise on Etymology, Philology, and Semantics*, critically edited from Original Manuscripts and translated for the First Time into English, with Introduction, Exegetical, and Critical Notes, Three Indexes and Eight Apendices by Laksman Sarup. 2nd Reprint, Delhi-Varanasi-Patna: Motilal Barnasidass.

Sarup. 1982. *Commentary of Skandas-Svāmin and Maheśvara on the Nirukta*, critically edited by Dr. Lakdhman Sarup. With Additions and Corrections by Acharya V. P. Limaye (Panini Vaidika Granthamala 11). New Delhi.

Śāstri, A. Chinnasvami. 1934. *Baudhāyana Dharmasūtra with the Vivaraṇa Commentary of Sri Govinda Swāmī* ed. with Notes, Introduction, Word Index, etc. by Pandit A. Chinnasvami Śastri (Kashi Shastri Series 104), Benares 1934.

Shastri. 1959. *The Siddhanta Kaumudi of Bhattoji Deekshit with the Tattvabodhini Commentary of Jnanendra Sarasvati, the Subodhini Commentary of Jayakrishna and the Chandrakala Commentary of Bhairava Misra with the Notes of Mahamahopadhyaya Pandit Sivadatta Shastri*, printed and published by Khemraj Shri Krishnadas. Bombay.

Shastri/Shukla. 1965-67. *Nyāsa or Pañcikā Commentary of Ācārya Jinendrabuddhipāda and Padamañjarī of Haradatta Miśra on the Kāśikāvṛtti of Vāmana-Jayāditya*. Critically ed. by Swami Dwarika Das Shastri and Pt. Kalika Prasad Shukla. 6 Vols. Varanasi: Prachya Bharati Prakashan.

Seyfort Ruegg, David. 1994. "*Pramāṇabhūta, *pramāṇa (bhūta)-puruṣa, pratyakṣadharman* and *sakṣatkṛtadharman* as Epithets of the *ṛṣi, ācārya* and *tathāgata* in grammatical, epistemological and Madhyamaka Texts", *Bulletin of the School of Oriental and African Studies* LVII, 303-320.

Sköld. 1926. *The Nirukta, its Place in Old Indian Literature, its Etymologies*. Lund: C. W. K. Gleerup (etc.).

Speyer, J. S. 1896. *Vedische und Sanskrit-Syntax* (Grundriss der Indo-Arischen Philologie und Altertumskunde I Bd. 6. Hft.) Strassburg: Trübner.

Staal, Frits. 1989. *Rules without Meaning. Essays on Ritual, Mantras and the Science of Man*. New York: Peter Lang.

———. 1990. *Jouer avec le Feu. Pratique et théorie du rituel Védique*. Paris: Collége de France, 1999.

von Stietencron, Heinrich. 1992. *Epic and Purāṇic Bibliography* (up to 1985) annotated and with indexes. Compiled under the chairmanship of H. v. Stietencron by ..... Edited by H. v. Stietencron, K.-P. Gritz, A. Malinar, A. Kollmann, P. Schreiner, M. Brockington. 2 Pts., Wiesbaden: O. Harrassowitz.

Subrahmanyam, P. S. 1999. *Paniniyam Linguistics*. Tokyo: Institute for the Study of Languages and Cultures, Asia and Africa.

Tarkatirtha/Tarkatirtha. 1936. *Nyāyadarśanam with Vātsyāyana's Bhāṣya, Uddyotakara's Vārttika, Vācaspati Miśra's Tātparyaṭīkā and Viśvanātha's Vṛtti, Chapter I, Section I*, Critically edited with notes of Taranatha Nyaya-Tarkatirtha and (Chapters I, II-VI) by Amarendramoha Tarkatirtha. Calcutta (Cal. S. S. 18), 1936 (Reprint: Kyoto 1982).

Thieme, Paul. 1958. "Review of L. Renou, Terminologie grammaticale de Sanskrit, Paris 1957", in: *Göttingische gelehrte Anzeigen* 212 (1958), 19-49 = Kleine Schriften, hrsg. v. Georg Buddruss. Wiesbaden: Steiner, 1975, 727-757.

Tichy, Eva. 1997. "Vom indogermanischen Tempus/Aspekt-System zum vedischen Zeitstufensystem", in: *Berthold Delbrück y la sintais indoeuropea*. Aetas del Coloquio de la Indogermanische Gesellschaft Madrid, 21-24 de septembre de 1994 editados por Emilio Crespo y José Luis García Ramón, Madrid (Ediciones de la Uam). Wiesbaden: Dr. Reichert, 589-609.

Ullmann, Stephen. 1973. *Semantik. Einführung in die Bedeutungslehre*. (Conditio humana. Ergebnisse aus den Wissenschaften vom Menschen), Frankfurt a M., S. Fischer (german translation of *Semantics. An Introduction in the Science of Meaning*, London 1962).

Weber, Albrecht. 1881. *Das Saptaçatakam des Hâla*. Hrsg. von Albrecht Weber (Abhandlungen zur Kunde des Morgenlandes VII.4), Leipzig.

Wezler, Albrecht. 1982. Review of G. Oberhammer (ed.), *Offenbarung, geistige Realität des Menschen*. Wien 1974, in: *Indo-Iranian Journal* 24, 142-155.

———. 1982/83. "Zum Verständnis von Chandogya-Upaniṣad 5.1.12", *Studien zur Indologie und Iranistik* 8/9, 147-168.

———. 1999a. "Medhātithi on *Sāmānyato Dṛṣṭam [Anumānam]*", *Journal of Indian Philosophy* 27 1/2, 139-157.

———. 1999b. "Über den sakramentalen Charakter des *Dharma* nachsinnend", in: G. Oberhammer, M. Schmücker (Hrsg.), *Raum-zeitliche Vermittlung der Transzendenz. Zur "sakramentalen" Dimension religiöser Tradition*. Wien: Verlag der Österreichischen Akademie der Wissenschaften, 63-114.

———. 2000. "Modes of reporting opinions in Verdic prose", to be published in the Proceedings of the 2nd Vedic Workshop, Kyoto.

Wezler/Motegi. 1998. *Yuktidīpikā. The Most Significant Commentary on the Sāṃkhyakārikā*. Critically edited by Albrecht Wezler and Shujun Motegi, Vol. I (Alt- u. Neu-Indische Studien 44). Stuttgart: Franz Steiner Verlag.

Witzel, Michael. 1987. "On the Origin of the Literary Device of the 'Frame Story' in Old Indian Literature", in: *Hinduismus und Buddhismus. Festschrift für Ulrich Schneider*, ed. by Harry Falk. Freiburg: Hedwig Falk, 386-414.

Contributors

Ashok Aklujkar, Professor of Sanskrit and Related Subjects in the Department of Asian Studies, University of British Columbia.

Bettina Bäumer, Professor of Religious Studies at the University of Vienna and Director of Research at the Alice Boner Foundation Varanasi.

James Benson, Lecturer of Sanskrit at the Oriental Institute Oxford.

Hermann Berger, Professor emeritus of Classical Indology at the South Asia Institute of the University of Heidelberg.

Johannes Bronkhorst, Professor of Sanskrit and Indian Studies at the University of Lausanne.

Madhav M. Deshpande, Professor of Sanskrit at the Department of Asian Languages and Culture, University of Michigan, Ann Arbor.

Harry Falk, Professor of Indology at the Freie Universität of Berlin.

Monika Horstmann, Professor of Modern Indology at the South Asia Institute of the University of Heidelberg.

Axel Michaels, Professor of Classical Indology at the South Asia Institute of the University of Heidelberg.

Christopher Z. Minkowski, Lecturer of Sanskrit at the Asian Studies Department of the Cornell University, Ithaca.

Gaya Caran Tripathi, Professor of Sanskrit at the Ganganath Jha Research Institute, Allahabad.

Albrecht Wezler, Professor of Indology at the University of Hamburg.

Publications by Pandit Dr. Parameswara Aithal

1. Review of Dharmarakshanam / by B. Lakshminarayana Rao. Adyar Library Bulletin : Brahmavidyā (ALB). Madras : Adyar Library and Research Centre, vol. 26 (1962), p. 126.
2. Review of Śrī Vanadurgā Mahāvidyā Pañcaśatī / compiled by Sri Viraraghava Swami, Sri Ramamurti and Sri Venkatarama Sastri. ALB, vol. 26 (1962), pp. 291-92.
3. Review of Non-Rigvedic Mantras in the Marriage Ceremonies / by Dr. P. K. Narayana Pillai. ALB, vol. 27 (1963), pp. 311-12.
4. Review of Vādirāja's Yaśodharacarita / edited by Dr. K. Krishnamoorthy. ALB, vol. 27 (1963), pp. 318-19.
5. Āśvalāyanagṛhyapariśiṣṭa : A rare and ancient Sanskrit text on Vedic rituals / critically edited with detailed Introduction, Appendixes, Indexes and Notes. ALB, vol. 27 (1963), pp. 217-87. (Adyar Library Pamphlet Series 36)
6. "Kārpāsa Cotton: Its Origin and Spread in Ancient India", A Research Paper in collaboration with V. Ramanatha Ayyar. ALB, vol. 28 (1964), pp. 1-40.
7. Review of Cāṇakya-Nīti-Text-Tradition (Cāṇakya-Nīti-Śākhā-Sampradāyaḥ) / edited by Ludwik Sternbach. ALB, vol. 28 (1964), pp. 154-56.
8. Review of Bhāshātattva aur Vākyapadīya / by Dr. Satyakam Varma. ALB, vol. 28 (1964), pp. 157-58.
9. Review of Rūpaka Samīkshā / edited by Dr. E. R. Sreekrishna Sarma. ALB, vol. 28 (1964), p.289.
10. Review of Saundaryalaharī of Śrī Śamkara-Bhagavatpāda / translated by Pandit S. Subrahmanya Sastri and T. R. Srinivasa Ayyangar. ALB, vol. 29 (1965), pp. 280-81.
11. Review of Tulasīdāsa / by Chandra Kumari Handoo. ALB, vol. 29 (1965), p. 286.
12. Review of Devatādhyāya-Saṃhitopaniṣad-Vaṃśa-Brāhmaṇas with commentaries / edited by Dr. B. R. Sharma. ALB, vol. 30 (1966), pp. 195-96.
13. Review of An Introduction to Hindu Symbolism / by Dr. I. K. Taimini. ALB, vol. 30 (1966), pp. 201-02.
14. Review of Veda Samīkṣā / edited by Dr. E. R. Sreekrishna Sarma. ALB, vol. 31-32, supplement (1967-68), pp. 11-13.
15. Review of Vedaśāstrasaṃgrahaḥ—an Anthology of the Vedas and Śāstras / edited by Vishva Bandhu. ALB, vol. 31-32, supplement (1967-68), pp. 15-16.
16. Descriptive Catalogue of Sanskrit Manuscripts in the Adyar Library. Vol. IV : Stotra-s. Madras : Adyar Library and Research Centre, 1968. Part I, xxxv, 623 pp.; Part II, 404 pp. (Adyar Library Series 96) (Description of 3244 manuscripts)
17. Stotra-Samuccayaḥ : A collection of 101 rare and unpublished philosophical and devotional Hymns / critically edited with Indexes and Notes: Vol. I, xvi, 309 pp. Vol. II, xix, 386 pp. Madras : Adyar Library and Research Centre, 1969. (Adyar Library Series 99)

18. "ṚgVeda Khila-s and the Sūtra-s of Āśvalāyana", : A Research paper on the relationship of Ṛgvedic Khila-s and Āśvalāyana's Sūtra works. ALB, vol. 33 (1969), pp. 182-94.
19. The Kṛṣṇabhāvaśatakam : A lyrical poem of 83 stanzas by Venkatācārya of Bukkapattanam (c. A.D. 1700) / critically edited on the basis of three manuscripts. ALB, vol. 33 (1969), pp. 365-82.
20. Review of Loka : World and Heaven in the Veda, 1966, 172 pp. and The Meaning of the Sanskrit Term Dhāman-, 1967, 100 pp. / Both by J. Gonda. ALB, vol. 33 (1969), pp. 387-89.
21. Review of A Survey of the Śrautasūtras / by C. G. Kashikar. ALB, vol. 33 (1969), pp. 392-93.
22. Review of Tattvanyāyavibhākaraḥ (with the commentary Nyāyaprakāśa) and of Sammatitattvasopānam / both by Vijayalabdhisūri. ALB, vol. 33 (1969), pp. 401-02.
23. Review of Advaita as Philosophy and Religion / by K. B. Ramakrishna Rao. ALB, vol. 33 (1969), p. 404.
24. Review of Camatkāracandrikā of Viśveśvarakavicandra / critically edited by Dr. P. Sriramamurti. ALB, vol. 33 (1969), pp. 415-16.
25. Review of Śivagītimālā of Candraśekharendrasarasvatī and Rāmāṣṭapadī of Rāmakavi / edited by Dr. V. Raghavan. ALB, vol. 33 (1969), p. 419.
26. Review of The Exposition of the Vedas / by Vidyanand 'videh'. ALB, vol. 33 (1969), p. 429.
27. Review of the Sāmavedīya Shashtyabdapūrtiśāntiḥ / by Mayuram Ramanatha Dikshita. ALB, vol. 33 (1969), p. 432.
28. Review of Guide to Indian Periodical Literature. ALB, vol. 33 (1969), pp. 435-36.
29. "The Yajñasiddhi of Īśāna : A rare and unpublished commentary on the Mantra-s of the Āśvalāyana Śrautasūtra", in : Pratibhānam : A collection of Research Papers Presented to Dr. P. K. Narayana Pillai. Trivandrum, 1970, pp. 23-28.
30. Descriptive Catalogue of Sanskrit Manuscripts in the Adyar Library. Vol. VIII : Sāmkhya, Yoga, Vaiśeṣika and Nyāya. Madras : Adyar Library and Research Centre, 1972. xxi, 552 pp. (Adyar Library Series 100) (1.616 manuscripts are described)
31. "Features of Localization in Contemporary Indian Fiction: Kannada", in : South Asian Digest of Regional Writing, vol. I. Heidelberg : South Asia Institute, 1972, pp. 66-73.
32. Review of Paribhāṣā IV, V and XV. Untersuchungen zur Geschichte der einheimischen grammatischen Scholastik / by Albrecht Wezler, in : Mundus : A quarterly Review of German Research Contributions on Asia, Africa and Latin America, vol. VIII. Stuttgart, 1972, pp. 39-41.
33. "The Making of a Poem Towords a Theory of Creativity in Contemporary Indian Poetry Kannada", in : South Asian Digest of Regional Writing, vol. II. Heidelberg : South Asia Institute, 1973, pp. 112-124.

34. "Religious Attitudes in Contemporary Kannada Literature", in : South Asian Digest of Regional Writing, vol. III. Heidelberg : South Asia Institute, 1974, pp. 41-52.
35. Review of Zur Frage nach der Urfassung des Pañcatantra / by Ruprecht Geib, in : Mundus, vol. XI. Stuttgart, 1975, pp. 301-02.
36. "Biographical Literature in Kannada", in : Biography and Autobiography in Modern South Asian Literatures, South Asian Digest of Regional Writing, vol. V. Heidelberg : South Asia Institute, 1976, pp. 48-53.
37. "Āśvalāyana and His Works", in : Proceedings of the 30th International Congress of Human Sciences in Asia and Africa (South Asia 3), Mexico, 1976, pp. 201-207.
38. "Über die Nicht-Rigvedischen Verse im Āśvalāyana Śrautasūtra", in : Zeitschrift der Morgenländischen Gesellschaft, Supplement III,2, Wiesbaden, 1977, pp. 763-69.
39. Review of Regionalismus in Südindien : Die Drawidische Bewegung / by Hans-Stefan Kruse, in : Mundus, vol. XIII, Stuttgart, 1977, pp. 301-02.
40. Descriptive Catalogue of Sanskrit Manuscripts in the Adyar Library, vol. II : Śrauta, Gṛhya, Smṛti and Dharmaśāstra; over 3.000 manuscripts described (in press).
41. "Prayogaratna of Nrisimhayajvan : Manuscript Notes", in : IVth World Sanskrit Conference of International Association of Sanskrit Studies, Weimar (GDR), May 1979. Berlin, 1985, pp. 416-19.
42. Āśvalāyana-Gṛhyasūtra-Bhāṣyam of Devasvāmin / critically edited on the basis of four South Indian manuscripts. Madras : Adyar Library and Research Centre, 1980. xxxix, 324 pp. (Adyar Library Series 111) (An ancient text on Hindu domestic rites with the rare commentary of Devasvāmin)
43. "On the Cāturmāsya-prayoga of Anantadeva : An analysis", in : Professor Kunjunni Raja Felicitation Volume. Madras : Adyar Library and Research Centre, 1980-81 (= ALB, vols. 44-45), pp. 486-505.
44. "Pānini and Vedic Ritual Literature", Proceedings of the International Seminar on Panini, Centre of Advanced Study of Sanskrit, University of Poona, July 1981.
45. "Devasvāmin : A Forgotten Jurist?", in : Indology and Law : Studies in Honour of Professor J. Duncan M. Derrett (of the School of Oriental and Afriacan Studies, University of London). / Edited by Günther-Dietz Sontheimer and Parameswara K. Aithal. Wiesbaden : Steiner, 1982, pp. 106-19, (Beiträge zur Südasienforschung, Band 77).
46. Indology and Law : Studies in Honour of Professor J. Duncan M. Derrett (of the School of Oriental and Afriacan Studies, University of London). / Edited with Günther-Dietz Sontheimer. Wiesbaden : Steiner, 1982, XI, 463 pp. (Beiträge zur Südasienforschung, Band 77).
47. "Āśvalāyana and His Works", in : Surabhi : Sreekrishna Sarma Felicitation Volume, Professor Sreekrishna Sarma Felicitation Committee. Tirupati, 1983, pp. 75-82.

48. "The Transmission of Sacred Texts in Traditional Hindu Society", in : Proceedings of the 31st International Congress of Human Sciences in Asia and North Africa, held in Tokyo-Kyoto, 31st August - 7th September 1983. Tokyo : The Institute of Eastern Culture, 1984, p. 538.
49. "On the Tradition of Vedic Recitation", Vth World Sanskrit Conference of International Association of Sanskrit Studies, Philadelphia, October, 1984.
50. Non-Ṛgvedic Citations in the Āśvalāyana Śrautasūtra : Doctoral Thesis. Varanasi : Chowhkamba Sanskrit Series Office, 1986. iv, lxxiv, 266 pp. (Chowkhamba Sanskrit Studies 100)
51. Veda-lakṣaṇa Vedic Ancillary Literature : A Descriptive Bibliography. A comprehensive catalogue of over 1600 works and authors, containing detailed information culled from original Sanskrit texts and over 160 volumes of catalogues of Sanskrit manuscripts of Libraries in India as well as in Europe. Wiesbaden : Steiner, 1991, VII, 725 pp. Indian edition: Delhi : Motilal Banarsidas, 1993.
52. "Indian Manuscripts in Germany" a paper read at the National Seminar on Preservation of Cultural Heritage : Manuscripts and Their Future (held on 8-10 March 1990 at the Asiatic Society, Calcutta). published in Ānanda Bhāratī – Dr. K. Krishnamoorthy Felicitaion Volume. Mysore : D. V. K. Murthy, 1995, pp. 300-18.
53. "Sanskrit Manuscript Collectoins in Europe (I)" paper read at the IXth World Sanskrit Conference (9-15 January 1994) in Melbourne / Australia.
54. "Sanskrit Manuscript Collections in Europe (II)" paper read at the Xth World Sanskrit Conference (3-9 January 1997) in Bangalore / India.

Index